THE CUNO GOVERNMENT AND REPARATIONS
1922–1923

Studies in Contemporary History

Volume 1

THE CUNO GOVERNMENT
AND REPARATIONS 1922-1923

POLITICS AND ECONOMICS

by

HERMANN J. RUPIEPER

1979

MARTINUS NIJHOFF

THE HAGUE / BOSTON / LONDON

ISBN 90 247 2114 8

PRINTED IN THE NETHERLANDS

CONTENTS

PREFACE

When the First World War ended, the political and economic system of prewar Europe lay in ruins. Though Allied politicians tried at various postwar conferences to create a new and stable European order they failed because of conflicting and competing national interests. The peace settlements neither established security from renewed attacks by the defeated nations nor did they lay the groundwork for a reconstruction of Europe's devastated economic system, because the members of the Allied war coalition could not agree on the goals to be pursued by the treaties or on the means to enforce their settlement. In this context, reparations played a most significant role. The conflict between the European protagonists France, Great Britain and Germany reached its peak at the beginning of 1923 when Franco-Belgian troops occupied the Ruhr district in a last attempt to implement strategies developed in 1919 for a control of the German economic potential until reparations had been paid and to show to the Anglo-Saxon powers that any modification of Allied policy toward Germany could not be attained against French objections or without a simultaneous adjustment of French war debts. By focusing on the reparation issue during the period of the Cuno Cabinet, this book attempts to contribute both to the literature on Cuno and to the interrelationship of political and economic problems after World War I.

The research for this study in the United States, in France, in Great Britain and in Germany was made possible by grants from the Center for Research in International Studies of Stanford University, the Newhouse Foundation Fund, the Stiftung Mitbestimmung Düsseldorf and the Historische Kommission zu Berlin. I am also indebted for assistance and cooperation to the staff of the National Archives, Washington; the Hoover Institution, Stanford; Thomas T. Thalken of the Herbert Hoover Presidential Library, West Branch, Iowa; the staff of the Library of Congress, Washington; the Public Record Office, London; the Ministère des Affaires Etrangères, Paris; the Bundesarchiv Koblenz and the Politisches Archiv des Auswärtigen Amtes, Bonn.

I am grateful to the following guardians of private collections: Bodo

Herzog who facilitated research at the Historisches Archiv der Gutehoff-nungshütte in Oberhausen; Frau Dr. Hoffmann of the Archiv der Hamburg-Amerika-Linie who allowed consultation of the Cuno papers; Frau Irmgard Denkinger of the Werkarchiv der MAN Augsburg who permitted the use of the Emil Guggenheimer papers; likewise to the staffs of the Westfälisches Wirtschaftsarchiv and the Institut für Zeitungsforschung, Dortmund, who placed valuable material at my disposal. Special thanks to Donald L. Kemmerer for the use of the papers of his father, Edwin W. Kemmerer, and to Mr. Gilbert W. Kahn who permitted the use of the Otto Kahn papers. The trustees of the John F. Dulles papers and the Fred I. Kent papers generously granted access to these collections at Princeton University. Mrs. Edith Hirsch vouchsafed the diary of her husband, Julius Hirsch. I am also greatly indebted to the family of the late Ambassador Alanson B. Houghton who made my research most enjoyable.

The manuscript was read by Barbara Jurca, and I am grateful to her for eliminating many ambiguities of style and infelicities of expression. My sincere thanks go also to Eva Furth, Ingrid Russau and Heike Siesslack who typed the manuscript at various stages of its development.

Gerald D. Feldman read an earlier version of this study and contributed a helpful critique. Finally, I want to express my particular gratitude to Gordon A. Craig for his understanding, critical guidance and advice through the preparation of this study. Without his constant encouragement and aid, this study would not have been possible.

Berlin, November 1977

THE CUNO GOVERNMENT AND REPARATIONS
1922-1923

INTRODUCTION: INTERNATIONAL ASPECTS OF
REPARATIONS 1919–1922

The inability of European statesmen to create a stable political and economic order from 1919 to 1924 has generally been attributed to German unwillingness to comply with the terms of the peace treaty. Contemporary politicians and later historians have argued that the period of extreme nationalistic agitation and continuing political struggle inflicted upon the people of Europe was basically caused by the wickedness of German political leaders and industrialists who attempted to evade the obligations imposed upon their country by the victorious powers. This long-suffering-creditor and dishonest-debtor theory certainly possesses a charming simplicity, but it is an oversimplification of complex economic and political problems which proves untenable if one examines it rigorously.

Political realities at Versailles had unfortunately proved less simple than politicians had expected. Because of conflicting ideas and aspirations, Woodrow Wilson, David Lloyd George, and Georges Clemenceau could not agree on a postwar system for Europe. The American President had hoped that international affairs would be transformed after the war by a system of collective security. Despite this goal, he thought that he could serve as a mediator between France and Great Britain, to develop a peace program for Europe and obtain the redemption of American war loans from the European Allies.[1] The main objectives for the French Prime Minister were the weakening of Germany, the collection of huge indemnities for the balancing of the war budget and the protection of French security by a permanent occupation of the left bank of the Rhine. British terms for a postwar system were partly contradictory to Clemenceau's, and Lloyd George attached great importance to British economic interests.[2] Furthermore, after years of wartime suffering,

---

[1] Of the many studies written about Wilson's policy the most important are Arno J. Mayer, *Politics and Diplomacy of Peacemaking: Containment and Counterrevolution at Versailles 1918–1919* (New York, 1967). Klaus Schwabe, *Deutsche Revolution und Wilson Frieden. Die amerikanische und deutsche Friedensstrategie zwischen Ideologie und Machtpolitik* (Düsseldorf, 1971).

[2] Jean Baptiste Duroselle/Pierre Renouvin, *Introduction to the History of International Relations* (New York, 1967), pp. 281–290. For the influence of the balance-of-power

a vindictive spirit shaped public statements of British and French politicians. The population in the Allied countries had been promised high indemnities and politicians were reluctant and often afraid to disappoint the expectations of a public aroused by wartime propaganda.[3]

However, when the Allies set out at Versailles to extract the total costs of the war from Germany, economic and financial advisers of the delegations soon ran into serious difficulties. Especially the Americans felt that French and British demands on Germany were totally unrealistic and tried to scale down the liability imposed on Germany according to the war-guilt clause of the treaty. Norman H. Davis and Bernard Baruch of the American delegation repeatedly urged their French and British colleagues to deal with reparations from a purely economic point of view. This was not an easy task, since in most delegations expert opinion differed as to Germany's capacity to pay. Nevertheless, the Americans finally succeeded in gaining support from their allied colleagues to reduce the previous figure of nearly 100 billion dollars to a sum of 15 billion dollars.[4]

concept upon Lloyd George see Karl-Heinz Menzel, "Die Gebundenheit der britischen Aussenpolitik am Ende der Regierungszeit Lloyd Georges und ihre Auswirkungen auf Deutschland," Phil. Diss. (Hamburg, 1951), pp. 15 ff. Arno Wolfers, *Britain and France between Two Wars. Conflicting Strategies of Peace from Versailles to World War II* (New York, 1940). W.M. Jordan, *Great Britain, France and the German Problem 1918–1939* (London, 1943). Neville Waites, (ed.), *Troubled Neighbours. Franco-British Relations in the Twentieth Century* (London, 1971). An excellent study of the French press and of parliamentary discussions in France during the peace negotiations is Pierre Miquel, *La Paix de Versailles et l'opinion publique française* (Paris, 1972).

[3] For the influence of public opinion on Allied statesmen cf: André Tardieu, *La Paix* (Paris, 1921) p. 322. Tardieu reports that in the light of the nationalistic spirit of the French Chamber reparations should be high. Alfred Sauvy, *Histoire Economique de la France entre les Deux Guerres* 1918–1931 (Paris, 1965), pp. 38–44, pp. 133–135. Sauvy describes the complete confusion of the French press towards postwar financial problems, and argues that French financial experts were unprepared to grasp the difficulties.

David Lloyd George, *The Truth about the Peace Treaties*, 2 vols. (London, 1938), I, pp. 461–467. E.M. House/Charles Seymour, *What really happened at Paris* (London, 1921), pp. 622 ff. On April 3, 1919 a resolution signed by 270 M.P.'s was sent to Paris reminding Lloyd George that he had promised to extract total war costs from Germany. Davis, one of the American reparation experts at Versailles and later Undersecretary of State, noted in his diary: "The peoples in most of the countries and especially in France and England had been entirely misled as to Germany's capacity to repair the damage she had done and in fact, as to the cost of such reparations which Germany, in the negotiations leading up to the Armistice, had agreed to make good." "Peace Conference Notes, July 5, 1919," *Norman H. Davis Papers*, Box 44. See also Clemenceau's letter to Général Mordacq of May 30, 1919 where he stated: "Lloyd George, comme toujours, se laissait beaucoup trop influencer à cette conférence de la Paix, par les considérations de politique intérieure." Quoted in Général Mordacq, *Le Ministère Clemenceau. Journal d'un Témoin*, t. 1–3 (Paris, 1930–1931), III, p. 298.

[4] Mayer, *op. cit.*, pp. 156–158. "Peace Conference Notes, July 5 and 15, 1919," *Davis Papers*, Box 44. Leonard P. Ayres reports that of all American advisers only Vance

These new figures were reported to Wilson, Lloyd George, and Clemenceau at a meeting on March 15, 1919 which is of special interest, because it demonstrated the gap that existed between the expectations of politicians and the estimates of their advisers. On this occasion, Davis argued on behalf of his colleagues that Germany's capacity depended upon the solution of the following difficult economic problems: First, a return to the stability of her prewar political order and to her prewar level of economic productivity were the preconditions for any sound appraisal of Germany's capacity to meet reparation payments. Second, German imports had to be sharply curtailed, while the world market had to be opened to German goods. This increase of German exports, the experts warned, although necessary for reparation purposes, would seriously affect export industries in Great Britain and France. These countries and the whole of Europe might become a dumping ground for cheap German goods. Thirdly, the experts did not think that it would do any good to force payments, but they suggested that the political leaders consider what Germany would willingly accept without Allied coercion.[5]

After the presentation of these preconditions for a final settlement with Germany, Davis told the heads of state that Loucheur, Montague, and he had reached the conclusion that Germany could pay from 10 to 20 billion dollars over a period of 20 to 30 years. But since the war damage done by Germany had been estimated at a total of 30 billion dollars, they felt that Germany was liable for this amount. Fearing, however, that this sum - which could only be acquired by Germany through increased exports – would destroy the trade of France and Britain and create an economic giant which might again try to overrun Europe, the experts recommended that half of the German liability should be paid in paper marks at the par of exchange. The

McCormick believed that the economic expectations of the political leaders were sound. "Memorandum on the American Attitude towards the Problem of Reparations during the Peace Conference," *Leonard P. Ayres Papers*, Box 2, Folder Misc. "American Committee to Negotiate Peace. Memos, Cables and Notes in Diary Form, March 20, 1919," p. 46, *Bernard Baruch Papers*. Hereafter cited as *Baruch Papers*. Louis Loucheur, the French expert on the Committee agreed, but was afraid to support his American colleagues. Cf. also Lloyd George, *op. cit.*, I, p. 474. André Tardieu, *The Truth about the Treaty* (Indianapolis, 1921). John Maynard Keynes, *The Economic Consequences of Peace* (New York, 1920). For the French side see Miquel, *op. cit.*, pp. 460–470.

[5] "Peace Conference Notes. Annex. Arguments presented by Norman Davis on Behalf of Himself and Messrs. Montague, and Loucheur, at a Meeting with the President, Messrs. Lloyd George, and Clemenceau at Paris, March 15, 1919," pp. 1–4, *Davis Papers*, Box 44; also "First Interim Report to the Commission on Reparations, by the 2nd Subcommittee, April 8, 1919," p. 4, *Baruch Papers*, American Committee to Negotiate Peace. Sauvy, *op. cit.*, reports that Loucheur's acceptance of this sum was kept secret from the French public.

remaining 15 billion dollars were to be paid in gold marks at the 1914 rate of exchange. Four or five billions of this sum could be paid within the next two or three years. According to this report, the Allies thus demanded about 60 billion gold marks and 60 billion paper marks. If the latter sum had been withdrawn from Germany immediately, serious monetary problems would have been created. In order to prevent such a development, the experts recommended that part of this sum could be reinvested in Germany and be withdrawn over a period of 30 to 60 years.[6] This report caused some uneasiness among Allied leaders, but both Lloyd George and Clemenceau claimed that they could not accept the figures because of "public opinion" at home. This may have been the case, but it should be noted that since December 1918 the European Powers had indicated to Wilson that a cancellation of interallied debts would enable their countries to reduce reparation demands on Germany. The Americans simply rejected any discussion of this issue. However, the close connection between interallied debts and reparations was obvious to all participants at the conference.[7]

In general, Allied disagreement on the amount of reparations and the connection of interallied debts and the German liability prevented an agreement at Versailles. However, insecurity about Germany's capacity to pay as well as confusion among the experts as to the evaluation of the Reich's potential also existed.[8] Thus, after long discussions, the Allied leaders decided that no final sum should be mentioned. Instead a Reparation Commission was to be created to decide on the liability, and apparently at least Lloyd George expected that a revision of the financial demands would be possible when the populace in France and Great Britain would come to recognize the impossibility of collecting total war costs from the defeated nations.[9] Davis aptly summarized the economic and financial problems

[6] "Peace Conference Notes. Annex . . .," p. 3 f. *Davis Papers*, Box 44.
[7] Germain Calmette, *Recueil des Documents sur l'Histoire de la Question des Réparations 1919–1921* (Paris, 1924), pp. IX–XX, Germain Calmette, *Les dettes Interalliées* (Paris, 1926), pp. 77–80. Mayer, *op. cit.*, p. 627. Laszlo Zsigmond, *Zur deutschen Frage 1918–1923* (Budapest, 1964), pp. 79–83.
[8] Already in 1919 Leonard Ayres recognized the importance of the transfer problem and reported of his colleagues: "The technical advisers of the other nations seemed at that time to be losing their estimates on figures showing the national wealth of Germany, and the war costs of the Allies, without giving close attention to the problem of getting the volume out of Germany, and making them available in the countries receiving them." "Memorandum on the American Attitude . . .," *Ayres Papers*, Box 2, Folder Misc.
[9] This sudden change was apparently caused by an attack of Jan C. Smuts, Prime Minister of South Africa, upon Lloyd George's reparation policy. See E.M. House, *The Intimate Diary of Colonel House*, ed. By Charles Seymour, 4 vols. (London, 1924), IV, p. 492. "Peace Conference Notes, July 5, 1919," pp. 8–11, *Davis Papers*, Box 44. Lloyd George to George Ridell, November 30, 1918 and March 30, 1919, George R. Ridell,

connected with reparations by stating: "The problem is not therefore so much what Germany can pay, but what the Allies can afford to have her pay," while French economic historian Albert Sauvy described Allied policy with the following words: "In short, the Allies wanted gold, but not goods."[10]

Although these statements show the gist of French and British policy in 1919, they underestimate the importance of reparation demands as a pledge for German well-behavior towards the execution of the peace terms and as a pledge for further Allied discussions about interallied debts.

If the American delegates warned of the dangers of huge indemnities for Allied industries, they were even more concerned about the economic provisions of the treaty. In their opinion Germany's ability to export was limited by the seizure of her merchant fleet, the territorial clauses of the treaty and preferential treatment for goods from Alsace-Lorraine, while the Allies introduced protective tariffs against German goods. Some of these provisions were written into the treaty despite the opposition of distinguished American advisers. Bernard Baruch, the chief American reparation expert, was so upset over the draconic and what he considered to be economically unsound conditions, that he warned President Wilson not to concede to a French exploitation of the Saar coal mines, because this would further impair the delivery of reparations. Disappointed about the obviously political demands of France and Great Britain Baruch warned that the United States should not place herself "in a position of agreeing with our associates in the war, that Germany is to pay a certain indemnity and yet making it impossible for her to pay."[11] These conflicting aspirations are also well described by Davis who wrote in the summer of 1919: "Some of the delegates wanted to destroy Germany, some wanted to collect reparations, and others wanted to do both. Some wanted to collect more than Germany had agreed to pay or could pay; and others wanted to take all her capital, destroy her and then collect a large reparation bill."[12] This criticism of Allied peace strategy was

Intimate Diary of the Peace Conference and after, 1918–1923 (New York, 1934), p. 3 and p. 42. Winston Churchill, *The Aftermath* (London, 1929), p. 944 f. For French expectations cf. Miquel, *op. cit.*, pp. 426–33.

[10] "Peace Conference Notes, July 5, 1919," p. 12, *Davis Papers*, Box 44. Also Mayer, *op. cit.*, p. 806. Sauvy, *op. cit.*, p. 136.

[11] Schwabe, *op. cit.*, p. 474. Baruch-Henry White, March 12, 1919, *Baruch Papers*, American Committee to Negotiate Peace, Folder 8.

[12] "Peace Conference Notes, July 5, 1919," p. 1, *Davis Papers*, Box 44. Cf. also "The Reparation Problem 1921." Address delivered to the League of Free Nations Association, March 12, 1921, *John F. Dulles Papers*, Box 8, Reparation Problem 1921. Interesting material about the purpose of French and British demands has been compiled by S.L. Bane/Ralph H. Lutz, eds., *The Blockade of Germany after the Armistice 1918–1919* (Stanford, 1919), pp. 579 ff.

certainly not less harsh than John Maynard Keynes' view, who has been held
partly responsible for Germany's attempts to evade reparation payments,
the only difference being that Keynes resigned from the British delegation
and then published his book questioning the economic validity of the Peace
Treaty.[13]

In the end, the German peace delegation had to sign a blank sheet and
could only hope for a modification of the economic and financial clauses of
the treaty over time, since their counterproposals and conditions were
considered inadequate. Two themes had dominated discussions with Germany: 1) reparations could only be paid through the export of German
manufactured goods; 2) an international loan was necessary to start payments. Naturally German politicians and experts from industry, trade and
banking who participated in the formulation of counter proposals had
attempted to keep the liability as low as possible.[14] This policy remained a
source of constant irritation for the Allies. But since the Reparation Commission had to decide by May 1921 on total Allied damages and consequently on final demands from Germany there remained some hope for a
reasonable settlement.[15]

However, the refusal of the United States Senate to ratify the Versailles
Treaty further complicated developments. Since the Americans from now
on were only represented "unofficially" on the Commission, it became a
French, British and Belgian agency to extract reparations from Germany.[16]

---

[13] Keynes, *op. cit.* Etienne Mantoux, *The Carthagenian Peace or the Economic Consequences of Mr. Keynes* (London, 1946).
[14] For the German attitude at Versailles see: Peter Krüger, *Deutschland und die Reparationen 1918–1919. Die Genesis des Reparationsproblems in Deutschland zwischen Waffenstillstand und Versailler Friedensschluss* (Stuttgart, 1973). Leo Haupts, *Deutsche Friedenspolitik 1918–1919. Eine Alternative zur Machtpolitik des Ersten Weltkriegs* (Düsseldorf,
1976). Max M. Warburg, *Aus meinen Aufzeichnungen* (New York, 1952), pp. 74–79. J.M.
Keynes, "Dr. Melchior: Ein besiegter Feind," *Vorträge und Aufsätze.* Herausgegeben
vom Verein für Hamburgische Geschichte, Bd. 15. *Carl Melchior. Ein Buch des Gedenkens
und der Freundschaft* (Tübingen, 1967), pp. 1–35. Schwabe, *op. cit.,* p. 526. Paul von
Schwabach, *Aus meinen Akten* (Berlin, 1927), pp. 370–376. Hermann Bücher, *Finanz- und
Wirtschaftsentwicklung Deutschlands in den Jahren 1921 bis 1925* (Berlin, 1925), pp. 7–29.
Carl Bergmann, "Wie können wir den Gegnern die Kriegsschäden ersetzen"? January 4,
1919, *Wilhelm Cuno Nachlaß*, Archiv des Vorsitzenden des Direktoriums. Hereafter cited
as *Cuno Nachlaß*. "Niederschrift über eine Besprechung betreffend der sich aus der Ent-
sendung einer Finanzkommission nach Paris ergebenden Fragen," March 27, 1919,
Bundesarchiv Koblenz, R2/188. Hereafter cited as *BA*.
[15] By May 1921 Germany would also be required to pay a first rate of 20 billion gold
marks and pay the costs of the Allied occupation armies. Charles S. Maier, *Recasting
Bourgeois Europe. Stabilization in France, Germany, and Italy in the Decade after World
War I* (Princeton, 1975). Etienne Weill-Raynal, *Les Réparations Allemandes et la France*,
3 vols. (Paris, 1947) vol. I, pp. 580 ff.
[16] James McNaughton Hester, *America and the Weimar Republic. A Study of the*

Reparation policy was further complicated by the intervention of Allied statesmen in the functions of the Commission when they tried at various postwar conferences to reach an agreement on Germany's liability. In these negotiations, British Prime Minister Lloyd George soon came to recognize the hazards of payments through German exports, urging reduction of claims in order not to destroy normal trade. Yet British proposals did not find support in France, where the government was issuing reconstruction loans budgeting them against eventual German reparation payments.[17] Nevertheless, when the Reparation Commission (*de jure* an independent agency) fixed the German liability in April 1921, demands had been significantly reduced over previous figures. Although the debt had been fixed at a nominal value of 132 billion gold marks, in reality it was even less. The final sum had been divided into three categories of A-, B-, and C-bonds. The A-bonds amounted to 12 billion gold marks, and the B-bonds to 38 billions, while the C-bonds covered the remaining 82 billion gold marks. However, the last bonds were only to be issued after payments sufficient to cover interest and sinking funds of the A- and B-bonds had been made. Payments for these bonds were to be made through a 26 percent charge on German exports. Of this sum reparations in kind were to be subtracted. Considering British fear of German industrial competition and the payments necessary for the A- and B-bonds, it is doubtful whether the experts thought that the C-bonds would ever be issued.[18] However, these bonds could be used, as later developments

---

Causes and Effects of American Policy and Action in Respect to Germany, 1918–1925, (Ph. D. thesis Oxford, 1955). Dieter Bruno Gescher, *Die Vereinigten Staaten von Nordamerika und die Reparationen 1920–1924* (Bonn, 1956). Werner Link, *Die amerikanische Stabilisierungspolitik in Deutschland 1921–1932* (Düsseldorf, 1970). Carl Bergmann, *Der Weg der Reparationen* (Frankfurt, 1926).

[17] For Lloyd George's proposals see for example: *Foreign Office, Documents on British Foreign Policy, 1919–1939*, First Series, vol. XV (London, 1967), No. 8, pp. 39 ff. (Hereafter cited as DBFP). Weill-Reynal, *op. cit.*, I. pp. 594–598. Gescher, *op. cit.*, pp. 49–50, and p. 60. Also Francis W. Hirst, *The Consequences of the War to Great Britain* (London, 1934), pp. 258 ff. Alfred Maizels, *Industrial Growth and World Trade. An Empirical Study of the Trends in Production, Consumption and Trade in Manufacturers from 1899–1959 with a Discussion of probable future Trends* (Cambridge, 1963), pp. 92–98, p. 220 and *passim*. Sidney Pollard, *The Development of the British Economy 1914–1967*, 2nd ed. (London, 1969), pp. 110–125. Already in February 27, 1919, the French Minister of Finance, Lucien Klotz, had declared that "French taxpayers would not be asked to pay anything before Germany had been charged the maximum of which she could pay." Cf. Miquel, *op. cit.*, p. 446. A similar statement was made by Paul Doumer, Minister of Finance in the Briand cabinet: "If any bankruptcy was to take place, he did not think that it was fair that it should be France that should incur such bankruptcy in order that Germany should escape paying this 12 billions per annum for the war." *DBFP*, vol. XV, No. 5 p. 39 f.

[18] Bergmann, *op. cit.*, p. 102 f. Sally Marks, "Reparations: A Reminder," *Central European History* 2 (1969), pp. 356–365 believes that the Allies tried to mislead public

showed, as a coercive means in the event of German misconduct. Furthermore, they could be traded for a reduction of French debts to Great Britain and the United States. Nevertheless, even the Allied reparation experts felt uncomfortable about their final decision, since they had, in face of expectations in their countries, only lumped together their estimates of Allied war damages, pensions and allowances.[19]

Germany accepted the Allied decision because it really had no other choice. The Fehrenbach cabinet resigned and the new Chancellor, Joseph Wirth, submitted to the London Schedule of Payments only because he feared that the threatened occupation of further German territory would lead to a dissolution of the Reich. Furthermore, all political groups in Germany, including the SPD and the trade unions, were convinced that the demands were impossible to fulfill or would at least seriously impair the economic development of the young republic. This situation did not create an appropriate atmosphere for the development of alternatives, but Wirth and later his Minister of Reconstruction and Foreign Affairs, Walther Rathenau, nevertheless attempted to introduce a policy of "fulfillment" hoping that the Allies would then further reduce their demands on Germany.[20] Since the Reich did not have ready cash for payments, Rathenau at first tried to increase reparations in kind through contracts with his French counterpart Louis Loucheur, Minister of Reconstruction in the Briand cabinet. But these negotiations did not result in significant deliveries because of industrial opposition in France and in Germany.[21] In domestic affairs the

opinions on purpose. Her views have been severely and justly criticized by David Felix, "Reparations Reconsidered with a vengeance," *ibid.*, 2 (1971), pp. 171–179.

[19] See especially the opinion of James A. Logan and Maurice Frère. Gescher, *op. cit.*, pp. 54 ff. "Notes by the Financial Secretary to the Treasury," July 30, 1923. Public Record Office, *Offices of Imperial Defense*, 24/161, C.P. 358. Hereafter cited as *Cab.*

[20] David Felix, *Walther Rathenau and the Weimar Republic: The Problem of Reparations* (Baltimore and London, 1971); Ernst Laubach, *Die Politik der Kabinette Wirth 1921–1922* (Lübeck and Hamburg, 1968).

[21] Weill-Raynal, *op. cit.*, II, pp. 28–68. Laubach, *op. cit.*, p. 73 f. Sauvy, *op. cit.*, p. 140; Richard Castillon, *Les Réparations Allemandes. Deux Expériences 1919–1932, 1945–1952* (Paris, 1953), p. 43. *Politisches Archiv des Auswärtigen Amtes, Wirtschafts Reparationen*, Abschluß von Abkommen mit Frankreich über Sachleistungen und Lauf der Sachlieferungen (Verhandlungen mit Tannery, Loucheur, Rathenau), November 10, 1921, K 444121–122. Hereafter cited as *PA AA. Papers Relating to the Agreement between the French and German Governments concerning the application of Part VIII of the Treaty of Versailles Regarding Deliveries in Kind* (London, 1921), p. 11 ff. For French industrial opposition cf. *Le Matin*, November 5, 1921. *Echo de Paris*, February 1, 1922. Weill-Raynal, *op. cit.*, II, p. 59. *L'Usine*, September 17 and September 24, 1921, "L'Accord de Wiesbaden au point de vue des sinistrés et de l'industrie française." *Journée Industrielle*, October 25, 1921. *L'Industrie Chimique*, September 9, 1921, *L'Exportateur Français*, September 15, 1921, "Les accords de Wiesbaden et l'exportation." *Bulletin Mensuel de la Chambre Syndicale des Constructeurs de Machines agricoles de France*, no. 8, December

cabinet also failed to raise sufficient taxes in order to balance the budget. Attempts to seize private agricultural and industrial property, which would have made revenues available for reparation purposes, were blocked by the bourgeois parties and industrialists.[22] Furthermore, payment of the liability became hopelessly entangled with the stabilization of the currency and a struggle over the future economic and social structure of the Weimar Republic. In the end the government had to resort to foreign aid for payment of the first reparation installments, i.e., to sell marks on the international money market in order to obtain the necessary foreign exchange. This of course further contributed to inflation. By 1921 the Reich's government thus saw in an international loan and in a moratorium the only way out of its financial difficulties.[23]

Although the Allies were totally disillusioned with the German performance, British politicians especially – fearing the effects of the postwar European political and economic crisis on British trade – renewed their attempts to reach a working agreement with Germany. However, they either submitted proposals which were doomed to fail from the beginning or isolated Britain among her European Allies. Thus in December 1921, Lloyd George again offered a renunciation of the war debts of Britain's European Allies under the condition that the United States would equally renounce British war debts to the United States; in that case the German liability could also be reduced. This proposal was supported by France, but American President Harding informed the European powers that the Republican administration could not undertake such a reduction in face of congressional opposition.[24] Another of Lloyd George's schemes, equally unrealistic, was discussed with Briand and Rathenau; it provided for a channelling of German exports to the Soviet Union where they could contribute to the reconstruction of Eastern Europe. German participation in an international financial syndicate for the financing of exports would, it was hoped, also afford an opportunity for reparation payments. The German government could, for example, take half of the shares of the syndicate and would then be entitled to dividends on them. Profits from this enterprise would automatically be applied to repara-

---

8, 1921. *Journée Industrielle*, July 21 and July 24, 1922, "La Réunion du Comité des Prestations en Nature." *L'Usine*, July 27, 1922, *Le Temps*, November 1, 1922, and *L'Echo Nationale*, November 13, 1922. For German industry see especially Jakob W. Reichert, *Rathenau's Reparationspolitik* (Berlin, 1922).

[22] Laubach, *op. cit.*, pp. 61 ff, pp. 145 ff. Julius Hirsch, *Die deutsche Währungsfrage* (Jena, 1924), pp. 58 ff.

[23] Maier, *op. cit.*, pp. 249 ff.

[24] Weill-Raynal, *op. cit.*, II, pp. 85–96.

tion payments.[25] Nothing came of these negotiations and other plans followed.

When Lloyd George, but also the American "unofficial" adviser on the Reparation Commission, Roland Boyden, suggested that Germany needed a moratorium and perhaps even an international loan in order to overcome difficulties, they were blocked by the new French Minister President Raymond Poincaré. While Poincaré also recognized that Germany was temporarily unable to pay, he would not agree to a moratorium without "productive pledges," nor did he intend to allow international bankers to decide on Germany's capacity to pay. In addition, in a meeting with German Ambassador Mayer, he stated the most important precondition for a final settlement with Germany: interallied debts had to be adjusted first.[26] Thus British Prime Minister Lloyd George might plead with Poincaré to regard their countries as "joint creditors of a bankrupt concern" or the Chancellor of the Exchequer Robert Horne, might argue to make Germany "a country fit for capitalists to live in" – Poincaré could not be moved.[27] He had identified his political future with the slogan of making Germany pay, a position he had endlessly repeated in his attacks on Briand who had been moving closer to British policy. In this context, the Reparation Commission, de jure responsible both for the control and revision of the German liability, played a crucial role. As long as unanimity existed among its members, it could be used as a weapon for the control of Germany, but once the British delegate, Sir John Bradbury, questioned the credibility of Allied policy and annihilated figures previously decided upon by Allied experts, the struggle was to take on new dimensions. Although Bradbury's statement that "the present total of 132 billion gold marks has the advantage of being ridiculous as well as absurd ... but if the Allies set themselves to collect 40 we should be passing from pure to applied lunacy"[28] has to be taken with some reservation, it nevertheless is an excellent example of the disillusionment existing among Allied experts in 1922. With British representatives in Allied negotiations generally recommending a new agreement or at least a moratorium,

---

[25] For the discussions see: *DBFP*, First Series, XV, No. 106, December 20, 1921; No. 108, December 21, 1921; No. 112–117, December 29–31, 1921.
[26] Weill-Raynal, *op. cit.*, pp. 162–182. Mayer-AA, *PA AA*, Büro RM, Reparationen, October 28, 1922, D 718392. *Ibid.*, October 5, 1922, D 718227–230. *Ibid.*, December 2, 1922, D 718402–406. Gescher, *op. cit.*, p. 131.
[27] Jean Loyrette, "The Foreign Policy of Poincaré: France and Great Britain in Relation with the German Problem 1919–1924," (Ph.D. thesis, Oxford University, 1955), pp. 133–135. See the reports on the London conference of August 1922. *Cab.*, 27/71, F.C. 40, July 31, 1922, and especially "Minutes of the London Conference on Reparations, August 1922," Public Record Office, *Foreign Office*, 371/7486. Hereafter cited as *FO*.
[28] Bradbury-Lloyd George, October 23, 1923, *ibid.*, C 14869. Also Felix, *op. cit.*, p. 109.

while Poincaré did not agree, the Allied coalition fell apart at the end of 1922.

While the Allies wrangled over their schemes, the Wirth government had invited international monetary experts to investigate Germany's financial and monetary situation. Contrary to German expectations, the majority of the experts (Keynes, Cassel, Jenks, and Brand) criticized the theory common-held in Germany that stabilization was impossible without international help. However, they did state that without German equality in international trade and without a moratorium, stabilization was unlikely. While these experts had proposed an attempt at stabilization of the currency through a domestic loan based on the gold reserves of the Reichsbank, a minority group (Dubois, Vissering, Kamenka) considered an international loan to be necessary. But despite this difference, they had agreed that a moratorium was necessary.[29] The German government tried to combine both reports in a memorandum submitted to the Reparation Commission on November 14, demanding a moratorium for three to four years for all cash payments and offering the issue of a foreign and domestic loan. By this time, however, only a complete acceptance of French demands for productive pledges in exchange for a moratorium would have influenced developments, but the Wirth government rejected these claims.

Thus, by the end of 1922, a stalemate had been reached both between Great Britain and France and between Germany and the Allies. The Germans pushed for a revision of the reparation clauses of the Versailles Treaty, hoping that an international inquiry would significantly reduce the liability and turn reparations from a political into a commercial debt. Great Britain was willing to grant certain reductions, at least temporarily, and was also prepared to initiate a broad, new approach towards the defeated nations, intending to reintroduce them into the European community of powers. This of course meant that negotiations for future settlements would be conducted among equals or at least, without a return to military coercion. For France, a number of political and financial problems (reparations, inter-allied debts, security and economic reconstruction) were intertwined and reaching new urgency in face of German determination to reduce reparations and British demands for a settlement of interallied debts.

[29] Laubach, *op. cit.*, pp. 303–306. Also J.W. Jenks-Edwin W. Kemmerer, January 26, 1923, *Edwin W. Kemmerer Papers*, Correspondence. Jenks believed that a unanimous report would have been possible. "It was our general opinion that if we had only three or four more days together, there would have been only one report, but as it was absolutely essential that Cassel and Keynes leave promptly, those of us who could handle English most readily got out one report as quickly as possible so that those two might sign it. The others preferred to state the subject in a somewhat different way, but there is little, if any difference in the fundamental principles."

This study will deal in detail with the domestic struggle between industry and the Reich government in Germany over reparations, with the various diplomatic initiatives of the Cuno cabinet at the end of 1922 and during 1923, Allied reactions to these proposals, and with the confrontation between the Allies (especially France and Great Britain) over a common policy towards Germany. In this context, the various initiatives which led to the creation of the Dawes Committee will also be examined. Furthermore, a significant part of this study will deal with Franco-Belgian goals during the occupation of the Ruhr.

CHAPTER I

THE FORMATION OF THE CUNO GOVERNMENT

Having failed to deal successfully with Germany's chief foreign policy problem, reparations, and her primary domestic difficulty, the control of monetary inflation, Chancellor Wirth felt in October 1922 that it was necessary
to rearrange his cabinet. Wirth hoped that by including the Deutsche Volkspartei (DVP) with its industrial backing in his cabinet, his policy towards
the Allies would be strengthened. He would be able to claim that his proposals for a final reparation settlement now had the support of German
industry. But the Social Democrats, who had just merged with the Independent Socialists, refused to cooperate with the representatives of industry
in the DVP.[1]

The failure to form a Great Coalition government immediately reinforced
the position of those who had argued since Wirth had become Chancellor
that his "policy of fulfillment" had been a mistake from the beginning. The
mark had further depreciated, Germany had delivered reparations up to the
limit of her capability. But all these efforts had not led to British or American
intervention on behalf of Germany.

Newspapers of the Right and even the liberal bourgeois press were thoroughly disgusted with party strife.[2] The resignation of Wirth was regarded
as a serious crisis of parliamentary democracy in the young republic.[3] The
inflexible "dogmatism" of the political parties was held responsible for the
impotence of parliamentary democracy in Germany.[4] While the newspapers
close to the bourgeois parties regretted the "crisis of parliamentarianism"[5]

---

[1] For a detailed account of Wirth's negotiations see the exhaustive study by Laubach,
op. cit., pp. 293–298, and pp. 307–331. President Ebert supported and might even have
initiated Wirth's plan.

[2] *Deutsche Allgemeine Zeitung*, November 16, No. 499/50; *Vossische Zeitung*, November
15, 1922, No. 641; *Frankfurter Zeitung*, November 17, 1922, No. 825.

[3] For example: *Rheinisch-Westfälische Zeitung*, November 17, 1922, No. 926; *Frankfurter Zeitung*, November 15, 1922, No. 820; *Germania*, November 19, 1922, No. 610.

[4] *Rheinisch-Westfälische Zeitung*, November 18, 1922, No. 931.

[5] *Germania*, November 19, 1922, No. 610 "Krise des Parlamentarismus." *Ibid.*, November 15, 1922, No. 610 "Der Sieg des Parteiengeistes." *Vossische Zeitung*, November 20,
1922, No. 542.

the conservative press was jubilant. The *Neue Preussische Zeitung* declared that the resignation of Wirth had shown that the transfer of a system of government alien to the German people had failed in the end.[6] Other papers of the Right were hardly less happy while the paper of the Stresemann party, *Die Zeit*, regarded the resignation of the cabinet as a definite sign that the policy of fulfillment had come to an end.[7]

From the beginning of the crisis it had been obvious that Wirth would not attempt the formation of another cabinet. Once he had resigned, the former coalition partners – Center, SPD, and DDP – were embarrassed to find out that nobody was willing to become Chancellor. Various persons were mentioned in connection with the formation of a cabinet, among them Konrad Adenauer, Lord Mayor of Cologne, Adam Stegerwald, who belonged to the right-wing of the Center, and Dr. Mayer, the German Ambassador to France.[8] The candidacy of Adenauer and Stegerwald proved to be impossible; even if Ebert had authorized them to form a cabinet, they would not have succeeded. The Reichstag delegation of the Center was annoyed over the fall of Wirth and refused to accept any responsibility for the formation of a cabinet.[9]

While there was still confusion among the political parties, President Ebert presented his own candidate. On November 16, 1922 he authorized Wilhelm Cuno, head of the Hamburg-Amerika shipping line, to form a cabinet.[10] This decision came as a surprise to most party leaders as well as the public, for normal parliamentary procedure would have called for Ebert to ask a member of one of the strongest parties in the Reichstag to form a new government. This, however, was rendered fruitless by the hardening attitude of the Center and the SPD. Ebert might have asked Gustav Stresemann of the DVP (apparently Stresemann expected such a move) and Stresemann might even have succeeded in forming a cabinet with the aid of the Center and the DDP. But his cabinet would never have gained the support of the SPD and without the support or at least toleration by the SPD, a Stresemann cabinet would have been doomed from the beginning.[11]

It appears that Ebert tried to overcome this deadlock by the designation

---

[6] *Neue Preussische Zeitung*, November 20, 1922, No. 522 was representative for the conservative press.
[7] *Die Zeit*, November 16, 1922, No. 407.
[8] *Vossische Zeitung*, November 16, 1922, No. 543.
[9] *Germania*, November 18, 1922, No. 606.
[10] According to Hans Luther, Ebert met Cuno in the Hapag office in Berlin. "Luther Erinnerungen," *Beiträge zur Geschichte von Stadt und Stift Essen*, Heft 73 (1958), p. 118.
[11] Gustav Stresemann, *Vermächtnis. Der Nachlaß in drei Bänden*, hrsg. von H. Bernhard (Berlin, 1932), I, p. 122; letter to Dingeldey, December 4, 1922.

of Cuno, perhaps on the recommendation of Carl Petersen, leader of the Democratic Party (DDP) and later on mayor of Hamburg.[12] But more important than the impasse between the political parties seems to have been Ebert's conviction – widely shared in Berlin government circles at the end of 1922 – that the approval of German business and industry was urgently needed to solve the Reich's pressing internal and external problems: reparations, an international loan, stabilization of the currency. The Social Democratic President had met Cuno several times. He had appreciated Cuno's opposition to the Rapallo Treaty, both of them fearing its repercussions upon Germany's relations with the West. Both had been upset by the disruption of financial negotiations at the Genoa conference as a result of the treaty. Furthermore, both were looking towards the United States and Great Britain for economic and financial aid.[13] Otherwise the President and the chancellor-designate did not have much in common.

Wilhelm Cuno was born in Suhl (Thuringia) in 1876. He had studied law in Heidelberg, Berlin and Breslau, completing his studies with a law degree.[14] In 1907 Cuno started his career as a *Regierungsassessor* in the *Reichsschatzamt* and in 1910 he became *Regierungsrat*. Only two years later, at the age of 36, Cuno was promoted to *Geheimer Regierungsrat*. During his time with the *Reichsschatzamt* he was occupied mainly with the drafting of bills and their presentation in the Reichstag. When the war broke out in 1914, Cuno was made head of the *Reichsgetreidestelle*. In July 1916 he became assistant to Secretary of State Adolf von Batocki with the special duty of organizing the *Kriegsernährungsamt*. In the same year Cuno took over the position of a special commissioner for questions concerning the organization of the war economy.[15]

---

[12] Max von Stockhausen, *Sechs Jahre Reichskanzlei. Von Rapallo bis Locarno. Erinnerungen und Tagebuchnotizen, 1922–1927*, hrsg. von Walter Görlitz (Bonn, 1954), p. 51. Friedrich Stampfer, *Die vierzehn Jahre der ersten Deutschen Republik* (Karlsbad, 1936), pp. 284–286. Otto Meissner, *Staatssekretär unter Ebert, Hindenburg, Hitler. Der Schicksalsweg des deutschen Volkes wie ich ihn erlebte*, 3rd ed. (Hamburg, 1950), p. 113; Arnold Brecht, *Aus nächster Nähe. Lebenserinnerungen 1884–1927* (Stuttgart, 1966), pp. 397 ff; Carl Severing, *Mein Lebensweg*, 2 vols. (Köln 1950), vol. I, pp. 376 ff.

[13] Meissner, *op. cit.*, p. 114. "Er [Ebert] war der Auffassung, daß nunmehr die Wirtschaft die Verpflichtung hätte, bei der Verständigung zwischen Deutschland und den Alliierten mitzuwirken, um auf dem Wege, den die internationalen Finanz- und Wirtschaftssachverständigen gewiesen hatten, eine Lösung der Reparationsfragen und zugleich eine Stabilisierung der deutschen Währung zu erreichen." Thus the cabinet should not be based upon a parliamentary majority, but should include "Vertreter der Wirtschaft und fachmännische Kräfte."

[14] Cuno received his doctorate in 1901 with a thesis "Übergang der Gefahr bei Gattungsproblemen nach dem bürgerlichen Gesetzbuch."

[15] This biography is mainly based on Heinz-Helmut Kohlhaus, *Die Hapag, Cuno*

On the basis of his education and early career Wilhelm Cuno would have ordinarily been destined to remain a civil servant. His work for the *Kriegs-ernährungsamt* had acquainted him with the problems of industrial organization. As an able administrator and excellent organizer, a career in the upper hierarchy of the German civil service was open to him.

Everything changed, however, when Cuno met Albert Ballin, head of the Hamburg-Amerika shipping line (HAPAG), in 1917. Ballin was so impressed with Cuno that he offered him a job on the board of directors of the HAPAG. Cuno accepted Ballin's offer and on November 1, 1917 left the civil service to go to Hamburg. Under the protection of Ballin, he soon made his way in the HAPAG. Obviously he was successful, for, after Ballin's death, Cuno – former civil servant, a Catholic, and a stranger to the Hamburg shipping business – became Ballin's successor on December 20, 1918.[16]

It was a difficult time for the start of a new career. Germany's defeat had an immediate impact on the future of the German merchant fleet and the HAPAG. Soon Cuno became one of the leading spokesmen of shipping industry, arguing that the delivery of the merchant fleet would mean the economic ruin of Germany. In his capacity as director of the HAPAG and as an official government adviser at Versailles and numerous other postwar conferences, Cuno stressed that the Allies were destroying any possibility for reparation payments if they did not allow Germany to earn foreign currency through exports. He objected to the delivery of the merchant fleet and suggested that, instead, Germany should build ships for the Allies.[17]

For Cuno, a contradiction existed between the economic and financial clauses of the Versailles Treaty and from 1919 he constantly worked for a revision of the peace terms:

In my opinion, all German counterproposals should stress the contradiction between the economic and financial clauses. We should stress Germany's readiness to pay an indemnity, but we should also make our position clear that if we are expected to pay, we must be allowed to work. Provided that it still exists and can work, German shipping industry is of course ready to contribute to the indemnity.[18]

When Cuno recognized that he could not save the merchant fleet, he resigned from the peace delegation and told Arndt von Holtzendorff, the HAPAG

---

und das Deutsche Reich 1920–1933, Phil. Diss. (Hamburg, 1952), pp. 167–187; also *Neue Deutsche Biographie*, III, pp. 438–439.

[16] Kohlhaus, *op. cit.*, pp. 167 ff.

[17] Wilhelm Cuno, "Friedensbedingungen die Schiffahrt betreffend." May 22, 1919, pp. 10–12, *Cuno Nachlaß*, Friedensvertragsverhandlungen 1919 ff.

[18] *Ibid.*, p. 13; also "Die Stellung der deutschen Seeschiffahrt zum Friedensvertrag." May 16, 1919, *ibid.*

representative in Berlin, that Versailles meant the end of an independent Germany. The Treaty had to be rejected, otherwise the Allies might as well treat Germany as a colony and take over the administration. This would have left them with the responsibility of feeding the population. Under these conditions he was no longer prepared to work as a government adviser.[19] His anger did not last long, however, and he tried to regain access to the world market for the HAPG through his personal connections. In June 1920 he signed a treaty with the American Ship and Commerce Company that facilitated the return of the HAPAG to her prewar activities as well as laying the foundation for further cooperation and friendship with Averell W. Harriman, owner of the American Ship and Commerce Company.[20]

After this success Cuno was regarded as an econonic wizard, after all, the contract had been signed before the United States had signed the peace treaty with Germany. Cuno's popularity among government circles rose, though he was hardly known to outsiders. From then on the HAPAG director participated at most German-Allied conferences. His theme at these meetings was based on the economic solidarity of nations and urgent appeals to political leaders to allow a conference of international experts to decide upon German reparation payments.[21]

As director of the HAPAG it was only natural that Cuno should seek the solution of Germany's financial and economic problems in an expansion of trade which would naturally help the Hamburg shipping industry. But more important than his immediate concern for the HAPAG were his ideas about the future of world trade. Cuno recognized that Germany's defeat had thoroughly changed the European political structure. But despite her defeat and the political and military predominance of France, Germany was still a great continental power. Cuno based his beliefs regarding Germany's strength not on her military or political potential, but on her economic power. Without Germany, world trade could not recuperate. The irrefutability of these economic facts was best expressed by the director of the HAPAG himself when he stated his credo before the Bruxelles Conference in December 1920: "Any extension of political power does not change basic economic facts."[22]

---

[19] Cuno's resignation was submitted on June 22, 1919. See *ibid.*, Akten von Holtzendorff 1921–1923.

[20] Link, *op. cit.*, pp. 67–70; also Kohlhaus, *op. cit.*, pp. 30–34.

[21] Cf. Cuno's speeches at the Brussels Conference in December 1920, *Cuno Nachlaß*, Brüsseler Konferenz, December 1920. The speech was made on December 18. *Ibid.*, "Konferenz von London. Exposés."

[22] "Brüsseler Conferenz," December 16–22, 1920, *ibid.*, Archiv des Vorsitzenden des Direktoriums.

Cuno was not only convinced that economic power was decisive in the struggle between states, but he believed in the superiority of businessmen over politicians as well. In his view, politicians were demagogues and their strictly ideological approach to political problems was alien to business. They tended to make inflammatory speeches, whereas for a businessman, only "sober calculations" counted.[23] In contrast to politicians, business-men would approach problems pragmatically; this in itself would always facilitate negotiations, and business partners would normally be able to reach a compromise. Though Cuno liked to see himself as a man free of all ideological prejudices, his point of view was actually an ideology in itself. Furthermore, Cuno strictly believed in the value of private enterprise and fought a violent battle against domestic attempts to nationalize the shipping industry. Thus, at the beginning of his career as director of the HAPAG, he successfully prevented its nationalization and managed to obtain an indem-nity from the Reich for the delivery of the merchant fleet amounting to 46.8% of the losses.[24]

Despite his peculiar ideas about the behavior of politicians and business-men, the myth about Cuno's political capabilities remained, and Max von Stockhausen, *Regierungsrat* in the Chancellory, described Cuno's attitude towards politics with the following words:

Cuno ... was above all a highly qualified expert from the old imperial bureau-cracy, who only knew one goal: to conduct business in a purely practical manner.[25]

But there were less flattering opinions about the political competence of this representative of Hamburg shipping interests. Moritz Bonn, economist and fellow government adviser, described Cuno as a charming man, who would have been an excellent reception clerk in a luxury hotel. Cuno, Bonn believed, knew less about politics than a "mittelmäßig begabter" trade union secre-tary who had suddenly found himself in charge of a ministry. Graf Kessler, a friend of Rathenau and observer of the Berlin literary and political scene, considered him to be "incapable" of filling a political office, while Rudolf Hilferding was doubtful about Cuno's political capabilities.[26]

[23] Cuno to King, February 14, 1922, *ibid.*, Briefe 1920–1922. Cuno wrote this letter to his British business partner after the Cannes conference.

[24] Kohlhaus, *op. cit.*, pp. 15 ff. and p. 48. The shipping companies received 12 billion paper marks and were obliged to rebuild 90% of the fleet on German shipyards. This had to be done within ten years from March 1921 onwards. Cf. Günther Leckebusch, *Die Beziehungen der deutschen Seeschiffswerften zur Eisenindustrie an der Ruhr in der Zeit von 1850–1930* (Köln, 1963), pp. 96 ff.

[25] Von Stockhausen, *op. cit.*, p. 53.

[26] Moritz J. Bonn, *So macht man Geschichte* (München, 1953), p. 274; Harry Graf Kessler, *Tagebuch, 1918–1937*, hrsg. v. Wolfgang Pfeiffer-Belli (Frankfurt/M., 1961), p. 346.

Nevertheless, Cuno's name was mentioned several times in connection with a cabinet post. When Matthias Erzberger was forced to resign in 1920, Cuno was offered the Ministry of Finance. In 1921 Ebert suggested that he became the first Ambassador to the United States, and in September 1922 Wirth asked him to become Foreign Minister in order to strengthen Germany's position at the coming reparation conferences through his American and British connections. Cuno declined all these appointments, though President Ebert intervened himself urging him to accept.[27]

The director of the HAPAG still believed that he could do more for Germany by remaining in the background and endeavoring to find a solution for Germany's problems with the help of his British and American business contacts.[28] By the summer of 1922 it had become clear that Germany could not wait for Allied politicians to create a feasible plan for a final reparation settlement. Otto Wiedfeldt, German Ambassador to Washington and former director of the Friedrich Krupp A.G., urged Wirth to develop a plan for an international conference of experts. Wiedfeldt proposed that the conference should take place before the end of the year.[29] For a man who believed as strongly as Cuno did in the superiority of business over politics, this was a plan he could support. He knew Wiedfeldt from their common work as government advisers, and appreciated him as a trustworthy and able partner. Cuno talked to Ebert and the members of Wirth's cabinet. At first, only Ebert and the Minister of Finance, Andreas Hermes, supported a final plan, while Wirth did not think that a plan mentioning a final sum was possible at all.[30]

But on September 29, 1922, Cuno could report to Wiedfeldt that a commission consisting of Carl Bergmann, Carl Melchior, and himself had been created for the preparatory work.[31] The purpose of the commission was to develop a plan which would allow an international loan to Germany. This loan would then be employed to pay France. Cuno intended to go to London

[27] Laubach, *op. cit.*, p. 282 reports that Ebert wanted Cuno as Foreign Minister. This is confirmed by Cuno. Cf. Cuno to J.P. Meyer, September 28, 1922, *Cuno Nachlaß*, Briefe 1919–1922. Carl Melchior to Wirth, August 31, 1922, *ibid.*, Politik, November 1920–Oktober 1922. The offer for the Ambassadorship in Washington is described in von Holtzendorff to Cuno, August 28, 1921, *ibid.*, Akten von Holtzendorff 1921–1923.

[28] Ebert and Wirth had sent Cuno to England and the United States in 1921–1922 to sound out politicians and businessmen about a conference. *Ibid.*, Politik, November 1920–October 1922.

[29] Otto Wiedfeldt to Cuno, July 27, 1922, *ibid.*, Briefe Cuno 1920–1922.

[30] Cuno to Wiedfeldt, August 4, 1922, *ibid.*, Archiv des Vorsitzenden des Direktoriums, Politik November 1920–October 1922.

[31] Carl Melchior – Reichskanzler, August 31, 1922, Aktennotiz vom 29.9. 1922, *BA*, R 38/179.

and talk the problem over with British financial experts and politicians, but nothing came of this plan as neither Britain nor the United States could be convinced that this plan would succeed in face of French opposition to a conference of international banking experts.[32] Still, Cuno had established himself in the inner circle of government experts, and by the end of 1922 his already considerable reputation was still rising. Despite this first set-back he seems to have impressed President Ebert as the man, who could do the impossible and arrange an international conference of financial experts to reconsider reparations.

Taking into consideration Cuno's ideas about politics and ideological differences between parties, it is no surprise that the chancellor-designate tried to form a cabinet based on the support of all parties. Cuno himself did not belong to any party, but probably sympathized with the DNVP and the DVP. However, both the Center Party and the DVP tried to gain Cuno as a candidate for the Reichstag elections in 1920. Cuno declined these offers. Undoubtedly he sympathized with the domestic program of the DVP, but above all he was a lobbyist for the HAPAG who wanted to cooperate with "all state-supporting parties."[33] Still, his inclination towards national-conservative groups had not prevented him in 1920 from writing to Ebert when rumors were rife that Ebert would not be a candidate for the presidency. Urging him to reconsider, Cuno explained that Ebert was the last link between the working class and the middle class. He feared the dissolution of the Reich and social unrest if Ebert resigned. In his opinion Ebert could guarantee that the Social Democrats would remain a stabilizing factor in the new republic.[34] But the decisive factor for Cuno's support of Ebert was his realization that cooperation within the new system offered the only means of achieving the preservation of the old economic order, the recovery of economic prosperity and the restoration of national power and prestige.

[32] Cuno-Dufour, October 26, 1922, *Cuno Nachlaß*, Briefe Cuno 1920–1922. Albert Dufour-Feronce was German attaché at the embassy in London; cf. Laubach, *op. cit.*, pp. 280 ff.

[33] S. William Halperin, *Germany Tried Democracy. A Political History of the Reich from 1918–1933* (New York, 1965), p. 224; Henry A. Turner, *Streseman and the Politics of the Weimar Republic* (Princeton, 1963), p. 103 and Stampfer, *op. cit.*, p. 185 maintain that Cuno had been a member of the DVP until the Kapp Putsch. Correct von Stockhausen, *op. cit.*, p. 52. For the 1920 elections see: Cuno–Dr. Rose, (DVP Landesverband Hamburg), January 1, 1920, *Cuno Nachlaß*, Politik, November 1919–October 1922; *ibid.*, Cuno's rejection of the Center approach. According to Hans Luther, Cuno was closest to the DNVP. Cf. "Luther Erinnerungen," *op. cit.*, p. 118; Paul Moldenhauer of the DVP believed that Cuno, an active Catholic, stood between Center and DVP. See *Paul Moldenhauer Nachlaß*, Nr. 1, p. 128.

[34] Cuno-Ebert, September 22, 1920, *ibid.*

Contrary to many other businessmen and politicians, Cuno thus accepted the republic from the beginning and tried to make the best of it.

Considering Cuno's ideas about politics, he was hardly prepared to fulfill Ebert's expectation. Cuno overestimated his own ability of bridging the gap between the different political parties; he did not understand the working of parliamentary democracy and wanted to run his cabinet by experts without party affiliation. Hoping to exclude the ideological differences between the parties from the working of his cabinet, he decided to form a "Kabinett der Arbeit."[35] He intended to unite all bourgeois parties and the SPD on a platform based upon a "sober and business-like" approach to the pending foreign and domestic problems. Though the name had changed, Cuno's "Kabinett der Arbeit" was nothing else than an attempt to form a Great Coalition. While he had been working for the HAPAG, he had sometimes regretted that the expertise of industrialists and businessmen was not represented on the executive level of government politics. His cabinet, Cuno hoped, would be the first government in the Weimar Republic that could rely upon the active collaboration of German business.[36] Cuno's high expectations – which were certainly unrealistic considering the intensity of the political struggle over economic, financial and foreign policy questions in the young republic – were soon destroyed by the parties. The Reich could not be run like the HAPAG office or the imperial bureaucracy. During his meetings with the parties, the Center and the SPD presented their conditions for cooperation. The Center voted against Cuno's intention to fill the post of foreign minister with Andreas Hermes. The majority of the Social Democrats was not prepared to support Cuno unless he agreed to exclude the DVP, considered to be the party of heavy industry, from his cabinet. In addition, the SPD requested that the Minister of Economics in the Wirth cabinet, Robert Schmidt (SPD), and his Secretary of State, Julius Hirsch, remain in their positions.[37]

These conditions were unacceptable to Cuno. Angered by the direct intervention of the parties, he wrote to Ebert on November 18 that he considered a "dispassionate collaboration" with the parties impossible. The conditions proposed by the parties had limited his responsibility as chancellor. Though Cuno did not underestimate the importance of a close cooperation between parliament and the cabinet, he felt that the final decision about the constitution of the cabinet lay with the chancellor alone. Since this was prevented

[35] Cuno-Ebert, November 18, 1922, *BA*, R 43I/1305.

[36] *Ibid.*

[37] *Vossische Zeitung*, November 18, 1922, No. 548/B 272. The unwillingness of the Center to allow Hermes to become Foreign Minister was due to frictions that had existed between Wirth and Hermes concerning foreign policy under the Wirth cabinet.

by the demands of the parties, the chancellor-designate returned his assignment.[38] Thus on November 18, only two days after Ebert had asked Cuno to form a cabinet, Cuno's attempt to do so had failed. Georg Bernard, one of the leading liberal journalists of the Weimar Republic and editor of the *Vossische Zeitung*, noted that Ebert should have dissolved the Reichstag and authorized new elections. But such a step would not have solved the stalemate, since Weimar electoral law rendered any clear parliamentary majority impossible.[39]

The Social Democratic President apparently never considered dissolving the Reichstag. Though a majority of the Social Democrats had rejected a coalition with the DVP against Ebert's advice, he was not willing to drop Cuno. The same evening, Ebert called another meeting between Cuno and the party leaders. As a result of these negotiations, Ebert authorized Cuno on November 20 to give the formation of a cabinet a second trial. At this point Cuno was given the opportunity to select a cabinet without the intrusion of the parties, which agreed to allow their members to decide if they wanted to work independently in a Cuno cabinet. After Cuno had made his choice the new cabinet would try to gain a vote of confidence in the Reichstag.[40]

Difficult negotiations followed and Cuno finally managed to form a "cabinet above parties."[41] This "Geschäftsministerium," as the new cabinet was called as well, was not a government "above parties."[42] It had been formed without the active support of the parties, but the parties, with the exception of the SPD, had at least not prevented their members from accepting cabinet posts. Cuno thus relied heavily on the bourgeois parties. Only four of his ministers did not belong to any party. The new Foreign Minister, Frederic von Rosenberg, a career diplomat, had been minister plenipotentiary to Denmark.[43] Wilhelm Groener, the Minister of Transport, did not belong to any party but had already been a member of both the Wirth and Fehrenbach cabinets. Heinrich Albert, the Minister of the Treasury, then Luther, who became Minister of Food and Agriculture after

[38] Cuno to Ebert, November 18, 1922, *BA*, R 43I/1305.

[39] *Vossische Zeitung*, November 19, 1922, No. 549 "Die Unvernunft der Logik."

[40] Rudolf Wertheimer, "Der Einfluß des Reichspräsidenten auf die Gestaltung der Reichsregierung"; Jur. Diss. (Heidelberg, 1929), pp. 62–65; Friedrich Glum, Das parlamentarische Regierungssystem in Deutschland, Großbritannien und Frankreich (München und Berlin, 1950), pp. 225–227. *Germania*, November 19, 1922 No. 610. Günther Arns, "Friedrich Ebert als Reichspräsident," *Historische Zeitschrift* Beiheft 1 (1971), p. 22.

[41] *Vossische Zeitung*, November 26, 1922, No. 560.

[42] *Vorwärts*, November 20, 1922, No. 549.

[43] Other persons mentioned for the post of Foreign Minister were Dr. Mayer (Ambassador to France) and von Neurath (Ambassador to Italy).

Cuno's first choice had to resign, did not have any party affiliation either.[44]

All other members of the cabinet belonged to the parties of the "bourgeois coalition." Andreas Hermes and Heinrich Brauns were members of the Center and remained in the positions they had had under Wirth. Rudolf Heinze and Dr. Johann Becker represented the DVP, while Otto Gessler, Rudolf Oeser and the Secretary of State in the Chancellory, Eduard Hamm, were members of the DDP. One minister belonged to the Bavarian People's Party (BVP).[45]

Even if the parties of the bourgeois *Arbeitsgemeinschaft* had voted for the cabinet, this would not have guaranteed a vote of confidence in the Reichstag, as the DNVP, the SPD, and the KPD could always overthrow the cabinet. Such a coalition, however, was unlikely. Nobody wanted a prolongation of the crisis, and the SPD delegation in the Reichstag decided to observe a policy of "benevolent neutrality" towards the new cabinet.[46]

The general relief of the parties over the formation of the cabinet was shown in the party press. To *Vorwärts*, the personal character of the new Chancellor was above reproach, and the paper expected that Cuno would be a "republican civil servant" who would work for the common good.[47] The Social Democrats would support the Chancellor, although his cabinet could only be considered a transitional government.[48] However, *Vorwärts* did not like the appointment of Dr. Johann Becker as Minister of Economics. Becker (former director of the *Rheinische Stahlwerke* and the DVP's finance expert) could not be trusted. He was known for his anti-labor position, and the SPD would have to keep an eye on his activities.[49]

The press of the Weimar coalition recognized that the crisis of parliamentary democracy had only been postponed. Most papers hoped that the Center and the SPD would finally support Cuno.[50] Papers close to the DDP warned the chancellor to give in to pressures exerted by the DNVP which

[44] Cuno's first appointment for Minister of Food and Agriculture had been Karl Müller. This appointment would cause the first crisis of the cabinet, and Müller had to resign on November 25, 1922.

[45] Hermes (Finance), Brauns (Labor), Oeser (Interior), Heinze (Justice), Becker (Economics), Gessler (Army), and Stingl (Postmaster General). See Uwe Oltmann, "Reichsarbeitsminister Heinrich Brauns in der Staats- und Währungskrise 1923–1924. Die Bedeutung der Sozialpolitik für die Inflation, den Ruhrkampf und die Stabilisierung," Phil. Diss. (Kiel, 1968), p. 21.

[46] *Vorwärts*, November 17, 1922, No. 544.

[47] *Ibid.*

[48] *Ibid.*, November 20, 1922, No. 549.

[49] *Ibid.*, November 22, 1922, No. 522 "Cuno zum Kanzler ernannt." *Ibid.*, November 23, 1922, No. 553 "An der Wende."

[50] Representative for this attitude is *Germania*, November 24, 1922, No. 617. The same expectations are shown in *Frankfurter Zeitung, Berliner Tageblatt* and *Vossische Zeitung*.

tried to push Cuno further to the Right.[51] In general, the papers of the bourgeois press were satisfied that Cuno had become chancellor. They expected that his close business connections with his former British and American business partners would facilitate a final settlement of the pending problems. This was the main reason for the existence of the Cuno cabinet.[52]

The conservative press was less enthusiastic and stressed that the DNVP was not represented in the cabinet and would be forced into opposition if Cuno should adhere to Wirth's policy of fulfillment.[53] For the Communist press, Cuno was simply the representative of Stinnes and heavy industry whom the Social Democrats had helped to form a bourgeois cabinet.[54]

When Cuno presented his cabinet in the Reichstag on November 24, 1922, he was greeted with warm applause from the Center, the DVP, and especially the DDP. The chancellor followed the presentation of his cabinet with a governmental program which emphasized the critical state of domestic and foreign affairs. Regretting that his government could not rely on the support of the SPD, he appealed to "a'l those parties who have the interest of the state at heart" to aid his cabinet. Governmental programs, Cuno told his audience, would not improve the situation if parties, interest groups, and the German people would not work together and forget party strife.[55]

Cuno's governmental program, which had been prepared by him in collaboration with his Secretary of State, Hamm, and the Syndic of the HAPAG and member of the DVP, Dr. Hasselmann, was an obvious attempt to gain the support of all parties and satisfy everbody. It proved to be easy for the parties to agree on Cuno's foreign policy program. Attacking the Versailles Treaty, the chancellor called for the return of German sovereignty and equal rights on the world market. He demanded a revision of the London Schedule of Payments which had been rendered obscure, he argued, according to the estimates of international experts at Cannes, Genoa, and later meetings. Relying on the estimate of international experts, he declared that Germany could not pay at the moment. The chancellor endorsed the Wirth note to the Allies of November 13, 1922 requesting an international loan (500 million gold marks) and a moratorium for 3 to 4 years.[56]

---

[51] For example *Vossische Zeitung*, November 25, 1922, No. 558 "Cuno's Grundproblem."

[52] These expectations were mentioned in most papers, but are best expressed by Georg Bernard in *ibid.*, November 26, 1922, No. 560 "Das parteifreie Kabinett."

[53] *Neue Preußische Zeitung*, November 21, 1922, No. 524. *Ibid.*, November 26, 1922, No. 531.

[54] *Rote Fahne*, November 25, 1922. Also *Westfälische Arbeiterzeitung*, November 28, 1922, No. 253.

[55] *Verhandlungen des Reichstags*, vol. 357, pp. 9099–9103. From now on *RT*.

[56] *Ibid.* Laubach, *op. cit.*, pp. 306–309 discusses the Wirth note of November 13.

At the same time he repeated Wirth's plan for the stabilization of the mark. For this purpose he would ask the Reichsbank to use 500 million gold marks of her reserves to support the mark on the international money market. In addition, measures would be taken to control and restrict the import of luxury goods.

Without a final reparation settlement, however, these German initiatives for the stabilization of their currency would be futile, and Cuno appealed to Great Britain and especially to the United States for help. In his opinion, constant French ultimata prevented the return of trust in the German currency, and he asked the Anglo-Saxon powers to aid Germany in her negotiations for the final settlement.[57] Good will towards Germany was all that was needed. Cuno hoped that his foreign policy would meet the approval of Great Britain and the United States.

No creditor, who considers reparations as an economic question and not as an instrument of power politics, can oppose such a policy.[58]

Although Cuno did not explicitly mention France, the object of his remarks was obvious.

Cuno had been attacked as the representative of Stinnes in the Reichstag. In order to show that his foreign policy was only a continuation of Wirth's and no turning point, Cuno stressed his predecessor's slogan "bread before reparations." This slogan would also be the guiding principle of his administration. It was Germany's duty to rebuild Northern France, but first the German people had to get over the next winter. This statement was especially applauded on the Right, but there was applause on the DDP and Center benches as well. Then Cuno turned to his domestic program and informed the Reichstag that in order to get Germany through the next difficult months, unproductive work – be it in industry, agriculture, or government service – had to be eliminated. An increase in agricultural production would furthermore reduce food and fat imports and would thus save foreign currency. Despite these proposals to cut expenditures, Cuno promised aid to pensioners and widows – in general to all those in need. In addition he pledged support to small craftsmen against competition from powerful trusts. He called for a tax reform, and promised to adjust the gap between wages and the sinking value of the mark.[59]

This ambitious program did not differ much from Wirth's designs. But the question remained whether Cuno would be able to and actually intended

[57] *RT.*, vol. 357, pp. 9103–9105.
[58] *Ibid.*, p. 9101.
[59] *Ibid.*, vol. 357, pp. 9103–9105.

to fulfill his rather vague promises. The discussion of his government program showed that Breitscheid (SPD), Marx (Z), Schiffer (DDP), and Stresemann (DVP), who spoke for their parties, could easily endorse the foreign policy platform with its attacks upon the Versailles Treaty. Most of the discussion however, was spent on the dissolution of the Wirth cabinet and the ensuing crisis. All parties felt uneasy about Wirth's resignation. They wanted to clarify and justify their own position before the public. Some party leaders seemed to doubt the wisdom of their previous decision. At a time when financial chaos loomed over Germany and the Allies were preparing a new conference on reparations, the parties had failed to form a strong government.[60]

While it had been easy to agree on the foreign policy platform, the discussion of Cuno's domestic program would show the real differences between the parties. Breitscheid supported Cuno's plan to increase agricultural and industrial production, but warned immediately that the SPD would never surrender the eight-hour day. Any attempt to abandon state control of basic industries and any efforts to relinquish rent control would force the SPD into opposition. He did not doubt Cuno's sincerity but questioned his ability to execute his program against the industrial group in the DVP. Breitscheid repeated the warning of *Vorwärts* that the SPD intended to watch carefully the activities of the Minister of Economics, Dr. Becker, who was known as an enemy of taxation of the material wealth of industry for reparation purposes.[61]

The attacks of Breitscheid and Sollmann (SPD) on the designation of Karl Müller as Minister of Food and Agriculture completed the criticism of Cuno's ministers. Though the cabinet stood behind Müller, he resigned because of accusations that he had been a member of the Separatist Movement in the Rhineland in 1919, advocating an independent Rhineland state within the Reich.[62] Hans Luther, the Oberbürgermeister of Essen, became his successor.[63]

Cuno did not try to obtain a vote of confidence in the Reichstag. The leader of the DDP group, Dr. Petersen, had prepared a motion in advance which stated that the Reichstag "had taken notice of Cuno's program and approved of his intention to base his policy on the note of November 13."[64]

---

[60] *Ibid.*, pp. 9105–9108, pp. 9115–9117, pp. 9221–2123, and pp. 9151–9156.
[61] *Ibid.*, pp. 9108–9114.
[62] *Ibid.*, pp. 9138–9139.
[63] Hans Luther, *Politiker ohne Partei* (Stuttgart, 1960), pp. 30–31. "Luther Erinnerungen," *op. cit.*, pp. 118 ff.
[64] *RT.*, vol. 357, pp. 316 ff. Dr. Petersen was Mayor of Hamburg. He seems to have

This tactical procedure allowed all parties to save face. It prevented the possibility of a new crisis if Cuno did attempt to gain the vote of confidence. A motion of the KPD to disapprove of Cuno's domestic and foreign policy platform was voted down by the SPD, the Center, the DVP and DDP, and the DNVP.[65]

Ten days after the Wirth government had been dissolved, the Weimar Republic had a new cabinet, the members of which were leaning a bit further to the right than the members of the Wirth cabinet. The policy of fulfillment had already failed under Wirth and recognizing this failure, Wirth had requested a moratorium and a revision of the London Schedule of Payments in November. In addition, he had tried to incorporate the DVP in his cabinet. If he had succeeded his cabinet would not have been much different from Cuno's with the important exception that the SPD was not represented in the new cabinet. Even now the SPD was not in opposition to Cuno but would regulate its attitude towards Cuno according to the issues involved.

The new chancellor had always been convinced that either economic lunatics or *Machtpolitiker*, set upon destruction of Germany's economic potential, had invented the reparation clauses. If the Allies wanted a solution to the European stalemate, Cuno was ready to negotiate and submit his own proposals. But he was under no circumstances prepared to continue reparation payments without a reduction of the London Schedule of Payments. Such payments would have only further diminished the substance of the German economy and would have only postponed a final struggle with Raymond Poincaré. In domestic politics, the formation of Cuno's cabinet subdued for the moment speculations about a dictatorship. But it is striking how naively the bourgeois press and the public had reacted to the stalemate between the parties. The desire for an impartial government that would set everything right and overcome pettifogging party divisions was an indicator for the weakness of parliamentary democracy in Germany.

Considering the unwillingness of the parties to cooperate in a Great Coalition, it is difficult to see how Cuno could have hoped to convince the Allies that his cabinet could participate in any serious negotiations. This weak cabinet was dependent upon shifting party coalitions. Furthermore, it is doubtful that it had the support of industry. True enough, Cuno could rely upon the judgement of members of the Hamburg banking community. Especially Carl Melchior of the Warburg Bank, finance adviser to several

taken the initiative after a meeting with Cuno. However nothing definite can be said about other participants of the meeting.

[65] *Ibid.*, vol. 357, pp. 3166 ff.

governments and known as a "moderate" among allied reparation experts supported Cuno.[66] However, there is no evidence of Cuno's having outstanding relations with heavy or light industries, and his being able to rally the support of these powerful interest groups to his cabinet before he became chancellor. As has been shown, he had Ebert's confidence and hoped to gain the support of Great Britain and the United States for a new approach towards reparations.[67] The latter hope did not seem to be too unrealistic at that point.

Lord d'Abernon, British Ambassador to Berlin, felt that Cuno was "a good choice – rather pro-English and still more pro-American." However, he doubted that Cuno was "nimble enough for party intrigues." In his opinion Cuno was "not at all a politician. Rather a Lohengrin." On the other hand, both D'Abernon and his French colleague in Berlin, Pierre de Margerie, believed that Cuno was an "honest man."[68] While doubts concerning Cuno's political competence existed with the British Ambassador, the American Ambassador, Alanson B. Houghton, had a very high opinion of Cuno. Since his arrival in Berlin in the spring of 1922, Houghton had met most leading German politicians, industrialists and bankers. During the summer of 1922, the American embassy had become one of the most popular meeting places of German and American politicians and businessmen, sometimes connections being arranged through the embassy. Himself a former businessman, Houghton looked upon reparations "from a broadly economic point of view."[69] On several occasions, Wirth and Rathenau asked for Houghton's advice concerning foreign policy initiatives, and Houghton's Berlin Diary reads like a compendium of German industry and banking. Houghton and his German visitors may not have agreed on many questions, yet this permanent exchange of ideas slowly created an intimacy which was both helpful and dangerous for German policy; it could be helpful in obtaining information on American attitudes, yet it could mean disaster if politicians and the business community relied too heavily on American ad-

[66] Carl Melchior-Wirth, August 31, 1922, *Cuno Nachlaß*, Politik, November 1919–Oktober 1922. Cf. Maier, *op. cit.*, p. 218.

[67] Jean-Claude Favez, *Le Reich devant l'occupation franco-belge de la Ruhr en 1923* (Genève, 1969), pp. 46 ff. Cuno certainly had not been "mis en place par des industriels"; cf. Pierre Miquel, *Poincaré* (Paris, 1961), p. 468. For a similar opinion see Jacques Bariéty, *Les relations franco-allemandes après la Première Guerre Mondiale* (Paris, 1977), p. 107; Kurt Gossweiler, *Ökonomie und Politik in Deutschland 1914–1932* (Berlin, 1971), p. 201.

[68] Viscount D'Abernon, *An Ambassador of Peace*, 3 vols. (London 1929–1930), vol. II, p. 132; de Margerie, December 12, 1922, *MAE*, Allemagne 477, fol. 57 ff.

[69] Castle-Dresel, March 25, 1922, *Ellis L. Dresel Papers*, Dresel was US representative in Berlin before diplomatic relations had been established. *Alanson B. Houghton Papers*, Diary.

vice, this being generously given by visiting bankers and businessmen.[70] Of all his Berlin contacts, Houghton developed a personal relationship only with Cuno. He visited Cuno in his Hamburg home and cabled back to Washington "Cuno is one of the really great constructive forces in Germany. His indirect power with the Government is tremendous. He is a man well worth knowing, and he will be a very considerable factor I think in helping me with such duties as you people may ask me to perform."[71] Warren D. Robbins of the US embassy, normally not a friend of Germany, agreed: "Of course we are delighted with this new Chief of Cabinet, as he seems to be not only well inclined towards us, but an able and efficient business head, who, if anyone can, should be able to succeed."[72] Cuno was not only held in high esteem by members of the American embassy, he had also discussed his accepting office with Averell Harriman and Houghton. As early as November 3, Harriman and Cuno had visited Houghton and talked about the "possibility of Cuno entering the Government." However, Harriman had urged Cuno not to accept "until the moment came, when, owing to a shift in the Government, his services would be made more valuable and more permanent. He [Harriman] seemed to think that under the Government as it stands, Cuno's hands would be tied and he would really be able to do little."[73] On November 18, the day Cuno had failed to form a Cabinet with the support of the parties, the American ambassador visited the HAPAG office in the Tiergarten upon Cuno's request. Again Cuno asked for advice. "Speaking as a friend and personally," but "not in any sense as the US ambassador," Houghton suggested that unless Cuno "could get a Cabinet of his own making and be given a free hand to do the things he wanted to do, it would be inadvisable for him to go further." In this friendly and intimate discussion, Cuno described his intentions. According to Houghton: "··· he believed it was possible to handle the reparations question as a business question, and that he meant, if made chancellor, to work definitely to that end."[74]

To France, reparations certainly was not a business question and Cuno's intentions would prove to be a gross miscalculation. However, this interpretation of the reparation issue was quite common among American businessmen and members of the Reparations Commission. As early as October

[70] *Houghton Papers*, Diary, May 12, meeting with Paul Schwabach; May 15, meeting with Kurt Sorge; May 17, Cuno and Gustav Krupp von Bohlen Halbach; June 1, Rathenau; June 2, Wirth; June 4, Felix Deutsch.
[71] Houghton-Castle, June 29, 1922, *William R. Castle Papers*, January 1922–June 1923. Castle was Undersecretary for European Affairs.
[72] Warren D. Robbins-Castle, December 11, 1922, *ibid.*
[73] *Houghton Papers*, Berlin Diary, November 3, 1922, p. 435.
[74] *Ibid.*, November 18, 1922.

1921, James Logan had stated frankly in a dinner conversation with Cuno, Paul Warburg and Dresel, that the London Schedule of Payments "is entirely unfulfillable."[75] Cuno and other German businessmen, industrialists and bankers were well informed of these opinions. They were convinced that in the end American financial and economic power would determine the outcome of reparations regardless of what France would do.[76] Without this conviction Cuno might not have had the courage to become chancellor. His immediate success, however, would not depend upon his personal relationship with American officials, but on the attitude of German industry and on France.

[75] Dresel-Castle, October 5, 1922, *Dresel Papers.*
[76] For American expectations see Werner Link, *Die amerikanische Stabilisierungspolitik in Deutschland 1921–1932* (Düsseldorf, 1970).

CHAPTER II

GERMAN INDUSTRY AND REPARATIONS

The reparation problem, complicated as it was, was made even more so by
the heightened role of industry in domestic politics, its attitude towards
party government, and its intervention into areas of foreign policy. However, this development was not only the result of industrial pressure upon
different German governments; rather politicians were only too willing to
allow the participation of industrial and banking experts in the formulation
of reparation initiatives. This development had of course started under the
Scheidemann cabinet. Demobilization, food supply, the delivery of the
merchant fleet, allied demands upon Germany, in short, the reconstruction
of the peace economy necessitated a close cooperation between the minis-
terial bureaucracy, labor and industry. In the pursuit of a domestic and
foreign peace policy, Weimar governments depended heavily upon the
expertise of bankers and industrialists. On one hand, the fact that the representatives of special interests acted as governmental advisers, predetermined
the search for feasible solutions; on the other hand, since the majority of the
Reichstag supported or at least did not have the power or will to reject the
influence of different interest groups upon governmental decision making,
the search for German reparation programs remained a source of constant
frustration for the Allies. Not only were Allied demands and German
counter proposals widely apart, but similar disagreements existed between
parties and interest groups whenever questions concerning the distribution
of the reparation burden were discussed in Berlin. While political parties,
labor, the banking community and industry might quarrel about the amount
of reparations and whether they should come from government revenues,
direct or indirect taxation, landed property, industrial stocks, international
and domestic loans or export surplus, all agreed that in the immediate future
German stocks were limited. The story of this struggle is largely known, and
there is no need to repeat it in detail here.[1] But in order to understand the

[1] For a discussion of these problems see: Lothar Albertin, *Liberalismus und Demokratie
am Anfang der Weimarer Republik. Eine vergleichende Analyse der Deutschen Demokratischen Partei und der Deutschen Volkspartei.* (Düsseldorf, 1972), pp. 41–45. Krüger, *op. cit.,*

developments that took place at the end of 1922, it is necessary to keep in mind some basic facts about industrial attitudes towards reparations since Versailles. Thus a general survey of opinions will be given here.

Full of resentment against Allied politicians, industrialists reasoned that the Versailles Treaty was the result of 19th century style cabinet politics. The war had hastened the dissolution of the old international economic system, and the creation of new states in Central and South-Eastern Europe had further added to the breakdown of European economic unity. Political decision-making at Versailles had stopped all attempts at a renewal of economic cooperation, and the demands imposed upon the defeated nations were a crime against economic common sense. Representatives of chemical and electrical industries in particular deplored these developments and argued that trade restrictions impoverished the European nations.[2]

The analysis of economic and political conditions in Europe led German industrialists to the conclusion that they had one important means for forcing a revision of Allied economic policy toward Germany, namely economic competition, and during the early period of the Weimar Republic German light industries attempted to obtain a revision of the Versailles Treaty through economic warfare. The measures for such a policy were openly discussed in the *Reichsverband der deutschen Industrie* (RdI), and its managing director, Hermann Bücher, proposed that Germany flood Allied markets with cheap goods. This would serve a double purpose: in the first place, it would hurt Allied industries, and thus might force these industries to collaborate with Germany and influence Allied policy towards reparations, and in the second place it would produce the foreign currency needed for

68–75; Laubach, *op. cit.*; Maier, *op. cit.*; Hans Schieck, "Der Kampf um die deutsche Wirtschaftspolitik nach dem Novembersturz 1919," Phil. Diss. (Heidelberg, 1958), pp. 140–155, 220 f; *Kab. Fehrenbach*, No. 168, February 2, 1921; No. 1, No. 6, June 1920; Kohlhaus, *op. cit.*, pp. 48–49. Richard Lewinsohn, *Die Umschichtung der europäischen Vermögen* (Berlin, 1925), pp. 116 ff. *Kab. Müller I*, No. 18, April 7, 1920; No. 66, April 26, 1920; No. 70, April 28, 1920; No. 77 May 3, 1920 and *passim*. Julius Hirsch, *Die deutsche Währungsfrage* (Jena, 1924), pp. 58–69. David Felix, *Walther Rathenau and the Weimar Republic. The Politics of Reparations* (Baltimore, 1971); Leo Haupts, *Deutsche Friedenspolitik 1918–1919. Eine Alternative zur Machtpolitik des Ersten Weltkrieges?* (Düsseldorf, 1976); Gerald D. Feldmann/Heidrun Homberg, *Industrie und Inflation. Studien und Dokumente zur Politik der deutschen Unternehmer 1916–1923* (Hamburg, 1977); Georges Soutou, "Problèmes concernant le Rétablissement des Relations Economiques Franco-Allemandes après la Première Guerre Mondiale," *Francia* 2 (1974).

[2] Duisberg, "Die wirtschaftliche Lage der deutschen Industrie," Duisberg, *op. cit.*, pp. 28–35; "Die wirtschaftliche Lage der chemischen Industrie 1921–1922," Duisberg, *Abhandlungen, Vorträge und Reden aus den Jahren 1882–1921* (Berlin und Leipzig, 1923), pp. 605–621. "Das internationale Wirtschaftsproblem unter dem Gesichtswinkel der Machtpolitik und der objektiven ökonomischen Erfordernisse," Hermann Bücher, *Finanz- und Wirtschaftspolitik Deutschlands 1921–1925* (Berlin, 1925), pp. 167–173.

reparation payments. Bücher recognized that the entry of German goods into Allied countries was hindered and in some cases prohibited by high tariffs, but he was convinced that a superior system of production and the high quality of German goods would overcome these difficulties.[3]

This scheme for a recovery of the status quo ante was not an isolated one, and Hans Jordan, tax specialist of the RdI and director of the *Vereinigte Glanzstoff Fabriken* Elberfeld, recommended similar steps. He expected a world-wide economic crisis, and urged the members of the RdI to prepare themselves for a final confrontation with the Allies, upon the outcome of which Germany's industrial and political future depended. If Germany could hold out longer than the other European nations, the economic crisis would force the Allies to admit that the liability they had imposed upon Germany endangered their own prosperity and had to be revised.[4]

These schemes did not mean that industry rejected reparations on principle. At different post-war conferences with the Allies and at numerous meetings with German government officials, industrialists and bankers had argued that they wanted reparations to be linked to the Reich's capacity to pay. Naturally nobody knew exactly what Germany could pay, since this depended both upon domestic financial and economic developments as well as upon reconstruction of the world market and its ability to absorb German goods. In Germany, demands for higher taxation or the mortgaging of private property for reparation purposes would have meant social and political conflict. In foreign affairs, the economic provisions of the Versailles Treaty had laid the basis for a shift in the economic balance of the continent. With the loss of Alsace-Lorraine, the Saar and later of Upper Silesia, German industry had suffered a severe set-back, while France now had the potential to become Europe's most important iron and steel producer. However, this would only happen if German industry cooperated and provided France with coal and coke for the smelting of the Lorraine iron ore. While France was thus dependent upon German cooperation, German industry had access to Swedish and Spanish ore as well and had been able to rebuild part of its lost steel mills in the Ruhr area and other parts of Germany. Ruhr heavy industry, knowing well that the withholding of reparation coal was a potent weapon against France, was unwilling to consent to payments without further compensation from the Allies.[5] The most important con-

---

[3] "Die internationale Wirtschaftslage in ihren Beziehungen zu Deutschland," Veröffentlichungen des RdI, 17. Oktober 1921, *Die deutsche Industrie und die Wiedergutmachungsfrage. Bericht über die dritte Mitgliederversammlung des RdI in München, September 1921* (Berlin, 1921), pp. 21–32.

[4] "Wiederaufbau und Steuerpolitik," *ibid.*, pp. 38–44.

[5] Soutou, *Problèmes*, pp. 580 ff.; Georges Soutou, "Die deutschen Reparationen und das

cessions demanded were the most favored nation clause for Germany; liberation of the Rhineland and the Saar from occupation and sanctions, and the reduction of reparation payments according to Germany's capacity. With this policy heavy industry tried to regain its prewar position. Apparently some Ruhr industrialists did not even fear a French occupation of the Ruhr. Since Allied demands were unfulfillable, they reasoned that it would come anyway and thus they were opposed to any attempt at temporary fulfillment.[6]

Different arguments were used against the Wiesbaden agreements of 1921 which had been signed by Walther Rathenau and the French Minister of Reconstruction in the Briand cabinet, Louis Loucheur, in order to substitute cash payments with reparations in kind. The RdI feared that national economic cooperation to allocate French orders would finally lead to nationalization. Furthermore, reparations in kind would destroy normal trade, and Rathenau had accepted a volume of deliveries in excess of the London Schedule of Payments.[7] When these contracts were modified, however, fears of state intervention decreased, but the argument persisted that reparations in kind were as detrimental as cash payments since in the end the Reich would have to reimburse industry.[8] By mid-1922, however, Hugo Stinnes, one of the most outspoken critics of Rathenau's policy, himself signed a contract with the Marquis de Lubersac, who represented French reconstruction cooperatives. Against a 6% fee, the Hoch- und Tiefbau A.G. Essen, a branch of the Stinnes combine, was authorized to organize and distribute orders for reconstruction material in Germany. In return, the French recon-

Seydoux Projekt 1920–1921," VjhZG (1975); Feldmann/Homburg, op. cit., pp. 67 ff.; Maier, op. cit., pp. 194 ff.; Reichert-Simons, February 24, 1921. "Erst dann, wenn Frankreich nicht mehr weiß, was es mit dem Überfluß an Erzen und Eisen machen kann ..." an acceptable agreement will perhaps be possible. PA AA, Büro RM, Reparationen, vol. 1; also Klöckner January 14, 1921, Aufzeichnung über die Besprechung im Auswärtigen Amt, ibid., vol. 3. Vereinbarungen mit Frankreich über die Lieferung von Koks und Kohle gegen Minette, Cuno Nachlaß, Friedensverhandlungen 1919 ff. Niederschrift Vorstandssitzung RdI, May 28, 1920, HA GHH 30019320/00.

[6] Reusch-Haniel von Haimhausen, May 1, 1921, HA GHH 300193000/11. "Meines Erachtens wäre es das Beste, wenn wir die Herrschaften ganz Deutschland besetzen lassen würden. Auf diese Weise hätten wir einige schwere Jahre vor uns, kämen aber am schnellsten aus der ganzen Misere heraus."

[7] RdI-Ministerium für Wiederaufbau, February 12, 1922,: ibid., 300120/5; Jakob W. Reichert, Rathenaus Reparationspolitik (Berlin, 1922; Maier, op. cit., pp. 262 ff.

[8] "Die deutschen Sachlieferungen," November 25, 1922, HA GHH, 300193023/0. For criticism of the AEG, the Siemens-Schuckert Werke and the MAN which delivered electrical equipment and machinery to Yugoslavia, see: Zweckverband Nordwestdeutscher Wirtschaftsvertretungen, "Rundschreiben," March 25, 1922, ibid., 300120/10; Schmerse-Reusch, March 10, 1922, ibid., 300193023/0; Schmerse-Dr. Koettgens (Siemens), October 25 and Dr. Koettgens-Schmerse, October 31, 1922,: ibid., 300120/10.

struction cooperatives would place at Stinnes' disposal the coal necessary for the production of cement and other reconstruction materials.[9] Similar contracts were soon signed between Paul Silverberg of the *Rheinische Braunkohlenbergbau- und Brikett AG* and the *Office Houillères Sinistrés*.[10]

What had brought about this sudden change of position? Apparently both economic and political motives played a role. By the summer of 1922, inland prices for coal and iron as well as wholesale prices for metal products had risen considerably and had nearly reached world market level, and processing industries began to complain about export problems.[11] At the same time, after the assassination of Rathenau and the failure of the international bankers meeting in June, foreign holders of mark deposits increasingly sold these deposits which led to a further deterioration of the German currency.[12] This development created serious difficulties for industry, but Stinnes, Sorge, Silverberg and Emil Guggenheimer of the MAN stressed the political implications of the new development. It was to become evident that Hugo Stinnes, who had become the protagonist of Germany's unwillingness to fulfill reparation demands, was supporting the reconstruction of Northern France. The agreement could become the starting point of Franco-German business cooperation on a private basis without government interference.[13] Stinnes

[9] *PA AA*, W. Rep. Lieferungsabkommen zwischen de Lubersac und Stinnes, K 246248–246251; letter Hoch-Tief-AG. – Ministerium für den Wiederaufbau, January 23, 1923, K. 246595 ff. For positive French reactions see: *Le Petit Parisien*, September 7, 1922 "Le premier accord." *Echo de Paris*, September 7; *Victoire*, September 7; *Eclair*, September 7; *Le Temps*, September 8; the agreements were criticized in *L'Ere Nouvelle*, November 14, 17 and 29.

[10] "Gründung einer Brikettverkaufsgesellschaft in Frankreich," October 10, 1922, *Silverberg Nachlass*, 60.

[11] Constantino Bresciani-Turroni, *The Economics of Inflation. A Study of Currency-Depreciation in Postwar Germany* (London, 1937), pp. 227–230; Karl Elster, *Von der Mark zur Reichsmark. Die Geschichte der deutschen Währung in den Jahren 1914–1924* (Jena, 1928), pp. 454–455. For the differences between industries see: Hermann Hesse, *Die deutsche Wirtschaftslage von 1914–1923. Krieg, Geldblähen und Wechsellagen* (Jena, 1928); pp. 227–234, pp. 287–290. Also "Monatliche Berichte der Niederrheinischen Handelskammer Duisburg." The reports for 1921–1923 are in *HA GHH*, 300123/6, 7. The monthly reports of the Ministerium für Handel und Gewerbe 1920–1925 are in *WWA*, Klc, Abt. II, 1a.

[12] Carl Ludwig Holtfrerich, "Internationale Verteilungsfolgen der deutschen Inflation 1918–1923," *Kyklos* vol. 30 (1977), p. 280. Hesse, *op. cit.*, p. 367; Bergmann, *op. cit.*, p. 139.

[13] For Silverberg see: "Die gegenwärtige Gesamtlage und ihre Auswirkungen auf die Politik der Verbände," October 12, 1922, *Silverberg Nachlaß*, vol. 1. Stinnes himself accepted an invitation by de Lubersac to visit Northern France once reconstruction was under way with material provided by him. Other industrialists (von Borsig, von Siemens, Deutsch, Vögler, Riepert, ten Hompel, Reusch, Duisberg, and Klöpfer) were expected to join him. *PA AA*, W. Rep. Lieferungsabkommen ... K 246507 ff. The participation of other interested groups was rejected. Cf. Reusch-Bücher, October 2, 1922 and Bücher-Hermann, September 25, 1922, *HA GHH*, 30019320/7. Emil Guggenheimer, "Das Stinnes-

was indeed trying to attain a separate deal with French heavy industry in mid-1922, but a unanimous attitude concerning German industrial priorities did not exist.[14] Business interests, regional peculiarities and party affiliations had determined industrial attitudes, but by the summer of 1922, the RdI tried to develop an industrial program which would both form the basis for co-operation between different industries as well as determine industrial attitudes towards foreign and domestic problems. In general, it was to become an industrial strategy for a revision of economic and social realities at home as well as of the Versailles Treaty.

I. THE RDI PROGRAM OF 1922

The initiative came from Hermann Bücher, spokesman of the RdI and previously employed by the Foreign Office, who for some time had tried to convince his colleagues that industry had to support the Reich in its struggle for an acceptable reparation offer.[15] His participation at different conferences as government adviser had convinced him that France was more in need of cash than of deliveries in kind. After his return from the Genoa conference, he made known his ideas at a meeting of the *Zweckverband Nordwestdeutscher Wirtschaftsvertretungen und Handelsvereinigungen in Essen*: only an international loan would make reparations possible. Bücher and foreign businessmen he had met were convinced that a solution to the

Lubersac Abkommen," November 24, 1922, speech held at the Überseeklub Hamburg, *Guggenheimer Nachlaß*, K 71/1922/23, Houghton-Department of State, September 15, 1922, *Houghton Papers*, Berlin correspondence. Report of a meeting with Sorge. According to Sorge, later meetings with other French industrialists (Eugene Schneider) were to follow. Under the precondition that 1) the occupied territory would be evacuated, 2) the Saar valley be returned to Germany and 3) all trade restrictions imposed at Versailles be removed, Ruhr industry would not only reconstruct Northern France, but would also form one "great cartel" with French heavy industry. These preconditions were of course totally unrealistic.

[14] Duisberg, *Abhandlungen, 1882–1921*, pp. 587 ff. and 606 ff. For Stinnes' attempts to contact Eugene Schneider through Silverberg and Emile Mayrisch see the correspondence in *Silverberg Nachlaß*, vol. 403.

[15] Laubach, *op. cit.*, p. 86. Cf. also: Veröffentlichungen des RdI, *Die deutsche Wirtschaft und die Wiedergutmachungsfrage. Bericht über die dritte Mitgliederversammlung des RdI, München 27–29 September 1921* (Berlin, 1921); Verein Deutscher Eisen und Stahl Industrieller, *Bericht über die Hauptversammlung der Mitglieder des Gesamtvereins am 6. 5. 1921* (Berlin, 1921), pp. 1–10. Verein deutscher Eisen- und Stahlindustrieller, *Bericht über die Hauptversammlung des Gesamtvereins am 2. 5. 1922* (Berlin, 1922). Dr. J. Herle, "Ziele der deutschen Industrie," Veröffentlichungen des RdI 1921, *op. cit.*, pp. 59–60; Gert von Klaas, *Albert Vögler* (Tübingen, 1958), p. 158. This is an uncritical study of Vögler, but it contains some material which is not available elsewhere.

pending problems could "only be found with the aid of the leading economists of the world, but not by the Ministers of Finance of excessively indebted states."

Bücher's appeal for international business cooperation was another attempt to free reparations of parliamentary influence. He expected that the conflict between Germany and the Allies would be decided in Germany's favor "when economic knowledge and the power of international capital will be more powerful than cabinet politics in the leading states." German industry did not have the power yet to force an "economically sound" decision, but he was confident that a change would come soon. The international economic recession which had set in in 1921 was Germany's greatest advantage. While the Allies could not be expected to completely renounce reparations, they would be significantly reduced. Until then Germany had to wait.[16]

In the meantime Bücher intended to develop a foreign policy program for industry as a guide line for all negotiations with the German government and the Allies. As a first step towards coordination in the RdI, a special committee was formed. At the first meeting on June 28, 1922, Bücher presented his ideas. Reminding his colleagues that Germany had lost the war and was in no position to evade payments, he urged them to participate in formulating a common industrial policy. To begin with, a propaganda campaign ought to be organized against domestic and foreign politicians who intervened on an issue mainly economic. The scheme that Bücher then suggested for a final solution of reparations placed the problem in a broader economic context. The first goal of industry ought to be a revision of Germany's external position. As compensation for industrial cooperation with the German government and the Allies, he demanded a repeal of all trade restrictions imposed at Versailles. The second goal would be a revision of the domestic situation. This included stabilization of the currency, balancing of the budget, reform of the tax system, repeal of the so-called demobilization laws, renovation of the public sector of the economy, and suspension of rent control. With the exception of rent control, all other proposals were unanimously accepted.[17]

[16] The quotations are from a speech held at a meeting of the *Zweckverband Nordwestdeutscher Wirtschaftsvertretungen und Handelsvereinigungen* in Essen on June 6, 1922, *Silverberg Nachlaß*, vol. 312.

[17] "Grundsätzliche Besprechung der vom Reichsverband zu befolgenden Wirtschaftspolitik," June 28, 1922, *Silverberg Nachlass*, vol. 312; also in *Guggenheimer Nachlaß*, K 71/RdI. The members of the committee were Bücher, Duisberg, Flechtheim, Frowein, Funcke, Guggenheimer, Jordan, Krämer, Lammers, von Raumer, Silverberg, Sorge, Stinnes, Vögler. Stinnes never attended the meetings.

But nothing else was accomplished and the meeting was adjourned. Two weeks later, Bücher again repeated his proposals and urged the members of the RdI to develop a positive program. At this meeting, his proposal for a foreign policy program and the creation of a committee of international financial and economic experts was attacked by Paul Silverberg, representative of Rhenish lignite industries, who insisted that the provision of supplies for Northern France was more important than international business collaboration. This discussion proved as futile as the first one as the majority of the subcommittee was more concerned with domestic problems, i.e. stabilization of the currency and labor problems. However, Bücher was to submit a detailed written proposal at the next meeting.[18] He set to work immediately and his program was ready by August 31.[19] It is the most complete scheme ever developed in the RdI, and deserves our special attention since it was only written for internal circulation. After attacks upon the economic provisions of the Versailles Treaty, Bücher stressed that Allied economic self-interest would prepare the way for a return to Germany's prewar position. Without German participation in world trade there would be no Allied recovery from the war. Since there was little point in waiting for an Allied initiative, it was necessary for German industry to create an additional stimulus for a revision of the treaty. Industrialists should declare that they acknowledged Allied rights to reparations. At the same time, Germany should demand equal rights on the world market. Without a repeal of export restrictions, Germany would not be able to earn the foreign currency necessary for reparations. If the Allies were not willing to help Germany to escape from this vicious circle, they could not expect payments.

Bücher's scheme did not leave much room for reparations. The Reich was bankrupt and could not fulfill its obligations. Private property was sacred and thus, in addition to a repeal of export restrictions, an international loan would be necessary to make immediate payments possible. Bücher also submitted an elaborate plan for domestic reform, since they were needed to facilitate a return to economic normalcy. First, an increase in productivity was necessary; second, the quality of manufactured goods had to be improved; third, the currency had to be stabilized in cooperation with industry; fourth, the tax system needed reform and especially property taxes had to be reduced; fifth, state intervention into the private sector of the economy had to be abolished and the public sector had to be organized under the

[18] "Niederschrift über die erste Sitzung des Sonderausschusses," July 21, 1922, *ibid.*
[19] "Entwurf Bücher," August 31, 1922, *ibid.* Now printed in: Feldmann/Homburg, *op. cit.*, pp. 328–332.

principle of highest productivity; and sixth, the Reich budget had to be stabilized.

The increase of industrial productivity was also Bücher's foremost goal. He suggested modernization of equipment, production of high quality goods and careful execution of business transactions as necessary to accelerate Germany's return to its prewar position. In short, he intended to create a powerful and efficient industrial machinery geared to higher and better productivity than was possible in Allied countries. This economic giant would be able to pay reparations, as well as regain its political influence.[20]

When this scheme was discussed in the special committee, several of the proposals did not find support. Paul Silverberg saw Germany's return to its prewar economic position in less positive terms – he simply did not believe it possible. Because of British weakness and American disinterest in European affairs, France would be able to prevent German recovery. In addition, he disputed the value of a foreign policy priority and argued that stronger emphasis on reform of the domestic situation was of greater importance. The foreign policy program should be postponed until the internal scene had been changed. Silverberg wanted a final showdown with the parties of the Left and hoped that the state bureaucracy would aid industry in this respect. As preparation for a policy of confrontation, he suggested the collection of coal and food stuffs in emergency stocks. When these precautionary measures had been taken, industry should start a compaign against the "socialist sins" of the government. A general strike would not matter. He did not fear a new revolution, but was convinced that a population provided with food and fuel for the winter would go along with demands for an increase of labor productivity. Silverberg stressed that stabilization would only be possible after labor productivity had been increased and a final decision on reparations had been reached. Acceptance of this program would have changed the social contract of the Republic, but it did not find the support of the majority who feared that publication of these demands would create political and social problems. Opinions on the preference of a domestic or foreign initiative were then significantly divided. The only agreement which was reached concerned the eight-hour day, and all participants agreed that longer hours and more intensive work was necessary.[21]

This general discussion showed that a more comprehensive study was needed. For this purpose two subcommittees were formed. The first dealt

[20] *Ibid.* A similar view had been held by Bücher's predecessor. *Veröffentlichungen des RdI*, Heft 8, 1920, pp. 34–35.
[21] "Niederschrift über die 2. Sitzung," August 9, 1922, *Silverberg Nachlass*, vol. 312; now Feldmann/Homburg, *op. cit.*, pp. 332–334.

with the private sector of the economy, specifically questions concerning an intensification of labor efficiency (Albert Vögler), increase of raw material supplies (Hans Krämer), modernization (Otto Funcke), capital shortage (Hans Jordan), unproductivity (Clemens Lammers) and prices (Emil Guggenheimer). The second subcommittee concerned itself with the study of the public sector of the economy, especially currency reform (Abraham Frowein), wages (Dr. Langen), exports and imports and the railway question (Dr. Frank), government controls of industry (Dr. Mann), taxation (Hans Jordan), reorganization of state administration (Julius Flechtheim) and public utilities (Paul Silverberg). Special reporters were named for foreign policy questions. Stinnes and Bücher examined relations with the United States, France and Great Britain, while Guggenheimer was responsible for the Soviet Union. Coordination within the RdI was arranged by Lammers. Hans von Raumer, former Minister of the Treasury in the Fehrenbach cabinet and member of the DVP, represented industry in negotiations with the parties.[22]

Reports of the subcommittees were presented on October 10, November 1, December 6 and December 12, 1922, but nothing happened at that time. Whether this was due to existing differences within the RdI or to the change of government cannot be said with certainty.[23] Differences did indeed exist within the RdI. Already on September 6, 1922, Stinnes and Silverberg had criticized Bücher's reliance on a foreign policy initiative, while Cuno had sided with Bücher.[24] As a result of Bücher's proposal Silverberg also developed a comprehensive plan of domestic confrontation with labor and the SPD, demanding the abolition of all laws introduced since the revolution which had reduced the total independence of the economy.[25] A similar plan was forwarded by Stinnes in October 1922, but only Silverberg's demands were discussed in the RdI and government circles and then rejected.[26] These differences show that any attempt to categorize industry under headings

---

[22] "An die Herren Mitglieder des Sonderausschusses für ein Wirtschaftsprogramm," September 11. 1922, *Silverberg Nachlass*, vol. 312.

[23] *Ibid.* Detailed reports do not exist.

[24] *HA GHH*, 3001240/4; cf. Feldmann/Homburg, *op. cit.*, pp. 313–323.

[25] *HA GHH*, 40012290/351. The plan was probably developed in November 1922 and sent to the Chancellor, the Minister of Economics and the Minister of Finance apparently at the latter's request. *Silverberg Nachlass*, vol. 412, fol. 112; Kempner-Hamm, January 6, 1923, *BA*, R 43I/1333.

[26] "Stinnes Niederschrift 14. Oktober 1922," *Houghton Papers*, Correspondence, Misc. 1922. The plan was handed over to the American Ambassador. Some basic demands are the return of the occupied territory to Germany, payment of reparations through longer work hours for 10 years and the liberation of the economy from all restrictions. Kempner-Hamm, January 6, 1923, *BA*, R 43I/1333. Silverberg-Hermes, December 26, 1922, *ibid.*

like "iron-coal-steel" or "chemical-electrical" blocks are as problematic as the terms "abenteuerlich-militaristisch" or "wendig-parlamentarisch."[27] These terms do not satisfactorily explain the attitudes of industrialists towards reparations although the former contribute much to an analysis of industrial demands. Individual attitudes, allegiance to parties or other organizations, and competition between industrialists will have to be analysed as well. For example, Paul Silverberg and Paul Reusch, both representative of heavy industry, differed in their approach towards Bücher's program. Reusch sided with Carl Duisberg, representative of the "chemical-electrical" block, both rejecting Silverberg's plan of confrontation with the SPD. The plan was considered unrealistic and not in the interest of industry. Duisburg believed that Silverberg's plan was an attempt to return to 19th century laissez-faire liberalism, which did not take into account the positive changes that had occurred in labor-industry relations. In his view, Silverberg had completely lost sight of the advantages of state arbitration in labor disputes and state intervention in questions of tariff policy. Duisberg also rejected the demand for a privately controlled railroad system, an old demand of heavy industry. In general, Reusch and Duisberg were convinced that Germany's external situation did not allow any risky confrontation with the working class. Both expected that British aid would be forthcoming and believed that foreign initiative would always have priority over a domestic one.[28]

Reusch was not satisfied with Bücher's program either. According to him, equality in international trade was less important than gaining strength. Even so, he sided with Bücher and Duisberg and repeatedly warned Silverberg that industry did not have the power to change the economic and social system of Weimar Germany. Complete cooperation between industrial groups was thus not possible within the RdI, and different personal and industrial interests determined the discussion of reparations. Duisberg and Reusch did not consider German-French cooperation was possible at the moment and always hoped for British intervention, preferably with the support of an international committee of financial and economic experts.[29] Discussions in the RdI had thus shown that a unanimous attitude towards reparations and connected problems was still impossible, and when Cuno became Chancellor, he had to reckon with different demands upon his

[27] Gossweiler, *op. cit.*, pp. 106–108.

[28] Duisberg-Silverberg, January 12, 1923; Reusch-Silverberg, January 13, 1923, *Silverberg Nachlass*, vol. 412.

[29] Reusch–Bücher, August 30, 1922, *HA GHH*, 30019320/2. Reusch-Silverberg, January 13, 1923, *Silverberg Nachlass*, vol. 412. Reusch-Karl Haniel, June 19, 1922, *HA GHH*, 300193/6.

government. Should he start with an initiative in France or in the Anglo-Saxon countries? Was a domestic plan for an increase of labor productivity, tax reform, abolition of demobilization laws, and stabilization of the currency more important than a reparation initiative? Cuno decided to approach France first.

2. GERMAN FEELERS IN PARIS

Only two weeks after Cuno had been asked to form a cabinet, Foreign Minister von Rosenberg tried to open direct negotiations between France and Germany, offering to discuss economic and financial problems.[30] A similar initiative had been undertaken by Wirth in October after he and President Ebert had met the Marquis de Lubersac through Stinnes, but Poincaré had refused to see either Stinnes, Silverberg or Klöckner. The French Minister would only deal with Berlin through official diplomatic contacts between governments.[31] Von Rosenberg also contacted de Lubersac, considered to be in close contact with Millerand and Poincaré, and the German Ambassador in Paris, Wilhelm Mayer, informed the French Foreign Office as well. However, Poincaré, busy with preparations for a conference with England on the future of reparations, was as unreceptive as in October. Mayer was told to leave his information with Peretti de la Rocca, political director of the French Foreign Office. After consulting the Stinnes representative in Paris, Mayer decided to wait for a meeting with Poincaré.[32] In the meantime, however, de Lubersac had already informed Jean Jacques Seydoux, economic specialist and reparation expert of the Quai d'Orsay. Mayer's decision did not find support in Berlin, and he was asked to see Poincaré at once.[33] Mayer was received by Peretti, who promised to inform Poincaré. When von Rosenberg had not obtained an answer after one week, he urged Mayer to inquire about the fate of the German proposal.[34]

Mayer rushed to see Peretti de la Rocca and pressed for an answer, but although Poincaré had been informed on December 7, there was no answer

[30] Von Rosenberg-de Lubersac, November 30, 1922, *PA AA*, Büro RM Reparationen, 5 secr., D 736179 f.
[31] "Aufzeichnung Stinnes," October 23, 1922, *ibid.*, D 736236 f, de Lubersac-Wirth, October 30, 1922, D 736162 ff.
[32] Mayer-AA, December 5, 1922, *ibid.*, D 736166 ff. von Rosenberg also intended to send Stinnes, Silverberg and Klöckner. If financial problems were discussed Max Warburg would join them.
[33] *Ibid.* Rosenberg-Mayer, December 7, 1922, *ibid.*, D 736168 ff.
[34] Rosenberg-Mayer, December 13, 1922, *ibid.*, D 736175.

yet. The London Conference of Allied Prime Ministers had interfered with this initiative to open negotiations with Paris through and with the support of Ruhr industry. However, Cuno had not only attempted to contact Paris, he also tried to present a German offer to the Allies assembled at London.

3. THE LONDON CONFERENCE

Any German government intending to develop an initiative in the reparation issue had to consider one major difficulty: Germany was a debtor to several Allied nations and their plans, therefore, had to make allowance for diverging interests. If Cuno had sought to adhere to normal diplomatic procedure, he would have officially approached the Allies and submitted a proposal. This overture had one important disadvantage: Several German governments had found out after 1919 that the formal exchange of written diplomatic notes was generally a futile exercise, since German and Allied reparation estimates were still too far apart or the Allies differed in their policy. However, since the beginning of 1922, several important personal contacts had been established between Allied members of the Reparation Commission and their German counterparts. Together with Sir John Bradbury, the British delegate, Leon Delacroix, his Belgian colleague, urged Germany to submit a new reparation plan to the conference of Allied Prime Ministers. It had been decided to arrange this meeting between Italy, Belgium, France, and Great Britain, after it had become clear that the United States was completely unwilling to participate in a conference that would deal with reparations and interallied debts. The London Conference, Delacroix and Bradbury suggested, would be an excellent chance to reopen negotiations. They recommended on November 21, 1922 that Germany should present a plan which should mention a final sum.[35] Three days later, however, Delacroix had changed his mind and explained to the German delegates of the *Kriegslastenkommission* (the German agency in charge of reparations) that a German offer would not have any chance "as long as Poincaré was in power." Convinced that the French Minister President would be overthrown soon, the Belgian delegate now recommended that Germany stabilize the mark with domestic loans signed by German industry while waiting for future developments.[36] Delacroix's view of France's irreconcilable attitude was shared by the British Prime Minister, Bonar Law, but he at least did not inform the Germans about his estimate of Poincaré's policy. However, he

[35] Bergmann-Reichsfinanzministerium, November 21, 1922, *BA*, R 43I/32.
[36] *Ibid.*

cabled to the American Secretary of State that no chance of agreement existed "while Poincaré stayed in office."[37] These estimates show the complete hopelessness of the German situation. The Belgian delegate had for some time been in favor of an international loan as a means of payment. Now, in face of French determination not to allow a loan without productive pledges – Poincaré's policy since August 1922 – he saw no way out.

Despite Delacroix's retreat, the members of the *Kriegslastenkommission* tried to find a compromise proposal which might open negotiations. Since the Belgian delegate knew that the Wirth note of November 14 (also the basis of Cuno's initiative) was not sufficient to change French policy, he suggested that Germany attempt stabilization with the aid of her own industry.[38] Carl Bergmann, former director of the Deutsche Bank and reparation expert, inquired whether Poincaré might not accept a moratorium in connection with a loan. The plan he had in mind had been written by Oscar Wassermann of the *Deutsche Bank* upon Cuno's request. It provided a cancellation of deliveries in kind for 1923. Under the condition that a German loan would extract 3 billion gold marks, Germany should be granted a moratorium for five years.[39] Delacroix immediately picked up this suggestion, closely resembling the conditions mentioned by Poincaré in his talk with a member of the *Kriegslastenkommission* in October,[40] and recommended that Bergmann cable Cuno suggesting an expansion of the Wirth note of November 14. The incorporation of the Wassermann plan into the note would be a great step towards closing the gap between German figures and Allied expectations. Bradbury, who was present at the meeting, did not have any grave objections either, but he had a different idea: Cuno should make a final offer. Twenty-five billion gold marks would naturally not be sufficient to satisfy Poincaré, but a little window dressing might help. Instead of a fixed sum, Germany should offer annuities payable over thirty years. Payments would begin after a moratorium of several years, then Germany should pay up to $3^1/_2$ billion gold marks per year. Including 5% interest, the present value of the German offer would be 45 billion gold marks payable through an international loan. In reality the sum would have been less, since Bradbury promised that Germany would be granted an 8% rate of

[37] *Charles E. Hughes Papers*, Box 175, Folder 76b, Great Britain, December 18, 1922.
[38] Fischer-AA, November 27, 1922, *PA AA*, Büro RM, Reparationen, D 718379 f.
[39] Bergmann-Reichsfinanzministerium, November 24, 1922, *Kab. Cuno*, No. 5, pp. 8 ff; Wassermann-Cuno, November 30, 1922, *BA*, R 43I/33.
[40] Meyer-AA, October 28, 1922, *PA AA*, Büro RM, Reparationen, D 718 392 ff. Poincaré knew that Germany was temporarily unable to pay and proposed a loan both for Germany and France. But there was one important precondition: interallied debts had to be adjusted first.

discount. Thus the real value of the German offer would be something like 25 billion gold marks.[41]

Bradbury could not convince Bergmann that the plan would work as the British delegate had suggested, but in order to get more information about Allied intentions, he went to see Roland Boyden and James Logan. Both "unofficial" American experts suggested that Cuno should not make an offer at all. The fact alone that it came from Germany would guarantee its failure.[42]

With the Reparation Commission divided, the chances of a favorable reception of a German offer were slim, but Cuno had decided to take the initiative. Despite these discouraging reports, he cabled Bergmann, requesting the latter's presence in Berlin.[43] Bergmann returned to Berlin immediately and several meetings with Cuno took place. After the SPD and the DVP had accepted the Wassermann plan, the Chancellor explained his initiative at a cabinet meeting on December 5. French reation to the German initiative, Cuno hoped, would show whether Poincaré really wanted reparations. Foreign Minister von Rosenberg then presented the details of a scheme which however differed slightly from the original Wassermann plan. The government would try to stabilize the currency without Allied aid. It would use 500 million gold marks from the Reichsbank reserves to this effect. At the same time, a 4 billion gold mark loan would be floated, half of it in Germany. The foreign part of the loan would go directly to the Reparation Commission. Of the 2 billions issued in Germany, half would be used to cover reparations, the other half would be employed to stabilize the budget. In return for this offer, the Allies were asked to grant a moratorium to Germany for two years. For each succeeding billion raised in Germany, the moratorium was to be extended for another year. In order to guarantee the success of the loan in Germany it should be tax free and carry 4% interest. It was also hoped that capital that had left Germany could be drawn back. However, these favorable terms for a provisional agreement with the Allies were nullified by a demand for equality in international trade, which France would never have accepted. The whole arrangement was not to last longer than five years – after this period, it was hoped, a final settlement would be reached.[44]

On December 7, Bergmann was back in Paris and informed Delacroix

[41] Bergmann-Reichsfinanzminister, November 24, 1922, *Kab. Cuno*, No. 5, pp. 12 ff.
[42] *Ibid.*, pp. 13 ff.
[43] November 29, 1922, *BA*, R 43I/32.
[44] "Kabinetssitzung 6. Dezember 1922," *Kab. Cuno*, No. 12, p. 37 f. Industry and banking did not participate in the formulation of the note. Cf. Note Hamm December 1, 1922, *BA*, R 43I/32.

about the German proposal for London. Delacroix was impressed and suggested that Cuno publicize the note one day before the Allied meeting. An identical note should be sent to the Reparation Commission at once. In this note Cuno should state that Germany was hoping for international credit, but since credit was not available, Berlin would act independently, hoping Allied credit would then become readily available.[45] From Paris, Bergmann went to London to meet Carl Melchior, who had arrived as Cuno's personal emissary to explain the details of the proposal. After a conference with the German Ambassador, Melchior, Bergmann, and Ambassador Sthamer paid a visit to Blackett and Bradbury, both of whom recommended that, instead of following the Belgian suggestion, Cuno should write a personal letter to the British Prime Minister Bonar Law. Without a letter of introduction from Cuno, Bonar Law would have to announce the German offer himself, and the idea of Anglo-German cooperation would needlessly anger Poincaré. It was better to eliminate any suspicion that Britain was plotting with Germany behind her Ally's back.[46] After this meeting the German delegation made its round, announcing its plan to anybody who cared to listen. When the scheme was shown to Bemelmans, the second Belgian delegate on the Reparation Commission, he maintained that it showed the way out of a cul-de-sac. After a temporary solution, which after all was the reason for the proposal, direct negotiations between Germany and the Allies would be possible. However, the conditions of the German offer could still be improved. It was not sufficient to offer 4% interest; the interest rate had to be raised. Furthermore, Cuno should declare that the scheme had been approved by German industry. This last suggestion came as no surprise. The Belgian government had repeatedly urged Berlin to guarantee that reparation policy was supported by industry.[47] The Belgians hoped that such a statement would destroy Poincaré's fears that German industry would oppose reparation payments. Bradbury and Delacroix also regarded the plan as a sincere effort to reach a temporary agreement with the Allies and to correct matters in Germany. But in order to frustrate French coercive measures, they suggested the same adjustments as Bemelmans.[48]

[45] Bergmann-Reichskanzler, December 7, 1922, *Kab. Cuno*, No. 15. For other Belgian hints cf. Landsberg-AA, November 29, 1922, *PA AA*, Büro RM, Reparationen, D 718379 ff. and November 14, 1922. For British suggestions: Fischer-AA, December 5, 1922, *ibid.*, D 718399 f.
[46] Sthamer-Cuno, December 8, 1923, *ibid.*, D 718423.
[47] Landsberg-AA, December 10, 1922, *ibid.*, D 718429.
[48] Already on November 29, the Belgian Foreign Minister had warned that only an offer supported by German industry could stop Poincaré. *Ibid.*, D 718377. Bergmann reported about Delacroix's and Bradbury's opinion in a letter to Cuno on December 10, 1922. *BA*, R 2/3124.

Bergmann tried to obtain a last minute change from Cuno, but the Chancellor refused. Arguing that it was useless to contact industry because a congruous attitude did not exist among industrialists, Cuno stressed that the offer had been worked out with representatives of German banking. Industry wanted a final settlement, while Wassermann's proposals only meant a provisional one. However, if a final arrangement could be obtained, he would consult industry. Cuno did not agree to an increase of the interest rate either; only Delacroix's first suggestion that Germany try stabilization without Allied support, if Allied credit was not immediately available, was incorporated in the note.[49]

Would it have made a difference if Cuno had agreed to include the above mentioned modifications? It is unlikely, since, when the British Prime Minister presented the German note on December 10, it was immediately rejected by Poincaré who wanted "productive pledges." Besides regarding the German note as a tactical overture to increase Allied disunity, Poincaré also rejected any reduction of the German debt, because he feared that without German payments France's financial situation would be hopeless. He stated: "There was · · · no chance of raising the money to balance the budget if nothing was done as regards Germany." Although he clearly recognized that Germany could not pay at the moment, he demanded that any future settlement would have to allow France, Italy, and Belgium "to relieve their financial embarrassment." Besides France's financial plight, Poincaré presented another reason for his policy: "in case of reduction" of the German debt, he would be "overthrown" because of the French Chamber's opposition to such a compromise.[50]

Although the British Prime Minister did agree with Poincaré's criticism that the German offer lacked sufficient securities and did not provide measures to halt the flight of German capital abroad (a matter which made Poincaré especially bitter, since he felt that industry was evading payments), Bonar Law considered the proposal to be a basis for a counterproposal. Furthermore, he did not believe that the Allies could prevent the flight of capital. In his opinion, the Allied problem was simple: they had to agree upon what they could get. Poincaré did not agree with this and when he

---

[49] Bergmann-Cuno, December 10, 1922, *ibid.* Also Sthamer-Cuno, December 10, 1922, *PA AA*, Büro RM, Reparationen, D 718423. Whether Cuno's proposal to use part of the *Reichsbank* reserves for stabilization could succeed is doubtful. The President of the *Reichsbank*, Rudolf Havenstein, had already warned on November 23 against such a policy. *BA*, R 43I/32; Bergmann, *op. cit.*, pp. 200–201.

[50] *FO.* 371/7489, C 16897 f., Notes of Allied meeting, December 9, 1922. Bariety, *op. cit.*, p. 108 also believes that the Anglo-French conferences of December and January were of no importance for the development of French plans.

demanded the occupation of the Ruhr, the conference broke up, despite Mussolini's attempt to find a compromise. Mussolini proposed to control the issue of German export and import licences, to create a customs border, and to control the delivery of coal and timber from German mines and state forests. However, Bonar Law rejected even this compromise. Britain would neither agree to an occupation of the Ruhr, nor to economic controls.[51]

Nevertheless, the Allies finally agreed to hold another conference in Paris to discuss interallied debts and reparations. Italy and Belgium hoped that the other powers would reconsider their positions and expected that Britain might allow a partial reduction of war debts, which would ease a modification of the French position upon reparations. The British government agreed to the conference for a different reason: it did not want to give the "Turks at Lausanne the impression of Allied disunity · · ·[52] At Lausanne Britain was negotiating for a settlement of the Greek-Turkish conflict in which France was supporting Turkey while Britain favored the Greek position. Remembering only too well the Anglo-French differences in this region before the war, the British Foreign Secretary, Lord Curzon, intended to preserve the Entente by all means, since a "hostile France over the whole of the Near East and in Egypt, in Morocco, and in Tangier," would create serious difficulties for the British Empire. Britain's European policy was thus submitted to its policy towards the Empire.[53]

When the final communiqué of the conference was published, nothing was said about Allied differences. Instead, the Allies announced that they had not reached an understanding about interallied debts and reparations but that further studies were necessary. As to the German plan, the communiqué stated that it had been rejected unanimously.[54]

Although Cuno's initiative did not improve the situation, he had shown that he wanted to negotiate, while Wirth had rejected any independent action and had been unwilling to employ part of the German gold reserves for stabilization. Cuno had promised to do so despite domestic opposition. This decision increased cooperation between Bradbury, Delacroix, and Bergmann. The German delegates in London, though not invited to participate in the conference, were informed about Allied negotiations. The Governor of the Bank of England, Montagu Norman, and Sir Robert Kindersley, one of its directors, who had already informed the German Ambassador

---

[51] FO., 371/7489, C 17026, December 10, 1922.
[52] Cab., 23/32, December 11, 1922.
[53] Harold Nicolson, Curzon: The Last Phase (London, 1934), pp. 212–214, pp. 275–304. Cab., 23/30, August 1, 1922; cf. also DBFP, vol. XVII, No. 508.
[54] Weill-Raynal, op. cit., II, pp. 323–324.

before the conference that Britain was seeking a way out of the temporary stalemate also belonged to Bergmann's British contacts.[55] Being rejected at the conference of Allied Prime ministers, Cuno immediately tried to contact Poincaré personally again. On December 15, von Rosenberg cabled the German embassy in Paris to inquire about French objections:

In order that we may be able to modify our future proposals accordingly, we would be grateful for any hints why and in which parts our proposals are insufficient.[56]

Von Rosenberg and Cuno were desperately looking for any signs that might indicate French willingness to hold oral negotiations with Germany. Rosenberg barely waited for Mayer's messages before he sent new cables. French threats had certainly influenced Berlin, but Rosenberg made it clear that a demand "to take productive pledges" would end his willingness to negotiate. Productive pledges were a violation of the Versailles Treaty and would be regarded as an attempt to annex German territory. Yet, in order to influence Poincaré, Cuno himself intervened and Mayer was to communicate to Poincaré that Cuno:

... was deeply convinced that the pressure that was effecting the whole world could only be removed by a reasonable understanding between Germany and the Western Powers, especially France.[57]

On December 16, Mayer talked to Poincaré for half an hour. In this conversation, he emphasized that 1) German industry was prepared to visit Paris and discuss its contribution to the reconstruction of Northern France, and 2) Cuno was trying to prepare the basis for a final solution of reparations. Mayer's presentation did not impress Poincaré. As to the first proposal, Poincaré had never liked the idea of direct German participation in reconstruction, and he argued that the state of public opinion in France was not ripe for collaboration. The French public was hostile toward German industry and did not want negotiations. However, the French Cabinet was prepared to examine any proposal forwarded by Cuno. When Mayer insisted that Germany's previous experiences with written communications had not been very successful, and then suggested that in the process of verbal negotiations progress would be made, Poincaré dodged and maintained that he had to consult his cabinet first but that Mayer would receive an answer the next day. After this meeting Mayer saw Seydoux, who confirmed that Poincaré was worried about the reaction of the French public if negotiations

---

[55] Sthamer-AA, December 1, 1922, *PA AA*, Büro RM, Reparationen, D 718383. For Norman's objections to French reparation policy see: Andrew Boyle, *Montagu Norman. A Biography* (London, 1967), pp. 138–148, 150–155, 166–169.

[56] Rosenberg-Mayer, December 15, 1922, *PA AA*, Büro RM, Reparationen D 736179 f.

[57] *Ibid.*

with industry became known. When Mayer left Seydoux, he had the impression that the latter would support the German proposal in the meeting of the Council of Ministers,[58] but on December 22 he was notified that direct negotiations with German industry were still impossible.[59] Thus, three weeks after Cuno had come into office, his first attempts to solve the reparation problem had failed. Neither his offers for industrial negotiations in Paris nor his reparation plan had been accepted. If France did indeed intend to take "productive pledges" an euphemism for a military occupation of the Ruhr – the Reparation Commission, the responsible agency in charge of the execution of treaty terms, would become the battleground. The delegates were to decide upon any default in German deliveries. Without such a decision, any occupation would have been an act of war. *De jure*, the Reparation Commission was an impartial and independent body for the control of Germany's capacity to pay and for the supervision of deliveries. *De facto*, it had become a French dominated agency after the withdrawal of American delegates due to the non-ratification of the Versailles Treaty. France nominated the President. With Belgium dependent on France, Italy and Great Britain could not prevent action even if they stood together, since the President had the casting vote. Nevertheless, it was important for Germany to present its case before the commission, since Belgium and Great Britain had repeatedly agreed to a more lenient treatment of Germany in the past.

4. THE REPARATION COMMISSION BEFORE THE OCCUPATION

The development of a new initiative by Cuno was aided by the British delegate, who, annoyed over the failure of the London conference, had indicated to Bergmann that it was impossible to work with Poincaré. The German note had been acceptable to Belgium and Great Britain, but Poincaré's fixation on productive pledges had destroyed an excellent opportunity to open negotiations. But in order to preserve the Entente, Bonar Law had been forced to reject the German offer as well. England wanted to prevent a break with France until the Lausanne conference had reached a settlement on the Greek-Turkish conflict. Combining wishful thinking with consolation, Bradbury maintained that British opposition to coercive measures had prevented French actions for the moment and that Poincaré might even be overthrown upon his return to Paris. But even if this should not happen, Britain would present a plan at the Allied Conference in Paris. The details

[58] Mayer-Rosenberg, December 16, 1922, *ibid.*, D 736182/183.
[59] Mayer-Rosenberg, December 22, 1922, *ibid.*, D 736187.

of the plan had been worked out by himself, and, promising that Bonar Law would present this plan in Paris in January, Bradbury informed Bergmann about its details.[60]

Bradbury's plan called for cancellation of all C bonds and reduction of the German debt to 50 billion gold marks nominal value. For the first four years, Germany would have to pay no interest; for the next four years, Bradbury demanded 4%, and only after 9 years should the interest rate be increased to 5%, the rate which had been fixed in the Versailles Treaty. The 1% redemption installment was to be completely omitted. After 10 years, an impartial court of arbitration, including a German and a British member, would have to decide whether Germany was able to pay the outstanding interest for the first eight years. If the court of arbitration could not agree upon a chairman, the President of the United States should be asked to name one.[61] Thus, one month before the Allied meeting was to take place in Paris, the Germans knew the outlines of the British scheme for a final reparation settlement. Apparently Bergmann believed that, if Bradbury kept all his promises, the plan might be acceptable to Germany.[62]

On December 23, the Belgian delegate to the Reparation Commission, Delacroix, intervened. He told Hans Meyer of the *Kriegslastenkommission* in Paris that, in order to prevent occupation, Cuno's initial offer should be improved. It should be presented to Poincaré one day before the Allied conference in Paris. A French refusal to deal with it would show that France did not want reparations. Instead, Poincaré was pursuing political goals.[63] On December 27, Bradbury, upon Bonar Law's request, met the counsellor of the German Embassy, Dufour-Feronce. The Prime Minister wanted to let Cuno know that Britain would appreciate the submission of a German plan acceptable to the Allies. This overture was the result of a previous meeting between David Fischer of the *Kriegslastenkommission* and Bradbury. Fischer had informed Bradbury that a plan was in the offing. Apparently Bonar Law now wanted to help. In order to prevent another rejection of a

---

[60] Bergmann-Cuno, December 10, 1922, *ibid.*, D 718432. Apparently the British delegate intended to submit a compromise proposal according to which Germany would have been granted a moratorium for 3 months. During this period the German government should issue a domestic loan. If 1 billion gold marks were signed, or, if industry and banking guaranteed the loan, Germany would receive a moratorium for three years. But the plan was never submitted.

[61] Bergmann-Cuno, December 11, 1923, *Kab. Cuno*, No. 19. The British plan is in *Cab.* 24/140. C.P. 4376; *FO.*, 371/8625, C 133, January 2, 1923 with slight modifications.

[62] *Ibid.*

[63] Meyer-AA, December 23, 1922, *PA AA*, Büro RM, Reparationen, D 718612 f. Cf. Landsberg-AA, December 21, 1922, D 718572 about a meeting with the Belgian Foreign Minister.

German offer, he suggested that 30 billion gold marks at 5% interest would be a basis for negotiations between the Allies and Germany.[64] The President of the Board of Trade, Sir Philip Lloyd Greame, whom Dufour-Feronce saw the same day, reinforced his impression that a German plan would facilitate British actions against Poincaré's intention to occupy the Ruhr. To the Germans, Bonar Law seemed prepared to cooperate in a common endeavor to solve the reparation issue.[65]

The general reluctance to join France in her coercive policy did not mean that the Reparation Commission could reject the French motion to declare Germany in default on Reparation deliveries. Several times the Commission had been able to postpone a decision, although, since July 1922, Poincaré had tried to gain a legal basis for coercive measures. On December 26 he finally succeeded, and Germany was declared in "voluntary default" for timber and telegraph pole deliveries.[66] When Meyer complained to Delacroix that he did not understand the Belgian attitude, since Belgium had received its full share of deliveries, Delacroix answered that, due to French political pressure, it had been impossible for him to vote against the motion. Though he had yielded to the French demand, he still believed that the Reparation Commission had not given Poincaré a legal basis for occupation. Paragraph 3 of the Commission's vote suggested proper Allied procedures.[67] Feeling uneasy about the French motion and being convinced that an occupation would not produce any cash payments, the Reparation Commission had fallen back on a note that had been sent to the Wirth government in March 1922. With this note, Germany had been granted a reduction of deliveries in kind for 1922. Uncertain whether it was possible to deliver the prescribed amounts, the Commission had also decided that in case of default, Germany would have to pay the difference in cash.[68] In paragraph 3 of the new decision, the Reparation Commission had inserted the March judgement. Thus Delacroix could justly argue that the decision on default alone did not give France a legal right to occupy German territory. The American observer to the Commission, James Logan, had reached the same conclusion:

[64] Dufour-Feronce-AA, December 27, 1922, *ibid.*, D 718655 f.
[65] *Ibid.*, D 718653.
[66] *Ibid.*, D 717949, July 21, 1922. Cf. *ibid.*, D 718612, December 23, 1922.
[67] *Ibid.*, D 718658-659, December 27, 1922.
[68] Reichstagsdrucksache, Nr. 2911, March 22, 1922, *RT*, vol. 356, the respective paragraph reads: "Si la Commission des Réparations constatait au cours de l'année 1922 que les livraisons en nature demandées . . ., n'étaient pas effectuées par suite d'une obstruction du Gouvernement allemand ou de ses organismes ou par suite d'infraction à la Commission des Réparations, des paiements supplémentaires équivalents en espèces seront exigés de l'Allemagne à la fin de l'année 1922 en remplacement des livraisons effectuées."

The facts are that at the time the demands were made on Germany in March 1922 for both coal and timber, the Commission itself was convinced that the German Government was not in a position to meet the demands and that a technical report of "default" was the only way out.[69]

But although Logan felt that a report on default would do no harm, he already doubted that an occupation of the Ruhr could be prevented. Belgium would join France despite certain misgivings:

The Belgians are gravely concerned by the present situation according to Delacroix and Bemelmans, for if Poincaré adopts his proposed policy and forces coercive measures against Germany, Belgium, for internal political reasons and as a measure of national economic safety against France, is practically forced to follow.[70]

Logan's interpretation of Belgian attitudes was correct. Not only Delacroix and Bemelmans doubted the wisdom of an occupation, but the Belgian Prime Minister, Georges Theunis, was convinced that Germany could not pay the sum requested.[71] On the other hand, Belgian suspicion of French Ruhr policy would lead her to join Poincaré. This ambivalence explains frantic Belgian steps at the end of 1922.

Though the Belgian delegate had voted with France on December 26, when Germany was declared to be in default, he did not give up his attempt to bring about a peaceful solution. Only three days after the decision had been made, he informed the *Kriegslastenkommission* about a separate Belgian plan for the Allied conference: According to this plan, the German debt was to be reduced to 60 billion gold marks; however, 30 billion would be discharged as war debts of Germany's former Allies, Austria and Hungary. Thus, Germany would only have to pay 30 billions.[72]

Delacroix's idea was another case of "political window dressing," so common after 1919. Everybody knew that Austria and Hungary, both financially bankrupt, could never and had never paid anything like 30 billion gold marks. Instead, Allied loans had prevented a complete financial and

---

[69] Logan-Hoover, December 22, 1922, *James A. Logan Papers*, Correspondence, October 1922–March 1923.

[70] Logan-Hoover, December 1, 1922, *ibid*.

[71] *Warren G. Harding Papers*, Microfilm, Roll 234, fol. 64–68, June 6, 1922, copy of a report from the American Ambassador to Brussels. Theunis had declared: "... Germany cannot live up to the London Schedule of Payments, and he estimated to me [Henry P. Fletcher] that M. de Lasteyrie, the French Minister of Finance, is of the same opinion, but as this question in France is political rather than practical, he believes that a settlement at the time along the lines recommended by the Committee of Financiers cannot be reached, and that some time gaining expedient will have to be found, if possible." Cf. also Logan-Hughes, March 1, 1923, *Henry P. Fletcher Papers*, Box 10 for a detailed analysis of Belgian difficulties.

[72] Meyer-Cuno, December 29, 1922, *PA AA*, Büro RM, Reparationen, D 718688.

political breakdown of the successor states of the Austro-Hungarian Empire. But obviously the fiction of a high German indemnity had to be maintained, even if Allied experts recognized that their own figures were hardly realistic. Delacroix's proposal was absurd, but it is difficult to say with certainty what he had anticipated when mentioning it to his German counterpart. Nevertheless, there is ample evidence that the Belgian government was reluctant to participate in an occupation of the Ruhr and went out of its way to prevent it. Thus, Delacroix's plan may be seen as a sign of Belgian determination to delay French action: hoping to prevent a decision which would not bring cash payments, Delacroix apparently clung to any straw that might postpone occupation. This plan, however, was never placed before the Paris conference. Instead, the Belgian Prime Minister decided upon another meeting with Poincaré, hoping to obtain French consent to a preliminary solution. Theunis proposed a two year moratorium for Germany under the condition that she would deliver $1^1/_2$ billion gold marks for the reparation account immediately. Since Germany did not have this amount in cash, the money would have had to be made available through an international loan.[73] Obviously Theunis hoped that a moratorium in connection with immediate cash payments to France would prevent military measures. Germany would obtain a breathing space, and perhaps, after some more time had passed, a final solution would be found acceptable to all powers.

But even before Germany had been declared in default, Bradbury had discussed other alternatives with the Germans. Sceptical about the outcome of the Allied meeting, he suggested to a member of the *Kriegslastenkommission* that a French occupation of the Ruhr would be a violation of the Versailles Treaty. Germany should thus revoke this interpretation of the treaty or file an application for admission to the League of Nations where reparations might then be discussed.[74] Apparently, Bradbury was determined to erect obstacles against French military action, but his advice was rather ambiguous. A rejection would not have changed anything. And France could always veto German admission to the League. A few days later, he came up with a different proposal: Germany should apply to the Reparation Commission and request an official interpretation of paragraph 18 of Annex 2, Part VIII of the Versailles Treaty, which was the basis for the French decision. The vote of the Commission would have to be unanimous, and Bradbury assured Bergmann in advance that unanimity would not be obtained. As a next step, Cuno should apply for admission to the League of

[73] Theunis, January 5, 1922, *ibid.*, W. Rep. Besetzung des Ruhrgebiets, H 276533 ff.; cf. Landsberg-AA, January 10, 1923, *ibid.*, H 276603.
[74] Fischer-AA, December 20, 1922, *ibid.*, H 276489.

Nations, requesting that an arbitration board of the League decide upon the matter.[75] Bradbury's plan would indeed have presented a severe threat to France if it had come before the Reparation Commission. British politicians had regarded the Commission as a judicial agency from the beginning, and in May 1920 Lord Curzon had made this clear in a dispute with Poincaré, at that time President of the Reparation Commission. According to Curzon, the Commission "had to decide questions not merely between Germany and the Allies, but between the Allies themselves."[76] The Cuno government did not follow Bradbury's advice. It did not believe that a new confrontation between France and Great Britain in the Commission would do any good. In addition, the Germans feared that the French-controlled League would not be an impartial agency while the Reparation Commission might not support Bradbury's interpretation.[77]

Although the Allies would meet again in Paris to discuss reparations, the important decision had already been made. The Reparation Commission had declared Germany in default on timber deliveries. It had thus paved the way for French action. However, there was still a chance that Cuno would again take the initiative and submit a new proposal to the Allied conference. A German proposal, however, had to be formulated in negotiations between the Government and parliamentary as well as industrial interest groups.

5. CUNO AND INDUSTRY

Most diplomatic communications reaching Berlin at the end of 1922 indicated that France was preparing military action against Germany. On November 27, the Council of Ministers had met in the Elysée Palace under President Millerand in the presence of the new delegate to the Reparation Commission, Louis Barthou, military experts (among them Marshal Foch), and representatives of the Coal Office.[78] Nothing definite became known about the meeting in Berlin but the French press announced that a decision concerning the Ruhr had been reached. This increased agitation in the French press and rumors about military measures did not fail to impress

---

[75] Bergmann-AA, January 4, 1923, *ibid.*, H 276531; Fischer-AA, January 18, 1923, *ibid.*, H 276724 f.; cf. Bergmann, *op. cit.*, p. 217. Bergmann reports that Delacroix was of the same opinion. But material which would support this statement could not be located.

[76] *DBFP*, First Series, vol. X, pp. 226–227; cf. Fletcher-Hughes, August 20, 1923, *Hughes Papers*, Correspondence, Box 21 for a report on discussions in Britain.

[77] Wiederaufbauministerium-AA, January 25, 1923, *PA AA*, W. Rep. Besetzung des Ruhrgebietes, H 276787 f.

[78] Mayer-Rosenberg, November 27, 1922, *ibid.*, Büro RM, Reparationen, D 718371.

Berlin. At a cabinet meeting on December 6, Cuno warned that French coercive action was imminent.[79] After Poincaré's flat refusal to grant a moratorium, the situation had become very serious. Of equal concern to Cuno was the fact that his foreign policy initiative was attacked both by the DNVP and the press of the Right. On December 11, the *Deutsche Allge-meine Zeitung* (*DAZ*), a Stinnes owned newspaper, published an article dis-approving of Cuno's reparation offers. Stating that industry had neither been asked nor been informed about the decision to solve reparations tempo-rarily through an international loan for payments and a domestic loan for stabilization, the *DAZ* indicated that industry would have attempted to negotiate a definite agreement, even if Cuno's proposal had been accepted by Poincaré.[80] It was rumored that the article had been inspired by Stinnes himself, and the liberal and social democratic press was angered over this attack.[81] Stinnes' opposition to a preliminary settlement of reparations was not new; he had clashed with Cuno's predecessors on a number of occasions, always demanding a final settlement.

From the beginning of his Chancellorship, Cuno had also stressed the necessity of a final settlement. He was rebelling against the policy of his predecessors, who, when confronted with an Allied ultimatum, had felt un-able to resist and consequently had been forced into successive demands for a respite. Cuno also knew that no government could successfully tackle repa-rations without the backing of industry and banking, and he was convinced that he would gain the support of these groups. In this respect, however, he was hardly more successful than Wirth or Fehrenbach, and from November 1922 until the fall of his government, he could seldom rely on the collabo-ration of industry, although he had the support of various former business associates.

When Cuno was still the director of the HAPAG, he himself had distrusted governmental decisions, since "as long as we [industry] are dependent on a government, in which there is nobody who knows the economy, we cannot expect that the situation will improve."[82] This had changed, Cuno felt, since his cabinet had been formed. On December 12, he made a speech be-fore the *Reichswirtschaftsrat*. For the first time since he had become Chan-cellor, he admitted that reparations were not only an economic problem, but that their „essential features and goals are political." After this clarification

[79] *Kab. Cuno*, No. 12.

[80] *DAZ*, December 11, 1922. Cf. Cuno-Bergmann, December 10, 1922, *PA AA*, Büro RM, Reparationen, D 718430 for industrial opposition towards a preliminary settlement.

[81] Georg Bernard, "Cuno's Gegner," *Vossische Zeitung*, December 10, 1922, No. 584.

[82] This statement was made at a meeting of the board of directors of the RdI on Sep-tember 6, 1922, *Silverberg Nachlass*, vol. 257.

Cuno turned directly to the *DAZ* article and rebuked the interference of industrial pressure groups with government politics. He stressed:

... that the Government leads and that industry supports the Government. There is no authority, no center of power in industry, which would be strong enough, to seize the initiative from the Government.[83]

The same afternoon he conferred with Dr. Sorge of the RdI. Two days later the news agency WTB printed a letter from Sorge stating that the *DAZ* article did not represent the position of the RdI. In addition, Sorge declared that "the RdI considered it to be its duty, to support the government at a time when Germany was in difficulties." Any rumors insinuating a difference between Cuno and the RdI were a crime against the Fatherland. Industry was willing to cooperate with Cuno.[84] The public denunciation of the article by the RdI was applauded in the liberal and social democratic press and for the moment silenced criticism of industrial behavior. However, Sorge had made it clear that the RdI wanted a definite settlement. In this respect, he had said nothing different from the *DAZ*, and even Cuno would have supported such a position. An important tactical difference existed between Cuno and the *DAZ*, though: the Chancellor's note to the Allied conference in London had been an attempt to open negotiations, and he trusted that once oral negotiations had begun, a definite settlement would be obtained. The *DAZ* article, however, rejected any provisional solutions and argued that it was useless to talk with the Allies unless they agreed in advance to a definite settlement.

After Cuno's first attempt for oral negotiations had failed, he had two alternatives. He could either fall back upon the fatalistic attitude, shared by many members of the administration, that any initiative was doomed to fail, since Poincaré would always reject a German plan which did not accept the French position; or, he could develop a plan that might be acceptable to one of the Allies. This plan might then be used as a basis for German-Allied negotiations. Cuno chose the second alternative, believing that without a concrete offer, France would march into the Ruhr. An occupation would destroy German economic unity, postpone reparation payments indefinitely, and thus prolong economic and political insecurity.

Cuno's conviction that only a final settlement would free Germany from the threat of Allied coercive measures caused him to accelerate preparations. His own view of the situation was reinforced by private and official communications from Paris, London and Washington. As important as this

---

[83] *Kab. Cuno*, No. 20, December 20, 1922.
[84] WTB, No. 2429, December 14, 1922, *BA*, R 43I/33.

information was the growing conviction in the cabinet that a foreign loan was not feasible at the moment. Cuno was kept well informed about conditions on the New York and London money markets. On December 6, Carl Melchior acquainted him with a letter he had received from J.M. Keynes, advising Melchior that attempts to place a German loan in New York would fail. This was a serious blow for Cuno, who had hoped for such a loan. But even worse, Keynes stated that British politicians and businessmen were disappointed about Cuno's weak domestic policy and his vague promises in his letter to Bonar Law. Ironically, although Keynes criticized Cuno for his inactivity in foreign policy, he did not see much hope for a settlement in any case. "The reparation question seems to be rapidly passing out of the economic sphere."[85]

With all these discouraging factors, it would not have been a surprise if Cuno had given up and resigned. But despite the rapidly deteriorating external situation, several branches of the government had become active at his request. On the basis of information received through Sir John Bradbury, the Ministry of Finance and the Ministry of Economics set out to prepare a comprehensive plan. But the result of their work showed that a common attitude did not exist. Many plans were developed during the next weeks. Most of them were never used, and apparently there were nearly as many plans as participants at the conferences. An unsigned memorandum in the files of the Ministry of Finance fixed the German debt at 45 billion gold marks. The plan was a combination of payments in kind and in cash; 800 million gold marks per year should be payed in reparations in kind. In addition to this amount, a percentage of custom receipts, the coal tax, and the export surplus should be used for cash payments. But apparently part of the money was also to be raised by an international loan, 2/3 of which should be placed on the international money market.[86]

Another draft was prepared by Ludwig Kastl, Secretary of State in the Ministry of Finance and later Geschäftsführer of the RdI. He fixed the German debt at 20 billion gold marks real value. Payments already made should be subtracted, and from January 1, 1923 onwards, cash payments

[85] Keynes-Melchior, December 1, 1922 and Melchior-Cuno, December 5, 1922, BA, R 43I/185. Max Warburg-Cuno, November 24, 1922, ibid., R 43I/32; Richard Merton-Cuno, November 29, 1922, ibid., R 43I/63, Schacht-Cuno, December 24, 1922, ibid., R 43I/33.
[86] BA, R 2/3158. Another proposal by Helphand fixed the German debt at 35 billions. Except reparations, all other liabilities (costs of occupation, indemnities for lost property, etc.) were to be cancelled. Eighteen billions should be guaranteed by the Reich through mortgages, the rest should be made available through an international loan; 10% of the loan should be assigned to stabilization. Kastl's plan was sent to Paul Reusch of the Gutehoffnungshütte. Cf. Kastl-Reusch, December 28, 1922, HA GHH, 300 193008/11.

should be made through an international loan at 5% interest and 1% sinking fund. The loan would be guaranteed by industry, agriculture, and trade. This plan was totally unrealistic. If payments already made were subtracted, not more than 12 to 13 billion would have remained for the Allies. He also demanded the repeal of all export restrictions and the evacuation of part of the Rhineland after 1/3 of the liability had been paid.[87]

Besides mentioning unrealistically low amounts, all plans had another common fault: their authors still believed in the possibility of a foreign loan for Germany. Similar expectations led to an initiative in the German Foreign Office, and von Rosenberg asked Wiedfeldt, the German Ambassador to Washington, to inquire whether the New York bank J.P. Morgan & Company was willing to organize a loan for Germany, and if so, how much could be raised. Morgan, of course, was not interested. A loan was impossible as long as the Allies and Germany had not come to a definite agreement about reparations. He also abstained from estimating Germany's capacity to pay. Such an estimate would have helped Cuno prepare an offer, but it could also have placed Morgan in a very embarrassing position, if the German government had used his estimate in public. A similar attempt to contact American business through the Chambers of Commerce also failed.[88]

But Cuno had at least managed to obtain information about British expectations. Thus it was decided to submit a new note. The *DAZ* affair had shown that the backing of industry was as important as the support of the banking community. Representatives of both groups were invited to separate meetings. The conference with the banking experts took place on December 19. Upon the invitation of the Minister of Finance and in the presence of Karl Ritter of the Foreign Office and Kastl and Alexander von Brandt of the Ministry of Finance, Oscar Wassermann (*Deutsche Bank*), Franz Urbig (*Diskonto-Gesellschaft*). Franz von Mendelssohn (a member of the Mendelssohn bank and President of the *Deutscher Industrie- und Handelstag*), Carl Melchior (Warburg & Co.), and Louis Hagen (Levy/Oppenheimer and representative of the occupied Rhineland) discussed a "final" reparation offer.[89]

In the discussion Hagen, supported by Urbig, immediately focused on the occupation of the Rhineland, arguing that the evacuation of the occupied

---

[87] *Ibid.*

[88] Rosenberg-Washington, December 13, 1922, *PA AA*, Büro RM, Reparationen, D 718462 f., Wiedfeldt-AA, December 19, 1922, *ibid.*, D 718550 f.; Link, *op. cit.*, pp. 160–162. For the Chamber of Commerce action cf. *PA AA*, Sonderreferat W. Die Aktion der amerikanischen Handelskammer with letters of Max Warburg, Mendelssohn and Melchior.

[89] "Niederschrift über eine Sachverständigenbesprechung wegen der Reparationsfrage," December 13, 1922, *BA*, R. 38/181 Also *ibid.*, R 43I/33.

territory had to be included in any negotiations with the Allies. Hermes, Wassermann, von Mendelssohn and Melchior objected to this proposal, which would have prejudiced the German position from the beginning. Instead, they favored an approach which would solve reparations first and then negotiate a Rhenish settlement which would contribute to French security.[90] This brief probe into the Rhenish questions showed that unanimity could not be reached. Hermes then opened the discussion on the Bradbury plan. Varying estimates about the real value of the 50 billions mentioned by Bradbury had been made. Wassermann had calculated that the real value of 50 billion gold marks, payable over 30 years at 5% interest and with a sinking fund of 1% was about 22 billion gold marks. If the period for payments were increased to 40 years, the actual value of 50 billions would be 21 billion gold marks, in 50 years only 20 billions.[91]

Hagen objected to Bradbury's plan which, in his opinion, was nothing but an attempt to help Poincaré in his domestic difficulties with the French Chamber which expected a high payment. He argued that the German offer should mention the real value. Wassermann and Urbig joined him in arguing that "absolute honesty" was necessary while Melchior, who during the negotiations was the most flexible and moderate and the most concerned about tactical procedures, favored Bradbury's plan. However, he also stated that "the high figures would only be a dressing to make the offer more palatable to the French public." Two plans should be developed: the first should offer a fixed sum, but, if Poincaré should reject it, a second plan offering annuities might perhaps be acceptable. This new proposal was supported by Wassermann and von Mendelssohn, while Urbig warned that annuities impaired German independence.[92]

Similar differences were revealed when Wassermann suggested that, because of existing chaotic economic conditions, an estimate of the capacity was impossible, and proposed a provisional arrangement. After the reconstruction of the German finance- and currency-system had been carried out, a final sum should be fixed. Franz Urbig did not agree. A provisional arrangement would not lead to a recovery of the currency. An increase in the value of the mark was only possible after an increase of industrial production.[93] Similar disagreements existed regarding guarantees. Hermes, Melchior, and von Mendelssohn argued that the details of German guarantees for an Allied loan should be worked out in negotiations with the Allies.

[90] Ibid.
[91] Wassermann-von Brandt, December 14, 1922, ibid., R 2/3168; cf. also R 2/2900 for other estimates.
[92] "Niederschrift ...," December 13, 1922, BA, R 38/181, p. 5, pp. 5–7, p. 14.
[93] Ibid., p. 8.

Hagen, Wassermann, and Urbig wanted the guarantees to be fixed by a German commission; the Allies could either take them or leave them.[94]

When this meeting had been arranged, the Minister of Finance had hoped that a common position could be found. But the discussion did not bring one about. Melchior suggested figures close to Bradbury's, while Urbig was unwilling to offer more than 20 billions payable in annuities of 1.25 billion gold marks within 36 years. In defence of this figure, Urbig cited a letter he had written to the French Minister of Finance in November. He did not mention that, while de Lasteyrie had indeed not opposed his estimate, he had not accepted it either.[95] At this point of the discussion, Karl Ritter from the Foreign Office intervened for the first time, declaring that different methods allowed fixing the debt at 20 billion gold marks real value. For example, Keynes had estimated Allied damages and German capacity at 20 billions, and Louis Loucheur had recently insisted that France had paid 12 billion gold marks for reconstruction and needed 14 more. If the sums already paid by Germany were subtracted, a debt of 20 billions would remain.[96] Ritter's plan was certainly misleading. It did not include debts to Great Britain, Italy and Belgium, and there was no indication that these powers would cancel German debts. But as a result of this meeting, the sum of 20 billion gold marks was accepted as an adequate offer, despite the warning of Melchior and von Mendelssohn.

On December 16 another meeting between the banking experts and the Ministry of Finance took place. They were joined by representatives of the Ministry of Economics and industry (Carl Duisberg, Paul Reusch, Paul Silverberg, Julius Flechtheim, Hermann Bücher, and Peter Klöckner) who originally had been scheduled to discuss reparations in a separate meeting but had been invited upon Hagen's recommendation, supported by all participants of the December 13 meeting. Carl Bergmann, who had just returned from London, also attended and reported in detail Bradbury's proposal for a meeting of the Allied Prime Ministers in January. Although this plan provided for a moratorium for four years, it meant a public renunciation of the C-bonds, thus reducing the capital value of the debts to 50 billion gold marks, the real value of which was lower. It also provided for

[94] *Ibid.*, p. 16.

[95] *Ibid.*, p. 17. Copies of Urbig's letters and the answer of de Lasteyrie are in *BA*, R 2/3175. Urbig-de Lasteyrie, November 15, and de Lasteyrie-Urbig, November 30, 1922. De Lasteyrie wrote: "J'ai également pris connaissance de vos suggestions, en ce qui concerne la solution dont le problème des réparations vous paraît susceptible, mais vous comprendrez qu'il ne me soit pas possible de les discuter actuellement."

[96] "Niederschrift ...," December 13, 1922, *ibid.*, R 38/181, p. 18. Keynes estimates are in *BA*, R 2/3159. The sum was not 20 but 21 billions payable in annuities of 1.260 million gold marks.

an international court of arbitration to decide if annuities should be raised from 2 billion to $2^1/_2$ billion after nine years. Nevertheless it was rejected by Bücher, Hagen, Reusch, Urbig, Klöckner, Silverberg and Wassermann, while Melchior, Bergmann and Flechtheim favored a German proposal close to the British figures.[97] When the Rhineland question was discussed, Klöckner, Bücher, Silverberg, Urbig and Hagen demanded that it ought to be part of the German plan, while Flechtheim, Melchior, Duisberg, and von Mendelssohn were against it. Reusch and Klöckner in particular were very pessimistic about the future of the Rhineland and argued that it would be lost forever if the occupation were not modified soon. Representatives of coal and iron industry in the Ruhr, with its close connections to the left bank of the Rhine, rejected negotiations without a modification of its status. Silverberg, Reusch and Klöckner recommended direct negotiations with France, while Duisberg, Flechtheim and Hagen did not want to make negotiations dependent upon an evacuation. They correctly estimated that French politicians would never agree to such a precondition.[98]

Other difficulties arose when the details of the German offer were discussed. Wassermann of the Deutsche Bank voted against the handling of a loan through foreign bankers. He demanded that the Reich should present bonds to the Allies. Allied governments should then attempt to place the bonds on the international money market, while Germany would pay the interest and provide securities for the loan. Wassermann's proposal was an ingenious move to put the burden for success of the transaction upon the British, French, and Belgian Governments. If they did not sell the bonds, it was their own fault. They could always put pressure upon their own bankers or ask the Treasuries to buy them. In addition, Wassermann maintained that direct negotiations with private foreign bankers would not allow Germany to place a loan at 5% interest, and he warned that up to 10% might have to be paid.[99] Wassermann's suggestion did not gain the support of the majority. Bücher and Reusch especially argued that participation of foreign bankers was important for tactical reasons. The bankers would not agree to any coercive actions by their Governments, since this would endanger their bonds. Both were convinced that international finance would not destroy a debtor and stressed the significance of foreign bankers as a means of pro-

---

[97] "Niederschrift über eine Sachverständigenbesprechung," December 16, 1922, ibid., R 38/181.

[98] Ibid., pp. 14, 17, 21–23, 28–33.

[99] Ibid., pp. 17–18, 37 f.; Gossweiler, op. cit., p. 185 argues that Wassermann wanted to make a profit himself and thus spoke against the participation of foreign bankers.

tection against the Allies. Reusch also hoped that they would demand reform of public finance and suspension of the 8-hour day.[100]

At the end of the morning session, Melchior and Bergmann tried to persuade the other experts to accept a motion close to Bradbury's plan. Both argued that in their meetings with French and British bankers and politicians, they had been advised to submit a plan with a high sum, even if this did not represent the real value of the indemnity. Large sums, Bergmann and Melchior repeatedly stressed, were important for tactical reasons. But Wassermann, Urbig, and the representatives of industry were not willing to follow such a course, stating that it would only be another attempt to help Poincaré. Wassermann expressed the opinion of most experts when he insisted:

It is true that our proposals will be rejected regardless of what form they take. But they have to be so constructed that their rejection does not harm Germany in the eyes of the world and that the impression remains that Germany had made a serious attempt to reach a solution.[101]

The conference was interrupted at 1.45 p.m. Hermes, Becker and Bergmann had to join Cuno and Rosenberg in a meeting with party leaders. The Chancellor had invited Stresemann and Zapf (DVP), Löbe, Wels, Breitscheid, Müller-Franken, and Dittmann (SPD), Koch-Weser, Erkelenz and Petersen (DDP), Spahn, Marx, and von Guerard (Center) and Emminger and Lang from the BVP, to discuss reparations. Bergmann informed them about London, and, apparently, the negotiations with financial and economic experts were also discussed.[102] Immediately after the meeting, Becker and Hermes went back to the conference. As in the morning session, disunity prevailed. Silverberg again insisted upon a Franco-German financial and economic agreement; Wassermann argued against the participation of foreign bankers, while Bücher and Reusch favored it. The only real contributions were made by Flechtheim, Bergmann, and Melchior. Flechtheim believed his colleagues underestimated German capacity:

We should not underestimate the extent of our capacity to pay. In the case of a provisional solution, our offer can of course not be low enough. In the case of a final solution, however, we could offer a substantially larger amount, since a final solution would lead to a healthy state of affairs in Germany. The size of the credit that can be granted to us, will be determined by the finality of the debt settlement.[103]

[100] "Niederschrift . . .," November 16, 1922, p. 28, *BA*, R 38/181, p. 37.
[101] *Ibid.*, p. 38.
[102] "Aktennotiz Kempner," December 16, 1922, *BA*, R 43I/33. A record about the meeting does not exist. According to information received from the *Deutsche Zentralarchiv Potsdam* the documents in the *DZA* do not contain any information either. Letter of May 15, 1973.
[103] *Ibid.*, p. 32.

Flechtheim's suggestion brought the discussion, which had turned more and more into monologues, back to reality. The meeting had been called to decide upon a comprehensive plan. The deadline for a plan was the Allied meeting in January, and Bergmann urged the participants to come to a decision. But despite his recommendation, he was no longer sure whether a plan would help. Poincaré "was absolutely negative and all previous attempts to deal with him had failed. He did not know why; nevertheless, a new attempt had to be made."[104] He criticized the figures mentioned by Urbig, Wassermann, and Klöckner. A sum representing a real value of 10, 15, or even 20 billion gold marks was below French expectations. France and even Great Britain anticipated an offer close to 50 billions. While France wanted the indemnity to be fixed at 50 billions real value, Bradbury's offer would mean less, and Bergmann appealed to his audience to accept the plan in a slightly modified form.

Despite objections which could justly be made, despite the high annuities, and despite the additional annuity, the present value of Bradbury's proposal was 20 billion gold marks at the most, if the discount rate of $8\frac{1}{3}\%$ would be available for a sufficient amount of time.[105]

Wassermann objected. To him Bradbury's plan was unacceptable because it required 1.75 billion gold marks for interest and amortisation alone. Even if Germany received a loan of 20 billions, the belief that interest and sinking fund could be paid was "utopian."[106] This exchange of arguments between Bergmann and Wassermann led to a deadlock of negotiations. At this point Carl Melchior proposed a compromise. Starting with Bradbury's 50 billions, he subtracted 10 billions for payments already made. This would leave 40 billions. According to the provisions of the Versailles Treaty, a loan could be issued at $2\frac{1}{2}\%$ interest for the first years. If the Reich requested a prolongation for a number of years, the annuity would amount to 1 billion gold marks per year. The highest annuity would be 2.4 billions. This enormous yearly payment would never be reached, but with this modification the German offer would come close to Bradbury's sum.[107]

The final responsibility for a proposal lay with the cabinet, and Hermes finally tried to obtain the support of the experts for the following statement which he had formulated: 1) Unanimity existed in regard to the active policy of Cuno; 2) a German proposal should be submitted to the Allied conference in January; 3) it should contain a final offer with a moratorium for

[104] *Ibid.*, p. 35.
[105] *Ibid.*
[106] *Ibid.*, p. 37 f.
[107] *Ibid.*, pp. 38–40.

4 years; 4) the debts should be paid as annuities; 5) if a final solution could not be obtained in January, Cuno could rely on industrial support for a provisional agreement as well; 6) the evacuation of the left bank of the Rhine should not be demanded as a precondition for negotiations. It should be made clear, however, that the evacuation was important for the establishment of German productivity and its economic independence; 7) political, financial, and economic guarantees should be offered; 8) the government was asked to prepare the ground for Franco-German industrial cooperation. With the exception of provision number six, all others were unanimously accepted. Klöckner and Reusch protested that evacuation of the Rhineland was indispensable. The Minister of Finance objected, arguing that any demand for evacuation as precondition for Germany's willingness to negotiate a final settlement would not be acceptable to the Allies. Regional or individual industrial interests had to be subordinated to the interests of the whole nation. "It was a matter involving the survival as a nation, and thus the demand could not be made that categorically."[108] Hagen and Duisberg supported Hermes. It seemed as if the meeting would break up without an agreement; however, the Minister of Economics, who had remained silent during the negotiations, now intervened and suggested a compromise. Although evacuation should not be the precondition for negotiations, it was the final goal, and Becker submitted a modified version of the disputed paragraph which should read:

A final settlement of the reparation question is only possible if an agreement is reached simultaneously that the occupation of the left bank of the Rhine be reduced, even if only in stages. The government is asked to take all necessary steps.[109]

With this compromise proposal, which was accepted, Becker, a former director of the *Rheinische Stahlwerke*, took sides with the Ruhr industrialists against the Minister of Finance and the majority of the banking representatives. But even worse, the demand for a simultaneous evacuation of the Rhineland would, if incorporated in a German offer, give Poincaré an excellent opportunity to attack it as an attempt to revise the Treaty of Versailles. Even the British, who were in favor of modification of the financial terms of the treaty, would never agree to this.

As a result of this meeting, the dispute between Melchior and Bergmann on the one side, and Wassermann and Urbig on the other about a loan con-

---

[108] *Ibid.*, pp. 42–44.
[109] *Ibid.*, p. 45. When this motion was accepted, Louis Hagen, who just previously had objected to any preconditions, now even demanded the evacuation of Duisburg, Düsseldorf and Ruhrort.

tinued. On December 18, Melchior warned Hermes not to rely on estimates made in the press and by other financial experts as to the amount of foreign currency hidden in Germany. Admitting that expert opinion differed in this respect, he explained that bankers close to the Deutsche Bank (Wassermann and Bergmann) had estimated that several billions could be extracted from hidden resources through a domestic loan. Melchior and another banker (probably von Mendelssohn) believed that 500–750 million gold marks would be an excellent result for a domestic loan, while a third banker (probably Urbig) figured that a domestic loan would not bring more than 100 million gold marks. Though Melchior was not certain of the result of a domestic loan, he believed that a domestic initiative was necessary. In order to show that Cuno intended to stabilize the currency to lay the foundation for a return to normalcy, Melchior proposed that Germany attempt stabilization with its own means. If the Allies would agree to a moratorium for several years, or if a final settlement was reached in January, the Reich could stabilize the currency without Allied aid. For this purpose, 500 million gold marks should be raised in Germany. For the control of stabilization measures, a committee consisting of the Minister of Finance, the Reichsbank, and a representative of banking and industry was to be formed. If foreign bankers were to participate, they should also be given a seat. The biggest problem for stabilization was, of course, the rate of the mark, and Melchior suggested that the market should determine its value. As soon as the preparations for the loan had been concluded, the plan should be published. The mark then ought to be stabilized at the rate of exchange existing on the international money market.[110]

Stabilization of the mark was only one part of Melchior's scheme. He also repeated the proposal that he had made at the meeting of the experts: the debt should be fixed at 40 billions payable in annuities between 1 and 2.4 billions over 50 years. Payments would begin after 4 years. As compensation for this delay, the Reich should immediately float a loan in Germany and abroad. Foreign returns would go completely, half the domestic returns would go to the reparation account. In addition to these cash payments, reparations in kind for the devastated regions should be made.[111]

Another proposal was submitted by Oscar Wassermann; it was based on the note to the London conference. He suggested a provisional agreement because 1) he believed that a definite solution was impossible, and 2) because any offer based on Germany's "real" situation would be rejected by the Allies.

---

[110] Melchior-Hermes, December 18, 1922, *ibid.*, also *PA AA*, Büro RM, Reparationen, D 718559 f.
[111] *Ibid.*

He proposed a 4 billion gold mark loan at 4% as compensation for a moratorium of 2 years. Three billions should be floated in Germany, one billion would be guaranteed by German industry. For every billion payed, the moratorium should be prolonged for another year. After the end of the moratorium, the Reich should pay annuities of 1 billion gold marks for 36 years. In addition to the loan, the Reich should work towards a budgetary surplus, and this amount would also go to the reparation account until 1925. This sum was to be paid in German currency. This last proposal was dangerous for stabilization, and Wassermann suggested that the money should not be transferred to the Allies. Instead, the Allies should buy raw materials for that amount in Germany. Furthermore, German property not already liquidated in the Allied countries ought to be placed in a fund and be sold; part of the returns should go to the Reich. In this proposal as well as in all others, repeal of all restrictions on trade was demanded.[112]

Differences among the experts were again exposed a few days later. On December 21, Duisberg and Flechtheim came forward with a new proposal. As soon as Wassermann had seen the scheme, he wrote to Cuno, Hermes, Becker, and Rosenberg, hailing it as the solution of all difficulties. Duisberg and Flechtheim started with the same amount as Melchior and Wassermann, i.e. 40 billions. But instead of annuities, they proposed that an international financial syndicate should immediately issue a loan of 15 billion gold marks at 5% interest and 1% amortization. For the payment of interest and amortization, Germany would raise 300 million gold marks per year; the sums missing should be taken from the returns of the loan and cover expenses for 4 years. If 15 billions could not be issued in one sum, several series should be used. The basic idea behind the proposal was "that Germany's capacity to pay can be most accurately measured by whatever credit is made available." Duisberg and Flechtheim were confident that international finance could be relied upon, and thus their proposal provided that another loan should be issued between January 1, 1927 and December 31, 1931 to cover the remaining indemnity. As a guarantee, they offered customs receipts, the property of the Reich and the estates: in other words, the returns of the fiscal mines, state forests and the railways.[113]

Wassermann's acceptance of the Duisberg-Flechtheim plan was a complete *volte face*. Two days earlier, he had still argued that an international loan was not available at the moment or would be too expensive. Apparently Wassermann was greatly disturbed by rumors of French action and seems to have sensed for the first time that Germany's foreign policy situation was

[112] Wassermann-Hermes, December 20, 1922, *ibid.*, D 718564 f.
[113] Wassermann-Hermes, December 23, 1922, *ibid.*, D 718599 f; also *BA*, R 2/3168.

really desperate. Obviously he expected that only the intervention of American finance could help. The Duisberg-Flechtheim suggestion meant immediate aid to the difficult French budgetary position and might block demands for occupation. As important was the provision that the international financial syndicate would determine Germany's future, and Wassermann told the Minister of Finance:

The syndicate will become the judge of Germany's capacity to pay and will have to vouch for its judgement by taking over the corresponding amount of German loans. We may be confident, that this syndicate will endanger neither its capital nor its reputation by allowing the issue of excessively high loans.

With the Duisberg-Flechtheim plan "irresponsible official experts" would be exchanged for experts "who must back up their judgement on moral and financial grounds."[114] Wassermann was far too enthusiastic. It is true that this new proposal went beyond Melchior's or his own. But the touchstone of any motion was its feasibility, and from this aspect the memorandum submitted to Hermes was hardly realistic. It only served to confuse the issue and led to more heated and futile discussions. As long as the French government did not accept a committee of financial experts, any German offer proposing such an initiative meant a rejection of negotiations. Furthermore, the deadline for a fixing of payments for 1923 was approaching fast. It was simply impossible to organize a syndicate for the issue of a loan within two weeks.

Any new reparation proposal had to be supported by German industry both for domestic and international credibility. On December 20, Cuno met the directorate of the Association of Industry, as a result of which an editorial committee for the formulation of an offer was created. The members were Bücher, Hagen, Melchior, Silverberg, Stinnes and Urbig.[115] The co-optation of Stinnes completely changed the direction of the discussion. Apparently he submitted his own plan, stating: 1) According to J.P. Morgan, the condition for an international loan was peace in Europe; 2) France needed money immediately; 3) if an agreement between France, England, and Germany would be reached, credit was available in the United States and in the neutral countries; 4) German debtors needed 15 billion gold marks which should be raised immediately, or, at least within four years; 5) interest and amortization should be paid according to the Versailles Treaty; 6) guarantees would be left to negotiations; 7) if a solution were not found soon,

---

[114] *Ibid.*
[115] "Votum der Redaktionskommission," *PA AA*, Büro RM, Reparationen, D 718708. Cuno mentioned the meeting in the cabinet on December 22, but no report was found. Cf. *BA* R 43I/1381. Apparently it was attempted to contact trade union leaders, but they could not be reached in time. A meeting took place on December 28. Cf. *Kab. Cuno*, No. 30.

payments would be made impossible; 8) in order to accelerate Germany's recovery, economic and political freedom was necessary; 9) international trade relations ought to be placed on equal terms; 10) German and French industries (coal, iron ore and steel) were dependent on one another and an adjustment of interests was necessary.[116]

This proposal was supported by a majority of the editorial committee; only number ten is missing in the final draft.[117] 15 million gold marks were of course a further reduction of German liabilities. Apparently, the Ministry of Finance was not satisfied with this reduction, and during the next days several other plans were developed fixing the debt at 20 and 30 billion marks.[118] Duisberg and Flechtheim also submitted a new plan on December 27. Instead of 15, twenty billions should now be raised through a loan.[119] The Minister of Economics and his Secretary of State, Trendelenburg, also prepared a memorandum, suggesting a provisional agreement based on a 4 billion gold mark loan which should cover reparation payments until 1927. From 1927 onwards Germany would then offer to pay up to 1 billion gold marks per year. Of the 4 billion gold mark loan, 1 billion would be signed by German industry.[120] On December 26, Paul Silverberg wrote a letter to Hermes suggesting that French demands should be satisfied through a combination of cash payments and economic collaboration. He urged direct negotiations with France.[121]

All these different and often only slightly modified proposals from earlier meetings make it nearly impossible to analyse the combinations and interests behind them. However, they are good indicators of the confusion and disagreement among industrialists, bankers, or even within the cabinet. Apparently differences of opinion, based on industrial self-interest and diverging interpretations of political necessities, prevented a common initiative. A comprehensive plan that would satisfy everybody was simply not available, and Paul Reusch complained in a letter to Cuno, after discussions had come to an end: "The result of last Friday's negotiations left a rather dissatisfied impression on all participants." Reusch especially regretted that, due to differences about the amount to be offered, no decision had been reached about securities for an Allied loan.[122]

---

[116] "Zehn Punkte Stinnes," *BA* R 2/2900. The document is undated.
[117] *PA AA*, Büro RM, Reparationen, D 718708 f.
[118] *Ibid.*, D 718715, D 718716, D 718720.
[119] "Letzte Fassung Duisberg-Flechtheim," *BA*, R 2/3168.
[120] "Plan Trendelenburg/Becker," December 29, 1922, *ibid.*
[121] Silverberg-Hermes, December 26, 1922, *ibid.*, R 43I/1333.
[122] Reusch-Cuno, December 31, 1922, *BA*, R 43I/33. It contains further suggestions for an offer.

The plan that was finally decided upon goes back to a proposal by Carl Melchior on December 29. As a result of the disagreement he did not fix the German debt, but proposed, instead, that a 20 billion gold mark loan be issued immediately. From December 1926 onwards, another loan of 5 billion should be issued, providing the international financial syndicate which had issued the first loan decided that it was possible and would not impair the recovery of the mark. Another loan was to be issued under the same condition from January 1931 onwards.[123] The same night, Cuno assembled his cabinet and obtained its consent. The next day, a meeting with the party leaders was held.[124]

In summary, the German note as written by Melchior was an attempt to satisfy different pressure groups. The fact that the last draft was formulated by a member of a Hamburg banking house and not by the Minister of Finance or by the Foreign Office, shows that a change had taken place in foreign policy matters. Though this alteration was doubtless influenced by the financial complexity of the problem, it seems to suggest that at this point of Weimar History private relations between Cuno and former business associates were most important for the formulation of foreign policy initiatives. On the other hand, Cuno had to take into account the attitudes of other industrial groups as well. The psychologically important offers of Melchior, Duisberg and Flechtheim, operating with 40 billions, were watered down to 20 billions. Even the prospect of another 10 billions in case of German solvency (which may have been inserted after an intervention of the British ambassador) could not influence the negative aspects of the note. As unfavorable was the insistence upon economic equality on the world market and the demand to liberate Germany from "her economic and political chains." This part of the proposal was directly taken from the Stinnes memorandum.[125] The influence of Ruhr industrialists and especially of Ruhr heavy industry is shown by the incorporation of the evacuation of Düsseldorf, Duisburg and Ruhrort as a precondition for settlement. In addition, the occupation of the Rhineland was to be terminated as soon as possible. This latter demand was a compromise, because at the first meetings, representatives from the Ruhr had still demanded evacuation as a precon-

---

[123] "Letzter Plan Melchior 29. 12. 22," *BA*, R 2/3168; cf. "Plan Duisberg, Wassermann, Flechtheim," *PA AA*, Büro RM, Reparationen, D 718645 f.
[124] *BA*, R 43I/1346.
[125] "Letzter Plan Melchior . . .," *BA*, R 2/3168. "Zehn Punkte Stinnes," *BA*, R 2/2900. Apparently the last draft was written by Kastl. Cf. *PA AA*, Büro RM, Reparationen, D 718651 f. For D'Abernon's suggestion see "Aufzeichnung" December 28, 1922, D 718620 and D 718700 f.

dition, and the proposal of the Minister of Economics of December 16, 1922 had requested evacuation in stages, beginning immediately.[126]

It was completely unrealistic to make the German offer dependent upon evacuation, and the inclusion of these demands rendered negotiations with France impossible. Though Melchior and Bergmann warned that securities had to be mentioned, the government did not offer any but merely stated its willingness to discuss securities with the financial syndicate. Whether this was due to a lack of time, as Reusch claimed in his letter to Cuno, or due to disagreements about the selection of guarantees, cannot be determined with certainty. However, as earlier discussions have shown, industry was opposed to private securities and had always requested that the property of the Reich was the first security. An exception was Paul Reusch, who reasoned that industry, agriculture, trade, banking, and transport should be used as securities for the German debt.[127]

6. THE PROPOSAL FOR A NON-AGGRESSION PACT

While these negotiations with industry and banking were going on, Cuno had made another attempt to contact Poincaré through the United States. Directly after the breakdown of the London conference, the Foreign Office had informed the American Secretary of State that Germany was prepared to sign a non-aggression pact with all countries bordering on the Rhine for 30 years. Peace was to be guaranteed by the United States and by the fact that the population of the concerned countries should decide in a referendum before going to war again.[128] With this plan, Cuno hoped to prevent occupation and to eliminate French fears of German military potential. The plan most probably originated from Cuno's discussions with the American Ambassador who had announced similar ideas about a 'people's referendum to end war" several times.[129]

The American Secretary of State gave the details of the plan to the French Ambassador in Washington and urged him to consider the German offer.[130] However, Poincaré could not be stopped any more. He rejected the peace

---

[126] Printed in *Kab. Cuno*, No. 34.
[127] *Ibid.*, No. 31.
[128] Rosenberg-Wiedfeldt, December 13, 1922, *PA AA*, Büro RM, Reparationen, D 718462 f.
[129] Houghton-Hughes, October 22, 1922, Coar-Houghton, August 13, 1922, Houghton-Coar, August 15, S.D. Weyer-Houghton, October 7, Houghton-Dwight, May 24, 1923, *Houghton Papers*, Correspondence.
[130] *Hughes Papers*, Box 174, Folder 74 a, France, December 14, 1922.

plan for several reasons: 1) It was an obvious attempt to prevent the occupation; 2) the power to declare war lay with the French Chamber, and the
German proposal would have necessitated a change of the French constitution; 3) article 10 of the League of Nations provided the necessary securities
against an attack; 4) he did not trust the Germans. He expected that the
German people might even vote for war with France, "because of the hatred
which they were instilling in the youth by the instruction in their schools,
they could easily provide for a plebiscite whenever they wanted it." Hughes
urged the French to reconsider, but Poincaré again rejected this approach.[131]

Although Cuno's offer was a move to prevent occupation, the offer was
not unreasonable at all, only "untimely". And when Cuno again repeated
his offer in a New Year's speech in Hamburg, the American Ambassador to
Berlin described the reaction of the diplomatic corps with the following
words: "They speak of it as naive, as the effort of a businessman to interfere
in statecraft, as containing much that is good but untimely in its utterances
…"[132] When Stresemann signed the Locarno treaty with Briand, Cuno's
idea was the basis of it, but in 1922, with Poincaré in power and determined
to occupy the Ruhr, the suggestion was indeed only a last desperate attempt
to change a policy on which Cuno did not have any influence. When he
summarized his policy on New Year's Eve, his speech, in which he mentioned
both the German reparation offer being prepared and the peace pact, was an
appeal to the nation and to world public opinion to show that he was willing
to negotiate. At midnight of New Year's Eve, he called the American Ambassador to wish him a Happy New Year and to extend it to Hughes. This
was a rather unusual procedure, but Cuno wanted to let Houghton know
that the duration of the peace pact was not 30 years, but could be extended
to 45 or even 60 years.[133] If Cuno was still hoping that the United States or
some other power could change French coercive policy, he was, as later developments show, to be disappointed. Before there could be peace, Poincaré
wanted to be paid.

7. THE GERMAN OFFER AND THE ALLIED MEETING

On December 30, Rosenberg informed the German embassies in Washing-

[131] *Ibid.*, December 21 and 26, 1922; *MAE*, Allemagne 477, December 23 and December
26, 1922, fol. 136–137, fol. 175–76. David G. White, *Einige Kapitel aus der großen
Politik zur Zeit der Ruhrbesetzung*. Phil. Diss. (Berlin, 1939), pp. 30–32.
[132] Houghton-Hughes, January 3, 1923, *Hughes Papers*, General Correspondence Box
46. *Kab. Cuno*, No. 32.
[133] Houghton-Hughes, January 3, 1923, *ibid.*

ton, London, Brussels, Rome, and Paris, that the proposal for the Paris conference was ready. At the same time, he asked the German Ambassador to London to contact the British government and find out about Bonar Law's attitude towards the plan.[134] Sthamer saw Bradbury and Sir Eyre Crowe, the Permanent Undersecretary in the Foreign Office, the same day. Crowe believed that Germany had made a "substantial offer," but warned to submit the note with its preconditions. Instead, he recommended that these preconditions should be included as economic necessities. Crowe was also skeptical about a 20 billion gold mark loan. He did not believe that such an enormous sum was available on the international money market. Crowe's criticism showed the weakness of the note, and after Bonar Law had been acquainted with the details through Bradbury, the British Prime Minister suggested that it should not be submitted. An offer well below 30 billions did not have a chance. The situation would of course be different if the German Government knew that it would be favorably received in the United States. If this were the case, it might also influence the Allied meeting in Paris.[135]

The announcement of a new German offer caused difficulties at the Quai d'Orsay. On December 31, Mayer informed Peretti de la Rocca that Carl Bergmann was on his way to Paris. He would, if asked to do so by the conference, explain and submit the note. The next day the official French news agency *HAVAS* reported that Mayer had announced a German note to France. Upon the intervention of Mayer, Peretti admitted that the *HAVAS* report was wrong, that the German note was addressed to the Allied conference.[136] Poincaré did not invite Bergmann to appear before the conference. Instead, the French Minister President declared at the opening meeting that he had received an offer to deal directly with German industry. This approach had been rejected. As to rumors about a new German note, Poincaré declared that it was even less precise than the last one addressed to the London conference. It was only a "démarche announcing a visit," and the Allies should wait until they had decided upon a common policy towards Germany.[137] When Poincaré explained the German approach, he was not truthful. On January 1, Ago von Maltzan, the Secretary of State in the German Foreign Office, had informed the French Ambassador that a note, offering 20 billions as a basis for negotiations, was to be sent to the

---

[134] Rosenberg-London, December 30, 1922, *PA AA*, Büro RM, Reparationen, D 718694 f. The notes to the other countries are in the same volume.
[135] Sthamer-Rosenberg, December 30, 1922, *ibid.*, D 718703 f.
[136] Mayer-AA, January 1, 1923, *ibid.*, D 718730 f. On January 1, Rosenberg cabled Bergmann to explain the financial aspects of the note and submit it if asked for. *Ibid.*, D 718734 f.

conference. One day later de Margerie received further information. Thus, one day before the conference, the French Foreign Office knew parts of the proposal, although it had not been submitted officially.[138] The Germans hesitated to submit the note themselves. Ambassador Mayer had already warned on December 22 that any offer with 15 or even 20 billion gold marks could not be accepted by France as long as French debts to the United States and Great Britain had not been reduced.[139] This impression was confirmed when Bergmann, who together with Melchior had gone to Paris, met Bradbury, Boyden, Delacroix and Raggi, all members of the Reparation Commission. Bradbury warned against its submission when he showed Bergmann the British proposal. The other delegates predicted that in face of Allied disunity, an insufficient offer would unite the Allies against Germany.[140] Only the American Ambassador to Germany, who had also been informed, praised the German plan.[141]

The German plan was never submitted. Instead the Allies agreed to Poincaré's suggestion to decide upon a common policy first, but then the conference took a turn which none of Britain's Allies had expected. Bonar Law submitted a plan which proposed to fix the German debt at 50 billion gold marks, while abolishing the C-bonds (82 billion gold marks). He estimated that the actual value of 50 billions was between 32 and 39 billion gold marks. However, if Germany could have paid immediately through an international loan, the value would not have been more than 25 billions, a fact which Poincaré severely criticized. But even worse, Britain demanded repeal of Belgian priority on German reparations and declared that French and Italian gold reserves in London were no longer available. They would be used to cover French and Italian debts to Great Britain. This was a rather brutal method of reminding these countries of their financial indebtedness to Great Britain and contributed to the failure of the conference.[142]

Although British politicians had hoped that a compromise between the

---

[137] Documents diplomatiques, *Conférence de Paris* (Paris, 1923), p. 75.

[138] De Margerie-MAE, January 1, and 2, 1923, *MAE*, Allemagne 478, fol. 1 f., 47 f.

[139] Mayer-AA, December 22, 1922, *PA AA*, Büro RM, Reparationen, D 718584 f.

[140] Bergmann-Cuno, January 2, 1923, *ibid.*, D 718750 f; Bergmann-AA, January 4, 1923, *ibid.*, D 718818.

[141] "Vermerk Maltzan," December 30, 1922, *ibid.*, D 718700. Mussolini recommended the acceptance of his proposal. Neurath-AA, January 3, 1923, *ibid.*, D 718812.

[142] Documents diplomatiques, *op. cit.*, pp. 104–112. Lucien Petit, *Histoire des Finances Extérieures de la France. Le Règlement des Dettes Interalliées* (Paris, 1932), pp. 417–423. For the development of British opinion and contacts with Paris *FO.*, 371/7491, C 17594, C 17747, C 17656, C 17814; *Cab.*, 24/140, C.P. 4344, 4345, 4348, 4376, *FO.*, 8625/C 133, January 2 with the British plan. Cf. Saint-Aulaire, December 24, 1922, *MAE*, Ruhr 3, fol. 246 f. for his estimate of British policy.

countries would finally be reached, the conference broke up. Neither Belgium nor Italy agreed to the British plan, and Poincaré informed his audience that France would never accept the fixing of the German debt along the lines suggested by Bonar Law. Such a policy would mean the economic and financial hegemony of Germany on the continent, a hegemony which the war had destroyed. Thus, Poincaré rejected the British proposal for a four year moratorium, and he also opposed the creation of an international financial syndicate to study Germany's capacity to pay:

As to the Banker's Committee, he did not quite know what Mr. Bonar Law had referred to. In any case, he was suffering under a misapprehension. The French Government had never dreamed in any circumstances of submitting its rights to consideration by any Committee of Bankers. Personally he thought they were people of very limited competence. They did not play any great role in relations with the French Government and never would. It would never be international financiers who would influence French policy.[143]

Poincaré's emotional and bitter rejection of the British proposal destroyed any chances for a settlement of reparations. The time was not ripe yet for a financial or economical solution. Supported by Belgium and Italy, who were incensed by the British demands, France and Belgium prepared their search for reparations in the Ruhr. The rejection of the British proposal showed that, for France, reparations were not only an economic problem. It was complicated through the developing French budgetary crisis and the attitude of the French Chamber, which severely limited France's foreign policy.

In Germany, the situation was different. The Reichstag hardly discussed reparations at the end of 1922, and the party leaders agreed to postpone the convocation of the Reichstag Foreign Policy Committee to give Cuno a free hand in reparations. Banking and industry in a way became the substitute for parliamentary control of the Government. The German offer was a compromise between demands of these interest groups and suggestions reaching Berlin through Bradbury and Delacroix or went back to proposals made by Keynes and Cassel in November 1922 when they had studied Germany's economic situation.

At any rate, the effect of the British plan had been disastrous for Germany. At the London conference in December, Poincaré had been isolated, in Paris Bonar Law was in the same position. One day after the conference had been dissolved *sine die*, the Belgian and Italian delegates to the Reparation

---

[143] Documents diplomatiques, *op. cit.*, p. 187. Cf. Weill-Raynal, *op. cit.*, II, pp. 325–368. Also Poincaré in a cable to Jusserand, December 23, 1922, *MAE*, Allemagne 477, fol. 175. "Nous sommes dans l'impossibilité de confier à des financiers l'examen des solutions dont nous devrons compte à notre Parlement."

Commission announced that they were forced to vote with France on Germany's default in coal deliveries. But despite their resentment of the British request, reason retained the upper hand for another two days. Against Poincaré's order to arrange a vote about the deficit immediately, Barthou allowed a discussion of the German request for a moratorium. The delegates reached the conclusion that a moratorium was needed, but they could not agree on the *modus procedendi* for a common plan. Bradbury rejected the French demand for "productive pledges" in case of a moratorium, and thus the Commission declared Germany in default, the British delegate voting against the motion.[144]

Germany had delivered coal at a level about 10% lower than prescribed by the Reparation Commission. But for months, the Reparation Commission had expected such a development and had not done anything. Now, under strong French pressure, it acted. Obviously this late decision was a political move independent of the actual default. The British decision to propose a final settlement of reparations and interallied-debts had finally carried Italy and Belgium over to the French side. Threatened by Bonar Law's claims upon their countries, Italy and Belgium followed France.[145]

The policy of "political window dressing" was thus carried to the extreme at the end of 1922. The eventual course of action was not determined by German default, but also by the unwillingness of the United States to abolish interallied debts and by British demands upon Belgium and Italy. Without a cancellation or at least partial reduction of interallied debts in connection with a reduction of the German debts, no European government, with the exception of Great Britain, would agree to negotiate a new settlement with Germany. In the emerging controversy, in which every power waited for a sacrifice on the part of the other Allies, Germany was a mere pawn of Allied policy and hardly a participant in this political game.

As to the amount of reparations, Allied estimates still differed at the end of 1922, but comparing the original sum of 132 billion gold marks with the new figures that had been mentioned, the Allies had reduced the German liability to between a half and a third of the original sum. Poincaré now demanded 40–50 billions and a cancellation of interallied debts, Britain demanded 50 billions (the real value being 32–39 billions, and if Germany had been able to pay immediately through a loan, only 25 billions), Belgium wanted 30 billions, and an international bankers committee had estimated Germany's capacity at 20–25 billions. The German note which was not sub-

---

[144] *PA AA*, W. Rep., Besetzung des Ruhrgebietes, January 7, 1923.
[145] Logan-Hoover, January 5, 1923, *Logan Papers*, Correspondence, October 1922–March 1923.

mitted had offered 30 billion gold marks nominal value, but only 12–15 billions real value.[146] Bergmann had felt uncomfortable about this low offer,[147] but as Poincaré's rejection of the British plan had shown, France could not have been satisfied anyway. Poincaré was determined to march into the Ruhr, and it is necessary to analyze his intentions at this point.

---

[146] These estimates are based upon an evaluation by Gaston A. Furst, *De Versailles aux Experts* (Paris, 1927), p. XXIV. Furst was a member of the Belgian Reparation Commission.

[147] *Kab. Cuno*, No. 144.

CHAPTER III

FRANCE BEFORE THE OCCUPATION

When the Reparation Commission declared Germany to be in "voluntary default" for timber and coal deliveries on December 26, 1922 and January 9, 1923 respectively, France had obtained a basis for the occupation of the Ruhr. Two days later French and Belgian troops began to execute their rights under paragraphs 17 and 18, Annex II of part VIII of the treaty. Paragraph 17 determined that the Reparation Commission would notify the Allies about any defaults. Paragraph 18 stated that in case of voluntary default the Allies had the right to take economic, financial, and other measures they deemed necessary.[1] The wording of paragraph 18 was certainly imprecise. John F. Dulles, who had formulated this provision at Versailles, later stated in a memorandum written for the Department of State that the words "other measures" would be "limited by the doctrine *sui generis* to economic measures of the type specifically contemplated."[2]

The British Government reached a similar conclusion. Thus it disputed the French right to take unilateral coercive measures. As early a May 1922, Cecil J.D. Hurst, legal adviser of the Foreign Office, had prepared a memorandum in which he rejected the French interpretation of paragraph 18.[3] However, in a final discussion with the permanent undersecretary, Sir Eyre Crowe, and Ralph Wigram, one of the senior clerks, it was decided that the British position was not unassailable. The officers of the Foreign Office felt

---

[1] The original text of paragraph 17 is: "En cas de manquement par l'Allemagne à l'exécution qui lui incombe de l'une quelconque des obligations visées à la présente partie du présent Traité, la Commission des Réparations signalera immédiatement cette exécution à chacune des Puissances intéressées en y joignant toutes propositions qui lui paraîtront opportunes au sujet des mesures à prendre en raison de cette inexécution." Paragraph 18: "Les mesures que les Puissances alliées et associées auront le droit de prendre en cas de manquement volontaire par l'Allemagne, et que l'Allemagne s'engage à ne pas considérer comme des actes d'hostilité, peuvent comprendre des actes de prohibitions et des représailles économiques et financières et, en général, telles autres mesures que les Gouvernements respectifs pourront estimer nécessitées par les circonstances." Weill-Raynal, *op. cit.*, II, pp. 368–370.

[2] J.F. Dulles, Memo on Reparation Clauses, August 11, 1923, *Dulles Papers*, II, Correspondence 1922. 1925, Box 135.

[3] *Cab.*, 24/136, C.P. 3987, May 23, 1922.

that the interpretation of paragraph 18 left the realm of legal disputes and was actually "a political question."[4] On May 24, the British Government had sent a note to Paris reminding Poincaré that the Foreign Office did not intend to follow him into "legal disquisitions." If he did not adhere to an understanding which had existed since 1920 when Millerand had "given a definite pledge" after the occupation of Frankfurt and Darmstadt that he would abstain from taking independent action in the future, France would commit a "deliberate breach of an honorable understanding."[5] Thus from May 1922 onwards Poincaré knew that although the meaning of the paragraph might be open to interpretation, he could not rely on British support in case of unilateral action.

The British position must have been a blow for Poincaré. When he succeeded Briand as Minister President in January 1922, he had promised that he would make Germany pay. In the meantime his own position had become more and more difficult at home. Instead of forcing Germany to pay reparations, the Allies had to grant several moratoria during 1922, and British politicians demanded a reduction of Germany's liability. This revisionist British approach towards the Versailles Treaty and the London Schedule of Payments did not mean that Britain was leaving the Entente with France and was turning towards Germany. Faced with the disruption of trade, rising unemployment and a German export offensive, British politicians were much concerned about the future of the European economic system. In 1921 and 1922 Lloyd George had developed several plans to reduce German reparation payments which, in his opinion, could only be made through increased exports. Thus, one ambitious plan provided for the opening of the Russian market for German goods.[6] Another proposal forwarded to France, cancelled all British reparation demands upon Germany based on pensions providing that the United States would "wipe out" her claims on Europe. France, Italy and the other powers would also have to abandon these demands. Only claims for devastation would remain, and Germany could pay her debts to France through a large loan.[7] These plans may not have been feasible due to the American position on war debts or

---

[4] *Ibid.*, C.P. 3992, May 24, 1922.

[5] *Ibid.*, C.P. 3992, Draft Dispatch to Hardinge, May 24, 1922. For discussion of the paragraphs at the Genoa conference between Louis Barthou and Lloyd George, and Lloyd George and Chancellor Wirth cf: *DBFP*, First Series, vol. XIX, No. 106, No. 111, No. 140. Lloyd George warned Wirth that Poincaré might „take unilateral action because he was only bound to discuss measures before initiating them. ... France would undoubtedly take the benefit of the doubt."

[6] Cf. *ibid.*, vol. XV, No. 106, 108, 112–117.

[7] *Ibid.*, vol. XIX, No. 101, April 29, 1922.

French difficulties with Russian war debts, but they showed that Great Britain was determined to reach a final understanding on reparations despite Germany's folly of signing the Rapallo-Treaty. To Lloyd George "there had been conferences at London, Paris, Spa, but no real settlement had yet been reached." Although Germany was to pay to "the utmost of her capacity" such a statement endangered the French position on reparations.[8] With Britain determined to deal with Germany and Russia on equal terms, as the Genoa conference had shown, and France in desperate need of payments to balance her budget, Poincaré was in a dilemma: neither would Russia repay her prewar debts and war loans, nor would German be in a position to make substantial reparation payments in the near future.

I. FRENCH PREPARATIONS FOR OCCUPATION

Since he had come to power, Poincaré had constantly demanded that the Ruhr be occupied if the Reich did not fulfill its obligations. During this early period he apparently hoped to convince Britain that such a step was necessary, but recognizing that British politicians were unwilling to follow his lead, he systematically prepared the ground for French action. Poincaré was an excellent lawyer, and he soon discovered that the clumsy formulation of paragraph 18 gave France a legal basis for coercive measures if the Reich did not fulfill the Schedule of Payments. Already in October 1922, three months before the Reparation Commission declared Germany in default, he ordered Louis Barthou, the new delegate to the Reparation Commission, to prepare the ground for French action. In a letter to Herriot, Barthou later described his policy, as follows:

As French delegate I could only be inspired by a policy that would give the French Government a satisfactory basis for the seizure of pledges, with all Allies if possible, but without them if needed.[9]

When the Reparation Commission declared Germany in default, Barthou believed that the French government now "had acquired the legal basis to execute its sanctions."[10]

Knowing well that legal advisers both of the US Department of State and British crown-lawyers had reached the conclusion that paragraph 18 was at least open to interpretation, Barthou did everything possible to prevent the

---

[8] *Ibid.*, No. 5 and No. 106.

[9] "Le Délégué de la France à la Commission des Réparations," June 15, 1924, *MAE*, Allemagne 487, fol. 22.

[10] *Ibid.*, fol. 25.

presentation of a motion before the Reparation Commission. Since the German Foreign Office had decided that an appeal to the Commission was futile, the French delegate even feared that Bradbury himself might initiate such a policy, but although the British considered such an action, it was not carried through.[11] Britain still needed French support in dealing with the Turkish question at Lausanne.

It is clear that the occupation of the Ruhr in 1923 was not the direct result of Germany's default in 1922. The occupation had been planned long before it became apparent that the Reich would or could not pay deliveries in kind for 1922. Propositions for an occupation of the Ruhr were not a new idea. In order to obtain coal from Germany such a step had been discussed by Millerand in November 1919. During 1920 the question of sanctions in the Ruhr were repeatedly discussed in French government and military circles.[12] In 1921, the Briand Government had studied the financial, economic, and military aspects of a French march into the Ruhr,[13] and General Nollet, a member of the French Military Commission in Germany, notified Briand that occupation was an excellent means to extract economic advantages from Germany. Among other measures, Nollet proposed the recovery of coal, the confiscation of industrial property and taxes, and the exchange of Ruhr coke for Lorraine iron ore.[14] Marshall Foch had also developed a comprehensive plan for the control of the Ruhr as a source of reparation payments, and on May 7, 1921 he had informed Briand that French troops were ready to move.[15]

But nothing came of French preparations, since the Wirth government had yielded to an Allied ultimatum agreeing to accept the London Schedule of Payments. But developments during 1921 and 1922 indicated that French politicians had given up all hope of bringing Germany to terms, and the occupation of the Ruhr became the *ultima ratio* of a French policy that tried to enforce the reparation clauses of the Treaty of Versailles by any means. True enough, Poincaré did not stumble into the Ruhr before he had tried to reach a peaceful understanding with the Allies. But by the summer of 1922, France was suffering one diplomatic defeat after another. Britain did not agree to a security treaty with France on French terms; international bankers

[11] *Cab.*, 24/140, C.P. 4377, December 28, 1922; *MAE*, Allemagne 487 fol. 26.

[12] Zimmermann, *op. cit.*, p. 33 f.

[13] April 15, 1921, *MAE*, Ruhr 1, fol. 151–152.

[14] "Considérations relatives à l'occupation de la Ruhr," Nollet-Briand, April 30, 1921, *ibid.*, fol. 318 ff.

[15] Foch-Briand, May 7, 1921, *ibid.*, Ruhr 2, fol. 81 ff. "Note au sujet de l'Attitude Probable de l'Allemagne en cas d'Occupation Prochaine Du Bassin de la Ruhr," April 26, 1921, *ibid.*, fol. 4–71, Zimmermann, *op. cit.*, pp. 38–42, pp. 73–76.

assembled at Paris had made it clear that Germany could not obtain loans for reparation purposes before Allied demands had been reduced and similar statements had been made by British politicians at the Genoa conference. Apparently the time had come for another reduction of German reparations; while Allied claims might not be as low as Germany hoped, any reduction would force the French Treasury to come to terms with the so-called recoverable budget.

France was indeed in a very difficult situation. Prospects of European economic and political hegemony and control of the German potential had been opened at Versailles. An occupation would have been relatively easy in 1920 or even in 1921, but in 1922 France had to consider the disillusionment with respect to reparations existing in Great Britain and other European countries. Nevertheless, in May 1922, several weeks before Germany appeared to fail on reparation payments due May 31, the French military began to renew its planning of military measures. General Degoutte, the French commanding general at Düsseldorf, urged the Ministry of War after Maginot's visit to the Rhineland to prepare the public for "notre opération éventuelle dans la Ruhr." Upset by the Rapallo-Treaty, seen as German preparation for a conflict with France, he proposed that France should make it clear that she neither intended to annex the Ruhr nor to destroy this highly organized industrial center of Germany. The sole purpose of a French Ruhr operation was to force Ruhr industrialists to pay the indemnity for the Reich. Industrialists should remain in possession of their property; and negotiations with industry, trade unions and representatives of the government should take place at Düsseldorf. If threats to occupy the Ruhr would not be sufficient to convince Germany that France meant business, customs controls should be erected, exports and imports be prevented and finally industrial property should be confiscated. However, Degoutte was convinced that Germany would give in to these threats as she had always done since 1919.[16] Despite this optimistic report about French possibilities, other military officers were well aware that an occupation, especially if executed without British support, was not an easy task. The Army did not fear military resistance. But since 1921 important changes had occurred in Germany. Not only were the Right and the bourgeois parties hostile to military measures in the Ruhr, but Communist and Social Democratic workers were attributing the rising cost of living and the financial chaos in Germany to French reparation policy. Since France already controlled Düsseldorf, Duisburg and Ruhrort, she had an excellent means to affect exports and

[16] Degoutte-Ministère de Guerre, May 2, 1922, *MAE*, Ruhr 3, fol. 22 ff; Zimmermann, *op. cit.*, pp. 78–80.

imports to Germany and a blockade of these important towns would have affected the whole Ruhr region. To some French officers, such an act was preferable to occupation, since it would have limited contacts between the population and the army.[17]

French planning for control of the Ruhr, however, went on. On May 29, representatives of several Ministries (War, Finance, Public Works) and the French Rhineland High Commissioner Tirard met to discuss means of extracting reparations from the Ruhr. Military plans provided for an encirclement of the Ruhr. Economic life was to be controlled by French engineers and government revenues were to be confiscated, among them the coal tax. On July 12, the Ruhr committee of 1921 was reinstated. When the Allied Prime Ministers were to discuss reparations in August, Poincaré wanted military plans to be ready.[18] At the same time, he gave the French reparation expert Louis Dubois detailed instructions for a new moratorium for Germany. As a member of the European concert of powers, France would prevent Germany from ruining herself and the rest of Europe through her ruthless exploitation of the mark devaluation. The Reparation Commission had to see that Germany would balance her budget. Without productive pledges, a new moratorium was not possible. If Germany should not agree to these demands, France would enforce sanctions in the Ruhr regardless of the other Allies.[19] Poincaré was annoyed that the Reparation Commission had not pressed the matter earlier. France could not wait, Poincaré told Dubois, until Germany had recovered from the war "pour recevoir les sommes qu'elle [France] a dépensées pour le compte allemand et qui empêchent l'equilibre de son budget."[19] Thus by the summer of 1922 Poincaré had decided upon sanctions in the Ruhr. He was talking about taking control of the Ruhr when he declared "ce n'est pas un contrôle provisoire qui peut avoir un effet utile sur les finances allemandes, c'est un contrôle permanent qui est nécessaire" to guarantee execution of French demands upon Germany.[20]

Before the French Minister President could present his far-reaching plans to the Allied conference, Britain made it clear to France that not only French financial plight was involved in reparations. On August 1, 1922 Lloyd George announced that Britain was to fund her war debts to the United

---

[17] "Note au sujet de l'Attitude Probable d'Allemagne en cas d'Occupation Prochaine du Bassin de la Ruhr," April 26, 1921, *MAE*, Ruhr 2, fol. 160 f.; Capitain Ployen, Chef de Poste de Contrôle de la Zone neutre Düsseldorf-Nollet, December 22, 1922, *ibid.*, Ruhr 4, fol. 15–19.

[18] Zimmermann, *op. cit.*, p. 83.

[19] Poincaré-Dubois, July 19, 1922, *MAE*, Allemagne 473, fol. 200 f.

[20] Poincaré-Dubois, August 3, 1922, *ibid.*, Allemagne 474, August 3, 1922, fol. 13–23.

States. Thus she must ask her Allies to pay their war debts to her as well.
Although the note, which became known as the Balfour Note, also mentioned a scheme for a cancellation of reparations and interallied debts, it only
increased French desire to extract reparations and her war debts from Germany.[21] When the European powers Italy, Belgium, France and Britain met
in London to discuss reparations again from August 7–14, the British decision
to extract war debts from her European Allies increased the differences between France and Britain. As to reparations, Poincaré now demanded the
enforcement of financial controls in Germany. In addition, he made French
agreement to a moratorium dependent upon the seizure of coal mines and
state forests which were to be exploited by the Allies. Other preconditions
for a moratorium were the establishment of a customs border on the Rhine,
a customs border around the Ruhr, and the collection of customs duties by
the Allies. Besides pledges for an execution of the peace, these measures
would also, Poincaré hoped, yield cash payments for the reparation account.
Reparation payments could be further increased by a transaction of 60% of
the stocks of German chemical industry located on the left bank of the
Rhine.[22]

This program would have meant the complete control of Germany's
richest industrial regions by the Allies, but it was rejected by Britain as well
as by Allied experts who studied its effect upon reparation payments and
Allied industries. With the exception of the French delegate the experts were
opposed to the collection of customs, the creation of customs barriers, and
the seizure of German stocks. The collection of customs was too expensive
and receipts would be insignificant. The seizure of German stocks was rejected
since the experts felt that the owners would have to be indemnified. The
Allies were of course unwilling to do that and thus the German government
would have to pay in papermarks. However, such a policy would furthermore react upon the exchange value of the mark. The British delegate considered the exploitation of German mines to be impractical while France and
Belgium demanded their control, and the Italian delegate wanted a further
investigation of the matter.[23]

2. THE RUHR COMMITTEE

With the Allies disagreeing upon the merit of sanctions the plan was blocked.

[21] Keith Middlemas and John Barnes, *Baldwin. A Biography* (London, 1969), p. 132 f.
[22] Weill-Raynal, *op. cit.*, II, pp. 201–205. Poincaré-Dubois, August 3, 1922, *MAE*,
Allemagne 474, fol. 13 ff.
[23] *Cab.* 24/138, C.P. 4151, August 9, 1922.

While Poincaré was in London, however the Ruhr committee held a meeting in Paris. Jean Jacques Seydoux, director of the economic branch of the Foreign Office and reparation specialist, presided over the first meeting, which was also attended by representatives of the Ministry of War and the Ministry of Public Works. The purpose of the discussion was the development of a plan for an occupation of the Ruhr district. Seydoux apparently felt uneasy about the effects of an occupation on Germany's financial and economic situation. He doubted the wisdom of military measures and argued that it was no longer sufficient to hold the Ruhr in order to control Germany. In his opinion, the situation had been complicated by a change in British policy. Even if France should succeed with the confiscation of coal, industrial production would not break down, since the Reich could always substitute Ruhr coal with imports from Great Britain. British industry would be only too willing to ship its coal to Germany.[24]

For General Desticker, who participated as personal representative of Marshal Foch, the purpose of the occupation had also changed. In 1920, a French move into the Ruhr would have primarily been a military action. In 1921, the purpose would have been economic, i.e. to put pressure upon German industry to collaborate with France. Now occupation had become a means "to study measures bringing about a profitable financial settlement."[25] The representative of the Ministry of Public Works and director of the Blanzy mines, Coste, stressed the importance of forcing German industry to come to terms with France. He believed that the control of the railways to Southern Germany and the confiscation of coal taxes were adequate means of putting pressure on Ruhr industry. In addition, Coste argued that France's Allies would not be opposed to these measures. Seydoux did not seem to be convinced, and he urged his collaborators to prevent disorganization of the Ruhr in case of occupation.[26]

The next day renewed discussions took place at the Quai d'Orsay. Representatives from all ministeries attended and delegates from the Rhine Army and the French High Commission in the Rhineland also participated. General Desticker submitted Marshall Foch's plan for occupation, which showed that a complete penetration of the district was unnecessary. Instead, Essen, seat of the Ruhr coal syndicate, should be occupied by a French detachment. No final decision was made at this conference, although special study committees on the seizure of customs duties, exports, and the issue of

[24] "Conférence relative aux mesures économiques et financères éventuelles à envisager en cas d'occupation du bassin de la Ruhr," August 9, 1922, *MAE*, Ruhr 3, fol. 147–149.
[25] *Ibid.*, fol. 148.
[26] *Ibid.*, fol. 152–157.

a special currency were formed.[27] On August 19, Seydoux summarized the results of these investigations in a report for Poincaré showing that it could be made a financial success or would at least break even. These optimistic expectations were severely criticized by the Minister of Finance, de Lasteyrie. To him, the Ruhr could only be a political pledge to exert pressure upon Germany.[28] When the French cabinet met on October 18 to discuss a British request for a German moratorium, de Lasteyrie was again out of line with the majority. He hesitated to allow the Reparation Commission to take over control of Germany's finances, as provided for in a French plan submitted by Mauclère of the French Reparation Commission. But more important than the differences between Poincaré and his Minister of Finance was Poincaré's demand on French delegates to make "reparations a political debt."[29]

3. FRENCH STRATEGIES AT THE END OF 1922

By August 1922, a course of action had been decided on: the French delegation on the Reparation Commission would force a showdown with Germany, and Poincaré could work on his Allies to support him. However, as Britain was not available, he started discussions with Belgium. Several times in September he informed Brussels that he would "seize pledges."[30] On November 23, a meeting between French and Belgian ministers took place in Paris. Poincaré warned Theunis and Jaspar that French troops would occupy the Ruhr if the Conference of Brussels, which had been arranged for December to discuss reparations and interallied debts, did not result in an agreement between the powers. According to Poincaré the French would then start an "opération d'huissier" under the protection of the army. Upon the interjection of Theunis that an occupation meant social disturbances in the Ruhr, the French Minister tried to comfort his Belgian colleagues by stating that French occupation authorities at Düsseldorf had good relations with the German working class.[31] This statement was false and cannot be supported by documents in the Foreign Office, which clearly

[27] *Ibid.*, fol. 159 f.
[28] Zimmermann, *op. cit.*, p. 84 f.
[29] "Réunion du 18 octobre 1922 sous la Présidence du Président du Conseil," *MAE*, Allemagne 476, fol. 17–25. Zimmermann, *op. cit.*, pp. 83–85.
[30] Poincaré-Herbette, September 2, 1922, *MAE*, Allemagne 475, fol. 30–31. Poincaré-Herbette, September 14, 1922, *ibid.*, fo. 129.
[31] "Réunion chez le Président du Conseil," November 23, 1922, *ibid.*, Allemagne 476, fol. 202–213.

show that French occupation officers had warned that the army would be confronted with a hostile population. Obviously Poincaré tried to diminish the problems of military action, hoping that Belgium could be influenced to follow France. The Belgian Ministers were not satisfied that easily, however. Theunis did not believe that Poincaré described French goals honestly when he declared the action as an "opération d'huissier." Theunis, who could not be convinced that occupation was an easy task, inquired repeatedly after the real motive of Poincaré's policy. Did the French, for example, intend to change the status of the Rhineland and create a Rhenish Republic after its army had entered the Ruhr? Poincaré took offense at such an interpretation of his policy and retorted that France neither intended to annex parts of Germany nor to create a new state. He admitted, however, that France planned the expulsion of Prussian civil servants and the confiscation of taxes if the Reich did not yield to French pressure. But contrary to his assurances, Poincaré was in fact hoping for the creation of a Rhenish state by the local population and added "it is another thing to have a Rhineland without Prussians: it would lead to the creation of a neutral zone" in which the population was friendly towards France.[32]

Without elaborating further on this issue Poincaré had partly lifted the veil which covered his policy towards Germany. He obviously hoped that the Rhenish population would establish special relations with France and loosen its ties with Prussia, but at the moment reparations and the Ruhr had priority. Furthermore, developments in the Rhineland would depend on British attitude. Correctly estimating British distrust of French Rhineland policy, he declared as to French goals: "··· on verrait ce que nous faisons: si les Anglais viennent avec nous, nous savons très bien que ce sera pour nous surveiller."[33] Poincaré's statement shows that his Rhineland policy had neither been decided upon, nor had he given up hopes for British participation. On November 11, he had bitterly complained in a telegram to London that France was willing to reach an agreement with England in the Middle East, but in return England could not "s'opposer aux voeux unanimes de la France dans la question des réparations ···"[34] France wanted Britain "to march" with her and in his meeting with the Belgians, Poincaré repeated this theme. Several days before occupation took place, he still expressed the hope that Britain would finally send "engineers" as well.[35]

[32] *Ibid.*, fol. 211.

[33] *Ibid.*, fol. 217.

[34] Poincaré-Saint-Aulaire, November 11, 1922, *ibid.*, fol. 175.

[35] January 9, 1923, *ibid.*, Ruhr 4, fol. 82. Bonar Law and Crowe were indeed willing to let France occupy the Ruhr. They did not want to participate but would afterwards "formulate reasonable demands" for a settlement. Cf. *FO.*, 371/7487 C 16116, November

If Britain was unwilling to agree to French coercive actions, international bankers were even more so. When the Belgians suggested that J.P. Morgan, the American banker who had placed French war loans in the United States, considered loans to Germany as a means to insure reparations payments, Poincaré rejected this intervention. He could not accept the banker's preconditions: a five year moratorium for Germany, the renunciation of future sanctions and a final reparation agreement between the Allies.[36] He himself was convinced that a moratorium and loans were necessary as he had announced in a meeting with a German delegate in Paris. But a loan and a moratorium could only be made available after France had received a pledge.[37]

The seizure of pledges, Poincaré stressed, was needed for domestic reasons as well: its purpose was to influence French public opinion. Without secure pledges in French hands, no government could grant a moratorium. Barthou, de Lasteyrie, and Reibel (the Minister for Reconstruction) supported him when he declared:

In any case ... the intended operation was the only means to make the French population accept a moratorium of two or three years; any cabinet that did not return with pledges would not survive an hour.[38]

Poincaré's domestic position was completely tied up with reparations. His warning that no government would survive the granting of a moratorium to Germany without the seizure of productive pledges was probably correct. But the agitated state of French public opinion and of both Houses were partly due to his own statements in 1922. He had become the prisoner of his own arguments. Nevertheless, when Poincaré tried to enforce reparation payments, he represented the majority of the French Chamber of Deputies and the French press.[39]

In May 1922, Adrien Dariac, President of the Finance Committee of the Chamber, had visited the Rhineland and the Saar to study French occupation expenditures.[40] Afterwards he presented a report describing the advantages of French control of the Ruhr, the Saar, and the Rhineland. He

---

22, 1922 about a meeting between Bonar Law and Bradbury and *ibid.*, 371/7490, C 17445, December 10, 1922, handwritten note by Crowe.

[36] "Réunion ...," *MAE*, Allemagne 476, fol. 204.

[37] Meyer-AA, October 28, 1922, *PA AA*, Büro RM, Reparationen, D 718392-393.

[38] "Réunion ...," *MAE*, Allemagne 476, fol. 212.

[39] George Bonnet, *Le Quai d'Orsay sous Trois Républiques* (Paris, 1961), pp. 58-68. Paul Cambon, *Correspondance, t. 1-3* (Paris, 1946), vol. 3, p. 418 and p. 432.

[40] "Rapport sur une mission de contrôle à l'Armée du Rhin" May 25, 1922, *MAE*, Rive gauche du Rhin, 6, fol. 192-219. The report became known in Germany cf. Hoesch-AA, August 12, 1922, *PA AA*, Besetzte Gebiete, Politische Angelegenheiten spec. die Reise des Herrn Dariac in das besetzte Rheinland und Saargebiet. Bariety, *op. cit.*, p. 97 f.

argued that while the Reich did not have sufficient means to pay an indemnity, Stinnes, Thyssen, Krupp, Haniel, Klöckner, Funke, and other Ruhr industrialists possessed an economic potential capable of carrying out reparation payments for the Reich. Thus, reparations would be simple if Ruhr industry could be forced to become a substitute for the Reich's liability. Industry would always receive credit abroad and was the only real source for the successful handling of reparations. Naturally, industry would have to be forced to accept this position. As a first step towards coercing industrialists, Dariac suggested that a customs barrier should be created between the French occupied bridgeheads and the Ruhr area. France should then begin to raise a levy on exports and imports payable to the reparation account. As a second measure, he proposed the compulsory creation of industrial shares representing one fourth to one fifth of the capital of certain companies. The shares should be assigned to the German government and controlled by the Reparation Commission. But far more important was the exchange of French ore for German coke. Dariac believed that such a policy was only natural since France could not live without German coke, while German industrial production could not reach half of its capacity without French ores.

Could France not consider the exchange of French minerals for German coke on a friendly basis? This would provide the foundation for a genuine association of their industries.[41]

The exchange of coke and iron ore would also enable control of German production. France would thus be in a position to profit from German prosperity while preventing the creation of an all-powerful economic giant. If France did collaborate with Germany, she would no longer have "to be worried by the vision of what German industry would look like, if it were in fact able to meet" reparation demands.[42]

This statement explains the ambivalence of French attitudes with respect to reparation payments, and shows their connection with the French notion of security. Dariac's scheme was probably based on ideas of the French High Commission in the Rhineland, but in contrast to Tirard, Dariac did not propose occupation. He felt that control of the bridgeheads Düsseldorf, Duisburg, Ruhrort and the Rhineland would be sufficient to force Ruhr industry to accept French demands. The Dariac report was widely discussed in the press. Le Journal recommended its execution,[43] and other papers also believed that it would be to France's advantage to follow the scheme.[44]

[41] "Rapport ...," MAE, Rive gauche du Rhin 6, fol. 211 f.
[42] Ibid., fol. 212.
[43] Le Journal, July 24, 1922 and August 4, 1922.
[44] For example L'Eclair, July 4, 1922 and Le Temps, July 4, 1922.

Dariac had addressed himself to those questions which had been of greatest importance since 1919: coal, reparations, the Rhineland and implicitly French security. Immediately after the war, French industry had hoped that prewar relations between Lorraine and the Ruhr would return and Germany would agree to an exchange of coal and coke against iron ore and steel. In 1920, French industrialists had suggested that the government put pressure on the Germans to hand over stock shares in Ruhr companies. Poincaré had made similar demands on German chemical industry in the Rhineland in August 1922.[45] Nevertheless, it would be wrong to assume that Poincaré went into the Ruhr to weave together Ruhr heavy industry and Lorraine under French control.[46] Even though French military presence in the Ruhr could be used to guarantee the delivery of coke and coal for the Lorraine iron and steel works, which was of utmost importance for French economic development, it would not provide France with the necessary cash payments to balance the budget. The same was true of deliveries in kind under the Wiesbaden Agreement and plans developed by the Minister of Public Works, which provided for the canalization of the Rhone, the Truyère and the Dordogne with German labour and equipment.[47] Nor was the Ruhr important for French security. French control of the Rhineland was an excellent assurance of security, since the Allied troops would remain in the Rhineland for 15 years, although occupation was to start in stages after 5 years. But this provision of the Versailles Treaty was also a pledge for Germany of treaty conditions. Thus, the period of occupation could be extended, as France used this provision to declare that due to German defaults the period of occupation had not really started yet.

[45] M. Brelet, *La Crise de la Métallurgie. La Politique Economique et Sociale du Comité des Forges* (Paris, 1923), p. 13 f. Maier, *op. cit.*, p. 201. Poincaré-Dubois, August 3, 1923, *MAE*, Allemagne 474, fol. 13 ff.

[46] *Les Informations Politiques et Financiers*, May 14, 1922, "L'Organisation technique de la Ruhr en cas d'occupation." *L'Humanité*. December 21, 1922. Raymond Recouly, "Après l'Occupation de la Ruhr," *La Revue de France*, February 1, 1923, pp. 659–663. A British observer in the Ruhr, the assistant director of the Coal Bureau of the Reparation Commission, Guy Greer, believed that occupation was the result of a "political and economic" deadlock between the European nations. Economic and political motives were intertwined, and he saw it as an attempt to secure an adequate supply of coal, to obtain security, and last, to obtain reparations from Germany. Cf. Guy Greer, *The Ruhr Lorraine Industrial Problem. A Study of the Economic Interdependence of Two Regions and Their Relations to the Reparation Question* (New York, 1925), pp. 178–179, pp. 183–200. Charles M.E. Nollet, *Une expérience de désarmement* (Paris, 1931), p. 146.

[47] AA-Fischer, October 12, 1922, *PA AA*, W. Rep. Vorschläge Le Trocqueur u.a. für den Wiederaufbau Frankreichs. Also "Bericht über Besprechung Reichsministerium für den Wiederaufbau," September 30, 1922, *ibid. Echo de Paris*, June 6, 1922 "Les Réparations Allemandes." *Journée Industrielle*, July 6, 1922. *Le Peuple*, September 1, 1922. *Le Populäon*, June 29, 1922, "Autour du Problème des Réparations. La grande idée de Napolèon Le Trocqueur."

If neither a Franco-German coal and steel syndicate, nor security were the object of the march into the Ruhr, what did Poincaré have in mind? Jules Laroche, deputy director of political and economic affairs at the Quai d'Orsay and André François-Poncet, at that time French economic observer at Düsseldorf, maintained that Poincaré was pushed into the Ruhr by President Millerand and a nationalistic Chamber.[48] The influence of Millerand, domestic difficulties with public opinion, and a Chamber which had been promised reparations cannot be denied. However, budgetary difficulties, Poincaré's worries concerning his personal future and foreign policy problems also played a role. The attitude of international bankers towards German debts, British and German demands for reparation loans, American attitudes and Poincaré's own evaluation of the situation had shown that another reduction of the liability was imminent. This Poincaré could not permit without a similar treatment of French debts to the United States and Great Britain.[49] While he hoped until the last minute that Britain would follow him into the Ruhr out of a distrust of French motives, did he really expect the United States to reduce French war debts? There certainly was no indication of this. When French plans became known in Washington, Secretary of State Hughes had made it clear that talks about a cancellation of war debts would be a "waste of time". Interallied debts were "irrelevant" to German reparations. Economic developments in Europe during 1922 had made it necessary, according to Hughes, to interpose between European governments "and their public the findings of an impartial" business committee to reach a final agreement on reparations.

Hughes' suggestions which had been reaching Paris since September 1922 through the French Ambassador to Washington, Jusserand, the American Ambassador to Paris, Herrick, and the American unofficial delegate to the Reparation Commission, Boyden, left no doubt about the American attitude towards reparations and interallied debts, although several hints were given that interallied debts might be reduced according to the financial capacities of the indebted nations.[50] On November 7, December 14, and in his famous New Haven speech on December 29, Hughes informally submitted proposals

---

[48] André François-Poncet, *De Versailles à Potsdam. La France et le Problème allemand contemporain 1919–1945* (Paris, 1948), p. 101. Jules Laroche, "Quelques Aspects de l'Affaire de la Ruhr," *Revue d'Histoire Diplomatique*, 63 (1949), pp. 180–182. Pierre Miquel, *Poincaré* (Paris, 1961), p. 471.

[49] For an excellent interpretation of Poincaré's motives see Denise Artaud, "A Propos de L'Occupation de la Ruhr," *Revue D'Histoire Moderne et Contemporaine* vol. XVII (1970), pp. 1–21. Artaud analyses Poincaré's speech before the Commission on Foreign Affairs on June 7, 1922.

[50] Hughes-Herrick and Boyden October 17, 1922, *Hughes Papers*, General Correspondence 1922–24, Box 4b; "Beerits Memo," *ibid.*, Box 172, Folder 27.

for fixing reparations through an independent international finance committee.[51] The American Secretary of State also urged Jusserand to consider Cuno's proposal for a non-aggression pact, but to no avail. Before an impartial body of experts could decide upon reparations, Poincaré informed Hughes, "it was deemed to be necessary to exhaust the opportunities that the French Government had of securing agreement with the other Governments."[52] On January 5, a heated discussion took place between Hughes and Jusserand. When Jusserand complained that Poincaré had not received an official proposal along the line of the New Haven speech, Hughes angrily retorted that he "didn't care about the matter or form", the French government was in possession of his proposals. Three days later, Hughes again tried to impress upon the French his position towards reparations and the Ruhr. He was ready to send a "formal note" if Poincaré should ask for it. If, however, "French troops started to go into the Ruhr, our troops would be withdrawn at once."[53] Information reaching Paris from Washington thus clearly indicate that an international committee of experts would have been made available at the end of 1922, if Poincaré had been willing to accept an impartial inquiry. In a press conference on December 29, President Harding himself announced that in case of failure of the Allied conference in Paris, the United States favored such an investigation. At the end of 1922, Poincaré rejected any intervention: "Nous sommes dans l'impossibilité de confier à des financiers l'examen de solutions dont nous devrons compte à notre Parlement."[54]

If Poincaré really believed that an international loan would finally solve reparation payments, could he expect that international bankers and the United States would grant such a loan with French and Belgian troops in the Ruhr? This was most unlikely. Poincaré occupied the Ruhr on the assumption that a connection existed between a moratorium and the seizure of pledges and between interallied debts and reparations. Great Britain rejected the first, the United States the second assumption.

[51] Memorandum of Interview with the French Ambassador, November 7, 1922, ibid., Box 174, Folder 74a, December 14, December 18. Link, op. cit., pp. 169 ff. Cf. Jusserand-Poincaré, December 15, 1922, MAE, Ruhr 3, fol. 234 in which Jusserand stated American opposition towards occupation and gave details about the impartial finance committee. Cf. Jusserand-Poincaré, December 26, 1922, fol. 258 ff. Also December 19, 1922, ibid., Allemagne, 477, fol. 113 ff; fol. 161 ff.

[52] Memorandum of Interview with the French Ambassador, December 21, 1922, Hughes Papers, Box 174, Folder 74a.

[53] Ibid., Box 174, 74b, and January 8, 1923, ibid. Cf. Jusserand-Poincaré, January 9, 1923, MAE, Ruhr 4, fol. 78 ff.

[54] Poincaré-Jusserand, December 23, 1922, ibid., Allemagne 477, fol. 175 f. Wiedfeldt-AA, December 29, 1922, PA AA, W. Rep. Amerikanische Vermittlung in der Reparationsfrage.

When Poincaré occupied the Ruhr, his policy was based upon several other wrong premises. The Belgians did not trust France, and followed her in order to avoid the consequences of letting "her take it alone."[55] This guaranteed some influence on future developments in Germany. But France's most reluctant ally was Italy. Mussolini feared that German coal supplies for Italy would be cut off, if France were to occupy the Ruhr alone.[56] The Italians did not send troops. They promised to participate with one or two engineers and were obviously interested in the quickest possible liquidation of the affair. Poincaré had pledged that negotiations with Germany would start as soon as the Ruhr had been occupied. On January 11, the first day of occupation, the Counsellor of the Italian Embassy in Paris visited the Quai d'Orsay, demanding that negotiations between France, Belgium, Germany, and Italy begin immediately.[57] The Italian Ambassador to Belgium also intervened and wanted to know when occupation would end.[58] Italy was not only a reluctant ally, but also played a double game. Mussolini told the Germans that he would try to check Poincaré's Ruhr policy. Occupation, he believed, was Poincaré's "last trump."[59] The Germans recognized the Italian position and, in contrast to their attitude towards France and Belgium, did not regard Italy as an aggressor. Diplomatic relations were not broken off, while ambassadors to France and Belgium were recalled. In addition, the German Foreign Office decided on January 13 that the delivery of reparation coal to Italy would not be stopped. "Special care" would be taken to guarantee these deliveries. One day later coal deliveries to France and Belgium were halted.[60]

In France several last minute attempts were made to prevent occupation. Jean Jacques Seydoux, who at one point had the most optimistic expectations concerning the financial result of French policy, submitted a plan in London which was based on the German note of November 14. This proposal did not envisage occupation at all. Instead, Germany should be granted a moratorium. Her finances and budget were to be placed under Allied control. Then, an international conference of financial experts should decide upon the level of the debt. In addition, an export levy of 26% on all German goods should contribute to reparation payments.[61]

[55] *FO.*, 371/7487, C 16101, November 25, 1922.
[56] Charles Roux-Poincaré, January 11, and 16, 1923, *MAE*, Ruhr 5, fol. 101 and 106.
[57] Note Peretti de la Rocca January 11, 1923, *ibid.*, Ruhr 4, fol. 206.
[58] Herbette-Poincaré, January 16, 1923, *ibid.*, Ruhr 5, fol. 95 f.
[59] Neurath-AA, January 10, 1923, *PA AA*, W. Rep. Besetzung des Ruhrgebietes, H 276601.
[60] AA-Rom, January 13, 1923, *ibid.*, H 276655 f. Cf. *Ibid.*, H 276675 and H 267707.
[61] Zimmermann, *op. cit.*, pp. 93–95. *FO.*, 371/7491, C 17273, December 17, 1922. The plan was not given to Germany. *Ibid.*, C 17579.

On January 4, Senators Dausset de Monzie and Henri de Jouvenel contacted Carl Melchior and informed him of their talks with Barthou and President Millerand. The Senators declared that never before had the situation been as favorable for direct Franco-German negotiations. They recommended that a plan should be submitted to the French Government alone. If Germany could guarantee 1 billion gold marks per year, an agreement was still possible.[62] Similar information reached the German Embassy a few days later. This time Dausset had informed a representative of the *Frankfurter Zeitung* that an immediate transfer of cash would stop coercive measures. The German Ambassador did not consider these unofficial contacts to be of much help; he was convinced that occupation could not be prevented any more.[63]

The young French deputy Paul Reynaud who in October had demanded occupation, visited Berlin on January 7. He claimed that a "rapprochement" was still possible, if Germany would agree to hand 30% of certain industrial shares over to France. Reynaud's plan was not a new one, and had already been rejected several times. Von Maltzan now told him that no Government would deal with France under military pressure.[64] These isolated attempts to extract concessions from Germany were doomed to fail. Reparations was not only a Franco-German problem, but interallied debts, France's financial and economic future and for some Frenchmen (Marshall Foch, Degoutte, Dariac, the Right in Parliament and Tirard)[65] security and the future of the Rhineland were also involved. For Poincaré, occupation was not directly connected with French security, although it was clearly understood that control of the Ruhr economy would reduce Germany's potential to make war. He did not intend to annex the Ruhr or the Rhineland, but announced that France was collecting reparations in the Ruhr for all Allies. This was an obvious step to calm British suspicion. On the other hand, he certainly was not opposed to the dissolution of the Reich, if this should re-

---

[62] Mayer-AA, January 4, 1923, *PA AA*, Büro RM, Reparationen, D 718852–853.

[63] *Ibid.*, January 6, 1923, D 718907–908.

[64] Note von Maltzan January 7, 1923, *ibid.*, D 718911. Besides these optimistic estimates of a possible Franco-German understanding, discouraging reports also reached Berlin. On December 24, Hjalmar Schacht arranged a meeting for December 26 between Senator Bergeon, a member of the French Senate Foreign Policy Committee, Cuno and von Rosenberg in Berlin. At this meeting, Bergeon informed the Germans that Poincaré would never reduce the London Schedule of Payments. Schacht-Cuno, December 24, 1922, *ibid.*, D 718606. Von Mutius-Hoesch, December 27, 1922, *ibid.*, D 718628 note Wever, December 26, 1922, *BA*, R 431/33.

[65] For the importance of the Rhine as a strategic border cf.: Raymond Recouly, *Foch. My Conversations with the Marshal* (New York, 1929), p. 252. Foch's opposition to Italian participation is shown by a handwritten note of December 7, 1922, *MAE*, Ruhr 3, fol. 217. Bariety, *op. cit.*, pp. 26 ff. Zimmermann, *op. cit.*, pp. 73–85.

sult from a Rhenish initiative or French pressure upon the population. As has been shown, he had said as much to the Belgians in November and French policy in 1923 supports this interpretation.

But Poincaré's primary long-term goal was to obtain a pledge for a final reparation settlement including interallied debts. Thus, occupation was a political pledge for a number of interallied and Franco-German problems. It could be used to extract cash payments for the balancing of the French budget, if the Allies and the international banking community could be convinced that loans to Germany required productive pledges. Without German cash payments, the French budgetary deficit could not be overcome. An increase of domestic taxation did not seem possible, since French politicians had promised the electorate that "L'Allemagne payera tout." Military penetration into the Ruhr was also a remedy for forcing financial reforms in Germany under French control and above all for controlling Ruhr heavy industry. France could disorganize the Ruhr, thus rendering industrial profits impossible. She could also organize deliveries in kind according to French economic interests. Poincaré held the view, widely accepted in France, that Ruhr industrialists were the "real masters" of Germany and should be coerced into accepting both reparations and stabilization of the currency. This concept of relations between industry and the government was, though it contained some truth, certainly simplistic. It completely neglects that a consensus existed that fulfillment of French demands would ruin Germany. Politicians were just as opposed to complete fulfillment as industrialists, with Walter Rathenau and Wirth no exceptions. The "policy of fulfillment" had been an attempt to create good will towards Germany, which then would lead to a significant reduction of Allied demands.

But Poincaré's greatest weakness seems to have been that he had only vague ideas about what would happen if industry, the population and the Government did not cooperate after the "seizure of pledges". According to Paul Cambon, former Ambassador to London, Poincaré had occupied the Ruhr on the hypothesis that Germany would yield to "a show of force."[66] General Degoutte had also been convinced that the Germans would yield to military force. Poincaré and Seydoux did recognize that Germany would certainly have yielded if France and Belgium had been accompanied by Great Britain, but they were willing to take the risk alone. That the seizure of pledges would not be an easy task was apparent as early as January 10, when it became known in Paris that the *Kohlensyndikat* at Essen, the agency responsible for the distribution of Ruhr coal, had left for Hamburg.[67]

[66] Bertrand de Jouvenel, *D'une Guerre à l'autre*, t. 1–2 (Paris, 1940/41), I, p. 211.
[67] Tirard-MAE, January 10, 1923, *MAE*, Ruhr 4, fol. 126. Also de Margerie-MAE, January 11, 1923, *ibid.*, fol. 168 f.

While according to Foch's original plan the occupation of Essen and the control of this organization had been the first stage of a "progressive penetration", by January 9 occupation plans were extended to the whole Ruhr region. Whether this was a reaction to rumors about the expected decision of the *Kohlensyndikat* or discussions among the military in Paris, cannot be said with certainty.[68]

These last minute changes were not of any importance for future developments. After occupation had been executed, Poincaré received the support of the majority of the Chamber, only parts of the Socialists and the Communists voting against him. Any opposition was regarded as disloyalty towards the French nation, and the political atmosphere in France reminded most observers of the first months after the German attack in 1914. The occupation became a symbol of a final struggle to uphold the principles laid down by the Versailles Treaty. The French Communist deputy Marcel Cachin, who attended a conference of the Third International in Germany and spoke out against occupation policy, was temporarily arrested.[69] Only four years after the end of the First World War, a war-like atmosphere again shook Europe. Nationalistic fervor in both Germany and France was running high and the presence of two infantry divisions, one cavalry division and a small Belgian unit in the Ruhr predicted future troubles.

---

[68] Foch's plan of November 20 in Zimmermann, *op. cit.*, pp. 88 f. Peretti de la Rocca January 9, 1923, *MAE*, Allemagne 478, fol. 171. Apparently Foch was dissatisfied with occupation procedures. "I had proposed a plan for the evacuation we eventually found necessary" ... "but it was carried out differently." "The Government wanted to swallow everything at one gulp. Consequently we choked and could not digest it." Cf. Raymond Recouly, *op. cit.*, p. 251 f.

[69] Wolfgang Ruge, *op. cit.*, p. 140.

CHAPTER IV

PROBLEMS OF PASSIVE RESISTANCE

I. REACTIONS TO THE OCCUPATION

On the morning of January 11, 1923 French and Belgian troops marched into the Ruhr and occupied the key-industrial cities. A French note delivered on January 10 had informed the German Government that the duty of the military was to protect the *Mission Interalliée de Contrôle des Usines et des Mines* (MICUM). This commission of 40 engineers was to control the future delivery of reparation coal to France. Mine owners and miners were asked to cooperate with the MICUM.[1]

Though Poincaré had announced his determination to occupy the Ruhr in advance, and though French troops had begun to move into position on January 6, the Germans had prepared remarkably little for such an emergency. One reason was that Cuno himself seems to have expected that occupation could be prevented. Although the German Ambassador to Paris was already convinced that this was no longer possible, Cuno still hoped for an international conference.[2] Barring this possibility, he did not have much choice. Military resistance was impossible. The Reichswehr was not strong enough to stop France, and an attempt to do so would have created political problems at home and abroad. The signatory powers of the Versailles Treaty might have considered active resistance as a breach of treaty, and Great Britain, which had just opposed coercive measures, might have been forced to join France at a moment when German politicians were hoping for an alienation between these countries.[3] In domestic politics, neither the SPD

---

[1] Mayer-AA, January 10, 1923, *PA AA*, W. Rep., *Besetzung des Ruhrgebietes* H 276 556 f. The Belgian Government delivered a similar note.

[2] The American Ambassador reported in his diary after a meeting with Cuno on January 10 that according to Cuno "the situation was, however, uncertain as the French troops were for the moment, evidently, being held back, and the French Ambassador had requested an audience with the Foreign Minister later today." But instead of a proposal for negotiations, the French note was delivered. *Houghton Papers*, Diary, p. 532.

[3] The British delegate at Cologne warned for example that a denunciation of the treaty would endanger British sympathies for Germany. Adenauer-Reichskanzler, January 9, 1923, *BA*, R 431/203.

nor the trade unions would have supported the Government on such a suicidal policy.

Germany's position was discussed at a cabinet council on January 9, at which President Ebert presided and the Prussian Minister President, Otto Braun, and the chief of the army, General von Seeckt, were present.[4] Ebert's appearance and his active support of Cuno, as well as the participation of Braun, seemed to guarantee that the SPD and Prussia with its social-democratic government would add additional weight to the formulation of a common policy. Cuno had based his rejection of French policy upon moral and legal grounds, but had also proposed that Poincaré's policy be met by a build-up of economic resistance. This meant that the supply of food-stuffs, the prevention of unemployment, the fight against usury, and the creation of a "united front" of employers and employees would be the basis of German policy. Furthermore, Cuno would base his rejection of invasion upon moral and legal arguments which would be presented to the Allies, the Churches and the International Trade Union movement.[5]

Ebert not only supported Cuno's proposals without hesitation, he also urged the cabinet to organize passive resistance against Poincaré's illegal action. For the social democratic President, it was necessary to show the world that Germany would not yield to military force. Ebert and Braun both anticipated that the *Kohlensyndikat* be moved, assuming that without the files of this organization, France could neither control production nor collect reparation coal. If the mine owners remained firm in face of French pressure, Ebert felt, the working class would soon rally to the support of Cuno. In order to facilitate such a development, he had contacted several leading members of the ADGB (the social democratic trade union association).[6] On January 8, Ebert met Leipart and others (known for their criticism of the Versailles Treaty as an "act of imperialism" against the German working class, endangering its social situation) in the presence of former Social Democratic Chancellor Gustav Bauer and Friedrich Stampfer, chief-editor of the SPD journal Vorwärts. While Ebert only wanted to investigate trade union opinion, Bauer stressed that "it was unthinkable to him, that the Unions would accept occupation without opposition." The same evening a meeting between representatives of the ADGB (Alexander Knoll, Rudolf Wissell), Cuno and Eduard Hamm took place in which the Chancellor

---

[4] "Niederschrift über den Kabinettsrat am 9.1.23," *Kab. Cuno*, No. 37. Heinrich Brauns the Minister of Labor did not attend due to illness.

[5] Undated and handwritten memo by Eduard Hamm, Secretary of State in the Chancellery. *BA*, R 43I/214. Printed in *Kab. Cuno*, No. 37, footnote 3.

[6] *Ibid.*, Ambassador Mayer had already suggested such a step on January 5. See *PA AA*, Büro RM, Reparationen, D 718893 f.

pledged trade union support. As in the previous meeting, the participants soon discussed whether a general strike should be announced. In order to clarify the question, contacts were immediately established between the ADGB and Bücher and Krämer of the RdI, both promising support. It was decided that the details of trade union action should be left to direct negotiations between industry and unions in the Ruhr. Ebert, having been kept informed continuously of these talks, totally agreed, suggesting that if a "Streikneigung vorhanden sei, man sie nicht zu dämpfen brauche, sie jedoch unter allen Umständen befristet werden müßte." Discussions about a strike were not continued that night, nor were the Christian Trade Unions (DGB) and the *Hirsch-Dunckersche Gewerkschaftsverband* informed – instead, upon Cuno's wish, Knoll immediately left Berlin to attend a conference of the *Bezirksausschüsse des ADGB Bezirks Rheinland-Westfalen* at Essen, where the strike debate continued. Uncertain about the attitude of Communists, Socialists, and Polish Miners, it was decided to announce a half-hour strike for January 15. At the end of the conference Knoll, Grassmann (representative of the Bundesvorstand), Waldhecker (Bergarbeiterverband) and Heinrich Meyer (*Bezirkssekretär* of the ADGB and later on most active in the organization of resistance) discussed strike measures with Stinnes, even though several trade unionists had been opposed to a cooperation with industry. Stinnes was in favor of a short strike, but rejected talks about the reimbursement of wages through employers. According to Knoll, these decisions were immediately made known to Ebert who approved of them.[7]

While the cabinet council was taking place in Berlin, the members of the coal syndicate met in a special session in Essen and decided to remove the files of the organization to Hamburg.[8] Immediately thereafter, Hugo Stinnes called Berlin and demanded that the Reich support the syndicate and guarantee its outstanding debts to the mines. Because of the transfer of the syndicate, it would have to delay payments for coal deliveries, meaning financial difficulties for the mines. The cabinet accepted Stinnes' proposal, and Ebert suggested, as a further means of increasing resistance, that the functionaries of the syndicate should also leave for Hamburg.[9] Whether this suggestion was taken up is unclear, but other organizations and industrial

---

[7] "Bericht über Besprechungen und Maßnahmen anläßlich der Besetzung des Ruhrgebietes vom 8.–10.1.1923," *August Bebel Archiv*, NB 166, fol. 0001 ff. Already in May 1922 union representatives from Berlin, the Rhineland and the Ruhr had discussed the advantages and disadvantages of a general strike in case of occupation. Cf. *Ibid.*, NB 144, fol. 0007 ff. Also "Rückschau auf den Ruhrkampf. Ein Nachtrag von A. Knoll," *ibid.*, NB 164, fol. 0025a.

[8] *Ursachen und Folgen*, vol. V, pp. 13 ff. Favez, *op. cit.*, p. 66.

[9] *Kab. Cuno*, No. 37.

enterprises removed their headquarters from the Ruhr as well.[10] The Ministry of Finance also transferred its office for the raising of coal taxes. Revenues from this tax alone amounted to 86.1 billion paper marks per month, while the value of all German coal deliveries to France, Belgium, and Luxemburg only amounted to 68.8 billions per month.[11]

The discussions within the cabinet, Ebert's attitude, the instantaneous reaction of the coal syndicate, the behavior of trade union representatives, and the approval of passive resistance by the Prussian Minister President seemed to indicate that unanimity existed. But future developments showed that French military action, though it had momentarily united different interests, prevented clashes neither between the Reich and Prussia, nor between the parties, nor within the cabinet itself.[12]

The first difference within the cabinet occurred over the advisability of the resistance of railway employees. In any struggle with France, the railways were of strategic and financial importance. Most exports from the Ruhr area went by rail, and the suspension of rail traffic would be a severe setback to the successful exploitation of productive pledges. Nevertheless, the Ministry of Transport decided that railway employees should not participate in passive resistance, on the grounds that to do so would not prevent French troops from running the railways themselves. The Foreign Office and the Ministry of the Interior supported this attitude,[13] but the decision caused protests among Ruhr industrialists who saw no reason why mining industry should refuse cooperation, while the Ministry of Transport was going to permit German personnel to facilitate the transport of French troops. The trade unions also protested.[14]

These objections led to further discussion within the cabinet, in which the Ministry of Transport again warned that the prohibition of the transport of French troops and Ruhr coal would result in French countermeasures. The railway system would be militarized, connections between occupied and unoccupied Germany would be cut off, and neither the supply of the Ruhr nor the supply of unoccupied Germany with coal would be possible. In addition, the railway administration would lose all influence upon its agencies in the Ruhr.[15] These arguments, which were not without substance, now

[10] Reusch-Woltmann, January 5, 1923, *HA GHH*, 3001900/3.
[11] *Kab. Cuno*, No. 45, January 16, 1923.
[12] *Ibid.*, No. 40, January 11, 1923. Oltmann, *op. cit.*, p. 46 f.
[13] *Kab. Cuno*, No. 38, January 10, 1923.
[14] Vögler-Becker, January 15, 1923, *BA*, R 43I/203. Cf. *Kab. Cuno*, No. 52, January 23, 1923.
[15] Stieler-Cuno, January 17, 1923, *BA*, R 43I/203.

proved to be ineffective. The cabinet, under other pressures, decided that railway employees would also participate in passive resistance.

Besides differences within the cabinet, Cuno also had to force industry into line. Despite public appeals for a common front of all Germans, some Ruhr industrialists did non intend to cut relations with France in the economic field. In negotiations between the MICUM and mine owners, the latter were prepared to deliver reparation coal if the French government paid for it,[16] and Hugo Stinnes declared that he would deliver coal to private French enterprises even if Berlin should order an export stop.[17] But it is doubtful whether Poincaré would have really accepted such a deal, even if mine owners had not been ordered to stop negotiations with French authorities.[18] Members of the *Nordwestdeutsche Gruppe des Vereins deutscher Eisen- und Stahlindustrieller* and other industrialist organizations in non-occupied Germany also favored the continuation of private commercial dealings with France. Otherwise, they argued, employment was endangered and this would lead to Communist agitation and serious social problems. On the other hand, they all agreed that the railways should stop delivering reparation coal to the occupation powers, even at the risk of an interruption of production and a closing down of all factories.[19]

In contrast to these differences about tactical procedures, the German press rallied to the support of the Fatherland, and condemned occupation as an act of imperialism and the renewal of the policy of Louis XIV. Rudolf Hilferding, writing in the SPD party organ *Vorwärts*, believed that a "new war had begun." Though Germany was helpless and could not defend herself, resistance was necessary. Poincaré was a danger for peace in Europe.[20] Karl Kautsky, Eduard Bernstein, and Friedrich Stampfer of the SPD similarly opposed occupation, arguing that the Treaty of Versailles had been broken. Bernstein demanded British intervention as a signatory power of the Treaty.[21] The SPD *Parteivorstand* also condemned "French imperialism"

---

[16] The details of these negotiations have been described in Favez, *op. cit.*, pp. 72–77. Cf. *BA*, R 43I/203, January 12, and January 16, 1923 for discussions between the MICUM and industry. Also *HA GHH*, 30019308/7, January 13, 1923 about a meeting of the Bergbau-Verein at Münster. *BA*, R 38/190, 162 f.

[17] *Der Nachlass des Reichskanzlers Wilhelm Marx*, 4 Bde, bearbeitet von Hugo Stehkaemper (Köln, 1969), III, No. 213, September 21, 1923. *Ibid.*, Hermes-Ersing, October 23, 1923.

[18] Bergmann, *op. cit.*, pp. 226–227. He criticizes that Cuno forbade deliveries and argues that payments would have made occupation even more expensive for France. There is no indication that Poincaré intended to pay for deliveries.

[19] Haniel-Reusch, January 30, 1923, *HA GHH*, 3001900/3. Woltmann-Reusch, January 18, 1923, *ibid.*, 300193008/7. Also *Richard Buz Nachlaß*, 32/271.

[20] "Poincaré's Pfänderspiele," *Vorwärts*, No. 12, January 9, 1923.

[21] *Ibid.*, No. 34, January 24; No. 36, January 23; No. 38, January 24, 1923.

and declared the invasion a contradiction of the treaty. The SPD made it clear that Germany was obliged to pay reparations, but military occupation would destroy German credit abroad and thus destroy the basis for payments.[22]

For the DDP and the Center, resistance became a fight for the "self-determination of the people,"[23] while the DNVP considered the French action an excellent chance for a final denunciation of the Versailles Treaty.[24] This attitude was not limited to the DVNP and some members of the DVP thought along the same lines. Abraham Frowein, co-chairman of the RdI and member of the DVP, claimed that Germany was no longer tied to the treaty. Poincaré was Napoleon on his way to Moscow and French coercive policy meant the resurrection of Germany.[25] But although the parties were united in their rejection of French action, a common front was not established, the SPD fearing that the Right would exploit the growing nationalistic mood in Germany.

Poincaré's official announcement that his sole motive in entering the Ruhr was to insure the continued payment of reparations was generally distrusted in Germany. The truth of the matter, in the opinion of the liberal *Frankfurter Zeitung* and the Social Democratic *Vorwärts*, was that France was seeking to reunite Ruhr coke and Lorraine iron ore in French hands.[26] At a meeting of the Center Party in Cologne, former Chancellor Wirth expressed the view that France intended to separate the Rhineland from the Reich and destroy German unity.[27] In a notice published in the *Münchener Neueste Nachrichten*, the DDP voiced similar fears,[28] and Gustav Stresemann described French policy – in a speech in the Reichstag – as an attempt to disorganize Germany: "France wants the destruction of Germany. She hopes either to destroy German unity by the permanent occupation of its territory and by economic strangulation or to force the German nation to accept her measures."[29] Cuno himself visited the occupied area on February 4 and asked representatives of the trade unions, the parties, and industry, to stand together in this final struggle with France. He did not leave any doubt that he was dismayed at being Chancellor in this moment of crisis, but since he had

---

[22] *Ursachen und Folgen*, V, pp. 24–25.
[23] Newspaper clippings in *BA*, R 43I/2657 and 2661.
[24] *Neue Preussische Zeitung*, No. 34, January 21, 1923.
[25] Geschäftliche Mitteilungen des RdI, No. 2, January 27, 1923, *BA*, R 43I/272.
[26] "Trustpläne. Die wirtschaftlichen Hintergründe der Ruhraktion," *Frankfurter Zeitung*, No. 101 and 104, February 8 and 9, 1923; "Der Kampf um die Kohle," *Vorwärts*, No. 28, January 28, 1923.
[27] *BA*, R 43I/2657, WTB, No. 51, January 8, 1923.
[28] *Ibid.*, R 43I/2661.
[29] Stresemann, *op. cit.*, I, p. 31.

accepted the job, he would carry it through. He also believed that Poincaré's real motive for occupation was the creation of a France-German industrial trust. If France should succeed, the Reich would break up.[30] In German opinion occupation was thus a war fought with economic means, and the liberal economist Moritz J. Bonn, who attacked Cuno in his memoirs for his lack of initiative, wrote in a letter to Walter I. Layton of the Economist in 1923, "we are in the midst of the greatest economic battle we have ever witnessed." Military occupation, he felt was nothing but a disguised attempt to control Germany's economic potential. As a result of this estimate, Bonn rejected negotiations with France and declared: "We are really fighting now for the principle of settling economic differences by reasonable negotiations and not by military braggadocio."[31]

The counsellor of the German embassy in Paris, Leopold von Hoesch, was less certain about French intentions. He reasoned that occupation was an attempt to force negotiations, but after one week of occupation he changed his opinion. He now feared that France might demand the Rhineland and the Ruhr as securities for future German conduct. If these were indeed French intentions, resistance was of course the only way out.[32]

Passive resistance thus became a fight for German existence and was identified with a struggle for the preservation of German unity. Besides, it was also a chance to destroy Germany's dependence upon the Allies, especially France. In this sense, resistance – if carried through successfully – could only end, it was hoped, with the restoration of Germany's prewar position in Europe. Germany would have to be treated as France's equal in all future negotiations. Once the insecure cabinet recognized that, despite some differences between the parties, a large part of the population and important organisations supported or at least were not opposed to countermeasures, the organization of passive resistance began.[33]

2. THE ORGANIZATION OF RESISTANCE

In the beginning, government intervention was only a reaction to French policy. On January 13, all reparation deliveries-in-kind to France and Bel-

---

[30] *Ibid.*, IV, pp. 122–130.

[31] Bonn-Layton, January 22, 1923, *Moritz J. Bonn Nachlaß*, vol. 49.

[32] "Überblick über die Lage," No. 62, January 23, 1923, *PA AA*, W. Rep., Besetzung des Ruhrgebietes, H. 276760 f.

[33] For public support of Cuno and protest resolution see *BA* 43I/203. Gewerkschaftsbund der Angestellten-Cuno, January 8, DGB-Cuno, January 16. Here also resolutions of the different Landtage. Also *ibid.*, 43I/205 and 206. *Kab. Cuno*, No. 51, 52 and 53.

gium were stopped. On January 19, civil servants in the occupied territory and the railway personnel were forbidden to follow orders of the occupation authorities. But the organization of passive resistance was not an easy task. It took several weeks before a special agency, the *Rhein-Ruhr-Zentrale* (first under the direction of *Ministerialrat* Kempner of the Chancellor's office, then under the expelled *Oberbürgermeister* of Düsseldorf, Schmid) was created to coordinate policy between the ministries, the parties, the trade unions, and industrial organizations.[34] At Cologne, Heidelberg and Dortmund "liaison offices" were created to establish close contacts between Berlin and the Ruhr. In these offices, government officials, trade union and industrial representatives cooperated, with the different trade unions becoming a most powerful weapon of resistance.[35] In April, a special export office was founded to control trade with the occupation powers, but not all commercial transactions were stopped and Ruhr industry complained that industries from unoccupied areas delivered goods to France and Belgium.[36]

Besides controlling and coordinating resistance, the Reich also provided Ruhr industry and the population with the necessary financial basis for resistance, and already on January 22 the Ministry of Finance put a first instalment of about 30 billion paper marks at their disposal.[37] From this money the government not only financed propaganda carried through by the parties, the trade unions, and the *Reichszentrale für Heimatdienst*, but also started to pay unemployment benefits, supported pensioners, and bought food stuffs for the Ruhr. Soon the Reich was spending billions of paper marks for resistance. These expenditures were made with the approval of the Reichstag which passed a bill on February 1 allowing the Minister of Finance to open another credit worth 500 billion marks for resistance.[38] At the beginning of occupation most of the money was spent on the support of industry, while expenditures for unemployment benefits remained relatively low. Fearing that resistance would break down if unemployment

Lothar Erdmann, *Die Gewerkschaften im Ruhrkampf* (Berlin, 1924), pp. 64–93. Hans Spethmann, *Zwölf Jahre Ruhrbergbau*, 5 Bde. (Berlin, 1930), vol. IV, p. 84 f, p. 118 f., p. 368. Favez, *op. cit.*, pp. 81 ff. "Vertreter der Bergarbeiterverbände bei der Internationalen Industrie-Kontrollkommission," *BA* 43I/203, p. 306 f.

[34] *Kab. Cuno*, No. 63, February 2 and No. 98, March 16, 1923. Favez, *op. cit.*, p. 133 f. Oltmann, *op. cit.*, p. 46 f. Cuno, January 18, 1923, *BA* 38/190, p. 145, Also *ibid.*, R 43I/1790.

[35] *BA*, R 43I/208 and 209, pp. 69 ff. *Kab. Cuno*, No. 71, February 12, 1923. Favez, *op. cit.*, p. 136 f.

[36] Favez, *op. cit.*, p. 142; Erich Maschke, *Es entsteht ein Konzern. Paul Reusch und die GHH* (Tübingen, 1969), p. 233.

[37] *BA*, R 43I/203.

[38] *Kab. Cuno*, No. 52, January 23; No. 59, January 30; No. 71, February 12, 1923. *RT*, vol. 376, No. 5508.

rose, the government had decided to aid industry to keep production going. After France had almost completely cut ties between occupied and unoccupied Germany, production still went on, even if goods could no longer be brought out of the Ruhr. As a result of this policy the MICUM started to confiscate coal, steel, and other goods which had been stock-piled. Government expenditure for industry soon caused great bitterness among employees, since they only obtained 2/3 of their wages.[39] Estimates of the actual government contribution to industrial wages differ, but from February until September 1923, 66 to 100% of industrial wages were paid by the Reich.[40]

From February until June the Ministry of Finance increased its credit for resistance. Not till June was a special Reichstag committee created which supervised government expenditure. It consisted of Dernburg (DDP), Hertz (SPD), Klöckner (Center), Leicht (BVP), Moldenhauer (DVP), Reichert (DNVP), and Schmidt-Berlin (SPD).[41] But by that time, most important decisions had already been made. In addition to governmental credit for "unproductive wages" which in theory was only to be made available after industry could no longer obtain credit itself, the Reich also paid financial compensation to keep the mines intact. A special commission consisting of representatives of the ministries, the trade unions, and mining industry decided in April that 60% of "unproductive costs" would be taken over by the Reich for February and March, while from April onwards 80% was to be paid.[42]

Until the end of May the Reich gave all credits in paper marks, a fact which significantly contributed to the inflation, since at least part of the sums could be made available only through the printing press. From May onwards credit was either based upon the pound sterling or the value of coal or steel prices at a fixed date.[43] In order to keep production going and to prevent unemployment which would be followed by increased social and political unrest, special financing companies were created for the coal and steel industries. Thus, in addition to normal credit, another 750 billion paper marks were made available for mining alone. The mines would sell their coal

[39] Meeting between Cuno and Leipart, February 26, 1923, *BA*, R 43I/201. "Kredithilfe im besetzten Gebiet." Report about a meeting between trade union representatives and the Ministry of Economics on March 12, 1923, *Bebel Archiv*, NB 166, fol. 0018 ff. *Kab. Cuno*, No. 87, March 1, 1923.

[40] Reichert-Reichsarbeitsministerium, August 26, 1923, *HA GHH*, 30019003/8. Reichert maintains that the Reich paid 66⅔% of "unproductive wages," while industry paid the rest. If a factory was closed down completely, the Reich paid everything. Favez,. *op. cit.*, p. 147.

[41] *RT*, vol. 360, p. 11205, June 6, 1923.

[42] *Ibid.*, vol. 471, No. 3615, p. 113 f.

[43] *Ibid.*, p. 231.

to the *Kohlefinanzierungsgesellschaft* and in return would receive credit. These bills of exchange carried an eight percent discount rate and an arbitrage of one percent. Overall the equivalent of 44,785,625 gold marks (1600 billion paper marks) was spent with the approval of the above mentioned Ruhr Committee.[44] Steel industry received a similar credit after difficult negotiations with the Ruhr's ten biggest steel companies. Apparently steel industry threatened to stop production if the Reich did not give credit at favorable terms. After several meetings between steel representatives and the Ministry of Economics and the Ministry of Finance, a credit worth 25,607,219 gold marks (560 billion paper marks) was made available at a discount rate of six percent.[45] After Stresemann had become Chancellor, lignite industries similarly received a credit.[46]

Government spending for resistance was investigated in 1925, and Hertz of the SPD, who had also been a member of the Ruhr Committee which had granted the credit, declared that industry had made a profit of 87 million Reichsmark; however, the majority of the investigation committee did not follow his estimate, arguing that it was impossible to prove how the money had been spent and whether all of it had been repaid. Nevertheless, they all agreed that laborers, white collar workers and small tradesmen had not been compensated for their losses.[47] Besides this direct support of mining and steel industries, further credit was distributed through the Chambers of Commerce in the Ruhr and the Rhineland. It is difficult to estimate the amount spent, since only incomplete records exist. According to them the Chamber of Commerce at Essen distributed credit worth 1,748,073 gold marks from February 1923 until October, while the Chamber of Commerce at Bochum spent 917, 914 gold marks over an unspecified period of time.[48] In addition to official government support, resistance was also financed through donations. Until April 27, the government had received 18 billion paper marks. This amount included 41,643 dollars, 4,719 pounds sterling, 17,571 Austrian crowns, and 18,419 Swiss francs. But in comparison to government expenditures, these sums were of minor importance.[49]

---

[44] *Ibid.*, vol. 398, No. 565, pp. 30–33. Favez, *op. cit.*, p. 151.

[45] *RT*, vol. 398, No. 565, pp. 35–39. Some material about negotiations and industrial demands is in *HA GHH*, 30019008/19. "Vertrag Reichswirtschaftsministerium-Stahl-finanzierungsgesellschaft."

[46] *RT*, vol. 398, No. 565, p. 34.

[47] *Ibid.*, vol. 417, No. 3615, pp. 3 ff.

[48] *WWA*, K 2, No. 463, Ruhrkampf. The report is undated. The figures for Essen are from Paul Wentzcke, *Ruhrkampf. Einbruch und Abwehr im rheinisch-westfälischen Industriegebiet*, 2 Bde. (Berlin, 1930/32), II, p. 445, note on page 119. See Favez, *op. cit.*, p. 150.

[49] *BA*, R 43I/219. When Cuno left office 200 billion marks had not been spent. However, considering the monetary inflation from April to August the amount is insignificant.

The financial organization of resistance was thus based mainly on cooperation between industry and different branches of the government. This development took place although the "Abwehrausschüsse" (the agencies that coordinated resistance) at Dortmund, Köln and Heidelberg were controlled by the trade unions.[50] Differences between industry and trade unions did not become visible when the members of the *Zentrale Arbeitsgemeinschaft* (*ZAG*) decided on January 24 to follow the Reich and the state governments in the announcement of a *Deutsches Volksopfer* in support of the occupied region. Unions and employers also created the *Ruhrhilfe*. Employees were asked to contribute 1/10 of an hourly pay, while employers would give four times as much as their workers. A joint finance committee consisting also of representatives of the churches, welfare organisations and government representatives would control the distribution of contributions.[51] However, the decision of the *Bundesvorstand* of the ADGB to cooperate with industry did not get the support of several local union organizations under the control of Independent Socialists and the *Deutscher Metallarbeiterverband* (*DMV*). As a result, different fund raising actions started, while at the same time members of the *Bundesvorstand* participated in conferences of the *Ruhrhilfe*.[52] Industry soon established independent collections as well and by April 1923 the *Ruhrhilfe* was dead. It merged with the *Deutsches Volksopfer*.[53] A "national front" had proved to be impossible in the face of unemployment, rising prices and a lack of food supplies.

3. PRELIMINARY "STABILIZATION" OF THE CURRENCY

From the beginning of resistance, it was clear that it could not be prolonged without the creation of a stable currency, which was of course made even

The collecting of donations also caused problems between the trade unions and industry. *Ibid.*, R 38/193, February 28, 1923. Favez, *op. cit.*, p. 154.

[50] Oltmann, *op. cit.*, p. 81.

[51] For the different resolutions cf. *BA*, 43I/219, WTB No. 210, January 26, 1923. *Ibid.*, "Das deutsche Volksopfer," February 14, 1923, fol. 210 ff. "Niederschrift über die Sitzung des Arbeitsausschusses des Deutschen Volksopfers im Reichsarbeitsministerium am 21. Februar 1923," *ibid.*, R 38/193, fol. 32 ff and fol. 65 ff for a distribution of payments. Erdmann, *op. cit.*, p. 110 f. for decisions within the ADGB.

[52] "An die deutschen Arbeiter und Angestellten," March 3, 1923, *Bebel Archiv*, NB 166, fol. 058 ff. This is a joint declaration by the ADGB and the Afa. "Aktennotiz Wissell," January 29, 1923, *ibid.*, NB 173, fol. 0005a about a meeting with industry (Bücher, Frank, Hoff, Huben, Tänzler) where the attitude of local unions was discussed. Leipart-Vorstände der Zentralverbände, February 8, 1923, *ibid.*, fol. 0011. Erdmann, *op. cit.*, p. 112 f.

[53] Cf. *Buz Nachlaß*, 32/271 and 271a for contributions of the MAN Augsburg and Nürnberg. Erdmann, *op. cit.*, p. 112 f.

more difficult through government spending in the Ruhr.[54] As a result of these expenses and the destruction of trade, prices rose and the supply of the population with food and raw materials for industrial production became more difficult. When the exchange rate of the mark fell from 27,000 to the dollar on January 28 to 49,000 on January 31, this was interpreted as a sign that industry and trade had lost all confidence in the German currency.[55] If the mark fell further, resistance would become impossible, and after a meeting between the government and the Reichsbank, it was decided that the Reichsbank would intervene in Amsterdam, London and New York and buy marks.[56] But neither its directorate nor the government expected that stabilization would last long. Rudolf Havenstein, President of the Reichsbank, believed that the rate of exchange could be held for 4 weeks, while Carl Bergmann expected that it would last 6–8 weeks.[57] Andreas Hermes was of the same opinion and they all agreed that within this limited period negotiations with the Allies would have to start.[58] When the Reichsbank had thrown about 100 million gold marks in foreign currency on the market, the exchange rate stabilized at 21,000 paper marks to the dollar.[59]

The decision to intervene despite certain misgivings indicates a development which characterized many decisions during 1923. It was made for political purposes, although it was recognized from the beginning that the mark would fall again if negotiations should not come about. In the case of Havenstein this was a complete *volte face*. At a meeting of the Reichsbank directorate in December he had declared:

After careful investigation we have reached the conclusion that stabilization is only possible if the reparation question is solved. Until then only supporting measures are feasible; but the gold reserves of the Reichsbank can only be employed for such a policy if a good chance for success exists. However, such a prospect is absolutely dependent upon our ability to regain confidence at home and abroad. An intervention that would be carried through by the Reichsbank alone, would be doomed from the beginning.[60]

[54] *Marx Nachlaß*, III, Note Hermes, September 21, 1923, p. 100.

[55] *Kab. Cuno*, No. 6, January 20, 1923.

[56] Bergmann, *op. cit.*, p. 233. *BA*, R 43I/2445 "Aufzeichnung Dollarsteigerung." *RT* vol. 380, No. 6591.

[57] *Kab. Cuno*, No. 128, April 19, 1923. "Untersuchungsausschuß Stützungsaktion, 4. Sitzung," June 4, 1923, *BA*, R 2/2419.

[58] *Marx Nachlaß*, III, note Hermes, p. 100.

[59] Bergmann, *op. cit.*, p. 233. Cf. Havenstein's report of May 29, 1923, *BA*, R 43I/632. French Mark purchases for occupation purposes may have also contributed. Cf. *MAE*. Ruhr 18, fol. 188.

[60] "Note Wolf," December 20, 1922, *BA*, R 43I/631. Havenstein justified his change of mind with political necessities on May 29, 1923. See *ibid.*, 2419, first meeting of the investigation committee.

At least one of Havenstein's preconditions for success did not exist. On the contrary, French occupation had even further destroyed domestic and foreign confidence in a recovery. But the German position was greatly strengthened by the attitude of the Bank of England, and the Central Banks in Switzerland and the Netherlands.[61] The Reichsbank borrowed money from these banks and gave her gold reserves as securities. Until April 19 the Bank of England and the Swiss Central Bank received 200 million gold marks and 116 millions respectively.[62] In London the Reichsbank paid three percent interest, which was the London bank rate. In a letter to Benjamin Strong, Governor of the American Federal Reserve Bank, Norman explained that he did not expect Germany to be able to repay British loans except through the sale of her gold, which happened during the summer of 1923.[63] The policy of the Bank of England and of other banks was not a mere banking transaction, it meant that these banks supported German resistance against France if only indirectly.[64] The importance of this policy can best be recognized if it is compared with British loans to France during the First World War, when the Bank of England took French gold and made credit available for the war against Germany.[65]

In addition to stabilization with the aid of foreign collaborators, the Ministry of Finance also placed a loan of 50 million dollars on the domestic market. The idea behind this initiative was to make foreign currency – held back by industry and trade – available for the financing of resistance. In contrast to the Minister of Finance, the Minister of Economics was in favor of a loan based on the pound sterling. He argued that German industry had close business connections with Great Britain. Thus it was advisable to base the loan on the exchange rate of the mark to the pound; but he did not succeed, and a dollar loan was issued.[66] In the beginning, the Reichsbank as well as the cabinet were rather hopeful that the loan would become a success. Havenstein visited the Ruhr and major industries agreed to put 2,250,000 dollars at the disposal of the Reichsbank. This amount was divided among the following companies: Deutsch-Luxemburgische Bergwerks- und Hütten-A.G. (400,000), August Thyssen-Hütte (300,000), Krupp (300,000), Phönix A.G. für Bergbau- und Hüttenbetrieb (300,000), GHH (200,000), Rheinische

[61] Benjamin Strong-Montagu Norman, May 2, 1923, *Strong-Norman Correspondence.*
[62] *BA*, R 43I/2435, April 19, 1923.
[63] Norman-Strong, May 2, 1923, *Strong-Norman Correspondence.*
[64] Strong-Norman, May 15, 1923, *ibid.*
[65] Germain Calmette, *Les dettes Interalliées.* (Paris, 1926), pp. 17–26.
[66] *BA*, R 43I/2445, February 22, and February 24, 1923, correspondence between Hermes and Becker. *Kab. Cuno*, No. 83, February 25, 1923.

Stahlwerke (200,000), Stumm (150,000), Hoesch (150,000), Klöckner (150,000), and Mannesmann-Röhrenwerke (100,000).[67]

But despite these expectations the loan did not become a success. The banks, which had guaranteed to sell fifty percent (25 billion dollars), only sold twenty-five. According to Havenstein, heavy industry had, in comparison with other industries, subscribed the most significant amount of the loan, while he was disappointed with contributions by trade.[68] Although this might have been the case, Hugo Stinnes, one of the most influential representatives of heavy industry, told both Stresemann and Hermes that he would not subscribe; "the only thing that could be expected from him was that he would not oppose the loan in public."[69]

Besides domestic reluctance and lack of confidence, France also seems to have contributed to the failure of the loan. A successful loan would have prolonged German resistance, and on March 23 *Le Temps* contested that the Reichsbank had the right to guarantee the redemption of the loan without prior approval from the Reparation Commission. This was not an empty threat. On March 27, the Committee of Guarantees of the Reparation Commission decided that it would not yield its priority on all revenues which the Reichsbank should use for the redemption of the dollar loan.[70] With this decision the Committee of Guarantees created insecurity for prospective subscribers, who could not be certain that they would receive their money back. But it is mere speculation to assess to what extent this decision influenced subscription. The Reichsbank and the *Centralverband der deutschen Banken und des Bankiergewerbes*, which propagandized subscription, believed that it did. Furthermore, the conditions of the loan were made public too late, and the lending rate could also have been improved. An article in the *Bankarchiv*, the organ of German banking interests, drew different conclusions from its failure. It had shown that the amount of foreign currency available in Germany had been overestimated.[71] Cuno himself was of a different opinion. When the mark started to fall again, he discussed countermeasures with the Reichsbank and leading private bankers. Apparently the Chancellor expected that more foreign currency could be made available through industry. If industry refused, he threatened to reveal the names of those who were responsible for the failure of stabilization measures.[72] How-

---

[67] "Niederschrift über Stahlfinanz," March 16, 1923, *HA GHH*, 300193008/19.
[68] *Kab, Cuno*, No. 128, April 4, 1923.
[69] *Marx-Nachlaß*, III, Note Hermes, September 21, 1923, p. 111; the quotation is from Stresemann, *op. cit.*, I, p. 42.
[70] *BA*, R 43I/36.
[71] *Bankarchiv*, No. 12, March 15, and No. 14, April 15, 1923.
[72] *Kab. Cuno*, No. 129, April 19, 1923.

ever just Cuno's criticism may have been, his policy had contributed to the fall of the mark, which set in on April 19 and could not be stopped again. The expenses for wages, unemployment benefits, credits for industry, and the purchase of raw materials and foodstuffs abroad – in short, the financing of passive resistance – had constantly increased the Reich's deficit. Higher taxation would have been a means to reduce the deficit, and Cuno had been in favor of such a policy. But since neither he nor any other member of the cabinet had expected that the French action would last longer than two to three months before Britain would intervene or a conference would be held on reparations, and since a tax reform was only possible after stabilization of the currency, with the exception of the loan no serious attempt was made to cover expenditures for the Ruhr struggle. When the Minister of Finance warned against the ever increasing spending, he was overruled. Political considerations were more important than budgetary ones.[73]

When a Reichstag investigation committee studied the developments which had led to the sudden fall of the mark in April 1923, a conclusive answer was not found. Several newspapers suspected that Hugo Stinnes had bought foreign exchange and this had started the renewed depreciation of the currency. Havenstein was also convinced that part of the Reich's credit for industry had been used to buy foreign exchange.[74] The investigations reveal that several companies, including Stinnes (60 000 pounds) and Eugen Bab & Co., had indeed bought foreign currency prior to the fall of the mark. These transactions had been carried through upon a request of the Ministry of Transport which needed foreign currency for the payment of coal supplies ordered for the Reichsbahn in England and Czechoslovakia.[75] To the great irritation of other cabinet members, the Ministry of Transport had the habit of realizing this policy without informing the *Devisenbeschaffungsstelle*.[76] The purchase of foreign currency against papermarks did of course react upon the value of the mark. In addition, some members of the Investigation Committee believed that since the sudden depreciation had first shown on foreign money markets, France was behind this policy. Whether this was the case cannot be said with certainty. On April 28, Poincaré had informed French occupation authorities, in need of marks despite confiscations, that it was inopportune "to retain the present exchange rate of the Mark." Thus he

---

[73] *Ibid.*, No. 193, June 16, and No. 216, July 11, 1923.
[74] *BA*, R 43I/2445. *Vorwärts*, No. 189, April 24, 1923; also *BZ* and *Vossische Zeitung*. *Kab. Cuno*, No. 138, April 23, 1923. For Havenstein's opinion see *BA*, R 2/2419, May 29, 1923.
[75] *Ibid.*, June 14, June 19, and June 20, 1923.
[76] Cf. Becker, December 6, 1922, *ibid.*, R 43I/2445. *Kab. Cuno*, No. 137, April 21, 1923. *RT*, vol. 380, No. 6591. "Auszug Bericht Havenstein. 8.12.22–7.3.23," *BA*, R 43I/632.

ordered further investigations in order to accelerate Germany's financial embarrassment.[77] Still, the depreciation of the mark had already started after von Rosenberg's speech in the Reichstag on April 16 in which he explained the German offer of January 2, and made the beginning of negotiation dependent upon a withdrawal of all occupation troops. As early as April 19, the mark reached a new low of 29,500 marks to the dollar, while on April 16 it had been at 21,000.[78] The meetings of the Investigation Committee reveal that neither its members nor government officials nor bankers knew exactly what had caused the sudden fall. Paul Loeb of the Mendelssohn Bank, which had executed the Reichsbank's interventions on the international money market, expressed an opinion which was basically shared by many of his colleagues when he declared that never before in his career as a banker had he been confronted with such a development.[79] Whatever the immediate cause of the currency depreciation in April, purchases of foreign currency for the Reichsbahn, coal orders, industrial orders for the payment of foreign or domestic contracts[80] or a loss of confidence for a solution of the Ruhr crisis within the near future after von Rosenberg's speech, preliminary stabilization had lasted longer than anybody had expected. While coal, food and raw material imports undoubtedly increased the deficit of the trade balance, they also contributed to the prolongation of resistance.

4. THE ECONOMIC WAR IN 1923

Since occupation had been perceived as an economic war against Germany rather than as an attempt merely to insure the collection of reparations, the government tried to made exploitation of Ruhr mines as difficult as possible, hoping that a Franco-Belgian failure would result in new negotiations and a reduction of Germany's liability. This attitude soon led to French countermeasures and to a complete breakdown of economic life during the summer of 1923.[81]

In this economic war, Cuno declared "bread and money" to be the coun-

---

[77] Poincaré-Degoutte, April 28, and April 29, 1923, *MAE*, Ruhr 18, fol. 188 and fol. 206 f. For confiscations see Wentzcke, *op. cit.*, II, p. 121.

[78] For Rosenberg's speech cf. *RT*, vol. 359, pp. 10539 ff. *Kab. Cuno*, No. 128, April 19, 1923. *BA*, R 2/2419, June 16, 1923.

[79] *BA*, R 2/2419, June 16, 1923.

[80] At the end of February the Gutehoffnungshütte bought 100 000 florin and resold them with profit. At the same time the Deutsch-Luxemburgische Bergwerk- und Hütten-AG was forced to sell 200 000 pound Sterling. Cf. Reusch-Haniel, February 25, 1923, *HA GHH*, 3001900/3. Also Woltmann-Reusch, February 26, 1923, *ibid.*, 300193003/8.

[81] Favez, *op. cit.*, pp. 157-173.

try's main ammunition.[82] One might have added, and raw materials, especially coal, as well. From the beginning Germany was at a disadvantage. As a highly industrialized country, it was dependent upon the export of manufactured goods and the import of raw materials and food stuffs. Eighty-five percent of German coal production came from the occupied area. When occupation started, the railways, for example, had coal reserves for seven weeks. Unoccupied Germany had coal reserves for four weeks, while coke would last for three weeks.[83] Cuno's problem was to keep industry going and prevent unemployment, since unhampered production was the basis of resistance. During the first weeks production in the Ruhr went on, and, because of the inefficiency of French controls, the railways were able to transport coal from the Ruhr until the end of January, when France cut connections between occupied and unoccupied Germany. But even with these additional reserves and the increase of production in the unoccupied part of the country Germany would not have lasted long if Poland, Czechoslovakia, and Great Britain had not increased their coal exports to Germany. While Poland had only delivered 2.9 million tons in 1922, exports to Germany reached 8.7 million tons in 1923. In 1924, after normal conditions had been partially restored, Poland still exported 6.5 million tons to Germany. Coal imports from Czechoslovakia also increased from 160,000 tons in 1922 to 802,000 tons in 1923. British coal exports to Germany doubled and rose from 7.7 million tons in 1922 to 15.4 million tons in 1923.[84] During 1923 Germany ordered about half of her coal from abroad, receiving credit from Britain for the purchase of British coal.

In other fields developments were similar. The import of pig-iron from France and Belgium decreased, while imports from Poland, Czechoslovakia, and Britain increased. Czech industry put more blast furnaces into operation to supply the German market with iron products. In the first three months of 1923, only five percent of German iron imports came from Czechoslovakia, while by June 1923 fifteen percent of Germany's total imports originated there.[85] In the textile market British goods replaced French and Belgian exports.[86]

[82] *Kab. Cuno*, No. 63, February 3, 1923. Oltmann, *op. cit.*, pp. 88 ff.

[83] *PA AA*, W. Rep. Besetzung des Ruhrgebietes, Aufzeichnung Lage Ruhr. 2. Besprechung, January 16, 1923. *BA*, R 2/2419, "Untersuchungsausschuss Stützungsaktion, 10. Sitzung," June 14, 1923. *Kab. Cuno*, No. 45, January 16, 1923. Reichskohlenkommissar Stutz only mentioned 29 days.

[84] Albert Wiedemann, "Die Wirkungen der Ruhrbesetzung auf die deutsche Volkswirtschaft," *Ruhrbesetzung und Weltwirtschaft. Eine internationale Untersuchung der Einwirkungen der Ruhrbesetzung auf die Weltwirtschaft.* Schriften des Weltwirtschaftsinstituts der Handelshochschule Leipzig, Bd. 3, hrsg. Ernst Schultze (Leipzig, 1927), pp. 23–24.

[85] J. Slemr, "Der Einfluß der Ruhrbesetzung auf das Wirtschaftsleben der Tschechoslowakischen Republik," *ibid.*, p. 134.

[86] Wiedemann, *ibid.*, p. 24.

The attitude of Poland and Czechoslovakia was a severe handicap to France. Poincaré had simply not foreseen that these members of the French alliance in Eastern Europe hesitated to cooperate, and he urged these countries to curtail their exports to Germany.[87] Both countries promised to do so, but hardly anything happened, and despite repeated intervention, deliveries continued as the above figures show.[88] Some upper Silesian mining companies also informed the Ministry of Transport in Berlin that they did not intend to break off trade relations, even if demanded to do so by the Polish government.[89] French control of the Ruhr was also hindered when Britain, the United States, the Netherlands, and other neutral countries complained about interference of trade with the occupied zone. Poincaré was especially sensitive to these protests and when London demanded that France stop meddling with British coal transports into the Ruhr, he ordered their immediate release.[90] Great Britain and other European countries with their depressed mining industries were only too willing to provide Germany with coal after France had halted the transport of Ruhr coal into unoccupied Germany. This economic "aid" greatly contributed to the strengthening of the German position and also led to a prolongation of the Franco-German struggle. Without sufficient coal supplies, Germany could never have been able to organize resistance.

Besides coal exports to Germany, France encountered further difficulties with Great Britain. Once the MICUM started to transport coal and coke from the Ruhr, Anglo-French differences began. The main railway-line from the Ruhr ran through the British zone of occupation. Without British cooperation the exploitation of productive pledges could not succeed, and General Degoutte asked his British colleague to allow the transport of coal through the Cologne zone. General Godley, the British representative, was not willing to help however, arguing that such a step would immediately lead to a strike of the German railway personnel. Britain was not interested in any complications and would have to leave the Rhineland if difficulties occurred.[91] Godley's attitude was a severe threat to French plans and Degoutte asked Paris for help. Without coke or coal transports through the Cologne zone, Poincaré would not have been able to prove at home that

[87] Poincaré-Prague, January 17, 1923, MAE, Ruhr 5, fol. 162–163. Ibid., January 18, 1923, fol. 232.

[88] Ibid., Ruhr 6, January 21, 1923, fol. 184. Ibid., Ruhr 7, January 24, 1923, fol. 102.

[89] PA AA, W. Rep., Besetzung des Ruhrgebietes, Sonderakte, Kohle, Koks, H 261885, February 24, 1923. According to another report, Polish mines cancelled contracts for coal transport on January 16. See BA, R 43I/205, January 16, 1923, "Ministerbesprechung."

[90] January 28, 1923, MAE, Ruhr 8, fol. 80–81.

[91] Poincaré-London, February 5, 1923, ibid., Ruhr 9, fol. 233–235.

occupation was a success, and he immediately intervened. If the British government would not agree to the French demand, he cabled to London, "irreparable damage" would be done to the Entente.[92] But the Foreign Office felt that cooperation might be regarded as British participation in the occupation. A question of such far-reaching importance could not be decided by the Foreign Office alone and consultations with the cabinet were necessary.[93]

When Poincaré had not received an answer after five days his impatience grew, and he angrily demanded a decision. He informed London that France had a legal right to use the railway net in the British zone of occupation as well, since the French Commanding General was responsible for the security of all troops. These legal arguments show Poincaré at his best, but he seems to have had second thoughts about his unfriendly cable and decided to send General Payot and Le Trocqueur to London, begging the British government not to make a final decision before the arrival of his delegates.[94] But neither this conciliatory letter nor the presence of the delegation in London changed much. Bonar Law and Curzon both refused to accept the interpretation that the Versailles Treaty or the ordinances of the Rhineland Agreement gave France any special rights. On the contrary, they maintained that the occupation had created a completely new situation not covered by the Treaty at all. This was a serious warning that Britain would not follow Poincaré into any legal arguments, and if he forced such an incident, the legality of occupation would also have to be discussed. French control of railway lines in the British zone could simply not be tolerated, but in order to show good will, the Foreign Office offered to cede one line which ran along the border of the British zone, also withdrawing troops from this area. If Poincaré did not accept this compromise "Britain was forced to withdraw her troops from the Rhineland, a fact which would seriously effect relations between the two countries.[95]

After this setback, Poincaré discussed the problem with his military advisers Foch, Weygand, and Paguenin. They considered the British proposal to be insufficient but accepted it for the moment, and French and British officers in the Rhineland negotiated the Payot-Godley agreement which

[92] *Ibid.*
[93] Saint-Aulaire-Poincaré, February 9, 1923, *ibid.*, Ruhr 10, fol. 190–192. *FO.*, 371/8749, C 20414, November 24, 1923 with a detailed description of British policy in the occupied regions.
[94] Poincaré-Saint-Aulaire, February 10, and February 11, 1923, *MAE*, Ruhr 10, fol. 242 ff., 280.
[95] February 15, 1923, *ibid.*, fol. 157–160.

arranged the crossing of 12 trains per day through the British zone and ceded the railway line Grevenbroich-Düren to France.[96]

While these negotiations had been going on in London, the British government kept Germany informed of the new developments. After hearing Captain Gregori, technical adviser to the British High Commissioner, report that Berlin would not oppose a certain number of trains per day, the above mentioned decision was made. Before the French delegation was notified, the cabinet waited for an affirmative answer from Berlin.[97] The Germans were indeed not interested in a withdrawal of British troops and were eager to find a modus vivendi in discussions with Lord D'Abernon.[98] The German Foreign Office was prepared to do everything to satisfy Britain, even though this might help France. The Reichsbahn office at Cologne notified its branches that 1) all supply trains for the occupation forces should continue to operate in order to prevent requisitions of food in the Ruhr; 2) all troop transports under the Rhineland agreement should also be run; and 3) trains in the British zone had to be run under any circumstances. Sabotage of Allied traffic in the Cologne zone was prohibited.[99]

These orders caused severe criticism of the Ministry of Transport, especially among trade unions. Members of the railway union met Lord Kilmanrock, British High Commissioner at Coblenz, and informed him that they would not participate in any activity detrimental to resistance.[100] The Ministry of Transport also reported that railway employees were angered about orders to run trains in the British zone, but fearing that resistance in the Cologne zone might result in British withdrawal, Germany did not oppose the Anglo-French agreement.[101]

True enough Britain threatened to withdraw her troops in case France or Germany created difficulties. But British politicians did not really want a withdrawal, since the British presence in Cologne was the only chance of controlling French policy. The Foreign Office had not yet clarified its own position towards French coercive measures. If France succeeded in extracting reparations from Germany, Britain would not object, but if Poincaré tried to bring the Ruhr under French political and economic hegemony,

---

[96] February 17, 1923, *ibid.*, Ruhr 11, fol. 278. This compromise was criticized in the British press. See White, *op. cit.*, p. 68. Weill-Raynal, *op. cit.*, II, p. 392.

[97] Cab., 23/45, February 15, and March 14, 1923.

[98] "Aufzeichnung Simon," February 2, 1923, *PA AA*, W. Rep., Besetzung des Ruhrgebietes H 276813–814.

[99] Von Guerard, January 30, 1923, *BA*, R 43I/207.

[100] Staatskommissar Mehlich-Hamm, February 7, 1923, *ibid.*, *Kab. Cuno*, No. 74, footnote 3.

[101] Reichsverkehrsministerium-AA, February 9, 1923, *BA Koblenz*, R 43I/207. Partly printed in *Kab. Cuno*, Nr. 74. footnote 2.

Britain could not stand by and watch. The importance of British presence in Cologne was well recognized by the Department of Overseas Trade in a memorandum concerning British policy. If British troops were withdrawn, its authors reasoned, British presence on the International Rhineland High Commission (IRHC) would also cease, thus damaging British trade. "If this country loses its footing in Cologne, it loses its footing in the occupied territory as a whole, and the occupied territory is that part of Germany which consumes British manufactured goods rather than British raw materials."[102]

Despite their insistence upon British rights, neither Bonar Law nor Curzon wanted a break with France over the Ruhr, since a rupture would also have influenced negotiations at Lausanne, where Britain was seeking an agreement on the tangled Turkish question. Curzon knew that he could wait, and despite his annoyance with Poincaré, he was prepared to deal with him at Lausanne and leave the conflict over the Ruhr for later discussions. After an agreement in that conflict, Britain would have a free hand in Europe. But if an agreement could not be obtained, French policy in the Near East would also lead to a rupture in Europe.[103] The consequence of the Anglo-French confrontation at Lausanne was a limitation of British freedom of action toward France at that moment, and when the zone of occupation was extended to include Appenweiler and Offenbach, the Foreign Office did not protest, although its legal adviser, Cecil Hurst, considered the action illegal.[104] But the British decision to stay in Cologne strengthened German hopes for future intervention, and Poincaré was convinced that the British Ambassador to Berlin was the prime mover behind Cuno's policy. Without Lord D'Abernon's backing, he reasoned, Germany was too "weak and disunited" to conduct resistance.[105]

[102] *FO.*, 371/8718, C.P. 3858, "The British Occupation of the Cologne Bridgehead and its Importance in Relation to British Commercial Interests," March 2, 1923.

[103] *Cab.*, 23/32, November 1, 1922, and Curzon-Lampson, January 31, 1923, *ibid.*, 24/158. To the anger of Curzon, the French delegation "entertained and informed" the Turks about everything. In a meeting with the British Ambassador Poincaré hinted that a connection between Lausanne and the Ruhr existed, and he warned London against supporting Germany: "The French were making every effort in the occupied districts to avoid any possible cause of friction with us, but if the Germans knew you [Curzon] had written of danger to the Entente, they would regard it as a direct encouragement." Curzon-Lampson, January 24, 1923, *ibid.*, 24/156. *DBFP*, First Series, vol. XVIII, No. 369, Crew-Curzon, February 2, 1923.

[104] Hurst felt it did not make "sense to stir up further mud." *FO.*, 371/8716, C 3597, February 22, 1923.

[105] *MAE*, Ruhr 7, January 23, 1923, fol. 6.

5. BRITISH AND AMERICAN ATTITUDES

From the beginning of occupation, it was clear that Germany stood alone and could not rely on foreign help. Neither the United States nor Great Britain could have stopped France and Belgium. But in a meeting with the American Secretary of State, the British Ambassador to Washington, Geddes, indicated that his country "must immediately take steps to secure better air protection." Both agreed that there was no danger of an attack upon Great Britain, but Geddes felt that in Britain "there was an apprehension and a feeling that there was a state of mind developing in France which made it desirable that the British should have better protection against air attack." Hughes similarly reasoned that neither the United States nor Great Britain could stand up to France at the moment:

The French knew perfectly well that there was no British force which could prevent their doing what they pleased in Germany; that the British had no force to oppose them, that the US had no force to oppose them, and they could overrun the whole of Germany if they desired.[106]

The United States did not intend to get involved in any Franco-German struggle, and as a protest against occupation withdrew her troops from the Rhineland.[107] The British Foreign Office investigated the advisability of a similar move, but concluded that it was unwise since Britain would then lose all influence upon future developments in Germany.[108] On the other hand, the Foreign Office feared a diminution of Germany's capacity, the "increased danger" of social disturbances and the effect on British trade. However, if Germany would succeed in refusing payments "owing to her inflationist proceedings" she would be "the one great industrial Power in Europe enjoying all the advantages accruing from the extinction of both foreign and internal debt." Official British policy thus remained one of "undiminished friendship" towards France while dissociating her actions from and denying all responsibility for occupation measures.[109] Britain was simply begging for time. Only the Soviet Union spoke out in favor of Germany and

---

[106] *Hughes Papers*, Box 175, Folder 77a, Great Britain, January 25, 1923. For discussions in the British Cabinet cf. *Cab.*, 23/45, January 26, 1923. *Ibid.*, 23/46, June 20, 1923, and especially *ibid.*, 24/160, C.P. 270, June 12, 1923 and C.P. 294 with an evaluation of French and British military potential.

[107] Hughes Papers, Box 174, Folder 24b, France, January 8, 1923, Gescher, *op. cit.*, pp. 150–153.

[108] Cab., 23/45, January 26, 1923.

[109] *Ibid.*, 24/140, C.P. 4348, December 5, 1922. *FO.*, 371/8627, C 5451, January 10, 1923.

sent money, wheat and political agitators, a fact, which made Cuno feel rather uncomfortable about this Ally.[110]

In spite of the increasingly clear indication that London and Washington would not intervene, the German government did not give up hope for intervention. This was partly due to the fact that although Germany was without Allies, it was not without foreign sympathizers. The American Ambassador in Berlin was one of them. Several times Houghton, who suspected Poincaré's motives, urged Washington to intervene on Germany's behalf. Before the occupation, he had been as uncertain as everybody else.

Does France desire reparations primarily? To ask for reparations but to gradually destroy the means by which reparations can be made possible, means of course, the destruction of Germany. If France wants reparations she will make reparations possible. If she merely wishes to talk reparations, while seeking Germany's destruction, that also will be made clear by her attitude.[111]

A few weeks later, he was convinced that Poincaré had "started a process of economic strangulation" hoping to obtain security after Germany had been broken up. Security, he reasoned, meant for France the destruction of German military, financial, and economic power. Besides these more general objectives an additional motive existed: Poincaré wanted to make France "independent in the production of an essential military necessity, – to wit steel."[112]

But neither these warnings nor the observation of Roland Boyden, who doubted "if we would ever see France out of Germany in our time,"[113] nor the suspicion of Warren D. Robbins, counsellor of the US embassy in Berlin, that Poincaré intended to keep Germany "crippled," caused the State Department to intervene.[114] Houghton's view that French policy was based upon economic, financial and political motives was accepted by William R. Castle, but the head of the European Division drew different conclusions than the Ambassador who suggested in March 1923:

... if France is not met by armed force in the shape of armies, it must be met by economic force in the shape of threatened ruin. That is the whole story. France must be met by force.[115]

This was a view neither Hughes nor Castle could accept. The latter felt that Houghton had been influenced by his Berlin contacts, while Hughes believed

[110] Cuno-Rosenberg, May 28, 1923 *BA*, R 43I/2669.
[111] Houghton-Boyden, January 5, 1923, *Houghton Papers*, Diary, p. 524.
[112] *Ibid.*, February 17, 1923, p. 546. Houghton-Castle, January 17, and February 12, 1923, *William R. Castle Papers*, Box 4.
[113] Warren D. Robbins-Castle, January 30, 1923, *ibid.*, Box 3.
[114] Robbins-Castle, January 30, 1923, *ibid.*
[115] Houghton-Castle, March 6, 1923, *Houghton Papers*, Diary, p. 580.

that these proposals involved Germany's return to her prewar status, a position which France would have never consented to. Houghton's ideas, the Secretary of State reasoned, were "fatuous."[116]

If the American Ambassador had kept his opinion to himself it would not have had any effect, but he apparently did not. He was in constant contact with German industrialists like Stinnes, Reusch, Sorge, Thyssen, and others. Cuno informed him about government initiatives in advance and met with him several times in the Berlin office of the Hapag being afraid to be seen "coming to the US Embassy."[117] Houghton regarded Cuno as his "friend," and there was at least one instance when he proposed a prolongation of passive resistance.[118] In contrast to Houghton, the counsellor of the embassy tried to point out the fallaciousness of German hopes for foreign intervention, but to no avail. Robbins partly blamed British representatives in Berlin for Cuno's attitude who, he felt, had made "a lot of foolish suggestions" which Britain was "not able to live up to." Otherwise "Germany would not be playing around" and "might already be fishing or cutting bait."[119]

The British Ambassador, Lord D'Abernon, who became known as the "Lord Protector" of Germany, suspected that Poincaré intended to establish French hegemony on the Continent. "To make supremacy complete, it was necessary for France to hold the Rhine and occupy the Ruhr."[120] The British delegate at Cologne, Piggott, informed Konrad Adenauer after his return from London that Britain would not intervene, but he hoped that, if German resistance lasted long enough, changes would occur in Paris.[121] Piggott was certainly not speaking for the government, but the indiscretion of such an announcement was obvious, and despite official discouragement in London and Washington,[122] Cuno expected intervention. In the long

[116] Castle-Houghton, March 17, 1923, *Castle Papers*, Box. 4. *Houghton Papers*, Mitchell Reference File. Interview with Hughes on November 11, 1941.

[117] *Ibid.*, interview with Houghton, March 6, 1941.

[118] *Hans von Seeckt Papers*, FM 132, reel 26, piece 289, January 20, 1923. According to this source Houghton took von Seeckt's wife aside at a party and "unofficially" congratulated her to Germany's resistance. "Er riet dringend durchzuhalten." Also *Cuno Nachlaß*, v. Holzendorff Akten, January 29, 1923.

[119] Robbins-Castle, April 17, 1923, *Castle Papers*, Box 4. Newson-Castle, August 18, 1923, *ibid.*

[120] D'Abernon, *op. cit.*, II, p. 21.

[121] *Kab. Cuno*, No. 58, January 27, 1923. For Bradbury's attitude cf. *ibid.*, No. 43, January 12, 1923. *PA AA* W. Rep., Konferenz in Brüssel zur Regelung der Reparationsfrage ... K 246814–815, January 11, 1923.

[122] Von Holtzendorff-Cuno, March 3, 1923, *PA AA*, Büro RM, Ruhrgebiet, Besatzungsprobleme, D 636806 f. "Aufzeichnung Dr. Breitscheid 21.2.1923 über Englandbesuch," *ibid.*, D 636543 ff. "Aufzeichnung von Schubert," January 23, 1923, *ibid.*, Büro RM, England, 490182 ff. Especially the report "Die englisch-französische Krise," Juli 8, 1923, *ibid.*, D 490406-420 with a description of different political opinions in England. Cf.

run these hopes were certainly justified, but it was another question whether resistance could last that long. Hoping for British and American good-will and trying to prevent Anglo-American support of French policy, the German Foreign Office tried to extract as many hints for the conduct of resistance from these countries as possible. Thus upon the recommendation of England, Italy and other countries, relations between Germany and the occupying powers were not broken off in February 1923, this step having been considered to force interventions.[123]

6. FRENCH REACTIONS TO PASSIVE RESISTANCE

During the first days of occupation, France and Belgium still hoped that Germany would yield and direct negotiations about the unhindered exploitation of productive pledges would take place. For the Belgian Foreign Minister, Henri Jaspar, these talks had been the main purpose of occupation, and on January 17 he informed the French Ambassador to Belgium, Jean Herbette, that he expected that talks would start within a month.[124] French Ambassador de Margerie sent similarly optimistic reports from Berlin, maintaining German industry would negotiate within three weeks.[125] But soon Poincaré recognized that the first attempt to force payments had failed, and as early as January 16 he warned publicly that he did not expect substantial revenues from the Ruhr, a statement which he had already made in a closed Senate meeting in November.[126]

While official contacts between Berlin and Paris were limited during the first weeks of occupation, many semi-official contacts remained intact. General Nollet approached Gustav Stresemann. Poincaré informed Professor Haguenin, French observer in Berlin, that he should keep in contact with the Germans claiming that negotiations with Berlin could start as soon as Cuno had given up supporting Ruhr industrialists. If Cuno would not

---

Hughes Papers, Box 175, 75b Germany. On the other hand, the American Envoy to Switzerland suggested to his German colleague that he was urging his government to intervene and stated "daß von uns, und sei es auch unter schwersten Opfern, durchgehalten werden muß, um die seiner Ansicht nach unausbleibliche Befreiung aus dem Reparationsjoch zu gewinnen." Müller-AA, February 9, 1923, *PA AA,* Büro RM, Ruhrgebiet, Besatzungsprobleme, D 638160.

[123] See the correspondence in *PA AA,* Büro RM, Frage des Abbruchs der Beziehungen, 8.2.1923–13.12.1923.

[124] January 17, 1923, *MAE,* Allemagne 479, fol. 107.

[125] January 25, 1923, *ibid.,* Ruhr 7, fol. 119 f. January 8, 1923, *ibid.,* Ruhr 8, fol. 6. Zimmermann, *op. cit.,* p. 100.

[126] *PA AA,* W. Rep., Besetzung des Ruhrgebietes, "Betrachtungen zur Lage," No. 363.

negotiate, France would enforce occupation, and neither a general strike nor other obstacles would prevent her from going "jusqu'au bout."[127]

Even more than by the attitude of the government, Poincaré was completely perplexed by the reaction of the SPD and the trade unions. He simply did not understand how representatives of the working class could support a bourgeois government after France had described the occupation as a showdown with the government and Ruhr heavy industry and even asked French observers in the Ruhr to enlighten the population about his intentions. Occupation authorities did indeed start a propaganda campaign arguing that Ruhr industry had enriched itself, while the population, which had French sympathies, had remained poor.[128] But the trade unions, although they were angered by the massive governmental support of industry, rejected any collaboration with France, despite pressure by the MICUM.[129]

When occupation did not bring results immediately parts of the French press grew restless. *Journée Industrielle* believed that this was the result of a lack of foresight. If France had only managed to seize the coal syndicate, Poincaré might have been spared an embarrassing situation. The paper regretted that an "economic war" had been started. Similar doubts appeared in other papers. *L'Oeuvre* reasoned that the only purpose of occupation had been the opening of direct negotiations with Germany. *Ere Nouvelle* was pessimistic, and regarded the operation as an "expedition to Mexico" which would end in Allied arbitration and consequently in a loss of prestige for France.[130] In contrast to these views the majority of the press, with the exception of the Left, demanded that there was no need to be pessimistic, France could win this struggle and be stronger than even ever before. The majority of the French Chamber also supported Poincaré and prevented the discussion of Ruhr policy demanded by the Left.[131]

Faced by a hostile population and recognizing that the first attempt to collect reparations had failed, the members of the MICUM panicked for a

[127] "Aufzeichnung 22.1.1923," *PA AA*, Büro RM, Ruhrgebiet, Besatzungsprobleme, D 636035. Poincaré-de Margerie, January 28, 1923, *MAE*, Ruhr 8, fol. 181 ff. For further contacts (Dausset-Jouvenel) see January 28, 1923, *PA AA*, Büro RM, Ruhrgebiet ..., D 636236. Cf. January 18, 1923, D 636011. Also "Aufzeichnung Maltzan" of a meeting with Hesnard of the French Embassy's Press Department. *Ibid.*, D 638338.
[128] January 28, and February 1, 1923, *MAE*, Ruhr 9, fol. 38 and Ruhr fol. 82 ff. Cf. a report about de Margerie's speech in a French Club in Berlin in which he stated that his government had "niemals an die Hartnäckigkeit des deutschen Widerstandes geglaubt." *PA AA*, Büro RM, Ruhrgebiet, January 28, 1923, D 636362 f.
[129] Spethmann, *op. cit.*, IV, p. 112 f.
[130] *Journée Industrielle*, January 14, 15 and 20, 1923. *L'Oeuvre*, January 17, 1923. *Ere Nouvelle*, January 17, 1923.
[131] *Annales de la Chambre des Députés*, vol. 119, February 1, 1923, p. 454. *Ibid.*, March 22, 1923, p. 1340. *Ibid.*, vol. 120, May 8, 1923, p. 6.

moment and suggested the retreat of French troops to the bridgeheads and a blockade of German coal exports. Otherwise the army of occupation would have to be increased, and France would have to run the railways herself. In contrast to the MICUM, General Degoutte voted against a retreat and proposed an increase of coercion.[132] Poincaré sent General Weygand and Le Trocqueur into the Ruhr to investigate further measures. On their return they suggested that France control the railways, the postal and the telegraph service, increase pressure upon mine owners and functionaries, and prepare everything for a disruption of all connections between the Ruhr and unoccupied Germany.[133] These proposals were discussed in a cabinet meeting and after Belgium had also agreed to them, coal exports from the Ruhr were interrupted on February 1, soon to be followed by an implementation of the other suggestions.[134] In other meetings with Belgian representatives the creation of a separate currency was also discussed, but no agreement could be reached since the Belgians distrusted French motives, suspecting that the creation of a currency was the first step towards the foundation of a new state. The French Minister of Finance also protested.[135]

A commission of French industrialists was sent into the Ruhr to investigate the situation, but since disunity prevailed between steel and coal mining industries, they hardly influenced the actual course of events, and French policy was determined by Poincaré. However, since many blast furnaces had to be blown out as a result of France's failure to collect coke, dissatisfaction grew among steel industry. It demanded that the government should accelerate its program of exploitation, and Weygand and Le Trocqueur were repeatedly sent into the Ruhr to encourage further preparations for an exploitation of pledges.[136] While these preparations were going on, new plans for a final settlement of reparations were developed. British abstention and the introduction of passive resistance had created a completely new situation. Before the beginning of resistance, occupation had mainly been regarded as an attempt to guarantee reparations from Germany, now additional motives became apparent.

[132] Zimmermann, *op. cit.*, pp. 103–104.
[133] *MAE*, Ruhr 8, January 28, 1923, fol. 75 f; *Petit Parisien*, January 25, 1923; Zimmermann, *op. cit.*, p. 104 f.
[134] *MAE*, Ruhr 8, January 29, 1923, fol. 94; Zimmermann, *op. cit.*, p. 107.
[135] *MAE*, Ruhr 7, January 26, 1923, fol. 209. *Ibid.*, Ruhr 8, January 27, and January 30m fol. 161. The plans worked out by Tirard and French bankers had several disadvantages. Thus Poincaré ordered renewed discussions in Paris. See *Ibid.*, January 28, 1923, fol. 80 f. *Ibid.*, Ruhr 9, February 5, 1923, fol. 164. *Journée Industrielle*, January 21, 1923.
[136] Peretti de la Rocca, February 12, 1923, *MAE*, Ruhr 11, fol. 50 ff. Zimmermann, *op. cit.*, p. 148; *L'Usine*, April 26, 1923; *Journée Industrielle*, April 21, 1923; *Echo Nationale*, April 20, 1923.

In a plan dated March 3, Marshal Foch suggested that occupation ought to have two results 1) to extract reparations from Germany and 2) to guarantee French security. His ideas about reparation payments were hopelessly unrealistic. He demanded that Germany pay 50 billion gold marks within 5 to 10 years instead of 36 years as prescribed in the London Schedule of Payments. However, certain reductions were possible. The remaining 82 billions were to be used for a settlement of interallied debts. The Ruhr was to be evacuated in three stages equalizing payment of the first 50 billions, but in order to guarantee payment of the rest, Essen would be kept as a pledge. In addition he demanded that the Saar mines should remain French property forever, and that an agreement guaranteeing coke deliveries to France would also have to be signed. If Cuno agreed to this plan, the economic strangulation of the Ruhr was to be halted, and France would negotiate with her Allies as to the distribution of the 50 billion gold marks. The Ruhr was a pledge for reparation deliveries, while the control of the Rhineland was important for French security. Thus Foch suggested that France influence her Allies into agreeing to permanent occupation of the left bank of the Rhine and the control of the bridgeheads on the right bank. In addition to these military measures to prevent a German attack, it was also necessary to control the railway system and place both the Rhineland as well as the railways under neutral control.[137]

This far-reaching plan contains all the elements of French policy towards Germany. A huge amount of reparations, the connection between reparations and interallied debts, concern for the exchange of coal and coke, and above all, the concern for security. The Rhine was the geostrategical border of Marshal Foch and the left bank of the Rhine was to become a neutralized buffer state between Germany and France. But did the French government support this solution? On March 6, 1923, the interministerial Ruhr committee discussed alternative policies under the direction of Seydoux who had also submitted a plan which did not differ much from Foch's. Seydoux demanded that the Ruhr be evacuated in stages according to payment of the A- and B-bonds. The Rhineland, however, would only be evacuated after security had been obtained and an agreement had been reached upon the remaining 82 billion C-bonds. But in contrast to Foch, Seydoux only demanded permanent Allied control of the Rhenish railways. As in the previous meetings, the representatives of the Ministry of Finance warned that the implementation of these suggestions meant that France would never leave the Ruhr again, since Germany could not fulfill the London Schedule of

---

[137] *MAE*, Allemagne 480, Comité Militaire Allié de Versailles, March 3, 1923, fol. 10 ff. For the development of Foch's ideas since 1918 cf. Bariéty, *op. cit.*, pp. 26 ff.

Payments. On the other hand, the Ministry of Public Works proposed to secure once and for all coke deliveries from Germany, and different schemes for such a policy were developed in the ministry.[138]

Future French plans partly depended on collaboration with Belgium, and on March 13 a meeting took place in Brussels in which the two countries decided not to leave the Ruhr before they had received all reparations from Germany.[139] As a result of this conference the French government increased preparations for a final settlement which would both guarantee reparations and security. General Serrigny (*directeur des Services du Secrétariat Général du Conseil Supérieur de la Défense Nationale*) wrote a questionnaire upon Poincaré's request in which he summarized the administrative, economic, financial, and military problems connected with the creation of a Rhenish state.[140] In a meeting of the *Conseil Supérieur de la Défense Nationale* the following general principles had been agreed upon: 1) an autonomous state within the Reich was to be created which included the Saar; 2) the state had to be viable, but should not become an economic danger to its neighbours; 3) it had to cover Belgian and French borders against a German attack. This new state was to cut its relations with the Reich and had to be controlled by the Allies initially, coming under League control at a later stage. Naturally the state had to contribute to German reparation payments. The detailed questionnaire which was then distributed to all ministries contained questions concerning the organization of the Rhineland, the most promising borders for France, the economic potential and its relations to the French economy and the Reich, administrative problems and military organization. Since Poincaré wanted the opinions of the ministries as early as possible, Serrigny demanded answers by April 3 at the latest.[141]

The French High Commissioner in the Rhineland naturally supported the scheme. Charles Brugère, Poincaré's *chef du cabinet*, did not doubt that a Rhenish state would greatly contribute to French security. He reasoned that French policy in 1866 and from 1917 onwards had been based upon demands for security, but although he favored an autonomous state outside the Reich, he clearly recognized that German participation in the foundation

---

[138] Zimmermann, *op. cit.*, pp. 162–163.

[139] Weill-Raynal, *op. cit.*, II, p. 400. On March 22, 1923 Poincaré stressed his determination that French troops stay until demands had been fulfilled. "La France et la Belgique sont alliéses dans la Ruhr pour obtenir un règlement définitif du problème des réparations." Poincaré-Saint-Aulaire, *MAE*, Ruhr 16, fol. 162 f.

[140] Général Serrigny-Brugère, "Organisation de la Rhénanie," March 26, 1923, *ibid.*, Rive gauche 29, fol. 257–264. Zimmermann, *op. cit.*, p. 165.

[141] *Ibid.*

of a Rhenish state was necessary. But since France was in the Ruhr and
controlled the administration of the Rhineland, he suggested that France
attempt to profit from the present chaos and extend the powers of the Rhineland Commission.[142] The political director of the Quai D'Orsay, Peretti de
la Rocca criticized Brugère's proposals. Great Britain would never allow
the creation of a new state, and the Rhenish population, though it might
want to create a separate state within the Reich, was not willing to collaborate with France. This meant that although he too was not unsympathetic
to the creation of a Rhenish state and supported French penetration into
the Rhineland, he stressed that an initiative for a revision of the status quo
would have to come from the population.[143]

By April 12, 1923, plans for French Ruhr and Rhineland policy were
summarized. Again, the close connection between reparations, interallied
debts and security prevailed. As to reparations, Germany was to pay 132
billion gold marks. French receipts from A- and B-bonds were 26 billion
gold marks, while her war debt amounted to 25 billions. France had a right
to receive 39 billions from the C-bonds, and was prepared to cancel 25 billions of this sum, provided the Allies cancelled French debts. This meant
that France would still receive 14 billions from the C-bonds while Belgium
had a priority on 4 billions from A and B and 6 from C. It was expected that
Germany could pay 2 billion gold marks per year, and if the Allies cancelled
25 billions of the C-bonds negotiations with Germany could start immediately. Germany would be asked to grant shares in the Ruhr mines, the value of
which were estimated at 3 to 4 billion gold marks. As soon as 1/3 of the A-
and B-bonds had been paid, part of the Ruhr would be evacuated. The remaining parts would be evacuated after the payment of the other instalments.[144]

Considering British and American ideas about interallied debts, this plan
was as unrealistic as all previous proposals. The United States did not intend
to reduce interallied debts, while Britain, although willing to reduce them,
would also have demanded a reduction of the German debt. Such a reduction was unlikely in face of French opposition. Furthermore, Italy and
Britain also had a right for reparation payments and would consequently
play an important role in fixing final demands upon Germany.

---

[142] "Note pour le Président du Conseil préparée par M. Brugère," March 30, 1923,
ibid., fol. 266–269. He also discussed Tirard's plan for several Rhenish states and compared
it with Serrigny's proposals. Cf. "Contribution à l'Etude de l'Organisation d'un Etat
Rhénan dans le Cadre du Reich," January 28, 1923, *ibid.*, fol. 270 ff.
[143] *Ibid.*,
[144] *Ibid.*, Ruhr 17, April 12, 1923, fol. 223–243. For the importance of the customs line
see Bariéty, *op. cit.*, pp. 180 ff.

The April plan not only discussed reparations, but provided for a final settlement of Franco-German industrial relations as well. France did not have sufficient coal. Thus the Saar mines would have to be handed over to France forever while she would give up her right to hold a plebiscite. In addition to coal, France also needed coke, and 7 million tons of Ruhr coke per year had to be delivered by the Reich. Payments would be attributed to the C-bonds. Later on, additional contracts between industries would guarantee France the delivery of 2.5 million tons of coke per year while Germany would receive iron ore and semi-finished products. The customs line between Alsace-Lorraine and Germany which had been abolished for a transitional period of 5 years after the signing of the peace treaty would not be brought into effect during the duration of the French plan. With these demands the economic program for a final peace with Germany was concluded. However, neither the Treaty of Versailles nor the League of Nations guaranteed French military security against Germany. Thus a new agreement on the Rhineland would also have to be reached. The Rhine, the memorandum stated, was France's military frontier, and the bridgeheads on the right bank of the Rhine guaranteed French security. This part of the program seems to have been directly taken from Marshal Foch's memorandum of March 3. The strategic plan which was then developed also provided for the neutralization of the railway system on the left bank of the Rhine and within the demilitarized zone on the right bank. The railway would have to be controlled by the League, and an autonomous Rhineland state and a Saar state would have to be set up. Both states would remain within the Reich, but would not have an army. Instead, an interallied police and later an international police under the control of the League of Nations would uphold neutrality. Nevertheless, the bridgeheads would remain under French control, although troops would be reduced once the railways were neutralized. If neutralization of the Rhineland should lead to German acts of aggression, they would have to be repressed immediately.[145]

This French plan – if carried out successfully – meant a revision of the Versailles Treaty. France would have received a military frontier on the Rhine with its strategic and economic advantages. Agreements between French and German industry would have guaranteed the development of France's economic potential. Ideas like those just described were widespread in France during 1923. With the exception of the newspapers of the Left, a great part of the press regarded occupation as a prelude to an "economic

---

[145] *MAE*, Ruhr 17, April 12, 1923, fol. 223 ff. For the payment of A- and B-bonds cf. "Paiement des Bons A et B." *Ibid.*, fol. 240 f.

alliance with Germany."[146] Others demanded that a military frontier should
be created on the Rhine which would be the frontier of "liberty and civili-
zation."[147] These two demands – the creation of a military frontier for
France and an economic alliance with Germany – were the most current
themes, while demands for an annexation of the Ruhr were not seriously
considered.[148]

The discussions in the French press and the April plan show the state of
mind existing in France, but they did not mean that the government had already decided to create an autonomous Rhineland state within the Reich.
The occupation of the Rhineland had been regulated in the Versailles
Treaty. It was to be evacuated in three stages within 15 years, but since
Germany had not fulfilled the disarmament agreements of the treaty to
Poincaré's satisfaction, he argued that the period of evacuation had not yet
started.[149] Thus troops could naturally stay on the left bank of the Rhine
longer than had been expected and within this prolonged occupation period
a solution would have to be found for the final destiny of the Rhineland.
Coke deliveries from the Ruhr were of course of greater urgency, and on
June 13 the Foreign Affairs Committee of the Chamber of Deputies passed
a motion demanding domestic industry increase the production of coke to
make France more independent of foreign supplies. The French mining
industry was not able to fulfill this demand completely, and thus the Committee suggested that coke imports from Germany would have to be made in
proportion to French needs.[150]

Whether France would be able to implement this policy depended upon
developments in Germany and on British policy. While Cuno did not intend
to yield to occupation, hoping for a reduction of reparations, he could not
have accepted French Rhineland plans, either. Although a separatist movement existed in the Rhineland, it could not claim the support of the population. Nor could Great Britain have accepted French revisionist demands.
In face of German opposition, they would have prevented a pacification of

[146] Jacques Rivière, "Pour une Entente économique avec l'Allemagne," La Nouvelle
Française, 116 (May 1, 1923), pp. 725–735.
[147] René Pinon, Le redressement de la Politique Française 1923 (Paris, 1923), p. 171.
Gaston Cadoux, "Etappes et résultats de la Bataille de la Ruhr," Revue Politique et
Parlementaire, 350 (January 1924), pp. 25–62. The quote is from André Chaumeix,
"L'Europe et la Question de la Ruhr", Revue de Paris, (March 15, 1923), p. 447. Raymond
Recouly, "La Barrière du Rhin: Droits et devoirs de la France pour assurer sa sécurité,"
La Revue de France (July 1, 1923), pp. 153–175.
[148] Biard D'Aunet, "Règlement de la Paix," Revue Economique Internationale, 2 (June
1923), pp. 7–40.
[149] Arnold Wolfers, Britain and France between Two Wars, 2nd ed. (New York, 1966),
p. 37.
[150] MAE, Ruhr 23, June 13, 1923, fol. 22.

Western Europe and would have meant constant British involvement on the Rhine, a policy which ran contrary to British interests. These facts must have been known to Poincaré and his advisers, but apparently extensive French plans would have one advantage in negotiations with Britain and the other wartime Allies: they could be used in bargaining. Thus, as in 1918, demands for an autonomous Rhineland could be traded against an Anglo-French security pact including both Western and Eastern Europe. Such a pact would have guaranteed French security and the security of her Allies in Eastern Europe against German attacks – a long-standing demand. On the other hand, despite rumors about neutralization of the Rhineland in Britain in 1923, there is no indication that any responsible government agency favored such a policy against German will nor that Great Britain would agree to French security plans, or had any knowledge of French planning. However, all developments seemed to favor Poincaré. He had the Ruhr as a pledge for reparations and interallied debts. He controlled the Rhineland and could wait to see how the population would react to the ever increasing difficulties of the Reich and French pressure through the International Rhineland High Commission. Nevertheless, these supposed advantages were also France's greatest weakness. She was dependent upon British collaboration, a reduction of interallied debts through the United States and Great Britain, international loans for Germany once Berlin agreed to pay reparations according to the French plans and developments in the Rhineland. Poincaré had started on a dangerous course of action when he occupied the Ruhr on the assumption that Germany would yield to force. He could create tremendous difficulties for Germany, but he nevertheless depended on negotiations for the realization of his plans. Success would also depend upon interpretation of French motives.

CHAPTER V

DIPLOMATIC INTERLUDES

I. GERMAN FEELERS IN WASHINGTON AND LONDON

With occupation troops in control of the Ruhr, the German government had
several alternatives: it could attempt to obtain British and American mediation, it could approach France and Belgium, and it could try to use private
feelers in Allied capitals both to investigate chances for mediation and to
extract opinions about practicable options. All alternatives were made use of
in 1923. Several days before the occupation began, the German Minister of
Finance had declared in an interview with the *Berliner Börsen Courier* that
Germany would gladly participate in a world conference on reparations in
Washington. For Hermes, the American Secretary of Commerce, Herbert
Hoover, was the appropriate person for the organization of such a confer-
ence. If Hoover could not accept, the position should be offered to D.
Rockefeller, Henry Ford, or Professor J.W. Jenks who should advise the
American Government.[1] This was an obvious demand for intervention and
Cuno also informed Ambassador Houghton that he himself supported
Hughes' suggestion of December 29 that "men of highest authority in
finance in their respective countries" should be chosen to study reparations –
"men of such prestige, experience and honor that their agreement upon the
amount to be paid, and upon a financial plan working out the payments,
would be accepted throughout the world as the most authoritative expression
available."[2]

Hughes' remarks were however, basically meant for home consumption.
The Secretary of State was disturbed by the fact that members of the Senate
and influential financial and industrial pressure groups had demanded a
more active policy towards Europe.[3] In addition, the speech also forshad-
owed his attitude towards future negotiations.

Later, when France entered the Ruhr, the State Department was protected against
demands for action from certain sections of American opinion, because Hughes

[1] *Berliner Börsen Courier*, No. 9, January 6, 1923.
[2] Gescher. *op. cit.*, p. 137; *Houghton Papers*, Diary, p. 532, January 10, 1923.
[3] Link, *op. cit.*, p. 169.

had made clear in advance what the USA was prepared to do. On the other hand, because of full negotiations with European countries, particularly France, well in advance of the New Haven speech, European countries could not take offense. The informality of the speech also prevented European nations from protesting.[4]

As Hughes had expected, neither France nor Great Britain reacted to his speech before the American Historical Association. It was simply ignored by these powers until the end of 1923.[5] Yet his statement incorporated everything Germany could have hoped for, and increased Cuno's and von Rosenberg's hopes for US intervention. Both were convinced that an international conference on reparations would lead to a reduction of the German liability. On January 27, Cuno visited Houghton and discussed plans for a new building for the US Embassy. This was not the main purpose of the visit, as Houghton soon found out. Cuno urged American intervention for an international conference on reparations. It could start immediately after France had withdrawn her troops from the Ruhr, and apparently Cuno was willing to allow the creation of a customs barrier around the Ruhr in order to facilitate a French retreat.[6] Foreign Minister von Rosenberg was similarly impressed by the New Haven speech, and he praised it as the "only reasonable way out of the problems all Europe was facing."[7]

Besides the German Foreign Office, members of political parties and private citizens also became active in search for mediators. Rudolf Breitscheid of the SPD was convinced that an understanding between Germany and Great Britain was necessary. He visited London in February and urged the Labour Party to use its political influence in Parliament to force the Conservative Government to put pressure upon France. He left with the impression that "insecurity and embarrassment" existed in London because of British impotence vis-à-vis France. Members of the Labour Party and the Liberal Party had both suggested that Germany bring the question of occupation before the League of Nations. Independent Labour favored the International Court in The Hague, and Bonar Law's personal secretary had proposed that Germany offer 1) cash payments to France 2) deliver securities upon agricultural and industrial property, 3) order her finances and agree to

---

[4] *Houghton Papers*, Mitchell Reference File, interview with Hughes, November 4, 1941. The late Professor Mitchell of Princeton University did preliminary research for the editing of Houghton's Berlin Diary. For this purpose he interviewed both Hughes and Houghton several times in 1941.

[5] *Ibid.*, Interview with Hughes, October 30, 1941. Hughes had also informed the British Ambassador to Washington, and he complained in 1941 that Britain did not react.

[6] *Ibid.*, Diary pp. 574 ff., January 27, 1923.

[7] *Ibid.*, Diary, p. 563, February 26, 1923. Link, *op. cit.*, p. 178 f.

Allied controls, and 4) allow a control of Germany's coal production. He also suggested that Germany ask for an international conference.[8]

Similar advice was received from Ambassador D'Abernon who wanted a declaration that international mediation was acceptable. The goal of resistance was an international conference.[9] The same information reached Berlin through Count Harry Kessler a friend of von Schubert in the German Foreign Office, who visited London and met with Liberal and Labour M.P.'s. Kessler's British contacts, John Simon, Fisher, Herbert Asquith, and Ramsay MacDonald all favored a clear statement that the Reich would abide by the decision of an impartial committee of experts. The British opposition parties intended to help, and Sir John Simon promised to submit an inquiry before the House of Commons. In addition, Cuno was advised to write a private letter to Bonar Law stating conditions for negotiations. As soon as this letter had been received, the opposition would immediately act and demand a debate on March 13. Simon also informed the German Ambassador, Sthamer, about his plan, and several days after the first meeting he again demanded that Cuno write a letter to Bonar Law.[10]

German collaboration with the British opposition behind the Government's back would have caused the gravest suspicions in London and might have led to a very embarrassing situation. It was thus better to inform the Foreign Office in advance. Consequently, von Rosenberg asked Sthamer to inquire unofficially whether a letter from Cuno to Bonar Law would be accepted if it contained the following proposals: First, Germany was ready to accept Hughes' plan. The committee of experts should determine a) what Germany had paid until now, b) what Germany must and could pay, and c) in which way payments could be made. Second, after the expert commission had reached a decision about these questions, Germany would try to raise an international loan. Every guarantee considered necessary by the loan consortium would be granted. Third, agricultural and industrial property would also be used as securities. An abandonment of passive resistance

---

[8] "Note Breitscheid," February 21, 1923, *ibid.*, Büro RM, Ruhrgebiet, Besatzungsprobleme, D 636543–548. "Zusammenstellung der von englischer Seite gegebenen Anregungen für Verhandlungen zwischen Deutschland und Frankreich," Breitscheid, February 21, 1923, *ibid.*, Handakten Direktoren, Schriftverkehr, L 418768 ff.

[9] *Ibid.*, L 418771, February 15, and L 418773, February 22, 1923. Report about a meeting between Lord D'Abernon and von Rheinbaben, February 27, 1923, *ibid.*, L 418780.

[10] Kessler-von Schubert, March 1, 1923, *ibid.*, L 418806 f. Sthamer-AA, March 1, 1923, *ibid.*, L 418801 f. Kessler-von Schubert, March 8, 1923, *ibid.*, L 418764 f. Karl von Schubert was director of the "Abteilung III" (Great Britain, America). For further contacts *ibid.*, Büro RM, Reparationen, February 28, 1923, D 719043 and *ibid.*, W. Rep., Besetzung des Ruhrgebietes, February 20, 1923, No. 20.

however was only possible if the status quo ante was established.[11] Although von Rosenberg's questions originated in Simon's suggestions, it is difficult to believe that the Foreign Minister really thought that the incorporation of French withdrawal as a precondition left a chance for talks. Nevertheless, Sthamer went to see Curzon, but since the Foreign Secretary was absent, he met Sir Eyre Crowe instead, who was sceptical of this proposal. A letter from Cuno, the undersecretary argued, would be very embarrassing to Bonar Law since Poincaré did not want intervention. However, he promised to let the Ambassador know the opinion of the British government as soon as he had contacted Curzon.[12] Despite this discouraging news, Cuno, who had also sent A. von Holtzendorff, head of the Hapag office in Berlin, to London to investigate British opinion, wrote a letter to Bonar Law stating that it had always been his intention to keep the economic questions of reparations apart from political controversies. Reparations should be dealt with according to the plan Sthamer had suggested at the Foreign Office. The government would provide the appropriate measures and laws to guarantee the support of this policy by German industry. With this letter Sthamer again attempted to contact Curzon, but failed to see him before the debate.[13]

The parliamentary debate took place on March 13, and Sir John Simon, demanding British intervention, inquired whether Germany was willing to negotiate. But since Bonar Law had not received Cuno's letter, it was easy to answer Simon.

The German attempt to collaborate with the opposition against the Conservative government had failed.[14] On March 14, Sthamer was finally able to deliver his letter. But even now Curzon did not accept it, and finally Sthamer only left a note. Though Curzon did not want to give any advice at all, he urged Germany to take the first step, since neither Britain nor anybody else could help. Cuno should make a reasonable offer and address it to all Allies; any other action would only create suspicion in France.[15] The next day Sthamer met both Curzon and Bonar Law, and the Prime Minister did

[11] Rosenberg-Sthamer, March 9, 1923, *PA AA*, Büro RM, Internationale Geschäftsleutekonferenz, D 739490.

[12] Sthamer-von Rosenberg, March 10, 1923, *ibid.*, D 739501. Cf. *FO.*, 371/8632, C 4876, March 12, 1923.

[13] *FO.*, 371/8626, C 1067, January 18, and C 1549, January 22. For von Holzendorff's reports cf. "Bericht über Aufenthalt in London," March 4, 1923, *PA AA*, Büro RM, Ruhrgebiet, Besatzungsprobleme, D 636806 ff. Cuno-Bonar Law, March 11, 1923, *ibid.*, Handakten, Direktoren, Schriftverkehr. L 418758.

[14] Harry Graf Kessler, *op. cit.*, p. 368.

[15] March 14, 1923, *PA AA*, Büro RM, Internationale Geschäftsleutekonferenz, D 739540 ff. For further contacts see especially Dufour-Ferroncea nd Kessler *ibid.*, Handakten Direktoren, Schriftverkehr.

not conceal his disappointment about the German note. It was simply insufficient – only the acceptance of his January proposal, Bonar Law felt, might open negotiations. Furthermore, the Germans would have to think about French security. This might include the demilitarization of the left bank of the Rhine and the control of the railways, League of Nation's control being sufficient.[16]

Considering Poincaré's rejection of Bonar Law's plan in January his proposal was hardly realistic, although a German acceptance might have created the basis for further cooperation despite strong pro-French forces in the British cabinet. On the other hand, Poincaré would have regarded any intervention as an "unfriendly act."[17] However, von Rosenberg also tried to sell his plan in Washington and informed both Houghton on March 3, and Hughes on March 16, of Cuno's letter. Although the information was to be kept confidential rumors about Anglo-American intervention were soon being spread. The American Secretary of State who believed that von Rosenberg was behind this leak was furious. The impression that the United States was siding with Germany could not be tolerated. To him there would have to be a "different disposition on both sides" before any impartial committee could be formed and before America would intervene.[18] Whether von Rosenberg, the German Embassy in Washington, American journalists in Berlin, or even members of the British opposition were behind these leaks is unimportant. But on March 14, Kessler had informed Simon about Cuno's letter. Simon immediately took Kessler to see Asquith, and the leader of the Liberal Party suggested a modification of Cuno's offer: occupation troops should be allowed to remain in the Ruhr until the banker's committee had reached an agreement upon a loan for Germany. This was a reasonable suggestion, but it was rejected by von Rosenberg, along with the Bonar Law plan.[19]

Attempts to open negotiations were also made along similar lines through the Pope, but they were likewise unsuccessful.[20] Despite the rejection of

---

[16] Sthamer-AA, March 16, 1923, *ibid.*, Büro RM, Internationale Geschäftsleutekonferenz, D 739558.

[17] Poincaré, March 10, 1923, *MAE*, Ruhr 13, fol. 94.

[18] Cf. the discussions between the German Ambassador in Washington and Hughes, February 24, 28, March, 16, 19, 23, 1923, *Hughes Papers*, 175, Folder 75 b, Germany. Also Gescher, *op. cit.*, pp. 168–170. Link, *op. cit.*, p. 181. For Houghton's many contacts with Cuno and Rosenberg cf. *Houghton Papers*, Diary, January 27, 28, February 6, 26, March 3, 15, 17, 18, 21, 25, 1923.

[19] Graf Kessler, *op. cit.*, pp. 366–373, p. 377. Kessler, March 15, 1923, *PA AA*, Handakten Direktoren, Schriftverkehr, L 418 724 ff. 1. Rosenberg-Sthamer, March 20, 1923, *ibid.*, Büro RM, Internationale Geschäftsleutekonferenz, D 73960 ff. White, *op. cit.*, p. 71.

mediation in London and Washington, von Rosenberg was not willing to deal directly with France, however, as this would have meant capitulation and total dependence on France.[21] On the other hand, he could again and again repeat demands for an international conference. The inquiry of the opposition in the British Parliament had reconfirmed von Rosenberg's expectation that changes might be forthcoming. Important parts of the British public and Parliament were growing impatient about the inactivity of the Conservative government, but opinions in the cabinet still wavered between different alternatives.[22] The Governor of the Bank of England, always prepared to give advice to German visitors, was rather pessimistic. Bonar Law, he informed the Counsellor of the German Embassy, could not intervene because the Cabinet was paralyzed due to a conflict between a pro-French and pro-German wing. On the other hand, Norman was convinced that Berlin could not make an offer which would be acceptable to France.[23] Lord D'Abernon was also of the opinion that nothing would satisfy France. Any German proposal with a fixed amount was pure nonsense. The international money market would never yield more than 2 billion gold marks yearly.[24] With the British cabinet divided, and the rather pessimistic estimates for a loan, Germany had to wait until a better opportunity for British intervention came about.

What the Germans could not know was that, despite his indignant rejection of mediation, Curzon obviously pushed by parliamentary events had tried to extract more information from Paris. Though he was desirous of preserving "benevolent neutrality," he warned the French that growing opposition in Parliament might necessitate a clear statement in the House of Commons. Before he made a speech, he wanted to know more about French goals.[25] But Poincaré was as intransigent as ever. A modification of the original sum (i.e. 132 billions) was impossible, but if interallied debts were cancelled, France would yield part of her receipts from the C-bonds. As to the occupation of the Ruhr, France would remain until she had been paid. "France and Belgium had gone into the Ruhr to obtain a definite regulation of reparations." When Curzon received this note, he was obvious-

[20] Cf. *ibid.*, Büro RM, Kurie, especially D 701542–566.

[21] Hoesch-AA, March 31, 1923, *ibid.*, W. Rep. Besetzung des Ruhrgebiets, No. 530 "Unsere Aussichten im Ruhrkonflikt."

[22] Maurice Cowling, *The Impact of Labour 1920–1924* (Cambridge, 1971), p. 303.

[23] Dufour-Feronce-von Schubert, March 24, 1923, *PA AA*, Handakten Direktoren, Schriftverkehr, L 418889. Sthamer-AA, March 20, 1923, *ibid.*, Büro RM, Reparationen, D 719104.

[24] Kessler, *op. cit.*, pp. 387 ff.

[25] Saint-Aulaire-Poincaré, March 20, 1923, *MAE*, Ruhr 16, fol. 112 f.

ly disappointed, but Saint-Aulaire begged him not to say anything in Parliament that might stimulate German resistance.[26] Although German feelers in London had failed, the changing atmosphere in London caused concern in Paris. Poincaré decided to send the former Minister of Reconstruction Louis Loucheur to London, to investigate the British attitude.

2. THE LOUCHEUR MISSION

In a speech before the *Association des producteurs des Alpes Françaises* in Grenoble, Loucheur had demanded on March 18, 1923 that the Rhineland ought to become a pledge for French security; he had suggested that this could be obtained through the expulsion of Prussian civil servants and the creation of an autonomous state within the Reich. Four days later, Loucheur met the Minister of Public Works, Le Trocquer, who suggested (upon Poincaré's initiative) that he visit London unofficially. Le Trocquer also arranged meetings with Millerand and Poincaré.[27] In his interlocution with Millerand, Loucheur developed a plan which he intended to discuss in London. It provided that 1) Germany pay France 26 billion gold marks in addition to whatever Britain and the United States would ask from France in interallied debts; 2) the Reich was to receive a moratorium in return for submitting to a control of her finances, for abandoning passive resistance, and for delivering guarantees. After this program had been implemented the Ruhr would be evacuated in stages according to reparations payment; 3) the Rhineland was to be demilitarized and separated from Prussia, while it should remain part of the Reich. The Rhineland as well as the Rhenish railway system were to be supervised by the League of Nations. Millerand endorsed the plan and asked Loucheur to include the creation of a separate Saar state. With the exception of Millerand's proposal, Poincaré approved of Loucheur's plan when they met the next day, and he provided him with a diplomatic passport.[28]

Loucheur went to London where he met Baldwin, Lloyd George and MacDonald. Although nobody suggested that France leave the Ruhr without a settlement of reparations, the security proposals were not accepted

[26] Poincaré-Saint-Aulaire, March 22, 1923, *ibid.*, fol. 162 f. Saint-Aulaire-Poincaré, March 27, 1923, *ibid.*, fol. 171 f.
[27] The speech is in *PA AA*, Büro RM, Ruhrgebiet, Besatzungsprobleme, D 637014 f. Louis Loucheur, *Carnets Secrets 1908–1932, présentés et annotés par Jacques de Launay* (Bruxelles, 1962), p. 117 f. Zimmermann, *op. cit.*, pp. 157 f.
[28] Weill-Raynal, *op. cit.*, II, p. 400 f; Loucheur, *op. cit.*, p. 118.

either.[29] When Miles Lampson and Wigram of the Foreign Office examined these proposals, they agreed that France wanted the dissolution of Germany, but fearing its political and social consequences, these officials felt obliged to reject the creation of such a state. Furthermore, they doubted that the League of Nations could control a Rhineland state and the railways. The status of the Saar could not be changed either, since it had been fixed in the Versailles Treaty.[30] Thus, a common Franco-British front could not be established. Even worse, when Loucheur's mission became known, the French press regarded it as a sign that Poincaré had changed his policy, and André Tardieu, always critical of the French Minister President, announced that the government no longer had faith in the Ruhr occupation.[31] The Belgian government, under pressure from a strong Flemish opposition, also resented that it had not been informed.[32] The whole affair proved to be embarrassing to Poincaré and in a number of meetings with Loucheur, representatives of the Paris press, and in his correspondence with London and Brussels, he attempted to reduce the damage this "unofficial inquiry" had done at home and abroad.[33] In communications to Saint-Aulaire and the British Ambassador to Paris, he declared that France didn't want British mediation, as this could only end in a dispute between the powers. The publication of details of Loucheur's proposals furthermore irritated Poincaré, but when the French Ambassador complained about the indiscretion in a meeting with the Prime Minister, Bonar Law – although he regretted publication – warned the French that chaos was approaching fast in Germany and that Cuno was to much engaged to yield now.[34] Both in Germany and France, governments had to take into account public opinion and other pressures.

3. PARLIAMENTARY DISCUSSIONS IN GERMANY

Cuno's reaction was not dissimilar to that of Poincaré when rumors were spread about German feelers in London. The reports led to attacks from the DNVP. Cuno also felt that any sign of weakness threatened the determi-

---

[29] *Ibid.*, pp. 119–120. Cf. *Loucheur Papers*, Box 7, Folder 2, April 10, 1923.

[30] *FO*, 371/8632, C 6300, April 7, 1923, White, *op. cit.*, pp. 76–77.

[31] *FO*, 371/8633, C 6481, April 10, 1923.

[32] Herbette, April 7, 1923, *MAE*, Ruhr 17, fol. 138 ff.

[33] Loucheur, *op. cit.*, pp. 120 ff. Poincaré-Herbette, April 7, 1923, *MAE*, Allemagne 480, fol. 137 f.

[34] *FO*, 311/8633, C 6482. Saint-Aulaire, April 12, 1923, *MAE*, Ruhr 17, fol. 210 f. Poincaré-Saint-Aulaire, April 14, 1923, *ibid.*, Fol. 285 ff.

nation to prolong passive resistance. On a trip through Bavaria, the Chancellor announced that passive resistance would only end after the status quo ante had been reestablished. This statement has to be seen as a direct answer to Loucheur's speech in Grenoble and to rumors about a weakening of resistance.[35] After this speech became known in Berlin, Müller-Franken of the SPD immediately demanded a convocation of the Reichstag Foreign affairs Committee.[36] In the ensuing discussion he agreed with Cuno that evacuation of the Ruhr was the ultimate goal, but warned that Germany had neither the political nor the economic power to force evacuation before negotiations about reparations had started. Breitscheid supported Müller-Franken and warned against prolonging resistance until the next winter or even longer, as Gothein of the DDP had suggested. It was doubtful whether Germany could continue that long. Von Rosenberg's argument that reparations were still the main problem, and that the government had to obtain an agreement on this issue, was contested by both Helfferich (DNVP) and Stresemann (DVP). Both were convinced that France intended to annex the Rhineland, but they drew different conclusions. Helfferich argued that Germany should prepare herself for a long struggle. If the cabinet yielded to French pressure, the Rhineland and the Ruhr would be lost forever, and though they might remain within the Reich, German military and economic sovereignty would be impaired. He criticized the fact that diplomatic relations with France had not been broken off completely and expected British intervention, considering public discussion over an increase of the British Air Force as a good sign for the changing mood in Britain. An increase of the air force could only be directed against France. In contrast to Helfferich, Stresemann did not expect British intervention, but he also opposed unconditional surrender and reasoned that the only way to get France and Belgium out of the Ruhr again was by means of an international discussion of reparations. Stresemann furthermore protected Cuno against attacks from the SPD, informing the committee that the Chancellor had stated his willingness to negotiate even before occupation troops had been withdrawn.[37] Cuno had indeed made a similar statement to the American Ambassador, but information coming out of the Foreign Office spoke a different language, or at least left doubts

[35] PA AA, W. Rep. öffentliche Reden deutscher und fremder Minister zur Reparationsfrage, WTB 678, March 23, 1923. Ibid., WTB 674. Kab. Cuno, No. 103.

[36] Stresemann Nachlaß, vol. 257, March 3, 1923.

[37] Kab. Cuno, No. 109, March 27, 1923. Helfferich probably referred to discussions in March. Cf. Schultheß, 1923, p. 263. Although the British Air Force was enforced against the "strongest Air Force within striking capability of this country," this decision was only made in June. Cab. 24/160, C.P. 270, June 12, 1923, and C.P. 294, June 15, 1923. The increase was discussed in the press at the end of June. The Economist, June 30, 1923, p. 1423, "Air Policy and European Problems."

about the exact procedure of negotiations.[38] For the cabinet it was a difficult situation. It had to find a line between nationalistic pressure from the DNVP and parts of the bourgeois parties demanding a withdrawal of occupation troops before negotiations started and resistance could be given up, and the SPD and the ADGB demanding negotiations while passive resistance was still at its peak.[39]

The increasingly difficult situation of the Reich was clearly recognized in the Chancellory, and already on February 18, Hamm had discussed Germany's alternatives including surrender and military countermeasures, but these discussions only led to a hardening of resistance and increased propaganda against French "imperialism." The cabinet labelled the Ruhr struggle to be a fight for self-determination and right against "nationalistic power politics" and tried to control military organization created by the Right.[40] But the cabinet did not come out with an offer. Instead semi-official contacts to show Germany's readiness for negotiations were established. Cuno travelled into the Ruhr to bolster resistance,[41] while another attempt was made to obtain an international inquiry.

4. THE MEETING OF THE INTERNATIONAL CHAMBER OF COMMERCE IN ROME

The meeting of the International Chamber of Commerce (ICC) in Rome from March 18–24, created a new possibility of discussing reparations with Allied bankers and businessmen. Though Germany was not a member of this organization, through a private American invitation Stinnes, Vögler, Burgers, Haniel, von Simson and Urbig went to Rome. The Foreign Office paid the costs for this trip and asked the German Ambassador in Rome to help the delegation in any way possible.[42] Already in December 1922, Berlin had tried to obtain an estimate of Germany's capacity to pay by members of the US Chamber of Commerce, but the intervention of Hughes and later

[38] *Houghton Papers*, Diary pp. 574 ff., January 27, 1923. *Kab. Cuno*, No. 130.
[39] Leipart-Cuno, February 26, 1923, *BA* 43 I/210, p. 59. *Ibid.*, March 28, p. 206. *Kab. Cuno*, No. January 25, 1923. *RT*, vol. 358, pp. 9526 ff, debate of January 26.
[40] *Kab. Cuno*, No. 78, February 1923. *Ibid.*, No. 82, "Der Reichskanzler an den Pressechef der Reichsregierung," February 23, 1923.
[41] *Ibid.*, No. 65, February 6, 1923. Weissmann, February 7, 1923, *BA*, 43I/212. Spethmann, *op. cit.*, IV, pp. 122 ff.
[42] *PA AA*, Büro RM, Ruhrgebiet, Besatzungsprobleme, D 637029. See especially Warburg's letter to Rosenberg in which he rejected participation and warned that the ICC could not influence politics. Rosenberg-Warburg, March 10, and Warburg-Rosenberg, March 12, 1923, *ibid.*, Sonderreferat W., Die Aktion der amerikanischen Handelskammer.

developments at the Paris conference had rendered such an investigation impossible.[43] One member of the US Chamber of Commerce, Fred I. Kent of the Bankers Trust Company, was especially disappointed about non-intervention, feeling that the United States could, through partly cancelling Allied war debts, bring about economic peace in Europe. Though he did not intend to create any difficulties for the Department of State, Kent was determined to make a speech in Rome along these lines. This intention, though he would speak as a private citizen, might not only have led to a rebuttal from the Department of State, but might also have annoyed Poincaré, if he had not been very careful to explain his plan as a private initiative.[44] Since his speech before the ICC in Rome led to his intervention in the Franco-German conflict and to several meetings with Cuno and French officials, including Poincaré, it is justifiable to discuss it here at length.

Since the United States was also affected by the situation in Europe, Kent suggested, in contrast to the well-known position of the Department of State, that a portion of interallied debts could be cancelled in exchange for agreements which would place Europe on a sound economic basis again. Against criticism from Washington, he reasoned that the buying power of Europe would far outweigh the outstanding debts from the Liberty Bonds. However, a cancellation of these debts would not be possible without certain compensations from the European countries. "Mere cancellation would have a tendency to encourage those forces in Europe which tend to extravagance in government expenditure in all of its departments, civil and military." As to the German situation, where civil government spending was excessive, he argued that it had to obtain a loan and give guarantees, while negotiations on interallied debts should be conducted simultaneously. With this statement, he had focused upon the real issue. Without a reduction of interallied debts France was not willing to reduce German reparations. On the other hand, without a reduction of the German liability, international finance was not willing to grant a loan to the Reich. This vicious circle could only be broken if the United States agreed to a cancellation of the debts, or if Poincaré allowed the fixing of German debt by an international expert committee. Kent admitted that the American government would not participate in negotiations at the moment. The intention of his speech was not immediate action, but he hoped to arouse the US public about the European stalemate. And if the American public reacted favorably to his speech, members of the new Congress might be influenced to propose a policy supporting American

---

[43] *Ibid.*,

[44] Kent-Hughes, February 9 and 20, 1923, and Seward Prosser-Kent, March 7, 1923, *Kent Papers*, Correspondence.

intervention in Europe. But since it would only convene in December, these statements would, he hoped, "warrant the Administration in undertaking negotiations subject to later ratification by Congress." An international committee of financial experts created by the ICC would greatly facilitate this task.[45]

Kent had already prepared a motion in advance which he submitted after his speech. It demanded a study of reparations, interallied debts, unbalanced government budgets and inflation, international credit, and abnormal exchange fluctuations. He recognized that it was inopportune to propose intervention of the ICC in a settlement between Germany and the Allies, but believed that at the proper time governments "may wish to avail themselves of the practical experience of business."[46] When the memorandum was discussed by the assembly, Sir Felix Schuster (Chairman of the Committee of London Banker's Clearing House), Maurice Despret (President of the Bank of Brussels), and representatives from Sweden, the Netherlands, and Italy supported the motion, while Maurice Lewandowski (Director of the *Comptoir National d'Escompte*, Paris) had certain reservations and stressed that the French government was solely responsible for political questions, but he also supported the motion which was accordingly passed.[47]

While the congress went on the German delegation had several meetings with the American members.[48] When both, the German Ambassador and the delegation found the resolution entirely acceptable, Kent decided to mediate between Germany and France. Two reasons seem to have influenced this decision. First, after his meeting with the German group, he had received information about their proposal for negotiations. Second, he had met Mussolini and officials of the French Embassy in Rome, and the French Ambassador had asked Poincaré to receive Kent in Paris, although he knew that several other members of the US delegation had felt that Kent had gone too far in his proposal.[49]

[45] "Speech Rome Meeting International Chamber of Commerce, March 1923," *ibid.*, Folder 1923.

[46] *Ibid.*, p. 14.

[47] "Proceedings of the Second Congress, Rome, March 18–24, 1923," *ibid.*, Reports, International Chamber of Commerce. Sir Felix Schuster suggested to hold a diplomatic and a financial conference.

[48] "Aufzeichnung Urbig über Romreise," April 4, 1923, *PA AA*, W. Rep., Amerikanische Vermittlung in der Reparationsfrage. Cf. Bergen-AA, March 26, 1923, *ibid.*, Büro RM, Reparationen, D 719122. Urbig-Kent, March 27, 1923, *ibid.*, Sonderreferat W., Die Internationale Handelskammer.

[49] Barrère-Poincaré, March 26 and 27, 1923, *MAE*. Allemagne 480, fol. 87 ff. Poincaré notified Barrère that he did not want to have anything to do with Stinnes. But when he was informed that Kent would not do anything against French interests, he seems to have changed his position.

Kent was not an unknown person in Paris. On behalf of the Bankers Trust Company he had been in the French capital at the end of 1919 to handle financial transactions between France and the United States. He had spent 10 months in Paris, and still had many acquaintances in governmental and financial circles.[50] Before he visited Paris, he travelled to Lausanne and Amsterdam where he met Dutch bankers (Vissering and Ter Meulen) and explained his plan.[51] In the meantime, Kent's friends in Paris had also been active. When he arrived on April 19, Paul de Vallombrosa of the Bankers Trust Office in Paris had arranged a meeting with Lucien Dior, the French Minister of Commerce. Kent also met Poincaré, who thanked him for his valuable services in Rome and made it clear that Cuno had to make a direct offer to France.[52]

When Kent offered to visit Berlin, Poincaré accepted. But he had learned from the outcry over Loucheur's mission and wrote a letter to be published if rumors should start, maintaining that he had not seen Kent.[53] After the American banker had agreed to this procedure, the French Minister explained his reparation and security demands: First, Germany should offer to pay the cost of reconstructing the devastated regions, estimated at 29–30 billion gold marks. Second, the Reich should pay any part of French debts to Britain and the United States that was not remitted by these countries. Third, in return the Ruhr was to be evacuated in three stages according to payments. Fourth, since France wanted to prevent any future war upon her territory but had lost all confidence in Germany, had no treaty with her Allies, and was unable to bear the burden of continued armament, the left bank of the Rhine should be controlled by an international police force. The Rhineland should not belong to any country, but might come under control of the League. Fifth, French financial interests in the Ruhr were necessary to "enable France to get coke with certainty." German interests in French industry were also possible in order to develop an exchange of coke and minerals. The purpose of this last demand, Poincaré explained to Kent, was to prevent "unfair competition" but not "to obtain unfair advantages." A majority interest was not requested, and an exchange of coke and minerals

[50] Material about Kent's stay in Paris in 1919 and 1920 is in *Kent Papers*, Box Writings 1909–1923.

[51] *Ibid.*

[52] Dior-Kent, April 19, 1923, *ibid.*, Correspondence, Alphabetical File, Foreign Correspondence 1919–1923. Poincaré-Kent, April 20, 1923, *ibid.*

[53] *Ibid.*, The respective paragraph reads: "J'ai appris le court séjour que vous faisiez parmi nous, et je tiens à vous dire combien je regrette qu'il ne me soit pas possible de vous recevoir." However, in a note Kent explains the origin of this letter. See *ibid.*, Carbon Copy, Economic conditions.

would be one "more way to keep peace as German commercial and industrial interests would not desire war under such conditions."[154]

Though this plan would have meant complete German submission, and might even have been opposed by Britain as later developments show, Kent went to Berlin. On April 24, he informally told Ambassador Houghton about his intentions,[55] and the next morning he met Cuno for $1^1/_2$ hours.[56] He also saw Bergmann, the bankers Wassermann, Urbig, Melchior and others and upon Cuno's suggestion he talked to von Maltzan of the Foreign Office, Hermes, and former Chancellor Wirth. He had a second conversation with Cuno and Hermes, and according to Kent they agreed to his plans.[57] However, it is doubtful whether he informed Cuno about all of Poincaré's demands. More likely, he omitted the most disagreeable section on the future of the Rhineland and suggested to his German contacts that, if the establishment of peaceful conditions throughout Europe were granted, an international loan committee "could immediately borrow sufficient amounts to make possible some substantial payments to France that would warrant her in withdrawing her troops from the Ruhr ..."[58] This was a wild speculation, contrary to every other suggestion received in Germany. Not only bankers but also the American Ambassador doubted that a loan to cover reparations was possible. Houghton, who was to leave Germany for a private visit in the United States, met von Maltzan prior to his departure and confirmed Kent's contacts with Poincaré. The American banker, Houghton felt, had some very good ideas about reparations, but when von Maltzan inquired about the amount Germany should offer, he considered any figure above 20 billions as a financially impracticable offer. It was better to leave the amount open and have it fixed by the banker's committee which would issue the loan. This committee, Houghton reasoned, would not ask more from Germany than could be raised. Since France had a hysterical fear of Germany, he advised an offer of cooperation between the two industries. As an ad-

[54] *Ibid.*, Writings, 1919–1923. This folder contains Kent's handwritten original of French conditions. The same folder has also several undated typed notes which give further information about Kent's intentions and his motives.

[55] *Houghton Papers*, Diary, p. 699, April 24, 1923.

[56] Kent-Seward, Prosser, May 5, 1923, *Kent Papers*, Correspondence 1919–1923.

[57] Kent-Cuno, April 27, 1923, *ibid.* Also Kent-Warburg, May 9, 1923, *ibid.*, Correspondence, Alphabetical File. According to this letter Kent also met Helfferich, von Gwinner, Blunzig, and von Simson.

[58] Kent-Cuno, April 27, 1923, *ibid.*, Correspondence 1919–1923. This letter contains several proposals based on Poincaré's suggestions. A detailed copy of the plan which was probably shown to Cuno or served as note for Kent's discussion is in *ibid.*, Writings 1919–1923. The memo is undated.

ditional security, Cuno should propose a peace treaty for 99 years and a pact of guarantees.[59]

The comparison between Kent's plan and Houghton's proposal shows the German dilemma. Though both suggested that a peaceful understanding including a peace pact was necessary, they differed as to the amount of reparations. Kent demanded a German offer with a fixed amount as had been requested by Poincaré; Houghton believed that such a procedure was unwise. A similar opinion was held by Lord Curzon. The British Foreign Secretary had made a speech in the House of Lords, demanding that Germany declare her readiness to pay the debts and offer securities. The amount to be paid should be fixed by an international committee.[60]

5. PRIVATE INITIATIVES OF GERMAN INDUSTRY

Thus by the middle of April 1923, demands for a German offer were increasing and, dissatisfied with the Foreign Office reliance upon Britain, representatives of German industry who felt that direct negotiations with France were of greater importance than waiting for British intervention became active, an approach Melchior had already suggested in February.[61] In a meeting with the French Consul at Düsseldorf, Otto Wolff and Werner Carp of the Phoenix AG für Bergbau- und Hüttenbetriebe criticized Cuno's inactivity. The purpose of their visit was to contact influential French industrialists with close connections with the French government. If the first encounter could become a success, official negotiations between industries could start at Düsseldorf and Cuno would be informed.[62] Poincaré, however, was unwilling to deal with industry now. He wanted a complete German submission.[63]

Several members of the French opposition as well as some industrialists were at least willing to talk to the Germans. Especially in Lorraine industrial circles, opposition to Poincaré had grown. As the result of resistance, Lorraine industry no longer received sufficient coke supplies from the Ruhr,

[59] "Aufzeichnung Maltzan," April 27, 1923, *PA AA*, Büro RM, Reparationen, D 719497.

[60] White, *op. cit.*, p. 82; Gescher, *op. cit.*, p. 171. Curzon's speech was made on April 20.

[61] Melchior-Cuno, February 2, 1923, *PA AA*, Büro RM, Ruhrgebiet Besatzungprobleme, D 636705.

[62] Genoyer-Paris, April 16, 1923, *MAE*, Allemagne 480, fol. 44.

[63] Already on March 15, Poincaré had informed Tirard that he was against a meeting between Stinnes and Paul Reynaud. *Ibid.*, fol. 40.

and more and more blast furnaces had to be blown out.[64] Contacts between German and French heavy industry were established through Stinnes' representative in Paris and a correspondent of the Stinnes-owned paper DAZ.[65] According to information received in Berlin, the *Comité des Forges* was split, Pinot and Schneider-Creusot supporting Poincaré, while Loucheur, de Wendel and other Lorraine industrialists took a more conciliatory attitude towards Germany.[66] Whatever the value of this information, Dr. Schmidt of the Stinnes bureau in Paris met with several members of the *Comité des Forges* in April. And Gustav Hervé, editor of *La Victoire*, informed Millerand about industrial feelers.[67] Though it cannot be said with certainty what Stinnes, who had severely criticized Cuno's reliance upon England and the United States,[68], really wanted, it seems that he was prepared to reach an understanding with France on the exchange of coal and iron. On the other hand, the Germans also hoped to isolate Poincaré, but neither Millerand, Herriot, or Loucheur, who had first been willing to meet Stinnes' representative, but then only sent a secretary, were willing to collaborate.[69] However, Hervé claimed that Millerand had informed him about Poincaré's reparation plans.

First, France expected to obtain the A- and B-bonds and a remission of her war debts by the United States and England. Second, after the payment of certain sums, the Ruhr would be evacuated with the exception of Essen, where French troops would remain until reparations had been paid. Third, for security reasons France demanded the internationalization of the Rhenish railway system and the creation of a Rhenish state within the Reich. This state would also have to include territory on the right bank of the Rhine.[70]

These demands must have confirmed Berlin's fears about French intentions in the Rhineland. At the same time, under pressure from the SPD, the ADGB, and representatives of the bourgeois parties (among them

[64] G.H. Bousquet, "Die wirtschaftlichen Wirkungen der Ruhrbesetzung auf Frankreich," *Ruhrbesetzung*, pp. 39–42. "La dissension au sein du Comité des Forges," Journal de Commerce, May 9, 1923, *BA*, 431/38.

[65] Zimmermann, *Deutsche Außenpolitik*, pp. 168–170. Hoesch-Rosenberg, March 20, 1923, *PA AA*, Büro RM, Reparationen, 5 secr., D 736 316 f. *Ibid.*, March 21, 1923, D 736349 f. *Ibid.*, April 24, 1923, D 736370 ff. This last report appears to be the most important.

[66] "Die Bedenken der französischen Industrie," March 12, 1923, *ibid.*, W. Rep. Besetzung des Ruhrgebietes, H 276819.

[67] Hoesch-Rosenberg, April 24, 1923, *ibid.*, Büro RM, Reparationen. 5 secr. D 736370 f.

[68] Stresemann, *op. cit.*, I, pp. 42–44. For Stinnes see also his correspondence with Arnold Rechberg, *PA AA*, Büro RM, Reparationen, 5 secr., D 736218 ff.

[69] Hoesch-Rosenberg, April 26, 27, and 30, 1923, *ibid.*, D 736735 ff. Zimmermann, *op. cit.*, p. 171.

[70] Hoesch-Rosenberg, April 24, 1923, *ibid.*, D 736374.

Gustav Stresemann), faced with an ever deteriorating economic situation and fearing Anglo-French rapprochement after the Loucheur mission, Cuno sent Paul Reusch, director of the Gutehoffnungshütte and an old acquaintance from the Chancellor's days in the HAPAG to London, the day after the Reichstag debate on April 16. Reusch was to contact the British Prime Minister through the former Minister of Transport in the Lloyd George Cabinet, Sir E. Geddes, and inform Bonar Law that Germany could not hold out for ever. Passive resistance would only last weeks, not months. Since the Reich was spending her revenues on resistance, thus reducing the amount available for reparations, it was in Britain's own interest to intervene now. Cuno again proposed that Britain and the United States call an international conference to fix reparations. A final sum could not yet be mentioned, but until the experts decided upon a fixed amount, he offered 16 billion gold marks to be raised immediately through a loan. The simultaneous abandonment of resistance and the beginning of evacuation could either begin after the Hughes proposal had been accepted by all the powers or after Germany and France had agreed to it. Cuno hoped that such a provisional settlement could be obtained within 4 to 6 weeks. At the same time deliveries would be resumed, and guarantees for a loan would also be given. The exact details of these guarantees should be left to the loan committee.[71]

This proposal had one serious weakness: the amount offered was too low, even if future payments were left to the decision of the loan committee. Poincaré could never have accepted it, since he had always demanded the complete costs for reconstruction and everything that the Allies would demand from France for interallied debts. On the other hand, the simultaneous abandonment of resistance and occupation was certainly an interesting offer, and Britain might have been willing to support it. However, in this context, it should not be forgotten that Cuno's proposal, if taken up, would certainly have created great difficulties with the nationalists at home. Nevertheless it was an important improvement. Despite domestic opposition from the Right, Cuno was prepared to deal with the Allies.

But the Chancellor's hopes for British interventions were futile. He soon learned that Curzon's speech in which he had suggested that Germany take the first step and submit a plan to France and Belgium did not signalize a

---

[71] *Kab. Cuno*, No. 133, April 20, 1923. Hamm, the Secretary of State in the Chancellory, travelled to The Hague and handed Reusch a letter from Cuno for his London contacts. It is possible that this new attempt was the results of a cabinet meeting on April 17, when the necessity of a German note had been discussed, *ibid.*, No. 125, April 14, 1923. Cf. Reusch-Cuno, April 17, 1923, *HA GHH* 400101290/119. Reusch-Cuno, April 22, 1923, *ibid.*

change of policy, but was basically meant to quieten domestic criticism of the inactivity of the Conservative cabinet in the reparation issue.[72] But as soon as Curzon's speech had become known in Paris, opposition to British intervention showed. According to *Le Matin* the French cabinet decided on April 26 that Germany had to submit proposals without any preconditions. The Reich had rebelled against the Versailles Treaty and before passive resistance was abandoned, any discussion of German proposals was out of the question. Now Curzon informed Sthamer that a note to Britain would not change anything.[73] Thus all efforts had failed. Neither official diplomatic contacts nor Cuno's private feelers, nor Stinnes' approach had led to foreign intervention. These different feelers may have even contributed to confusion both in Berlin and abroad. Under these circumstances, the Foreign Office decided to submit an official plan.

6. PREPARATIONS FOR THE GERMAN NOTE OF MAY 2

Discussions in the cabinet and in the Foreign Office soon showed that unanimity did not exist. The Foreign Office tried to develop a plan out of the different pieces of information received during the last months. Von Maltzan discussed a German proposal at a dinner with Hilferding, Stresemann, Bernard, and Lord D'Abernon, suggesting a compromise as to the amount of reparations. Germany would mention the highest figure deemed possible, but as a sign of her willingness to come to an agreement, she would leave it to international authorities mentioned by Curzon to fix the exact amount. Breitscheid, Stresemann, and the British Ambassador were impressed by this idea.[74]

But when discussions were resumed in the Cabinet, other differences became apparent. The Minister of Transport was opposed to using the railway system as guarantee. He feared that a mortgaging of the railways would endanger the Reich's tariff sovereignty and thus allow Allied influence on Germany's economic autonomy.[75] Foreign Minister von Rosenberg did not

---

[72] Gescher, *op. cit.*, pp. 172 ff. Reusch-Cuno, personally, April 26, 1923, *PA AA*, Büro RM, Reparationen D 719468. Sthamer-von Schubert, April 27, 1923, *ibid.*, Büro RM, Ruhrgebiet, Besatzungsprobleme, D 638403.

[73] *Le Matin*, April 27, 1923; Hoesch-AA, April 27, 1923, *ibid.*, Büro RM., Reparationen, D 719506.

[74] "Aufzeichnung Maltzan," April 27, 1923 *ibid.*, D 719495 f. Sthamer had also reported from London that Lampson and Vansittart of the Foreign Office had suggested that it was better not to offer anything at all, if a substantial amount could not be offered.

[75] *Kab. Cuno*, No. 140, April 25, 1923.

intend to submit an acceptable offer at all. He regarded the note as a tactical step to stress the economic absurdity of the Franco-Belgian action, and foster alienation between Belgium and France on one side and France and Great Britain on the other. The note was also to serve a domestic purpose. If the government had shown its willingness to negotiate, growing domestic criticism from the SPD and the ADGB that passive resistance did not bring any solution, would be silenced. Becker, the Minister of Economics, was also opposed to placing the railway into allied hands as a mortgage. He also objected to an extension of the German offer of January 2, which had mentioned 30 billion gold marks, while Brauns, Luther, Gessler, and Secretary of State Schröder representing the Minister of Finance, were prepared to go higher than this amount.[76]

No final decision was made at this meeting, but von Rosenberg was asked to prepare a note. The Foreign Office could refer back to a number of plans which had been developed since the fiasco of the German plan in January. One important proposal had tried to find a middle line between British and Italian plans mentioned at the Allied conference in January.[77] Moritz Bonn, Carl Melchior, and the legal expert of the Foreign Office, Gaus, had submitted proposals.[78] Eduard Hamm of the Chancellor's Office had summarized these suggestions in a paper which dealt with the amount of reparations, mortgages upon state and private property (the most important being the mortgaging of the Reichsbahn) stabilization of the currency and a security pact.[79] However, when the cabinet discussed a draft proposal which had been written by Carl Bergmann, it did not even receive written copies, but had to rely on von Rosenberg's explanations. Bergmann's offer provided for 30 billion gold marks payable through loans. Twenty billions (15 billions in cash and 5 billions for deliveries in kind) were to be issued until 1927, the remaining ten billions would follow in two instalments. After a moratorium of four years, Germany would thus have to pay 1.2 billions per year. This was a significant improvement over the January plan, since, including interest, the nominal value of the sum could amount to nearly 40 billions. However, Cuno, Becker, and von Rosenberg objected; they favored the old January plan, while Brauns, Albert and Schröder of the

[76] *Ibid.*, No. 142, April 28, 1923. Becker and von Rosenberg did not want an offer at all. Cf. *ibid.*, No. 125, April, 17, 1923. *Ibid.*, No. 120, April 14, and No. 135, April 21, 1923.

[77] The plan was submitted on February 26, 1923. See *PA AA*, Büro RM, Reparationen, D 718972-992.

[78] *Ibid.*, April 25, 1924, D 719280. "Vorschläge für einen Reparationsplan," *BA.*, 43I/36. Cf. also Richard Merton-Cuno, April 28, and Cuno-Merton, May 5, 1923, *ibid.*

[79] *Kab. Cuno*, No. 122, April 15, 1923.

Ministry of Finance supported Bergmann. Finally the January plan was submitted with several minor modifications. While it had only offered 20 billions and had made the additional 10 billions dependent on the decision of an international committee, the May note offered 30 billions in three instalments. However, since interest for the reimbursement of the loans was to be taken out of the loan itself, the real value of the offer had only been increased from 12 to 15 billion gold marks, while Bonar Law's plan of January 4 under the most favorable conditions for Germany had a real value of at least 25 billions. But even this amount had been rejected by Poincaré and the Germans knew from their contacts in London that Britain also expected more than 30 billions.[80]

Bergmann thus did not have any illusions about the effect of this proposal. On the other hand, although he considered von Rosenberg's proposal insufficient, he was also convinced that Germany could not propose a sum which France would accept.[81] Von Rosenberg and von Maltzan were of the same opinion.[82] When the Minister of Finance returned to Berlin after ten days absence owing to illness, Bergmann and Schröder acquainted him with the details of the plan. Completely dissatisfied with the amount offered, Hermes went to Cuno immediately and suggested changes, but the Chancellor rejected any substantial modifications.[83] Cuno was also opposed to the inclusion of mortgages on private property and political securities for France as suggested by the Prussian Minister President.[84] Not even the mortgaging of the railways to which the Ministry of Transport had finally agreed was incorporated in the note. Instead, only unspecified guarantees were offered. The details were to be left to direct negotiations.

The drafting of the note shows one serious weakness of the cabinet: it did not have a sound parliamentary basis and von Rosenberg, Becker and to a certain extent Cuno, relied upon the support from the DNVP or did at least take into account the attitude of this party to broaden the cabinet's basis as

[80] *Ibid.*, No. 144, April 30, 1923. Sthamer-AA, April 20, 1923, *PA AA*, Büro RM, Reparationen, D 719432 f. Also *ibid.*, D 719440. Oltmann, *op. cit.*, pp. 64 ff.

[81] *Kab. Cuno*, No. 144, April 30, 1923.

[82] Rosenberg-von Neurath, undated, *PA AA*, Büro RM Reparationen, D 719477. Von Maltzan, May 1, 1923, *ibid.*, D 719537. Back from a visit to London Lord D'Abernon mentioned to von Rosenberg on April 18 that France would not accept any sum coming from Germany be it 20, 50, or 70 billions. "Aufzeichnung von Rosenberg," *ibid.*, D 719345.

[83] Bergmann, *op. cit.*, p. 240; *Marx Nachlaß*, III, p. 106 f. Hermes later on maintained that he even considered to resign.

[84] *Kab. Cuno*, No. 145, April 30, 1923.

[85] John G. Williamson, *Karl Helfferich 1872-1924. Economist, Financier, Politician* (Princeton, 1971), pp. 373 ff. Williamson describes Helfferich's relations to Cuno, von Rosenberg, and Becker.

far as possible. On the other hand, in face of information reaching the Foreign Office from London and Paris, it could be argued that any offer but total submission to French demands would fail. In any case, the cabinet tried to obtain support from the Minister Presidents of the German states. Instead of being supported, the proposal was severely criticized by Braun (Prussia), Ulrich (Hesse), Zeigner (Thuringia) and Froelich (Saxony), Hieber (Württemberg) und Remmele (Baden) who were not satisfied, while the Minister President of Bavaria objected to the note arguing that it went too far.[86] When it became known in the press it was also criticized by the Right and the Left.[87]

If Cuno had hoped to obtain a positive answer from the Allies, he was also to be disappointed. After the note had been prepared, he informed Kent, who had remained in Berlin all this time, of the details. Kent immediately warned that the plan would defeat its own purpose, and Cuno, who seems to have had second thoughts about the proposal, asked the American banker to visit Paris "to offset the harm that it might carry." When Kent arrived in Paris, he met Barthou and Seydoux; but all agreed that this note did not offer a basis for negotiations.[88]

When the German note was discussed in the British Foreign Office it was not rejected immediately. Since the last Allied conference in January, the British Treasury had made a new estimate of German capacity and had reached the conclusion that after five months of government spending for passive resistance, the Reich could not pay as much as in January.[89] Sir John Bradbury had revised the original plan, and now he argued in a letter to the Prime Minister that it was "unwise" to ask more than 30–32 billion gold marks real value.[90] After an examination of the financial aspect of the German note, Bradbury and Sir Otto Niemeyer of the Treasury reached the conclusion that an international loan of 20 billions was impossible at the

[86] *Kab. Cuno*, No. 146, May 1 and May 2, 1923. The note is printed in *Ursachen und Folgen*, V, pp. 121–124. The content of the note shows that it was pieced together and tried to satisfy several interests at home and abroad. White, *op. cit.*, p. 85 believes that the German note meant a reduction of the debts from 132 to 30 billions. This is wrong.

[87] White, *op. cit.*, p. 85. The industrial paper *Rheinisch-Westfälische Zeitung*, No. 262, May 3, 1923 also criticized the note. Cuno had endangered German Sovereignty. The KPD organ in the Ruhr, the *Westfälische Arbeiterzeitung*, No. 101, May 3, 1923 attacked Cuno who had capitulated before foreign imperialists. This was high treason and the working class had to overthrow Cuno and then unite with the Soviet Union.

[88] Kent-Warburg, May 9, 1923, *Kent Papers*, Correspondence, Alphabetical File. Kent-Prosser, May 28, 1923, *ibid.*, Foreign Correspondence 1919–1923. An understanding seems to have existed between Cuno and Kent according to which Kent was to inform his Paris partners that Cuno wanted an international conference.

[89] *FO*, 371/8633, C 7301, April 18, 1923. Memo Niemeyer.

[90] Bradbury-Bonar Law, April 23, 1923, *ibid.*, C 7649.

moment. But even though the amount offered was only sixty percent of the original Bonar Law plan, they suggested taking Cuno's note as a "jumping point" for further discussions with Germany.[91] The Senior Officers in the Foreign Office also felt that the note was the first sign of a possible understanding and ordered the British Ambassador to Paris to ask for an audience at the Quai d'Orsay in order to formulate a common answer of the Allies. Though the offer was insufficient, it might lead to a further exchange of notes and, hopefully, to a final solution.[92]

The outcome of Crewe's consultations at the Quai d'Orsay did not come as a surprise: Poincaré simply refused any concerted action with Great Britain.[93] Obviously he feared being drawn into negotiations where France might be as isolated as in August 1922, when Belgium, Italy and Britain had rejected all French proposals for a settlement of reparations and a control of German industry and finance as unfeasible.[94] Poincaré was especially indignant about these inquiries, since Saint-Aulaire had already told Crowe on April 30 that the German note would be a farce. "Whatever it was, it would not be accepted." France had a veto in all questions concerning the Ruhr, and Britain had no right to complain about the French attitude since she had done the same in Syria and the Orient.[95]

Without French approval, mediation was thus impossible. However, Britain was no longer as isolated as in January. British-Italian negotiations had been going on in London for some time. An Italian delegation in London discussed a variety of topics including the Italian debts to Great Britain, German debts to Italy, and British support for Italy in financial questions. Though these talks had not been concluded the powers reached an understanding about the necessity of a new German offer.[96] At the moment, however, the Foreign Office was not satisfied with the German note. This feeling of irritation increased when Sthamer explained to Crowe on May 6, that the Chancellor was ready to go beyond the 30 billions mentioned. The amount had only been named as a basis for discussions. Crowe was simply disgusted with the quality of the note. He now told Sthamer that Cuno "could not be

[91] *Ibid.*, 8634, C 7984, May 4, 1923.
[92] *Ibid.*, comments by Wigram, Lampson, and Crowe.
[93] *Ibid.*, C 7966, C 7966, May 4, 1923. Already on May 2, 1923 Crewe had reported that the Quai d'Orsay was "hostile" and "higly incensed" about the German note. *Ibid.*, C 7833.
[94] See White, *op. cit.*, p. 89. The British Ambassador to Belgium confirmed Poincaré's fears after a talk with Belgian officials. *FO*, 371/8634, C 8048, May 5, 1923.
[95] *Ibid.*, 8633, C 7387, April 30, 1923. Poincaré-Saint-Aulaire, May 4, and May 6, 1923, *MAE*, Ruhr 17, fol. 130 f, and fol. 166 f.
[96] White, *op. cit.*, p. 90. *FO*, 371/8633 C 6473, April 9, 1923. *Ibid.*, 8634, C 8037, May 2, 1923.

congratulated upon a note which needed explanation within days of delivery." France and Belgium rejected the note as completely unsatisfactory on May 6, and Italy and Britain also turned down the note on May 12 and May 13, but the latter powers demanded a new offer; that is exactly what Poincaré had feared, and why he had opposed the Belgian demand for a common Allied reply.[97]

After this failure to divide France and Britain, rumors about Cuno's resignation were circulating in Berlin. Such step was informally discussed between the Reich's representative in Bavaria von Haniel, and the Bavarian Minister President. Von Knilling, strictly opposed to resignation, threatened to recall the Bavarian minister from Berlin, if the Social Democrats formed a government.[98] But neither the SPD nor the members of the bourgeois coalition were ready to assume the burden of forming a new cabinet at a moment when a solution of the crisis was not yet in sight. Instead, the SPD, the DDP, the Center, and part of the DVP demanded new proposals, while the DNVP was opposed to any further concessions.[99] Cuno himself seems to have believed in a miracle. He even stayed in Berlin, hoping that Kent would return from Paris with new information as to French views for a settlement. Kent did indeed return after he had met Montagu Norman in London and had also visited Brussels, suggesting another attempt.[100]

7. NEW REPARATION PLANS

After the disaster of the May note, the *Wilhelmstraße* increased its activities in London. As before, the Germans tried to work through various channels. British opposition leaders and bankers were again approached, and Harry Kessler revisited London. Upon the invitation of several British industrialists who were also members of the Conservative Party, Hermann Bücher of the RdI went to London to investigate British-German industrial cooperation. His British partners were suspicious that as a result of occupation, Franco-German industrial cooperation would ensue, and wanted to make sure that they were informed about any private deals between French and German industry. At these meetings reparations were also discussed.[101] The

---

[97] *FO*, 371/8634, C 8044, May 6, 1923. White, *op. cit.*, p. 89.

[98] *Ibid.*, p. 91; D'Abernon, *op. cit.*, II, p. 145. *Kab. Cuno*, No. 153, May 7, 1923.

[99] White, *op. cit.*, p. 90 f.

[100] *Houghton-Papers*, Correspondence, May 16, 1923. Kent-Theunis, May 23, Kent-Whasburn July 19, Norman-Kent, July 20, and Kent-Norman, July 16 and 25, 1923, *Kent-Papers*, Correspondence 1919–1923.

[101] Material about this visit is in *PA AA*, Büro RM, Deutsch-Englische-Industrie-

German visitors to London informed British politicians about the content of a new proposal which was being prepared at the end of May. Lord Curzon was asked informally to give his opinion, but this time he wisely abstained; Ramsay MacDonald, Snowden, Norman and others, however, considered the new draft to be a great step forward. John Maynard Keynes, who had been to Berlin informed Stanley Baldwin, who had become Prime Minister after Bonar Law – being mortal ill – had resigned on May 22. Baldwin although not approving of the draft, did not say anything against it either.[102]

Hugo Stinnes also tried to renew discussions with his French contacts, and after a meeting with Bücher, he decided to send a personal emissary to Paris. The official purpose was to examine the Stinnes-de Lubersac agreement, but in reality, the agent should establish contacts with French politicians and industrialists. Cuno, von Rosenberg, and President Ebert were informed of this initiative, and they all supported it.[103] Thus G. Brecht, a civil servant in the coal office, was sent to France where he met Herriot. This meeting between the leader of the Radical-Socialist Party and Brecht was as fruitless as earlier contacts. Herriot was not prepared to collaborate with the Germans; instead he recommended that German industry submit a substantial offer as the only way to negotiations. However, in contrast to official French policy, the opposition leader suggested that he was prepared to leave the Ruhr before payments had ended. Herriot also hinted that no fixed amount should be named, Germany's capacity to pay to be determined by the international committee which would issue the loan.[104] Though these suggestions were certainly of great value for future negotiations the problem was that Herriot had proposed just the opposite from what Poincaré expected.

Unofficial contacts in France had thus totally failed, and the Germans were thrown back on their own imagination. Cuno had already demanded an investigation of reparations, the same day the May note had been delivered. He had asked the Ministries to prepare 1) a memorandum on pre-

Kooperation. The British participants were Sir Allan Smith, P.J. Hannon, Michael Dewar. Sthamer-AA, May 29, 1923, *ibid.*, Büro RM Reparationen, D 720225 f, May 30, 1923, *ibid.*, D 720228.

[102] Memo June 4, 1923, *ibid.*, D 720256 f, and D 720270. "Aufzeichnung Dufour," June 6, 1923, *ibid.*, D 7203048 f.

[103] "Aktennotiz" G. Brecht, May 15, 1923, *ibid.*, Büro RM, Reparationen, 5 secr., D 736384 f. *MAE*, Allemagne 481, Note pour le Président du Conseil, May 29, 1923, fol. 15 f. According to this report German industry submitted a reparation plan and agreed to pay 20–25 billion gold marks through annuities.

[104] "Aktennotiz Brecht über Reise nach Paris, 22.5.–2.6.23," June 6, 1923, *ibid.*, D 736406–415. Hoesch-Rosenberg, May 25, and June 1, 1923, *ibid.*, D 736388, and D 736400 f.

vious German deliveries (the Ministries of Economics, Finance, and Reconstruction were still operating with different estimates); 2) an estimate of the
damage caused by the Ruhr occupation; 3) a study of the financial position
of the involved countries; and 4) to consider legal preparations necessary
to obtain domestic guarantees for a German offer of payments.[105] As a
result of this request a special committee for the study of reparations was
created under Karl Ritter of the Foreign office.[106] At the same time, representatives from the SPD, the Center, and the DVP met in the office of Hans
von Raumer (DVP) and reached an agreement on the urgency of a new
initiative. Upon Stresemann's suggestion, the new plan would also have to
incorporate concrete guarantees. However, even now unanimity could not
be obtained. Obviously out of protest against the study of mortgages upon
private property, Florian Klöckner of the Center abstained from the meeting.
The DVP was also split on this issue.[107]

    When the cabinet discussed a new proposal on May 15, von Rosenberg
threatened to resign when the majority suggested that Germany offer more
than the 30 billions already mentioned. If the cabinet would now, after five
months of resistance propose conditions going beyond the old note, this
might be regarded as a sign that the first offer had been dishonest, or that
Germany would yield to military force. Cuno, who seems to have been
willing to go beyond this amount if it was fixed by an international committee
succumbed to von Rosenberg's pressure. Von Rosenberg's opposition to an
extension of the draft led to several clashes with the Minister of Finance, the
disagreement being based on contradictory evaluations of the Reich's financial position. Warning that financial chaos was imminent, Hermes argued
that Germany could no longer wait for British intervention and should make
a substantial offer close to the Bonar Law plan. Von Rosenberg, on the
contrary, did not take into account the financial situation at all and still
clung to his original plan to foster a break between France and Great
Britain.[108] Hermes was especially incensed about von Rosenberg's attitude
since both his Ministry and the Ministry for Food and Agriculture were
operating with figures showing that hardly any difference existed between
the Bonar Law plan and the German offer of May 2, if the latter would be
modified in respect to the rate of interest. However, the cabinet being divided,

---

[105] Cuno, May 2, 1923, *ibid.*, W. Rep., Kommissionsarbeiten zur Bereitstellung des
Reparationsmaterials, K 242722.
[106] *Ibid.* This volume contains several proposals which were used as a basis for discussions within the commission. The first meeting took place on May 7, 1923, K 242725.
[107] *Marx Nachlass*, II, p. 284.
[108] *Kab. Cuno*, No. 159, May 15, 1923.

it was necessary to obtain further clarification about the attitude of the parties.[109] But neither Cuno nor von Rosenberg wanted a public discussion of Germany's foreign policy situation, and they tried to prevent debate in the Reichstag. Before the budget of the Foreign Office was discussed on May 16, Cuno and von Rosenberg met Wels, Müller-Franken, Dittmann, and Breitscheid of the SPD. Müller-Franken was especially critical of the emphasis placed upon passive resistance, but he could not convince Cuno and von Rosenberg that a significantly different offer was necessary.[110] Thus an understanding with the SPD was impossible. After the SPD delegation had left, Cuno received representatives of the Center, the DDP, the DVP, and the BVP. In contrast to von Rosenberg, Stresemann and Marx argued that any proposal should be addressed to the French mood rather than the British, while Marx, Becker (Center) and Zapf objected to the mortgaging of the railways. Despite differences as to the content of the note, they all agreed that a foreign policy debate should not take place.[111]

When the last Reichstag session prior to the holidays opened, Müller-Franken demanded a discussion of foreign policy. Criticizing the tactical inability of the cabinet and demanding that industry and agriculture contribute to reparation payments, he argued that a compromise between the Bonar Law plan and the German figures was necessary. The Reich should offer the revenues from customs, the railways, and the liquor monopoly as a means of payment. Negotiations about coke and coal deliveries to France should be dealt with in direct negotiations between the German and the French governments. In addition, Cuno should offer political securities along the lines of a "Rhine Pact." The goal of negotiations ought to be a "fast evacuation." With this program, the SPD had laid down the condition for a settlement with the Allies. Although it was a great step forward in comparison with the position of the Foreign Office, Müller-Franken's ideas were hardly more realistic. Poincaré had already rejected the British plan in January. Thus a mere repetition of the old offer was useless. But von Rosenberg did not have to explain the cabinet's policy before the Reichstag. According to the understanding which had been reached the same morning with Cuno, Leicht of the BVP announced in the name of the DDP, the DVP, the Center, and his party that they would not participate in a discussion about foreign policy. The government needed more time to study Allied demands in detail. As previously the DNVP was against another offer.[112]

---

[109] *Ibid.* Cf. *BA*, R2/3167 and 2904 for differed evaluations of the plans.
[110] *Kab. Cuno*, No. 160, May 16, 1923.
[111] *BA*, R 43I/37, p. 76. The meeting took place in the Chancellor's office.
[112] *RT*, vol. 260, pp. 11125 ff.

With this statement a discussion of reparations had become impossible, and the Reichstag adjourned until the end of the Whitsun holidays.

When the cabinet met the next day, the search for a compromise proposal went on, but the positions of Hermes and von Rosenberg could not be reconciled. The Minister of Finance renewed his warning against another "diplomatic interlude," while von Rosenberg remained stubborn and rejected the Bonar Law plan. Hermes again tried to convince him that a final solution was impossible at the moment and declared that an offer of 30 billions was doomed to fail. He justly pointed out that since Germany had accepted an international committee, she had in fact agreed to pay more than 30 billions, if the experts should demand it. But although the majority of the cabinet supported Hermes no decision was made.[113]

The cabinet had reached a breaking-point. Further meetings took place during the next few days, and on May 19, Cuno, who until now had abstained from interfering with Hermes and von Rosenberg, urged his colleagues to make up their minds. The question whether Germany should accept the Bonar Law plan or submit the old proposal in a modified form, "was of critical importance for future collaboration" within the cabinet.[114] After Cuno had finished, von Rosenberg spoke first. The extension of the note of May 2 was a matter of principle, but he would accept any scheme of annuities which would remain within the original figures. He was also prepared to offer concrete securities, and suggested that, at the beginning of negotiations, the Ruhr could be given to a trustee consisting either of an international "engineering commission" or to a single power like Sweden, the Netherlands, or Italy. Naturally, the trustee had the duty to return the Ruhr. With this statement he had given the conditions for his cooperation. Hermes' reaction was weak. The Minister of Finance did not bring up the Bonar Law plan. He stressed the importance of guarantees for German deliveries, and declared that industry would also have to contribute to guarantees. But even more important were direct payments to France, and Hermes suggested, for the first time, the taxation of private property for reparation purposes. His plan meant a confrontation with industry and apparently the cabinet did not intend to discuss it at the moment, while Cuno was also hoping that business contacts in Great Britain would aid the formulation of a plan.[115]

---

[113] *Kab. Cuno*, No. 161, May 17, 1923. Rudolf Oeser, the Minister of the Interior, informed his colleagues that two parties had demanded that Ebert should participate at these discussions. Cuno promised to invite Ebert after the cabinet had clarified its own ideas.

[114] *Ibid.*, No. 162, May 19, 1923.

[115] During the next days several meeting took place, but there are hardly any reports.

While these negotiations were taking place and proving that the mort-gaging of private property was one of the most controversial problems, Cuno had met representatives of the RdI on May 15 to discuss this topic with the industrialists. Stinnes, Bücher, and Peter Klöckner all agreed that direct Allied participation was impossible, but they were prepared to accept mortgages. However, Stinnes stressed that the first pledge could only be the Reich and repeated his preconditions of the previous year.[116] In contrast to the German note in January, the May note had not been discussed with industrial representatives in advance, although both Bücher and Sorge were informed of its content. The directorate of the RdI regretted that the May note had increased Germany's liability and Emil Guggenheimer of the MAN angrily claimed that the Cuno Cabinet, although generally considered to be a "Kabinett der deutschen Wirtschaft" did not deserve this title at all.[117] Hugo Stinnes also opposed the May plan, but in general, industrialists agreed that they would participate in the formulation of a final plan, although the last offer was ridiculously high.[118]

Nevertheless when Cuno's demand was discussed in a meeting of the RdI directorate, it was clear from the beginning that industrial contributions would be of minor importance. As early as January, Hermann Bücher had suggested that the Reichsbahn be used as a security for an international loan. But in order to guarantee the receipt of about 600 million gold marks from the railways per year, its status had to be changed. It could no longer be run as a state enterprise, but it would have to be run as a company in which all branches of industry had their shares. In return for this change, industry, agriculture, and real estate would provide the railway company with a capital of 10 billion gold marks in the form of mortgages upon their property.[119]

Since January, Bücher's position had hardly changed, and when the RdI met in May to discuss Cuno's demand, he submitted a slightly modified plan. Several other plans were submitted by Lammers and Silverberg,[120] and as a result of these discussions Cuno received a letter signed by 18 in-

Cf. *ibid., Marx Nachlaß,* I, p. 284, *and PA AA,* W. Rep., Kommissionsarbeiten zur Bereitstellung des Reparationsmaterials, K 242773 ff.

[116] "Niederschrift, 15.5.1923," *HA GHH,* 30019320/7. For Stinnes, see discussion of the January note.

[117] "Aktennotiz über Besprechung mit Dr. Krukenberg vom RdI," May 17, 1923, *Guggenheimer Nachlaß,* K 71/RdI. See "Zur Lage," May 16, 1923, *ibid.*

[118] *PA AA,* Büro RM, Reparationen, 5 secr. May 6, 1923, D 736380.

[119] *Silverberg Nachlaß,* vol. 315, January 11, 1923 "Zur Sicherheits- und Garantie-frage."

[120] *Ibid.,* vol. 239.

dustrialists.[121] Speaking for the RdI, they declared that they had not participated in the preparation of the May 2 note and stressed that the property of
the Reich and the *Länder* was the first pledge for reparations payments. If
this should not be sufficient, all Germans should be encumbered equally before any special group or class was selected. But these were not the only
preconditions for industrial participation. They also demanded that reparations should be solved once and for all. But first, irresponsible government
spending had to be stopped, and state enterprises had to be run according
to private business principles. Then these companies would yield from 600
millions to 1 billion gold marks per year. Industrial contributions would
depend on revenues from state enterprises. According to industrial estimates,
industry, agriculture, trade, and banking could guarantee 500 million gold
marks per year. Only 40% of this amount would be raised by industry. But
even this insignificant amount was made dependent upon several preconditions. Germany would have to be granted the most-favored nation clause
and a moratorium for several years. In domestic affairs the following preconditions were also made: state intervention into private business, export
controls, and demobilization laws had to be abolished, and the efficiency of
labor had to be increased.[122]

These industrial demands would have meant a complete submission of the
Government to industry. Besides disunity within the cabinet, the attitude of
the RdI furthermore complicated Cuno's domestic position. During the
next days Berlin was in a turmoil. The ADGB protested and meetings with
the SPD and the bourgeois parties took place.[123] Again it seemed as if the
Cabinet would fall apart but the bourgeois parties rallied to the support of
the government. Stresemann published an unsigned article in *Die Zeit*,
defending Cuno against all attacks and declaring that foreign policy activities did not allow a change of government.[124] Stresemann's support of the
cabinet and his acceptance of the original 30 billions as the basis for another
German offer probably saved Cuno. Without support from the DVP and
without Stresemann's intervention the cabinet might have been forced to
resign, since Hermes and other members of the Center Party were completely
disillusioned with Cuno, whom they held responsible for the failure of the

[121] *Kab. Cuno*, No. 168, May 25, 1923. Upon Cuno's request the letter had been slightly
modified, but the RdI had not agreed to a reduction of the demands upon state enterprises.
Bücher/Sorge – Cuno, May 28, 1923, *BA* 43I/37.
[122] *Kab. Cuno*, No. 168, May 25, 1923.
[123] *Ibid.*, No. 168, May 26, 1923. *Marx Nachlaß*, I, p. 284; Stresemann, *op. cit.*, I, p. 65.
Kab. Cuno, No. 177, June 1, 1923.
[124] *Kab. Cuno*, No. 169; Stresemann's article of May 29 is printed in Stresemann, *op.
cit.*, I, p. 65.

May note.[125] Relations between the Minister of Finance and Cuno became even more strained when rumors of a conspiracy between Hermes and the SPD were brought to Cuno's knowledge.[126]

On the other hand, relations between the Minister of Finance and the Minister of Foreign Affairs also remained at a low ebb. Relying upon Bergmann's evaluation, Hermes had estimated Bonar Law's demands at 49 billions. Both believed that it was advisable to go beyond 30 billions and come as close to British figures as possible.[127] On May 30, Cuno had been forced by the Prussian Minister President to inform the *Länder* of the new plan. When von Rosenberg told his audience that the Foreign Office had studied the Bonar Law proposal in detail and maintained that the annuities went far beyond those of the German offer, Hermes left the room. The Minister Presidents of Prussia, Thuringia, Saxony, and Hesse also urged to extend the offer, but to no avail – von Rosenberg defended his position. An extension of the note would be interpreted by France as a sign that Germany would yield to pressure.[128]

Hermes' attack as well as the opposition of the Social Democratic Minister Presidents caused von Rosenberg to increase his activities in London. Sthamer, Dufour-Feronce, and Kessler were again instructed to obtain an official statement of a sum acceptable to Great Britain. Though officially the British Foreign Office abstained from giving any advice, Berlin received a hint that a fixed sum was useless. It was better to base the note upon annuities.[129] Several hectic meetings between Cuno and the party leaders followed, but the parties could not agree on the details of the offer due to conflicting suggestions from London.[130] Hermann Bücher intervened again and suggested that if the Reich intended to go beyond the guarantees mentioned in the RdI memorandum, it should offer the receipts from excise taxes on tobacco and liquor while customs receipts should not be used. He believed however, that the guarantees mentioned by the RdI were sufficient.

---

[125] *Marx Nachlaß*, I, p. 285 and p. 299.

[126] *Kab. Cuno*, No. 175, May 31, 1923, and *ibid.*, No. 178, June 2, 1923.

[127] Entwurf Bergmann-Hermes, undated, but written about May 24, 1923, *PA AA*, Büro RM, Reparationen, D 719914 ff. There are also several other drafts by Luther, Dr. Becker, Groener, and Hermes. D 719894 ff. Cf. also "Leistungen für die 50 Milliarden," *BA*, R2/3168 and "Möglichkeiten einer Lösung," *ibid.*, R2/3159, pp. 22 ff.

[128] *Kab. Cuno*, No. 173, May 30, 1923.

[129] For example Rosenberg-Sthamer May 28, 1923, *PA AA*, Büro RM, Reparationen, D 720202. *Marx Nachlaß*, I, pp. 284 and 300.

[130] Already on May 17 Hjalmar Schacht had informed Cuno about British attitudes. Members of the Conservative Party had suggested that Germany should offer 20–50 (Dawson and Hannon) and 30–60 billions (Smith). "Bericht über Londonaufenthalt," *Cuno Nachlaß*, Archiv des Vorsitzenden des Direktoriums. Geheime Schriftstücke. *PA AA*, Büro RM, Reparationen, May 16, 1923, D 719819 and May 19, 1923, D 719853.

In addition, he warned that the RdI proposal could not be modified without prior approval by industry. If the RdI was not informed of all changes, Cuno could not expect industrial support.[131] Cuno answered Bücher's letter on June 7 after the final draft of the note had been prepared, declaring that the conditions would be acceptable to industry.[132] But by then Bücher probably knew the details of the note, since upon the invitation of Becker he had attended a conference between the Ministry of Economics and the Ministry of Justice at which the legal aspects of the mortgaging of private property were discussed.[133]

While the RdI was thus constantly kept informed of developments, Cuno received representatives of agriculture for the first time on May 29 and asked for their cooperation which was granted. But similar to industrial demands support was not given unconditionally. It was made dependent upon protection of private property, a final solution of reparations, and other demands which were later on specified in letters from the *Reichslandbund* and the *Vereinigung der deutschen Bauernvereine*.[134]

When the German proposal was finally submitted on June 7, Cuno as well as von Rosenberg knew already that it would not be rejected by Great Britain. Considering the opposition from the DNVP, the differences within the cabinet, and the preconditions of industry, the note was remarkably moderate. Passive resistance was not mentioned at all, and the legality of the occupation was not discussed either. The decision about the capacity for payments was left to an international committee of experts, Germany would cooperate with the committee to fix the liability. The best method of payment was a loan, but as long as a loan was impossible, Germany would agree to annuities. For the first time, concrete mortgages were offered. The Reichsbahn was to be made independent within the Reich fiscal system and would be placed under special administration. The Reichsbahn would issue bonds worth 10 billion gold marks which would be used as a first charge upon the assets of the railways. From July 1, 1927 onwards five percent interest would be charged on these bonds. Thus the Allies would receive 500 millions gold marks per year from the railway system alone.[135]

---

[131] *Kab. Cuno*, No. 174, May 31, 1923.

[132] *BA*, R 43I/37.

[133] *PA AA*, W. Rep., Kommissionsarbeiten zur Bereitstellung des Reparationsmaterials, K 242880, note June 8, 1923. Kempner criticized Bücher's participation. *BA*, R 43I/37, June 4, 1923.

[134] *Kab. Cuno*, No. 171, May 29, 1923. *Ibid.*, No. 187, June 12, 1923. *BA*, R 43I/38. The demands of both organizations are almost identical, but the *Vereinigung der deutschen Bauernvereine* does not stress that the May note had been sent without prior consultations.

[135] *Ursachen und Folgen*, V, p. 145 f. Originally the Reichsbahn was to guarantee 15 billions. See "3. Sitzung zur Bereitstellung des Reparationsmaterials," May 17, 1923, *PA*

Another 500 million gold mark would be guaranteed by industry, trade, agriculture, and banking. This sum was either to be raised as a tax, or directly through a mortgage upon industrial and agricultural property and upon real estate. In addition the revenues from customs receipts, excise taxes on beer, tobacco, wine, sugar and the receipts of the liquor monopoly would also be used as a mortgage. Before the war these revenues had brought 800 million gold marks per year. Though they had decreased to about 200 millions after the war, it was expected that they would increase again after normalcy had been established. Finally the memorandum demanded oral negotiations and admitted Germany's duty to pay reparations.[136]

If this note had only been addressed to the United States, Great Britain and Italy, it would have become a success immediately, for it contained hardly anything to which these powers could have objected. Even considering the annuities later on established by the Dawes plan, the memorandum offered sizeable yearly payments from 1927 onwards. It is true that according to the Dawes plan German payments began after a year. But during the first two years the Reich did not have to pay anything, and even industry only had to start payments in the second year. The bulk of the first two annuities was to be raised by an external loan and interest on railway bonds.[137]

For Great Britain and Belgium the German plan was an honest effort to reach an understanding, but the French attitude was of course different. At a meeting in Brussels, Poincaré tried to prevent a Belgian initiative for a common answer of all Allies. However, now the Belgians did not give in that easily, arguing that their Parliament favored cooperation with Great Britain and that Belgium's economic situation was also becoming increasingly difficult. But Poincaré would not be won over. As a result the occupation powers informed Britain separately of their positions, Belgium only de-

---

AA, W. Rep., Kommissionsarbeiten zur Bereitstellung des Reparationsmaterials, K 242277–286. For final preparations see: "Vorschläge Bergmann, Schubert, Becker, Hilferding," *ibid.*, W. Rep., Allgemeine Reparationsfrage, H 259672 ff. "Memorandum Melchior," June 1, 1923, *ibid.*, H 259834 f. For British contacts (Norman, MacDonald, Dewar) cf. *ibid.*, Handakten Direktoren, Schriftverkehr, L 419016–087. Keynes showed the memo to McKenna and Baldwin. *Ibid.*, Büro RM, Reparationen, D 720345, June 6, 1923.

[136] *Ursachen und Folgen*, V, p. 145 f. These 500 millions were exactly the amount offered by industry on May 28. Cf. M.J. Bonn, "Vorschläge für einen Reparationsplan," May 19, 1923, *BA*, R 43I/36.

[137] Harry G. Moulton, *The Reparation Plan* (New York, 1924), pp. 31–36; Weill-Raynal. *op. cit.*, II, pp. 552–555; Bergmann, *op. cit.*, p. 296 f. The annuities for the first 4 years were 1, 1.2, 1.2, and 1.75 billions. From the fifth year onwards 2.5 billions were to be payed, while the German note offered 1.8 billions as the highest possible amount. The British representative on the Reparation Commission had proposed 2 billions from 1928 onwards, but he was voted down.

manding the end of passive resistance before negotiations could take place. Poincaré considered the June memorandum to be completely unacceptable because it did not contain an obligation to abandon passive resistance, because it failed to offer a concrete sum, and because it assumed the elimination of the Reparation Commission, replacing it with a committee of experts and, finally, because it failed to give the debtors concrete securities, offering them only theoretical pledges.[138] When the French objections became known in London, Sir Eyre Crowe informed the French and Belgian Ambassadors that his country could not demand the end of passive resistance without offering Germany something in return. Furthermore, British lawyers considered occupation to be illegal in any case.[139]

With France demanding the termination of resistance, and Britain not yet willing to intervene, von Rosenberg reconsidered and offered to abandon resistance in stages. First, Germany would advise its citizens against further sabotage of traffic, it would take over the railways again, provide occupation troops with supplies and start the transport of coal. In return, France was to free all prisoners. Second, three weeks after the beginning of negotiations, the Reichsbahn and real estate would be mortgaged. Within the same period, evacuation was to start. Third, within an additional three weeks the Reichsbank would deliver its gold reserves to a trustee. After the gold had been delivered, Essen was to be evacuated as well.[140] With these concessions von Rosenberg hoped to accelerate intervention. London was informed of the suggestion, and Friedrich Gaus, legal expert of the Foreign Office, prepared another proposal for the abolition of passive resistance. But after Cuno had met representatives of the Ruhr population on a trip to Westphalia, the situation changed again. Now Karl von Schubert informed the embassies in Paris and London that resistance could not be given up. According to Schubert, President Ebert had also threatened to resign together with the cabinet, if such a step was taken.[141] Whatever the validity of this statement, passive resistance was becoming more and more difficult. Still, the new German offer increased for the moment hopes of British inter-

---

[138] Herbette-MAE, June 8, 1923, *MAE*, Ruhr 21, fol. 210 ff. Poincaré, June 9, 1923, *ibid.*, fol. 250 ff. *Ursachen und Folgen*, V, p. 147, Cf. *FO.*, 371/8638, C 9749, June 6; 8639, C 10067, June 8, 1923.

[139] Report about a meeting in the Foreign Office. *FO*, 371/8639, C 10185, June 11, 1923.

[140] Rosenberg-Hoesch, June 10, 1923, *PA AA*, Büro RM, Reparationen, D 720371 f. Cf. Schubert-Kessler, June 6, 1923, *ibid.*, Handakten Direktoren, Schriftverkehr, L 419082 ff.

[141] "Projekt Gaus," June 13, 1923, *ibid.*, Handakten Direktoren, Schriftverkehr, L 419079 f., *ibid.*, L 419078, June 13, 1923. Schubert-Sthamer, June 13, 1923, *ibid.*, L. 419073 ff.

vention in the trade unions as well. However, criticism of the Cuno cabinet among union officials was also growing.[142]

While reactions to the note of June 7 seemed in the beginning to justify hopes for British intervention, they were soon destroyed by Allied disagreement.[143] According to Keynes:

The note has done all it was capable of doing and has ranged virtually the whole of British opinion on its side. I don't know when the Press has been more unanimous in quiet approval. Germany having done what she can, the game is now between England and France. It is impossible to be particularly hopeful.[144]

Keynes' evaluation of the ensuing struggle between France and Britain was only too realistic. Even now, Poincaré could prevent immediate British intervention. Considering the fact that the struggle between Germany and France had been expected in January not to last longer than two or three months at the most, the German offer came too late. However, before Anglo-French differences finally led to British counteractions, another attempt to mediate between Cuno and the occupation powers took place.

8. JOHN F. DULLES AS MEDIATOR

For some time the Belgians had been dissatisfied with the results of occupation both from the economic and the political point of view, and the Socialist as well as the Flemish press accused the government of relegating Belgium to a French satellite which was not being kept informed of Poincaré's intentions.[145] The opposition of these groups in parliament had grown since the first German note in May. Thus the Belgian government tried again to obtain a common basis for a Franco-Belgian proposal, but Poincaré had rejected the initiative. He could wait for another German offer.[146] This was a position Belgium could not accept, and the Belgian delegate to the Reparation Commission informed the Germans that his country hoped nego-

---

[142] Erdmann, *op. cit.*, pp. 66 ff.Favez, *op. cit.*, pp. 130 ff. Spethmann, *op. cit.*, IV, pp. 84 ff, 118 ff, 368. Oltmann, *op. cit.*, pp. 142 ff. For trade union attempts to influence public opinion and unions in the Allied countries cf. *Bebel Archiv*, NB 169 and 173. For discussions of resistance see "Niederschrift der Verhandlungen über die Gesamtlage im besetzten Gebiet, insbesondere im Ruhrgebiet, am 26. Mai 1923 im Büro des ADGB," *ibid.*, NB 166, fol. 0034. Cf. "Sitzung der Verbandsvorstände vom 20. Mai 1923 im Rathaussaal in Schwerte," *ibid.*, fol. 0036 ff. Also NB 167, fol. 0038 f.

[143] *PA AA*, Büro RM, Reparationen, D 720345 f., June 6, 1923 and D 720442 f, June 14, 1923.

[144] Keynes-Max Warburg, June 21, 1923, *ibid.*, Büro RM, Ruhrgebiet, Besatzungsprobleme, D 637552.

[145] Herbette, April 7, 1923, *MAE*, Ruhr 17, fol. 138.

[146] Weill-Raynal, *op. cit.*, II, pp. 408–415.

tiations would start soon.[147] As the following developments show, the government's concern about its domestic position was all too justified. Only a few weeks later on June 15, it was overthrown. Though the immediate cause of its fall was not Ruhr policy, and although Theunis managed to form a new cabinet by the end of June, the warning was obvious and the Belgian cabinet increased its activities to reach a solution of the stalemate.[148]

The chance of Belgian mediation grew when John F. Dulles visited Germany. Dulles had been engaged by the *Juristische Gesellschaft Essen* to defend German industrialists in French courts.[149] Before his departure from the United States he had talked with both Hughes and Hoover about his assignment, and as a result, felt that it was inadvisable for him to become involved in problems "that might be objectionable to Washington."[150] Obviously the Republican Administration wanted to prevent this trip from being considered as American mediation. When Dulles was later asked by the Belgian Prime Minister to act as an intermediary between France, Germany, and Belgium, he made it clear that he was acting as a private citizen upon Theunis' suggestion.[151]

After Dulles arrived in Essen, the occupation powers made it known that they would not allow his participation at the trials.[152] Upon Max Warburg's invitation Dulles went to Hamburg, where a meeting with Cuno and Carl Melchior had been arranged in the office of the HAPAG. At this encounter Cuno explained that he earnestly sought a solution, but, "the only thing he [Cuno] would not do" was to

sign an obligation which he honestly believed to be unfulfillable. Previous German government had done that. It may have been necessary under all the circumstances. He was not disposed to criticize them. But as far as he was concerned, he would never do that. The previous practice had resulted in giving an impression of Germany's bad faith, and while temporary respites had been attained, ultimately it had to be paid for and was now being paid for.[153]

---

[147] Note von Schubert, May 29, 1923, "Unterredung Rieth mit D. [Delacroix]," *PA AA*, Büro RM, Reparationen, D 720216 ff. The details of the Belgian activities are also described in Furst, *op. cit.*, pp. 166 ff.

[148] White, *op. cit.*, pp. 103 ff.

[149] Barret-Max Warburg, May 16 and May 28, 1923, *Dulles Papers*, Supplement 1971, II. Correspondence European Trip 1923.

[150] Dulles-Cromwell, June 6, 1923, *ibid.*

[151] Dulles-Allan W. Dulles, August 2, 1923, *ibid.* Dulles-Georges Jouasset, September 25, 1923, *ibid.*, II, Correspondence, Box 134, Folder Reparation Questions 1921–1924.

[152] Dulles-Ladycourt, July 4, 1923, *ibid.*, Supplement 1971, II, Correspondence, European Trip 1923. Ladycourt was the code for the Law Office of Sullivan & Cromwell, New York.

[153] Memo of a conference with Cuno and Melchior in Hamburg, July 2, 1923, *ibid.*

At the end of the meeting Cuno suggested that Dulles return to Germany if he had any information after his trip to Paris and Brussels. The discussion was typical of Cuno's state of mind in July 1923. After 4 weeks without a reply from Britain to his memorandum of June 7, time was running out, Germany's economic and financial difficulties increased from day to day, but despite this development, he clung to his idea of the "honest business-man."[154] With such an attitude political decisions were rendered virtually impossible.

From Hamburg Dulles went to Brussels. A former member of the US peace delegation at Versailles and a brilliant lawyer, although without any experience in international politics, he discussed reparations with the Belgian Prime Minister who was glad to see his old aquaintance from the Versailles days. Theunis described his country's difficulties in gloomy terms. Politically, Belgium was allied with France, but contrary to France, his country had no self-contained economy and was economically in the same position as Great Britain. Both countries needed a revival of trade in Europe. The present European situation was intolerable, but what could a small country like Belgium do? Though Belgium was "uncomfortably" yoked with France, she "was not willing to give this up unless assured of at least a good seat with Great Britain. There was danger of being left standing between these two, which would be even more uncomfortable."

Theunis felt that the political situation was simply impossible owing to the personal animosity of Poincaré and Lord Curzon. As to reparations he informed Dulles that France wanted 26 billions above interallied debts. Belgium must have 5 billions, and Italy would also have to get something. "Italy always needs a tip." England would also have to receive her share. In contrast to public announcements Theunis admitted that the Ruhr had proved to be unsatisfactory as an economic pledge. Real economic securities, he believed, could only be obtained through monopolies and mortgages under the control of the Reparation Commission.[155]

When they spoke about the German situation, Dulles mentioned his meeting with Cuno. Being convinced that disintegration was approaching fast in Germany, he warned Theunis that if that happened the reparation problem would also be postponed and the Allies would not receive anything in the near future. Believing Cuno to be a reasonable and honest man and not having much hope in a change of government, he suggested cooperation. Cuno needed "a reciprocal evacuation or change in the character of occu-pation in the Ruhr, to keep his political position secure" in case of a termi-

---

[154] Lord D'Abernon also criticized this attitude. D'Abernon, *op. cit.*, II, p. 238.
[155] Memo, July 5, 1923, *Dulles-Papers, ibid.* The meeting took place in Theunis' office.

nation of resistance. Unconditional surrender of Germany was not in the interest of the Allies at all. To keep the nationalists under control, passive resistance was necessary until a program had been developed by the Allies. Whether Cuno had furnished Dulles with these arguments, or whether the American lawyer had simply given his own opinion, is unknown. But whatever the origin of his arguments, Theunis agreed and when Dulles suggested that he would be willing to visit Cuno again if Theunis thought it might be useful, the Belgian Prime Minister asked him to visit Paris first. In the meantime, he would discuss the question with Jaspar.[156]

Dulles did indeed go to Paris. During a three-day stay, he met Louis Barthou and Louis Loucheur whom he also knew from Versailles. In his meeting with Barthou, Dulles also suggested that the Allies should help Cuno. For example, if Germany should announce its intention to resume deliveries in kind, the Allied Powers should make a statement within 24 hours which permitted Cuno to remain in office. Barthou was convinced that Cuno could not give up passive resistance without being overthrown, but he argued that it was also very difficult to reason with Poincaré. Barthou also confirmed what Theunis had already explained – Poincaré wanted 26 billions,[157] while Loucheur believed that France needed 29 to 30 billions.[158]

When Dulles returned to Brussels he had recognized that interallied debts, i.e. American unwillingness to abolish or reduce the Allies' war debts, was the real stumbling block, while all other problems could be solved.[159] The Belgian Prime Minister did not quite agree, suggesting that though European war debts in the United States influenced reparations, their elimination was not a prerequisite. Far more important for a settlement was the cancellation of French debts to Great Britain. It was rather awkward for France to remain a debtor of "a daily companion" and a "financial equal." Thus a Franco-British understanding was necessary. As to the Germans, Theunis asked Dulles to visit Berlin and warn the Chancellor that a break between France and Britain "would be absolutely fatal to Germany." Cuno "should implore Great Britain to prevent this." Furthermore, Theunis suggested,

the Cuno government should resign. Cuno has good intentions, but is not strong enough. Only a more socialistic government can make the necessary sacrifices and take the necessary action against the great industrialists. If Cuno should try, he

---

[156] *Ibid.*

[157] Memo July 7, 1923, *ibid.*

[158] Memo July 7, 1923 (Loucheur), *ibid.* Loucheur believed that Germany could pay 3 billion gold marks per year, 1 billion should be paid in kind. (700 millions to France, 300 to Belgium.) When Theunis was informed about this, he objected. Belgium did not want more than 200 millions in kind.

[159] Memo, July 10, 1923 (Conference with Theunis), *ibid.*

would fail and be assassinated. It is often necessary to resort to governmental tricks to accomplish serious steps. The Germans know this. They did the same trick at the signature of the Versailles Treaty.[160]

With these rather peculiar instructions Dulles travelled to Berlin where he met Carl Melchior. It was not difficult to convince the German banker that a final settlement could not be obtained in the near future. Since Great Britain had not yet reacted, Dulles suggested a provisional settlement. Germany should offer the resumption of deliveries in kind and the cessation of resistance. At the same time mortgages upon private property and the railroads should be created and pledged with the Reparation Commission. The collection of taxes on beer, wine and tobacco and other goods for reparation purposes should also be offered. Finally, a serious effort had to be made concerning the balancing of the budget and the stabilization of the mark. The proposal was to appear to be free of conditions, but there would be "the private understanding that a reciprocal announcement would immediately be made by the Allies, containing assurances regarding changing the character of the Ruhr occupations, so as to save the German government from disastrous political consequences."[161]

Melchior completely agreed with this suggestion. He immediately arranged a meeting with Cuno. The same night Dulles, Melchior, and Cuno had dinner in the HAPAG office in Berlin. Dulles repeated his proposals and Cuno "expressed his general acceptance" and asked him "to work out with his [Cuno's] technical advisers, a detailed and concrete course of action." For the next day, the Chancellor arranged a meeting with von Maltzan who was in charge of the Foreign Office owing to von Rosenberg's absence. Cuno himself introduced Dulles to von Maltzan, and he also asked the Foreign Minister to return from his vacation. Before leaving for Hamburg Cuno begged Dulles to inform him of the results of his discussions with the Foreign Office.[162]

In the presence of Melchior, Dulles met von Maltzan, Ritter and Gaus, the economic and legal experts of the Wilhelmstraße. The Germans brought with them two papers, one indicating their views on mortgage laws for 20 billion gold marks. The other was Gaus' project concerning the progressive evacuation of the Ruhr in return for abandonment of resistance. Out of these proposals and Dulle's plan, they prepared a common draft. Four points could not be agreed upon during this session. First, Dulles insisted that the mortgage bonds should be enforceable in case of Germany defaulting im-

---

[160] *Ibid.*
[161] Memo of Conference in Berlin, July 12–17, 1923, *ibid.*
[162] *Ibid.*, The meeting with von Maltzan took place on July 13. Cf. *ibid.*

mediately, and that interests, which according to the German memorandum were only due at the end of 1927, should start earlier. Second, the German officials wanted to place the securities in a trustee organization of which Germany was a member, rather than directly with the Reparation Commission. Third, the Foreign Office officials also desired to avoid any references to monopolies of beer, tobacco, etc., "because of strong socialist objections to this form." Fourth, the question of a fulfillment of deliveries in kind also remained open. As to the question of evacuation, Dulles made it clear that in his opinion complete evacuation was impossible, while "invisible occupation" (meaning a retreat of troops from the cities) would probably be accepted by France.[163]

At this point Gaus and von Maltzan left, while Melchior, Ritter and Dulles went to the HAPAG office and tried to work out a compromise on these four points. Apparently all problems were solved with the exception of the enforceability of the bonds. Ritter considered this to be a matter of principle and did not want to decide on his own.[164]

The next day von Rosenberg was back in Berlin to meet Dulles and Melchior. With the appearance of von Rosenberg, difficulties began anew.[165] The Foreign Minister, who had always hoped for British intervention and a break of the Entente, now presented a new reason to reject all negotiations with either France or Belgium. On July 12, Curzon and Baldwin had finally broken their silence on the German note of June 7. In speeches before the House of Commons and the House of Lords respectively, they had announced that Britain would invite the Allied powers to discuss reparations. It did not make sense at all to wait for a complete German collapse, since such a development would also ruin the reconstruction of German credit and postpone payments indefinitely. All European powers were suffering in different ways through this unsatisfactory state of affairs, be it either through a depreciation of currency, a decrease of trade or an increase of unemployment, and the British politicians warned that the reconstruction of the world

---

[163] *Ibid.*, According to a note in the files of the Foreign Office, the first meeting had already taken place the night before. Note July 14, 1923, *PA AA*, Büro RM, Reparationen, D 720629. The draft laws for the mortgages had been worked out by a committee under Ritter. See "4. Sitzung Kommission zur Bereitstellung Reparationsmaterials," July 17, 1923, *ibid.*, D 720343 f. Also *ibid.*, W. Rep., Kommissionsarbeiten . . ., K 242853.

[164] Memo of Conferences in Berlin, July 12–17, 1923, *Dulles Papers, ibid.* The files of the Foreign Office contain a note Maltzan of July 15, 1923 and a copy of Dulles' draft. *PA AA*, Büro RM, Reparationen, D 720659–662, and "Memorandum D.[ulles] in der abgeänderten Fassung," D 720642–650. The copy contains several changes and marginal notes in German and English.

[165] Memo of Conferences in Berlin, July 12–17, 1923, *Dulles Papers, ibid.*

and the peace of the world were endangered if reparations were not solved soon.[166]

After weeks of waiting for a British declaration, this speech was regarded as intervention and von Rosenberg's expectations seemed to become reality. Britain would stop France, the policy of the German Foreign Office would be justified in the end, and passive resistance would have fulfilled its function – to prevent exploitation of productive pledges in the Ruhr and to obtain a new settlement of reparations before an international tribunal. With this development negotiations with France and Belgium would only weaken the German position. Thus von Rosenberg asked Dulles, though his own answer was obviously negative, whether Germany could "wisely seek to intervene or influence the situation as long as Great Britain indicated an intention to take initiatives in a sense favorable or at least satisfactory to Germany." On the other hand, he also objected to several other parts of Dulles' proposal. A provisional settlement could not be accepted and he doubted that the cabinet could "politically enact the necessary legislation," for the creation of bonds and mortgages, "except as part of a general and final settlement on satisfactory terms."[167]

Von Rosenberg hoped for a break between France and Britain as a result of the speeches in the Houses. On the other hand, Dulles agreed with von Rosenberg that a final settlement was preferable but it was simply impossible at the moment. Either France and Britain would disagree which meant "disaster" for Germany, or, if they did agree, the reparation liability would be fixed at a figure unacceptable to Germany. This would be at least 40 billions, but more probably 45 billions which Cuno had assured Dulles he would not accept.[168] Von Rosenberg only promised to study the proposal again. He would then inform Cuno about his decision. Together with Melchior, Dulles travelled to Hamburg. Upon their arrival the Chancellor mentioned a phone call from the Foreign Minister, but did not inform them of its content. Instead he suggested that they reconsider Dulles' draft immediately. The examination resulted in further changes. Upon Cuno's demand the reference to full delivery of reparations in kind according to the London Schedule of Payments was omitted in favor of less precise language, which made them dependent upon "rapid" change of occupation. When the date of the enforceability of the guarantees (to be handed to a board of trustees appointed by the Reparation Commission, of which Germany and

[166] *Cab.*, 23/24 July 12, 1923. Stresemann, *op. cit.*, I, p. 71 has an excerpt of Baldwin's speech.
[167] Memo of Conferences in Berlin, July 12–17, 1923, *Dulles Papers, ibid.*
[168] *Ibid.*

the United States would also be members) was discussed, Melchior proposed that the date should be left open, to which all agreed. Furthermore, it was decided that the balancing of the budget and stabilization of the mark would be part of the deal. In order to avoid the impression as if Germany was working with France and Belgium behind Baldwin's and Curzon's back, Cuno demanded that the Dulles' plan be made known in London so as to allow the British cabinet to incorporate the German ideas in its reply to the memorandum of June 7. In addition, it was to be presented in Brussels only if British politicians thought it might help. At the end of the meeting, Cuno again stressed that he was prepared to sign an agreement which could be fulfilled. Repeatedly he asked Dulles whether he really was convinced that France wanted a financial settlement.[169]

The next morning, Dulles and Cuno returned to Berlin together while Carl Melchior remained in Hamburg. Again, they discussed the plan and according to Dulles a "substantial agreement" existed as to the proposal and the course of action.[170] After their arrival in Berlin, Cuno informed von Rosenberg, but when they met again in the presence of von Rosenberg, Cuno's attitude had completely changed. The Chancellor now told Dulles that notification of the British government was impossible at the moment, while Theunis could be informed. After this opening statement, Cuno was silent for most of the rest of the meeting, while von Rosenberg declared that Germany could not make another offer and could not influence Britain in her relations with France. As to France, he maintained she did not want a financial settlement at all. If he should go "to Poincaré today and say out of newly discovered gold mines in Germany they had extracted 132 billion gold marks which would be delivered at 4 p.m. tomorrow, Poincaré would say it is due today, you are in default, and I seize your railroads so that you cannot make delivery tomorrow." France was determined, he reasoned, to "humiliate and crush" Germany, but the Reich simply would not be humiliated any more. After this emotional outbreak by von Rosenberg, Dulles again tried to convince him that even though he might be correct as to Poincaré's intentions, the cabinet should make another offer. Although von Rosenberg objected, he considered Dulles' visit an excellent chance for a diplomatic intrigue. He intended to inform Lord Curzon that an American citizen

[169] *Ibid.* This meeting took place on July 16, 1923.
[170] *Ibid.* Dulles' Papers contain a memorandum "German memo in form of July 16, 1923 as approved by Cuno, Maltzan, Ritter, and Gauss." However, it is unclear when this memo was written. On July 16, Dulles was in Hamburg. On July 17 he was back in Berlin. The memo contains all the changes suggested by Cuno in Hamburg. The essential points are the acceptance of a provisional settlement, the demand for a fixation of the German debt according to article 234 of the Versailles Treaty and concrete guarantees.

was on his way to Brussels where he would present "two papers." Dulles immediately refused to have his name mentioned in such an undertaking, correctly estimating that "Lord Curzon might draw the conclusion that my government was at least cognizant of my actions." Von Rosenberg of course hoped to create such an impression. Now he demanded that Dulles should not inform Theunis of the present meeting. The American lawyer did not want to participate any longer in von Rosenberg's diplomatic intrigues, and when Cuno broke his silence proposing that he return to Berlin if he received further information about developments in Belgium, Dulles simply rejected the suggestion.[171]

When Dulles saw Theunis in Brussels on July 19, he handed him the draft note which had been worked out in cooperation with Cuno as well as a paper with three offers regarding the evacuation of the Ruhr as laid down in von Rosenberg's cables to Hoesch and Sthamer at the beginning of June. After a conversation with Jaspar, Theunis rejected the conditions for evacuation.[172] Dulles also went to Paris and informed Loucheur about the result of his conversations in Brussels and Berlin. The former French Minister of Reconstruction confirmed that Dulles' memorandum would appeal very much to the French government. But he believed that Poincaré

did not want to agree to any program with Great Britain before Germany capitulated in the Ruhr, as Great Britain would thus gain the political prestige of having been the influence which determined Germany to give in. Poincaré was deliberately dragging the negotiations to this end.[173]

Nevertheless, Loucheur was prepared to arrange a meeting between Poincaré and Dulles, but the latter refused. When Loucheur suggested that Poincaré should be informed of the negotiations in Berlin, Dulles agreed under the condition that Loucheur did not leave any doubt that the Republican Administration had nothing to do with his visit.[174] With this meeting in Paris, Dulles' European trip came to an end. Another attempt to mediate between Germany, Belgium, and France had failed.

The intransigence of von Rosenberg against a modification of the terms of resistance did not help Germany at all. Even Lord Curzon, who only a few weeks before had not demanded unconditional surrender to French con-

[171] *Ibid.* In a letter to Melchior, Dulles confirmed on August 3 that although Cuno did not express concurrence with von Rosenberg's views, he agreed with the Foreign Minister that nothing should be done at the moment.

[172] Memo of Conference with Theunis, July 19, and Memo of Conference with Theunis, July 21, 1923, *ibid.* Jaspar was also present.

[173] Memo of Conference with Loucheur, July 25, 1923, *ibid.* Also *Loucheur Papers,* Box 12, Folder 4, July 25, 1923.

[174] Memo of Conference with Loucheur, July 25, 1923, *Dulles Papers, ibid.*

ditions, urged the German Foreign Office on July 19, to make concessions and withdraw the ordinances concerning passive resistance. Without concessions from all sides, a solution of the Ruhr crisis was impossible. Von Rosenberg was not yet willing to yield.[175] But just ten days later, on July 29, in the midst of domestic crisis, he instructed London that Germany's domestic situation was hopeless. The cabinet had to fight domestic unrest caused by the depreciation of the mark and the lack of food-stuffs. It would defend the Reich against any attacks from the Left or the Right, but it was important to know whether the government could hope for British aid now. In his desperation the Foreign Minister even considered moral aid or sympathy as an improvement over British silence. Upon Cuno's initiative, he also inquired what Germany could do herself to end the stalemate. Should the Reich, for example, demand admission to the League of Nations, or submit the legality of the Ruhr occupation to the International Court in The Hague? With this inquiry von Rosenberg admitted that he saw no way out. Domestic development forced him to petition for British aid. But Lord Curzon was simply not moved by these entreaties. Neither the admission to the League of Nations nor the submission of the Ruhr occupation to the International Court in The Hague would help. The inquiry was completely unrealistic, since both steps would be prevented by France.[176] Though Curzon had been informed that Germany could not last much longer, he did not explain to Sthamer that a British note to France had already been prepared and would be sent soon. Von Rosenberg's foreign policy, the purpose of which had been to obtain British intervention before the economy broke down, had failed. He had both overestimated British willingness to break with her war time ally and Germany's economic and financial strength. The combination of these factors together with the growing dissatisfaction with internal developments among the population finally led to the fall of the Cuno Cabinet. Von Rosenberg's foreign policy had greatly contributed to this development.

On the other hand, members of the British opposition, representatives of British industry, and especially the Governor of the Bank of England, who on July 31, still warned Germany not to capitulate and suggested to Sthamer that persons close to the Prime Minister also hoped that resistance would last at least until the opening of the French Chamber, contributed, if only

---

[175] Sthamer-AA, July 19, 1923, *PA AA*, Büro RM, Reparationen, D 720722. Von Rosenberg-Sthamer, July 19, 1923, *ibid.*, D 720727.

[176] Von Rosenberg-Sthamer, "Lagebericht," July 29, 1923, *ibid.*, Büro RM, Ruhrgebiet, Besatzungsprobleme, D 637780. Also Zimmermann, *Deutsche Außenpolitik*, p. 184.

indirectly, to the illusionary policy of von Rosenberg.[177] It is understandable that in face of these conflicting suggestions from private and official sources, von Rosenberg did not give up hope for British mediation. Politically disunited and facing financial chaos, Germany could not wait until Curzon had finished his long, skilful, but increasingly acrimonious correspondence with Poincaré. On the other hand, as all previous cabinets, Cuno had to carry through negotiations for an acceptable reparation offer against the interference of strong industrial groups, denying the government the right to pledge private property for reparation purposes or demanding preconditions for cooperation, which would not have been acceptable to either the SPD or the trade unions. Furthermore, despite certain misgivings about developments since May the parties were still united behind resistance, fearing French policy in the Rhineland and control of the Ruhr until reparations had been paid. Thus besides being a struggle for a revision of reparation payments, the Ruhr occupation also became identified with a fight for the independence and integrity of the Reich after Allied decisions in Upper Silesia had further reduced German territory. Under these circumstances it could hardly be expected that Germany would yield unconditionally before its financial and economic resources had been exhausted. The limits of these sources being known, a reasonable policy would have been to open negotiations earlier, a policy which had been urged by the SPD, the ADGB and isolated members of the bourgeois parties, but was prevented by von Rosenberg.

[177] Sthamer-AA, July 31, 1923, *PA AA*, Büro RM. Ruhrgebiet, Besatzungsprobleme, D 637806.

CHAPTER VI

FINANCIAL CHAOS AND THE RESIGNATION OF CUNO

I. PARTY ATTITUDES TOWARDS TAXATION

Besides foreign policy problems, the Cuno cabinet had also inherited unsolved domestic problems from its predecessors. While reparations remained the single most important issue in foreign affairs, the cabinet slowly overcame its domestic paralysis during the summer of 1923 and endeavored to tackle the country's major domestic problem – the adaptation of taxation to monetary inflation. The constant depreciation of the mark followed by a decline of its purchasing power had made the balancing of the budget more and more difficult during 1922. When the Reich's budget for 1923 was discussed in the Ministry of Finance, it had become clear that growing inflation had made calculations of expenditures and revenues nearly impossible. The Ministry's bureaucracy clearly recognized the effect of currency depreciation upon the Reich's fiscal system. Indeed, this system was the result of Matthias Erzberger's reforms in 1919 and had been developed under the precondition that the currency could be stabilized and that reparations would be adjusted to Germany's capacity to pay.[1] Nevertheless, the bureaucracy proved unwilling or unable to base taxation upon gold marks or any other stable standard of values. Instead, a draft bill, prepared by the Wirth cabinet, which proposed an increase of tax rates and modified the basis of assessment for income, property, corporation income, and inheritance taxes, was submitted to the Reichstag several days after the Cuno cabinet had been formed.[2] The change of the cabinet had not brought any significant alterations in the taxation policy of the Reich, since Wirth's Minister of Finance retained this post under Cuno as well.

When the government's proposals were discussed by the Taxation Com-

---

[1] See especially: Klaus Epstein, *Matthias Erzberger und das Dilemma der deutschen Demokratie* (Frankfurt, Berlin, Wien 1976²), 2nd ed., pp. 373–391. Peter Christian Witt, "Finanzpolitik und sozialer Wandel in Krieg und Inflation," *Industrielles System und politische Entwicklung in der Weimarer Republik*, hrsg. von Hans Mommsen, Dietmar Petzina. Bernd Weisbrod (Düsseldorf, 1974) pp. 395–426.

[2] *RT*, vol. 375, No. 5195, pp. 5639 ff.

mittee of the Reichstag, significant changes were written into the bill by the bourgeois tax specialists on the committee. These modifications amounted to a substantial increase of tax exemptions, which, the SPD felt, was not justified at all. But the majority of the Taxation Committee voted down all the SPD's proposals to amend the government bill and finally accepted the draft with several modifications.[3] When this new proposal was discussed in the Reichstag on December 14 and 16, even the Minister of Finance cautiously criticized the changes written into the bill by the Taxation Committee, while the SPD strongly disapproved of the attitude of the bourgeois parties and declared that even the government draft was insufficient. Hermes' criticism of the Taxation Committee finally led to a motion submitted by members of the Center, the DDP, and the DVP which modified the proposals of the Taxation Committee but did not restore the government bill. This compromise proposal, which was accepted against the opposition of the SPD and the KPD, still allowed a substantial increase of tax exemptions.[4]

Similar difficulties arose when the Ministry of Finance submitted a bill to adapt taxation to monetary inflation. The draft bill reveals that the Ministry itself was opposed to the creation of a stable standard of values for the Reich's fiscal system. As justification for this policy, the drafters of the bill pointed out that introduction of such a system could only be part of a more complex reform including the stabilization of the mark. Until this final goal had been achieved, the creation of stable rates would serve to undermine the position of the mark, since similar steps in other fields – especially wages, salaries and commercial contracts – would follow. Such a development would, the authors of the bill maintained, lead to a "premature curtailment of the paper mark" as lawful money. Besides this effect, they feared that a stable standard of values would not contribute anything to an increase of the exchange rate of the mark either. The financial experts of the Ministry of Finance had further reasons for opposing the introduction of gold taxes, arguing that, in comparison to the prewar period, an adequate standard for price movements did not exist, since inflation did not allow a sound fixation of tax indices. Without safe estimates or indices fair taxation was impossible.[5]

---

[3] *Ibid.* No., 5335, pp. 5778 ff. For example, the government draft started with the collection of income tax from 250,000 marks and introduced new tax rates for the next three additional 125,000 marks, while the proposal of the Taxation Committee began with 300,000 marks, and introduced new tax rates at additional 300,000, 100,000, and 500,000 marks. The higher rates also differed.

[4] *Ibid.*, pp. 9308 ff. The compromise proposal started with 400,000, but then increased the tax rate for every 200,000 for the next three tax classes.

[5] *Ibid.*, vol. 376, No. 5490, pp. 5639 ff. The cabinet had agreed to the proposal on December 22. *Kab. Cuno*, No. 29.

The preparations for the bill had been finished by December 18: that is, at a moment when the Ruhr had not yet been occupied, when the rate of exchange of the mark to the dollar had been far above the rate that was reached by the end of January, and when the purchasing power of the mark had still been higher. Thus when discussion of the bill began in the Taxation Committee, calculations of the new tax rates were already based on faulty premises. Although it could not possibly have been foreseen, the debates in the committee revealed that the parties did not even make allowances for this new development after it had set in. Instead, significant modifications, which in fact reduced the tax receipts of the Reich, were written into the bill by the majority of the Taxation Committee, while all proposals of the SPD to adapt taxation to monetary inflation and introduce a stable standard of values were voted down.[6]

True enough, the representative of the DDP had demanded the introduction of tariffs based upon gold marks, but his colleagues from the DVP and the DNVP had both argued that this was inconceivable as long as excessive reparations, being the basic cause of inflation, were not reduced. However, the position of the DVP differed slightly from that of the DNVP, and the DVP representative demanded the automatic adaptation of taxation to monetary inflation. This suggestion was simply rejected by Johannes Popitz, *Ministerialdirigent* in the Ministry of Finance, who disputed that a "miracle formula" for adaptation existed, and also warned that expert studies in the Ministry of Finance had shown conclusively that a fair index did not exist and that the mark would lose its function as a currency, if taxes based upon gold were introduced.[7] With the Ministry of Finance opposed to taxes based upon gold, the bourgeois parties gladly accepted the government's proposals. While unanimity had not existed about the necessity of a stable standard of values, the members of the Taxation Committee unanimously protested against the increase of the exchange stamp tax [Wechselsteuer]. This time, Popitz blocked demands to modify the government bill by arguing that the Reichsbank and the *Centralverband des deutschen Banken- und Bankiergewerbes*, which had both been informed of the provisions of the bill in advance, had accepted the new rates.[8]

Popitz's statement throws an interesting light on the functioning of the Reich's bureaucracy and its cooperation, or at least its intimacy with private interest groups. It was obvious that officials in the Ministry of Finance felt

---

[6] *RT*, Vol. 375, No. 5600, pp. 6327 ff.

[7] *Ibid.*, pp. 6327 ff. For Popitz' activities see Hildemarie Dieckmann, *Johannes Popitz, Entwicklung und Wirksamkeit in der Weimarer Republik*, (Berlin, 1960), pp. 19–41.

[8] *RT*, vol. 376, No. 5600, pp. 6329 ff.

compelled to consider the attitude of these groups in the drafting of new bills. On the other hand, the Ministry of Finance, responsible for the Reich's budget, also needed revenues to cover expenditures, and when the tax specialists of the DDP and the DVP supported a motion of the DNVP demanding that stocks of industry and trade should be taxed at the end of the year according to their purchase price minus a deduction for a deterioration in value, the representatives of the Ministry of Finance objected and defended the government proposal which did not allow deductions. They disputed the justification of the motion on two grounds. First, deductions would exempt solvent taxpayers from carrying an adequate tax burden, and second, the proposal would create additional problems for the revenue offices. Who was going to decide on the amount of deterioration? Was it possible to find a fair index for these deductions at all? The revenue offices were already overburdened with constant changes which had become necessary because of the adaptation of taxation to inflation and simply could not control or introduce any new modus of payments. But despite protests of the Ministry of Finance, changes were made.[9]

This was not the only instance when government proposals were modified. The draft bill also included provisions which liberated existing banking laws. Forced deposits and customer lists that had been introduced in 1919 were cancelled. Industry, trade, banking, and the Reichsbank had been opposed to these decrees from the beginning, arguing that the provisions had led to a flight of capital abroad and had severely limited credit, while the original intention of the law – to control tax evasion – had not been achieved either.[10] When the DDP, the DNVP, and the DVP demanded that the obligation of the banks to inform the revenue offices of the holdings of their clients should

---

[9] *Ibid.*, pp. 6333 ff. The assessment of stocks for property taxes was indeed one of the most complicated issues during the inflation. The bourgeois parties felt that the value of stocks which had been increased in absolute figures because of the depreciation of the mark should not be assessed at all, since these figures only constituted "sham profits." On the other hand, the parties recognized that profits were possible, if stocks had been used for production and had been supplemented again. In order to find some basis for assessment, they suggested that only permanent stocks should be taxed according to a very complicated system which was criticized by both Popitz and the SPD.

[10] *Ibid.* For the attitude of banking see a letter of the *Centralverband des deutschen Banken- und Bankiergewerbes*, the *Genossenschaftsverband der deutschen Raiffeisengenossenschaften*, the *Deutsche Genossenschaftsverband*, the *Deutsche Sparkassenbund*, the *Reichsverband der deutschen landwirtschaftlichen Genossenschaften* and the *Verband deutscher öffentlicher Kreditanstalten* to Cuno, *BA*, R 43I/2357, January 9, 1923. The *Deutscher Industrie- und Handelstag*, the *Hauptgemeinschaft des deutschen Handels*, the *Reichsausschuß des deutschen Handwerks*, the *Reichsverband der deutschen Industrie* and the *Inlandsverband des deutschen Großhandels* demanded on January 20 that only if serious grounds for suspicion existed the banks should cooperate. *Ibid.*

also be abolished, Popitz refused this concession, since the Reich needed these provisions in order to prosecute tax evaders. The representatives of the bourgeois parties were not satisfied with Popitz, and in order to strengthen their arguments they invited the President of the Reichsbank to a committee meeting. Havenstein, having always been opposed to these decrees, was only too willing to accept. When he appeared before the Taxation Committee, he reasoned that these laws did not prevent tax evasions at all. Instead, the supervision of bank accounts by the revenue offices had led to the withdrawal of holdings, excessive spending, and the purchase of commodities. This development, he pointed out, had completely destroyed the individual drive to save and had thus further contributed to inflation. This interpretation of one of the causes of inflation was immediately disputed by the Secretary of State in the Ministry of Finance, Zapf, who stressed that it was not the banking laws but the constant depreciation of the mark that had led to the withdrawal of savings. However, representatives of the DDP, the DVP, and BVP, and the DNVP supported Havenstein, demanding that the secrecy of banking transactions be re-introduced.

In general, with only a few exceptions where the government bill was improved, the bourgeois parties modified the original bill so that tax receipts for the Reich dropped. As in December the committee increased tax exemptions on property taxes from 500,000 marks in the government bill to 1.5 billion marks. The same happened with the inheritance tax where the appropriate figures for the lowest and highest rates were 200,000 and 400,000 marks respectively.[11]

When Keinath of the DDP explained the bill before the Reichstag, he admitted that the tax rates did not correspond with the rate of inflation but argued that, because of differences between the experts as to an appropriate tax index, only a provisional solution had been found.[12]

The new bill was only an emergency measure, but the question still remained whether the laws would provide sufficient revenues to balance the budget. Without exception, representatives of the bourgeois parties who spoke in the Reichstag ignored this question. Instead, they argued that calculation of taxes was impossible as long as the depreciation of the currency continued. From this interpretation, however, they did not draw the conclusion that the government ought to stop the inflation, but they reasoned that inflation was the result of German reparation payments and the negative balance of payments. Cuno himself was of the opinion that even without reparation payments, the German currency would have depreciated because

[11] *RT*, vol. 376, No. 5600, pp. 6346 ff.
[12] *Ibid.*, vol. 358, pp. 10003 ff, March 8, 1923.

of the negative balance of payments.[13] Keinath maintained that German citizens payed higher taxes than Allied citizens, and Zapf claimed that the German tax system was "exhausted." Hermes, Moldenhauer (DVP), Helfferich (DNVP), and Herold (Z) warned that an increase in taxation above the rates of the bill would immediately lead to a serious economic crisis. The demands of the SPD to increase tax rates would, in their opinion, curtail Germany's export capability and lead to unemployment. Against this strong opposition, the SPD, which agreed with the majority that a final reform of the tax system was not yet possible, vainly argued in favor of an increase in taxes for solvent taxpayers. A motion demanding the reintroduction of the government bill in those areas where it yielded more than the modified draft was simply voted down. The same happened with other proposals which went beyond the bill submitted.[14]

These parliamentary discussions reveal that the parties, with the exception of the SPD, the KPD and some members of the Center, were not in favor of higher taxation. After the Cuno cabinet had resigned, the Minister of Finance complained in a private letter that the bourgeois parties had simply been unwilling to support the government. Hermes' own party, the Center, had not been an exception, and he reported that his party did not want to accept the "ungrateful duty towards its electorate, to vote confiscatory taxes together with the SPD." Instead the Center had always demanded that the cabinet obtain the support of the other bourgeois parties for its taxation policy.[15]

Besides the parties, representatives of other interest groups also influenced the shaping of the cabinet's fiscal policy, and on July 22, a member of the Center Party wrote that because of the "ruthless" policy of pressure groups governmental proposals had been demolished. Twice Cuno intervened personally to obtain the support of the DNVP and the BVP for his cabinet's tax measures.[16] On the other hand, the Minister of Finance himself informed Helfferich and Reichert of the DNVP about tax bills in advance, and apparently took note of their wishes.[17] The parties in the Reichstag were more interested in handing out preferential treatment to interest groups represent-

[13] Ibid., vol. 357, pp. 9100 ff, November 24, 1922.
[14] Ibid., vol. 358, 10009 ff, pp. 10029 ff, and 10085 ff, March 9, 1923, Ibid., vol. 376, No. 5601 ff.
[15] Marx Nachlaß, III, September 21, 1923, p. 91.
[16] Ibid., p. 92 f. Cf. petitions, BA, R 431/2357.
[17] "Vertraulicher Bericht über die neuen Steuern." In this meeting, Hermes informed Helfferich, Reichert, and Reusch about the forced loan. Helfferich demanded that the term "speculation profits" had to be defined in the new law. Only sales within three months after the purchase should by included. Reichert demanded a modification of the heritage tax which was too high. HA GHH, 3001930/16. Also RT, vol. 358, p. 10040.

ed by their parties than in a sound fiscal policy for the Reich. In other words, while the bourgeois majority prevented the collection of adequate taxes from income and corporation-income taxpayers, wage and salary earners carried a disproportional part of the tax burden.[18] The Dawes Committee later criticised this policy with the following words:

It can be said with confidence that the wealthier classes have escaped with far less than their proper share of the national burden, and we have put it as a matter for serious consideration of the German government whether they should not, facing even the admitted administrative difficulties, review the assessments of recent years in the case of those particular classes of taxpayers and reassess their liability upon a gold basis.[19]

2. FINANCIAL ALTERNATIVES IN THE SUMMER OF 1923

Although criticism of the Reich's fiscal policy – further complicated through the attitude of the Länder – is only too justified, it has to be noted that several attempts were made during the summer of 1923 to change this state of affairs, unfortunately coming too late. The ever growing inflation, the growing disillusionment of great parts of the population with the fiscal policy, and the fear of a complete break-down of the Reich's finances finally led to a renewed examination of its fiscal system. In this context it is important to note that the initiative was developed in the Chancellory. In a memorandum prepared for Cuno, Secretary of State Hamm stressed that the destruction of the currency, which he regarded as the basis of all financial problems, had to be prevented by all means, otherwise social unrest and unpredictable developments might be the result. Immediate changes had become obligatory, and Hamm strongly urged the introduction of financial and economic measures by the Minister of Finance and the Minister of Economics that would contribute to a stabilization of the mark. As a first step he suggested that opportunities for stable investments had to be created, wages and salaries had to be adapted to the inflation, the collection of direct taxes had to be facilitated, luxury spending and unnecessary imports had to be curtailed, and exports had to be subsidized.[20]

[18] According to Hertz of the SPD the percentage of wage taxes among income taxes rose from 20% in 1920, 33% in 1921 to about 57% in August 1922. *RT*, vol. 357, pp. 9308 ff.

[19] Report of the First Committee of Experts," printed in Harold G. Moulton, *The Reparation Plan. An Interpretation of the Reports of the Expert Committees Appointed by the Reparation Commission*, repr. (Westport, 1970), p. 198.

[20] *Kab. Cuno*, No. 192, June 16, 1923. Cf. letter Becker, Heinze, Luther to the Länder governments, June 9, 1923, *BA*, R 431/2435.

With the internal situation deteriorating rapidly and with foreign intervention still not in sight, the Minister of Finance warned at about the same time, that, because of the depreciating currency and government spending for the Ruhr struggle, the budgetary deficit of the Reich was constantly increasing. Until June 11, the Minister of Labor had received 1.346 billion paper marks for social welfare work in the Ruhr, the Minister of Interior had obtained 160 billions to indemnify requisitions by the occupation troops, while the railway administration had needed 1.710 billions. With credits to industry and sums already guaranteed, Ruhr expenditures had risen to 5 trillion paper marks. In the same period, the floating debt of the Reich had increased from 1.495 billions in January to 10.275 billions by June. Hermes estimated that the Ministry of Labor alone would need another 1.2 trillion marks for wages until the end of July.[21]

With this statement Hermes finally admitted that the Reich's fiscal system was not able to carry the burden of passive resistance any longer, since receipts did not cover expenditures. However, this was not a new development, the gap between revenues and expenditures, with few exceptions, having constantly increased since the war. It had only widened after the Ruhr occupation, and when the tax program was discussed before the Reichstag, expenditures were already seven times as high as revenues. It should be remembered that at that time Hermes still defended his tax legislation and apparently considered it to be adequate to cover at least a substantial amount of the budget, while he now rejected any responsibility for the Reich's fiscal developments if government spending were not limited.[22]

The situation had indeed become intolerable, and only two days later Cuno announced in a letter to the Minister Presidents of the Länder demanding cooperation, that the cabinet would now fight the growing inflation and promised that the adaptation of wages and salaries would be accelerated. He openly admitted that wage and salary earners as well as pensioners were especially handicapped by the monthly collection of income taxes, and he declared his readiness to enforce a similar policy upon all those members of society which until now had been favored by a less frequent collection of taxes.[23] The program outlined in Cuno's letter was a mere promise for future action and it did not contain a detailed plan. Although these announcements obviously served to quieten criticism of the cabinet, the following weeks

[21] *Kab. Cuno*, No. 193, June 16, 1923. For the adaption of wages and unemployment benefits to the inflation cf. Oltmann, *op. cit.*, pp. 88 ff. Cf. *Kab. Cuno*, No. 147, May 2, 1923. Erdmann, *op. cit.*, p. 152.
[22] *Kab. Cuno*, No. 193, June 16, 1923.
[23] *Ibid.*, No. 196, June 18, 1923. At a meeting with members of the *Verband Sächsischer Industrieller* Cuno discussed conditions in Saxony. *Ibid.*, No. 197, June 19, 1923.

reveal that the Chancellor and his Secretary of State were seriously considering currency reform and an adaptation of taxation to the growing inflation. Britain had not yet answered the German note of June 6, and if the Reich wanted to hold out until Britain intervened, immediate action was necessary.

Speculation against the mark was another problem, and here the cabinet became active again in order to obtain the means for an extension of resistance. On July 20 a first meeting with members of the banking community and the Reichswirtschaftsrat was held under the presidency of the Minister of Economics.[24] According to Kempner the participants agreed to the following points: 1) trade with foreign exchange should be stopped despite overwhelming economic objections and although such a measure could not be enforced in the occupied area; 2) the purchase of foreign stocks with paper marks from foreigners had to be discontinued, although exceptions were possible in order to secure a German majority in foreign enterprises, and a fixed rate of exchange was proposed despite the opposition from import trade; 3) the Chambers of Commerce which issued certificates for the purchase of foreign exchange were advised to restrict the issue.[25]

A second meeting of the same group was held on June 21, and now the creation of a central exchange office [Devisenzentrale] was discussed. With the exception of Rudolf Hilferding, all opposed such an institution, Samuel Ritscher of the Dresdener Bank arguing that the Austrian experience with such an office hardly suggested a repetition in Germany. According to Ritscher, the creation of this office had only led to a depreciation of the currency, a decrease of imports, and a rise in prices, while Austria's financial and monetary situation had only improved after foreign credits had been made available.[26] Another argument was brought forward by Wassermann of the Deutsche Bank when the limitation of foreign exchange trade was discussed. He felt that it was hardly realistic to leave the control to individual bankers:

The banks cannot and will not control requirements for foreign exchange more severely. They only fulfill the orders of their clients. This is a misunderstanding of the economic function of the banks and is subordinate, but these facts have to be recognized.[27]

---

[24] *BA*, R 43I/2445, June 16, 1923. According to this list Hilferding, Schmidt, Wassermann, Melchior, Hagen, Lehnel, Lindgens, Böhm, Frowein, Witthöft, Kotzenberg, Loeb, Urbig, Ritscher, Maron, Mersbach, Krämer, Schwarz, and Cramer were invited. Whether they all participated in unclear.
[25] "Besprechung im Reichstag über Devisenfragen, June 20, 1923," *ibid.*
[26] "Devisenzentrale und wertbeständige Anlagen," *ibid.*, undated.
[27] *Ibid.*, fol. 165–166, undated and unsigned note.

Even if a control of the trade in foreign exchange had been accepted, serious difficulties would have remained. Between three to four thousand private bankers had to be controlled. On the other hand, if trade with foreign exchange was limited to a selected group, who was going to decide upon the selection? It would certainly have been a difficult decision, and one proposal suggesting the foundation date of the banks as an adequate criterion was not taken seriously. However, Kempner was convinced that something had to be done, and he proposed that the granting of export licences and the control of foreign exchange deliveries by the Reichsbank should be handled less liberally, and that deliveries should be increased.[28]

Export controls already existed, but the amount of foreign exchange which had to be delivered to the Export Trade Office [Außenhandelsstelle] differed according to the goods exported. For example, sixty to ninety percent of foreign currency earned through the export of China had to be delivered to this office, while the rates for cables (basically consisting of copper and rubber which had to be reimported) was only ten percent. According to Kemper the average rate was forty percent, and he felt that these scales could be increased through a strict control of industry. A second measure would be the enforcing of foreign exchange deliveries. After the Export Trade Office had received information about exports, it would inform the Reichsbank of the quotas which had to be delivered. This system, however, had one serious weakness: the Reichsbank only checked every two or three months whether these quotas had actually been transferred. But even if a company did deliver and obtained paper marks in return, it could immediately buy foreign exchange again with a Chamber of Commerce licence. This system of course allowed the uncontrolled purchase of foreign exchange, a factor which contributed to the depreciation of the currency. But since industry needed foreign exchange for the purchase of raw materials abroad, it is only too understandable for industrialists to hold foreign exchange accounts in order to guarantee the solvency of their enterprises. The situation was of course different if foreign exchange was hoarded abroad or used for domestic business transactions, a practice quite common among industrialists.[29]

While these discussions were going on, Cuno held several meetings with the Reichsbank, urging intervention in support of the mark, both in order to gain time for further negotiations with the Allies and to allow a prolon-

---

[28] *BA*, R 43I/2445, Kempner, June 19, 1923, and *ibid.*, fol. 163.

[29] *Ibid.* For the consequences of foreign exchange laws on business transactions cf. *WWA*, Klc, HK Dortmund, Abt. XVI, Nr. 10, "Gesetz über den Verkehr mit ausländischen Zahlungsmitteln." Maier, *op. cit.*, pp. 68 ff.

gation of resistance. As on previous occasions, Havenstein surrendered to what he considered political necessities, only demanding that the Reichsbank fix the exchange rate of the mark to the dollar. This policy would of course have an immediate impact on export and import trade, and before the cabinet decided upon a government decree, Cuno informed representatives of industry and trade in separate meetings about his intentions.[30] As the following developments show, various bankers and industrialists were opposed to these measures. The Minister of Economics also objected, arguing that the decree would impede import trade and enforce the tendency to buy foreign currency on the black market in the occupied area. The Reich simply did not have the power to enforce the decree there. There was indeed good reason to believe it would not function, since the Reichsbank could not affect notations in New York, Paris, or London either. While most cabinet members recognized that preliminary stabilization was necessary for political reasons, hardly anybody believed that it would function.[31]

The relevance of the decree for a prolongation of resistance has already been mentioned above, but obviously the decree was also of immense domestic importance. The catastrophic fall of the mark and its effect on the population had led to increased criticism of the cabinet in the liberal, social-democratic, and communist press. A fixed rate of exchange could be considered a first step towards limitation of the trade in foreign exchange and might thus have a positive effect upon the SPD, which had long demanded such a move. The support of the SPD was important to keep the mass of the working class united behind the policy of passive resistance. On the other hand, Cuno's decision to introduce a fixed rate of exchange would certainly lead to difficulties with the banking community, which had always been opposed to such a policy.[32] But the cabinet did not have time for further discussion of its policy measures, and in order to prevent delay through parliamentary discussions, the decree was passed under the emergency legislation of Article 48 of the constitution.

The publication of the decree did indeed cause protests, especially from

---

[30] *BA* 43I/2445. The list of invitation for industry has the following names: Stinnes, Raabe (Thyssen Konzern), Reusch (did not attend), Schäffer (Krupp), Deutsch, Frowein, Rosenthal, Friedrich von Siemens, Berckemeyer, Hartmann, Simson, Hirsch, Eichberg (Linke-Hoffmann). At 6 p.m. trade representatives appeared: Münchmeyer (President of the Chamber of Commerce, Hamburg), Bromberg (Hamburg), Stimming (Norddeutscher Lloyd), Carl Adler (Adler Werke), Cramer (President of the Chamber of Commerce, Bremen), Blumenstein. A report about the meeting could not be located, but cf. "Besprechung im Reichstag über Devisenfragen am 20. Juni 1923," *ibid.*, p. 160.

[31] *Kab. Cuno*, No. 200, June 22, 1923.

[32] Jakob Riesser in the Reichstag on April 20, 1923, *RT*, vol. 358, pp. 10088 ff. Also *Bankarchiv*, No. 12, March 15, 1923, p. 193 f.

bankers in the occupied area. Louis Hagen, Robert Pferdmenges, and other bankers from Cologne had already informed the Ministry of Economics on June 22 that they did not intend to observe the government decree. Hagen, one of the participants of the first meeting with Cuno on June 20, had pointed out at that time that the decree would create serious difficulties for import trade. In addition, because of communication difficulties with Berlin (it took two days for a cable to reach Cologne), the decree would destroy the functioning of the economy in the occupied areas. The Chamber of Commerce at Duisburg also protested and warned that the purchase of food stuffs would be endangered if the decree were enforced.[33]

If the Reichsbank had allowed these groups to buy foreign exchange at a rate different from the one fixed daily in Berlin, or before the exchange opened or after it closed, the decree would have lost all meaning. The attempt to control the purchase of foreign currency and thus ease the pressure on the mark would have been doomed to fail even before it started. The government was therefore in no mood to yield to the opposition and, as it became manifest, Kempner arranged a meeting between Becker, von Rosenberg, Schröder (of the Ministry of Finance), and a representative of the Reichsbank, at which it was decided to hold a conference with representatives of the main banks the next day and to ask them to cooperate with the Reichsbank and influence their branches in the occupied area.[34]

Of those bankers who participated at the conference Wassermann (Deutsche Bank), Mosler (Diskonto-Gesellschaft), Ritscher (Dresdener Bank), and Goldschmidt (Darmstädter & Nationalbank) promised to support the government decree, Wassermann suggesting that the Reichsbank liquidate the deposit accounts of those banks that did not support the measure. The Vice-President of the Reichsbank, von Glasenapp, was especially incensed about the cables from Cologne and threatened not only to liquidate the deposit accounts but also warned that he would freeze all credits if the Cologne bankers did not "withdraw their declarations." One other banker believed that Pferdmenges, Hagen and foreign banks in the occupied area could not be influenced, which led von Glasenapp to repeat his threats. The Minister of Economics was more cautious, suggesting that Cuno should talk to bankers and industrialists from the occupied area first, making clear his own doubts about the practicability of the decree.[35]

---

[33] Telegram Hagen/Pferdmenges-Becker, June 22, 1923, *BA*, R 43I/2445. The cable also mentions Deichmann, Delbrück, von der Heydt, Levy, Oppenheim, Seligmann and Stein. Pferdmenges-Becker, June 24, 1923, *ibid.*

[34] *Kab. Cuno*, No. 203, June 25, 1923.

[35] Besides the above mentioned banks, deputies from *Mendelssohn & Co., Berliner Handels-Gesellschaft, Mitteldeutsche Creditbank, J. Dreyfus & Co., Kretschmar, S.*

When Cuno met representatives from the occupied area the next day, Louis Hagen preferred not to appear.[36] Even without him bankers and industrialists came out strongly against the decree, and Robert Pferdmenges again stressed that it was impractical. Although most were opposed to the form in which Hagen had announced his opposition, they did not leave any doubt that from a "technical" point of view the government's action was a mistake. Abraham Frowein, textile manufacturer from the Rhineland and member of the *RdI* directorate, was especially outspoken in his criticism and demanded, together with Pferdmenges, Herren, and Hohenemser (Rheinische Kreditbank, Mannheim), that the decree be modified.[37]

Although Cuno and von Glasenapp repeatedly stressed that the government and the Reichsbank would use all means, including credit restrictions and the liquidation of deposit accounts and would make public the names of the opposition, several members of the conference tried to convince Cuno that they needed a preferential assignment of foreign exchange, otherwise employment was endangered. But the Reichsbank was opposed to such a policy, although Kauffmann admitted that import trade would be especially hurt. On the other hand, he warned that the "banks sell marks in foreign countries for import trade." This was harmful for the currency and could not be tolerated.[38] Even though the Reichsbank had demanded complete subordination, a compromise was finally reached and orders for foreign exchange were to be collected in Mannheim, Cologne, and Frankfurt and then forwarded to Berlin. The Reichsbank also agreed to fulfill demands if they should arrive late in Berlin because of postal difficulties.[39] Besides these domestic attempts to stabilize the currency, Havenstein again attempted to

Bleichröder, Hardy & Co. and the *Commerz- und Privatbank* also attended. The handwritten note is partly printed *ibid.*, footnote 4. One whole page was not printed. Cf. *BA*, R 43I/2445.

[36] Invitations were sent to the *Rheinische Kreditbank*, the *Bankhaus* J.H. Stein (x), the *Süddeutsche Discontogesellschaft* (x), the *Handelskammer Düsseldorf* (x) and Langen, Duisberg (x), Stinnes, Silverberg, Reusch (x), von Oppenheim (x), Hagen (x), Wolff, Herren, Carp (x), Karl Haniel, *Pferdmenges, Tengelmann*, Schäffer (Krupp), *Hirschland, Vögler*, Sorge, *Frowein, Kaufmann, Deichmann*, Most, Hasslacher, Bierwes. Of these the underlined did appear and participated in the discussion, those marked (x) cabled that they could not attend. See *Kab. Cuno*, No. 203, footnotes 6 and 7.

[37] *Ibid.*, and *BA*, R 43I/2445. Part of the handwritten note is unreadable.

[38] *BA*, R 43I/2445. Vögler, who wanted the export tax to be abolished, argued that it was a political measure and not an economic one. Only Hirschland did not directly oppose the decree, maintaining that he could not yet evaluate the consequences.

[39] *Ibid.* On July 17 Bavarian banks also demanded that their foreign exchange orders should be treated similarly to those of the occupied area. The Reichsbank agreed. *Ibid.*, R 43I/2446. It is possible that Cuno met Hagen and tried to overcome his opposition. See *Kab. Cuno*, No. 200, footnote II. Cuno cabled Hagen to come to Elberfeld on June 28, but it is uncertain whether this meeting took place.

obtain foreign help. But the Bank of England, which had given credit against gold securities during the first months of 1923, was no longer willing to help. Montagu Norman felt that the mark could not be saved any more, and since the public had lost all confidence in the currency, it did not really matter whether it stood at 700,000 or 2 billion marks to the dollar. If this development had not set in, Norman would have helped "out of friendship for Havenstein."[40]

Within the next weeks, several other attempts were made to control speculation,[41] but the Minister of Economics believed that all these decrees would be futile, arguing not without justification that industry and trade could not even be blamed for investing its working capital in foreign currency, since without such investments the turnover of goods was unrealizable during the inflation. Becker was convinced that only one way existed to stop this development: gold accounts had to be created and all credit transactions had to be converted to a gold standard, or any other stable standard of value. Economic problems connected with the introduction of a stable currency had been discussed in the Ministry of Economics for some time, and after a meeting with representatives of the Association of German Industry on April 19, Becker expounded in a letter to Cuno that the RdI was prepared to accept gold accounts.[42] The attitude of the RdI was the consequence of a development which had started long before. While inflation had favored German exports on the world market since 1918, the growing depreciation of the currency also led to the introduction of accounting based on gold, the dollar, or the pound sterling. The Deutsch-Luxemburgische Bergwerks- und Hütten-AG, for example, had not had any mark balances since the spring of 1921.[43] In other big companies the situation was probably the same, and the Gutehoffnungshütte demanded that all branches of the concern pay each other in foreign currency.[44] Thus in normal business transactions, the mark had partly lost its value as legal tender.

In a memorandum prepared in the Ministry of Economics at the beginning of 1923, the causes for this development were summarized and a solution to the pending problem was proposed. Since this memorandum explains the position of the Ministry in detail and also served as a basis for discussions

[40] Sthamer-AA, June 18, 29, and July 31, 1923, *PA AA*, Handakten Direktoren, Schriftverkehr, D 419177–179, D 419140.

[41] See *Reichsgesetzblatt* (RGBl), I 1923, p. 401 f, p. 507 f, p. 549, p. 765.

[42] Becker-Cuno, *BA*, R 43I/2435,

[43] Peter Czada, "Ursachen und Folgen der Inflation," *Finanz- und wirtschaftspolitische Fragen der Zwischenkriegszeit*, Verein für Sozialpolitik. Gesellschaft für Wirtschafts- und Sozialwissenschaften, Neue Folge Band 73, 1973, pp. 28 ff. Maier, *op. cit.*, pp. 68 ff.

[44] "Bericht über die 4. Konzernsitzung," Oberhausen, February 6, 1922, *HA GHH*, 3001900/1.

within the Ministry, it deserves to be quoted at some length. Its author, Ministerialdirektor Rudolf Dalberg, began by outlining the negative effects of the continued depreciation of the currency upon economic life. The non-existence of a stable currency had, he maintained, led to a "progressive consumption of the working capital" of industry and trade. The destruction of the currency as a standard of value had in the beginning created "self-deception about profits, and had furthermore destroyed the basis of all contracts based upon marks." Following this development the economy had "disengaged itself from paper marks" during the last few years. Initially it had started in the field of imports; export trade had followed, and in the end, since nobody was willing or able to carry the risks of trading with a depreciating currency, even calculations for domestic contracts had been based upon foreign exchange.[45]

As a result of this development even small trade and domestic industries not dependent upon imports or exports had been forced to invest their working capital in foreign exchange. Thus purchase of foreign currency was of course a "burden on the balance of payments" and already in February 1923 Dalberg had suggested that "an embargo on foreign exchange will improve the balance of payments and have a favorable effect on the rate of exchange of the mark."[46] Dalberg had correctly evaluated the effect of the purchase of foreign exchange against paper marks, and it is interesting to follow his arguments a little further. It could not be denied that industry and trade needed working capital in order to keep the economy going. On the other hand, prohibition of the purchase of foreign currency would be of little value, since it simply would not be obeyed. Therefore, only the creation of stable investments for industry would solve the problem.

Several experiments with long-term capital investments based on coal or rye had already been successful in Germany, and Dalberg was convinced that a basis for short-term investments of capital existed as well.

There are already large German industries who are working with foreign exchange credit [Valutakredit], who have no objection to debts in foreign exchange. They can carry the burden, because their profits correspond to the value of foreign exchange, whether they are made abroad or at home.[47]

---

[45] Cf. Rudolf Dalberg, *Die Entwertung des Geldes*, Berlin 1918. He worked as a Regierungsdirektor in the Reichswirtschaftsministerium. For his proposal see: "Zur Einführung der Banko-Mark (Goldkonten bei den Banken)," *BA* R 43I/2435, February 2, 1923, Dalberg.

[46] *Ibid.*

[47] *Ibid.* Rudolf Stucken, "Die wertbeständigen Anleihen in finanzieller Betrachtung," *Schriften des Vereins für Sozialpolitik*, 160 (1924), counts 20 loans in 1923 alone.

In addition, he was convinced that foreign exchange credits in Germany were still higher than paper mark credits of the Reichsbank and, in order to support his estimate, he pointed to the Dutch credit of 120 million gulden, which had been given to Germany at the beginning of 1921.[48]

Considering the demand for safe investments and the availability of foreign exchange in Germany, Dalberg saw no reason why a system based upon a stable value, which he called "Banko-Mark" would not work, and that technical difficulties, e.g. the problem of securing the solvency of banks, could be solved. As an example, he mentioned a co-operative in Baden which had based saving accounts and loans on the value of wheat. He was convinced that a similar system might be arranged for the Reich, the only difference being that, instead of wheat, about 20–25 million gold marks, which were necessary as basic capital and would have to be raised by industry, trade and banking, would be used. As soon as this basis had been established, he believed, owners of foreign exchange would invest their money in these accounts, while at the same time industry, trade and agriculture, always in need of credit, would obtain paper mark credit repayable at a fixed rate based upon gold. This was an important difference to the policy of the Reichsbank which was criticized by Dalberg, because the bank's issue of paper mark credits allowed their repayment with depreciated currency and because they could only be made available through an "ever increasing use of the printing press." Thus the Reichsbank itself had contributed to the use of its credits to the advantage of private interests.

In his analysis of the currency situation, Dalberg also tried to deal with one of the most significant reasons for an inflationary policy – the financing of government expenditures. According to his scheme, prices might be based upon gold, but payments would still be made in paper marks. Thus the Reich would keep its means of payment. In addition, if public debts were not to be based upon gold, or if there were a lack of confidence in the currency, the Reich should give part of its property as security. He believed that a pledging of the railway system alone would provide enough paper marks to make monetary inflation unlikely. Naturally the introduction of gold accounts would also lead to wages based upon gold, and Dalberg maintained that several industrialists had declared their readiness to agree to gold wages. These wages would still be lower than wages in other countries, and he

---

[48] *RGBl* I 1923, p. 55 f. Dalberg's figure is wrong. The credit amounted to 200 million gulden at 6% interest. Sixty millions had to be spent in the Netherlands for the purchase of food stuffs, the rest could be used at Germany's will. In return Germany promised to deliver coal. Based upon a rate of 2.45 gulden to the dollar, 120 millions are about 201 million gold marks. See also *Kab. Müller* I, No. 55, April 19, 1920.

warned "the longer the establishing of stable values is dragged out, the heavier the crisis will set in later on because of the progressive exhaustion of capital."

Dalberg had also analysed the possibilities of a new fixed rate of exchange, suggesting that it should be linked to the pound sterling at a rate of £ 0.01 to the mark. This was most favorable for German industry and trade, since, if another European monetary crisis occurred, the British currency would also be affected. This meant that the export of German goods, which mostly went to Great Britain or countries connected with the pound sterling, would not be hurt. The creation of a "Banko-Mark" at the value of £ 0.01 also had an additional domestic advantage which was of great psychological and political importance. Since the war, wages expressed in gold figures were lower than they had been before the war, and Dalberg pointed out that wages based upon the above mentioned rate would, in absolute figures, be above peace rates. The logic of this argument is self-evident: a wage or salary earner might resent a drop of his income from 1000 gold marks in 1913 to 300 gold marks in 1923, but he might be satisfied with 1200–1400 "Banko-Marks."[49]

Dalberg's analysis was accepted by the Minister of Economics, and after consultation with the RdI Becker urged Cuno to support the plan. If the Reichsbank was unwilling to participate, he suggested that the Foreign Exchange Purchasing Office [Devisenbeschaffungsstelle], which already existed, could create the kind of institution described in Dalberg's memorandum.[50] Cuno agreed and on April 23 he forwarded a copy of Becker's letter to the Minister of Finance. On June 20, and again on July 11, the Secretary of State in the Chancellory, Hamm, had to remind the sick Hermes that Cuno had received no reply to the letter.[51]

When Hermes finally answered on July 13, nearly three precious months had been lost. Commenting on Becker's proposal, he agreed with the analysis in principle but argued that introduction of a central foreign exchange office and creation of gold accounts was impossible at the moment. The Reichsbank was emphatically opposed to the introduction of such a system for practical reasons. In order to protect the liquidity of the bank, any money

---

[49] *Ibid.* For discussion of wages based upon gold see Fritz Tarnow in *Korrespondenzblatt des ADGB* 1922, No. 41 S. 585; *ibid.*, No. 40 p. 577; *ibid.*, 1923, No. 11, p. 122, No. 25, p. 281, No. 26, 292. Oltmann, *op. cit.*, pp. 135 ff. Bernhard Bußmann, "Die Freien Gewerkschaften während der Inflation. Die Politik des Allgemeinen Deutschen Gewerkschaftsbundes und die soziale Entwicklung in den Jahren 1920–1923," Diss. Phil. (Kiel, 1965), p. 155 f.

[50] Becker-Cuno, April 20, 1923, *BA* 43I/2435, p. 170.

[51] *Ibid.*

accepted at a stable rate would have to be reinvested on the same basis. But even then problems arose, and he suggested that a notice of at least four weeks was needed to prevent the sudden withdrawal of deposits. Nevertheless, despite such a precautionary measure a bank might be unable to procure the money for reimbursements in case of sudden withdrawals, since the bank itself would be unable to recall all her investments. Such an emergency situation could only be overcome if the bank had foreign currency at its disposal, or if the Reichsbank discounted gold bills. But "the Reichsbank would never resolve to such a step, since in that case an enormous speculation would develop on the back of the Reichsbank." In addition to these practical difficulties, Hermes, in contrast to the Minister of Economics, argued that introduction of gold accounts would accelerate the adaption of domestic prices to prices on the world market. However, he promised to review the matter again, but there was no doubt in his mind as to what his experts' studies would reveal:

The real difficulties have been caused by the upsetting of Germany's economic equilibrium by the Versailles Treaty, which led to a negative balance of payments and a disproportion between revenues and expenditures.[52]

The attitude of the Ministry of Finance corresponded exactly with similar statements of the Reichsbank, the *Centralverband des deutschen Banken- und Bankiergewerbes*, and individual bankers. In a slightly modified version, Dalberg's memorandum had been published in *Bankarchiv* on March 1.[53] As early as March 17, the *Centralverband* passed a resolution against the creation of gold accounts as long as the reparation problem remained unsolved and a change in the existing insecurity as to Germany's financial and economic future had not been brought about.[54] Dalberg's proposal was also criticized by Max von Schinkel, prominent Hamburg banker, and other attacks in *Bankarchiv* followed.[55] At this early stage in the discussion Havenstein did not intervene, but he made his opposition to the scheme clear by arguing that introduction of gold accounts meant the financial breakdown of the Reich which could only pay its expenditures in paper marks.[56] The former Minister of Finance in the Scheidemann cabinet, Bernard Dernburg,

[52] Hermes-Hamm, July 13, 1923, *ibid*.
[53] *Bankarchiv*, No. 13, April 1, 1923, p. 165 f. E.W. Schmidt, "Die Wahrheit von heute. Bemerkungen zur Goldmarkrechnung."
[54] *Ibid*., No. 11, March 1, 1923, p. 141 f.
[55] *Ibid*., No. 12, March 15, p. 153 f "Zur sogenannten Bankowährung"; *ibid*., No. 14, April 15, 1923, p. 172 f.
[56] "43. Untersuchungsausschuss, Stützungsaktion, 7. Sitzung," June 7, 1923, *BA*, R 2/2419.

expounded in a letter to Hamm on June 16, that "any businessman worth his salt had to oppose such plans."[57] Walter Dauch, a member of the DVP and representative of the Hamburg export and import trade, was less certain than Dernburg, and after a discussion with Cuno informed the Chancellor that gold accounts would be necessary as soon as the Ruhr was liberated. On the other hand, Dauch admitted that it was advisable to start with such action even earlier. In this context, it was also of great domestic significance that export, shipping, and other industries already accounting with gold should also pay gold wages. Such a policy, he felt, was necessary to contain public unrest, and he reasoned that in Hamburg alone 30–40,000 men could be "pulled out of radical tracks and be turned into reliable citizens." In his opinion a combination of factors – the negative balance of trade, the negative balance of payments, the lack of confidence in the country's economic and political future, and insecurity regarding the confiscation of property – were the cause for the depreciation of the currency. In his view only two ways of improving the situation existed: 1) an export offensive to obtain foreign currency, and 2) the creation of stable investments in Germany. He also warned that the present financing of the Reich's budget through the printing press did not bring any long-term advantages and suspected that undue considerations for the Reich had until now prevented stabilization.[58]

The attitude of the Ministry of Economics, the discussions in the press, and the upcoming debates in the Reichstag led Cuno to write a letter to the Ministry of Economics the day after his talk with Dauch, demanding that the Ministry accelerate its study of gold accounts.[59]

In this debate, the Reichsbank directorate was in the defensive and already on June 15, one of its Vice-Presidents, Dr. Friedrich, summarized in a long and detailed article, appearing in *Bankarchiv*, the reasons for its opposition to the introduction of gold accounts and a "Banko-Mark."[60] Friedrich used the by now already familiar arguments expounded in *Bankarchiv* and in Hermes' letter to Cuno. But he went beyond the Minister of Finance and tried to demolish Dalberg's scheme completely. He warned against launching "useless and economically or politically risky experiments," before the main causes of inflation – the negative balance of payments and

[57] Dernburg-Hamm, June 16, 1923, *ibid.*, R 43I/2435. Instead of gold accounts Dernburg suggested rye or potash as equivalents.

[58] Dauch-Cuno, July 12, 1923, *ibid.*, For Cuno's answer of cf. Cuno-Dauch, August 6, 1923, *ibid.*

[59] Cuno-Becker, July 10, 1923, *ibid.*, Cuno had met Dauch on July 9, when they travelled to Berlin together. Daugh-Cuno, June 12, 1923, *ibid.*

[60] "Goldmarkkredite und Goldmarkrechnung im Bankverkehr," *Bankarchiv*, No. 18, June 15, 1923, pp. 218 ff.

excessive reparation demands which were the basis of Germany's budgetary deficit – had been removed. What Friedrich and the Reichsbank directorate, for whom he obviously spoke, wanted to show was that the implementation of Dalberg's proposal would create insuperable problems for the banks. Friedrich contested the practicability of the scheme, which in his view destroyed a fundamental rule of banking, i.e. the balancing of all liabilities through assets. In his opinion, the implementation of this scheme would not stop speculation. Instead of industry and trade or other groups which until now had speculated to the detriment of the mark, the banks would be forced to do the same; introduction of gold accounts and gold credits only meant a shifting of speculation from banking clients to the banks themselves. Friedrich admitted, however, that as long as the mark continued to depreciate, the risks of such a banking policy were insignificant. But as soon as the value of the mark rose again, even temporarily, the existence of any bank that had accepted gold accounts or issued gold credits without sufficient funds in hand would naturally be endangered.

Friedrich was also convinced that nobody would deliberately create gold debts as long as paper mark credits were readily available. Ironically, this was an excellent criticism of Havenstein's policy, but he claimed that the Reichsbank could not have acted differently. If he stopped the issue of credits, industry and trade would still be able to obtain credits in other places which the Reichsbank could not control. Other problems also existed. Who was going to determine the need for gold credits, and who would see to it that besides "official" gold credit, the debtor did not receive credits from other institutions as well? In general, Friedrich emphatically rejected the idea that the Reichsbank should only issue gold mark credits. Such a policy was "not ripe yet for serious consideration."[61]

From a strictly technical point of view, Friedrich's arguments did indeed reveal the possible dangers of gold accounts. On the other hand, he did not have any positive suggestions as to how Germany's difficulties could be solved. Although he explained that a low discount rate for gold loans and an increased rate for paper mark loans might be a solution to force those groups that held foreign exchange to invest their holdings on a gold basis, he himself destroyed this notion by stating that an increase of the normal Reichsbank discount rate to 30, 40, or 50 percent, resulting in an increase of private bank rates, would render credit too expensive for industry.

The economy has to be able to continue to operate, and it is the overriding necessity of the economy to maintain a constant turnover of goods and to insure that unemployment does not exceed certain limits. Against this factor, the question

[61] *Ibid.*

whether paper mark debtors have profited as a result of their paper mark debts is with due consideration a question of minor importance.[62]

With this statement Friedrich had enunciated the crucial motive for the policy of easy credits. Without these credits, the public and the private sector of the economy would have broken down, and unemployment would have been the result. Havenstein also argued along these lines, and stated that without credits the Reich would go bankrupt.[63] On the other hand, they recognized that their policy was being exploited by industry and trade, and at the meetings of the *Zentralausschuß der Reichsbank*, Havenstein and von Glasenapp had warned against the abuse of Reichsbank credits, but except for an insignificant increase of the discount rate and appeals to its debtors, they had done hardly anything to stop or control credits. Fearing that an increase of the discount rate would lead to bankruptcy of the Reich, the rate had remained at 5% until June 1922 and was only raised to 10% on November 13. On January 18, 1923 it was increased to 12% and on April 24 to 18%.[64]

This last increase had been decided upon after the sudden fall of the mark which had set in on April 19. The increase of the discount rate was the "strongest warning the Reichsbank possessed," and Havenstein entertained the hope that it would be sufficient to restrict credits. In addition, he strongly urged private banks not to issue credit which was not absolutely indispensable.[65] Obviously, the banking community did not intend to follow this appeal, and what was true of the trade with foreign currency applied to credit as well – the banking community fulfilled the orders of its clients and did not limit credits as long as their clients were solvent.

When the next increase in the discount rate to 25 percent was put through, for "psychological reasons," the *Zentralausschuß* with the exception of Carl Fürstenberg voted against it, arguing that an increase of the discount rate for paper mark credits would only lead to higher prices, since industry would shift the burden of increased credit rates to the consumer.[66] When the Reichsbank decided upon another increase to 30% on August 2, the *Zentralausschuß* again voted against it with an overwhelming majority.[67] Although it had only an advisory function and thus could not block the introduction of increased discount rates, the opposition of prominent

---

[62] *Ibid.*

[63] "Sitzung Reichsbankrat," June 19, 1923, *BA*, R 43I/633; *ibid.*, R 2/2419, June 7, 1923, 7th meeting "Stützungsaktion."

[64] *Ibid.*, R 43I/640, October 28, 1922, November 13, December 23, 1922, January 18, 1923.

[65] *Ibid.*, April 24, 1923.

bankers to an increase of the rates also contributed to the policy of the Reichsbank.

Although paper mark credits to industry and trade had increased during 1923, credits for the Reich were still higher. In order to support the policy of easy credits, von Glasenapp quoted the following figures in July 1923: until April 15, 1923, the Reichsbank had issued 5.4 billion paper marks in treasury bills, while 2.6 billions had been issued in commercial bills; on June 30 treasury bills had increased to 18.3 billion marks, while commercial bills had increased to 6.9 billions. In percentage, this meant an increase of about 338% for treasury bills and only 265% for commercial bills. The latter increase was at least partly connected with the Ruhr occupation.[68] It is obvious that the Reichsbank directorate felt obliged not to deny credit to the Reich, and in justification of his policy Havenstein stressed that he could not have acted differently. Without these credits the position of the Reich would have become "untenable." He denied that the "policy of easy credits was the main source of inflation," such a statement was both "incorrect and exaggerated." Instead, he reasoned that the basic cause of inflation was the "uncontrolled increase of the floating debt and its conversion into currency deposit accounts through the discounting of treasury bills at the Reichsbank." The cause for the increase of Germany's debts, however, were reparations and insufficient revenues for the regular budget.[69]

This was a remarkable statement. It showed that Havenstein clearly recognized the effect of the floating debt on inflation. It also proves that the President of the Reichsbank, who had been attacked as an adherent of the balance of payment theory, did not attribute Germany's financial situation to one single factor, but to a number of developments. In earlier statements, especially immediately after the war, the Reichsbank had repeatedly warned that a connection existed between the floating debt of the Reich and inflation. Nevertheless Havenstein had felt obliged to finance government expenditures through the printing press instead of forcing the Reich to return to sound financing either through taxation or loans.[70] Apparently, fear of a

---

[66] *Ibid.*, July 11, 1923.

[67] *Ibid.*, August 2, 1923. The Minister of Economics favored an increase of the discount rate. "Eine wesentliche Erhöhung des Diskontsatzes der Reichsbank wird sich nicht vermeiden lassen, wenn man der spekulativen Ausnutzung von Reichsbankkrediten wirksam entgegen treten will. Die Bedenken wegen der damit verbundenen Erschwerung des wirtschaftlich notwendigen Kredits müssen zurückgestellt werden." Becker-Hamm, July 4, 1923, *ibid.*, R 43I/2435.

[68] *Ibid.*, R 43I/640, July 11, 1923.

[69] *Ibid.*, August 25, 1923.

[70] See *ibid.*, R 2/1894, July 1, 1919, pp. 4 ff; *ibid.*, R 43I/638, March 31, 1919. "Verwaltungsbericht der Reichsbank für das Jahr 1919," p. 4.

deflationary policy and its consequences on the social and political stability of the young republic played an important role in this decision. Furthermore, as soon as Allied reparation demands became known, Havenstein not believing that they could be fulfilled, could further argue that reparations were the main cause of inflation, thus supporting governmental attempts to obtain a reduction of the liability. Although this seems to be a logical policy, it is not quite clear whether the Reichsbank did not place domestic and foreign causes of inflation side by side. This may have been especially true since the theoretical basis of German Economic Science was not of much help for the solution of Germany's pressing financial and monetary problems. Only outsiders like Friedrich Bendixen, Ludwig Albert Hahn, Ludwig Pohle, or the young *Privatdozent* at the University of Berlin, Walter Eucken, criticized the balance of payment theory upon which most arguments were based, while accepted economists like Georg Friedrich Knapp, Karl Diehl, Frank Eulenburg, Herbert Beckerath, and Robert Liefmann, as well as the former director of the Deutsche Bank, Karl Helfferich, were the most prominent advocates of the balance of payment theory.[71] Of this latter group, Karl Helfferich, although not an economist, had the greatest influence on discussions, and statements by Havenstein, Hermes, or others very often seem to have been taken directly from Helfferich's voluminous study "Das Geld."[72]

On the other hand, academic battles were fought between supporters of the balance of payment theory and adherents of the inflation theory. In an article in *Bankarchiv*, Professor Liefmann attacked Albert Lansburgh for the spreading of an erroneous monetary theory. Although Liefmann admitted that German economists had not yet theoretically solved problems of monetary inflation belonging in the field of price theory, he vigorously attacked all those arguing that government spending and not the negative balance of payments and the provisions of the Versailles "Diktat" were responsible for the state of affairs in Germany. "It seems almost unbelievable that the experts [of the Reich Economic Council] can be of the opinion that, without a radical change of Germany's foreign situation, the return to a stable currency and even to gold marks is possible. There must exist a lack

[71] Howard S. Ellis, *German Monetary Theory 1905-1933* (Cambridge, 1937), *passim.* Czada, *op. cit.*, pp. 15 ff.

[72] Karl Helfferich, *Das Geld, 6th ed.* (Leipzig, 1923). Cf. Claus-Dieter Krohn, "Helfferich contra Hilferding. Konservative Geldpolitik und die sozialen Folgen der deutschen Inflation 1918-1923," VjhZG, Bd. 62, 1975; Claus-Dieter Krohn, *Stabilisierung und ökonomische Interessen. Die Finanzpolitik des Deutschen Reiches 1923-1927* (Düsseldorf, 1974), pp. 13 ff. For the influence of Helfferich on Havenstein see: "Im Kampf um die deutsche Währung," *Hirsch Papers*. The statement was written on October 26, 1959 and draws upon Hirsch's diary as "Unterstaatssekretär" in the "Reichsschatzamt."

of understanding of economic interrelations which I would not have deemed possible."[73]

Considering the academic struggle between the adherents of the balance of payments theory and the inflation theory (or quantity theory), it is difficult to determine precisely whether German politicians clearly recognized the faults of the balance of payments theory or simply used it as the most appropriate justification of German monetary policy. On the other hand, even leaving these theoretical questions aside, Havenstein, Friedrich, and other members of the Reichsbank directorate were convinced that they had to discount Reich treasury bills and keep the discount rate low, even at the danger of an abuse by speculators. What would have happened if the Reichsbank had not discounted Reich treasury bills after 1919? A clue to the apprehension of politicians may be found in a memorandum about Germany's financial position in 1919 prepared by the Minister of Finance in the Scheidemann cabinet, Bernard Dernburg. Dernburg, expecting a financial catastrophe because of war-time spending and reparation demands, felt that German negotiators at Versailles should explain the situation to the Allies, but warned that the real financial position of the Reich should not become public: otherwise the German people might lose all courage to tackle these difficult problems and become "victims of pessimism," feeling that the simplest way to get out of this chaotic financial situation was "Communism."[74]

Even Ludwig Albert Hahn, otherwise a severe critic of the Reichsbank, could still argue in the summer of 1923: "We have ... an extraordinarily large budgetary deficit, which at the moment, if a social catastrophe is to be prevented, must be financed through inflation by means of the printing press."[75] Friedrich Bendixen had suggested the same in 1919,[76] and a Berlin banker admitted that political motives had primarily caused the Reichsbank to finance government expenditures through the printing press. The latter argued in 1923 that if the Reichsbank had not discounted treasury bills in 1919, higher taxation would have been the result and the economy would have returned to normalcy far slower than it in fact did. He recognized that profits would have been smaller and that the enrichment through easy credits would not have been possible. On the other hand, he argued that such a course of action as just described was only of theoretical value, since even if

[73] *Bankarchiv*, No. 1, October 5, 1923, pp. 1 ff.
[74] *Kab. Scheidemann*, No. 54b, April 26, 1919.
[75] *Bankarchiv*, No. 11, March 1, 1923, p. 154.
[76] Cf. Czada, *op. cit.*, p. 23.

political motives had not existed in 1919, he seriously doubted that the printing press method could have been stopped at that point.[77]

Political deliberations were apparently the most important motive for the policy of inflation. The American Ambassador to Germany, who discussed monetary policy with several industrialists and bankers, reported that Walter Rathenau had declared that inflation had been necessary to "transfer capital from one class to another," and that under the conditions created by the war "the German people were so poor that this transfer became necessary."[78] Hugo Stinnes gave a slightly different reason for inflation. He told Houghton that "it was politically necessary in order to put at work the three million men coming back from the war." This, Stinnes argued, could only be done with easy credit from the Reich.

It was necessary both to turn industry back from the production of war materials and into the production of peace materials. It was also necessary to buy raw materials. Germany had not in hand the gold or credit to meet these demands.[79]

Carl Melchior also stressed the political necessity of an inflationary policy after the war. Although "economically inadvisable," he believed that it was

politically and socially necessary at the time and that, could it have been controlled, no permanent harm would have occurred. It [the inflation] was not planned. It came about first from a tremendous budgetary deficiency at the close of the war, when they had no funds. It became involved later in the creation of new capital to enable industry to hire the returning soldiers. It grew out of control owing to the demands on German resources made from abroad.[80]

Fear of a social and political revolution seems to have caused respective governments and the Reichsbank to finance expenditures through the printing press. But in the summer of 1923, Bernard Dernburg reasoned that an inflationary policy was also unavoidable for monetary reasons:

The mark is now worth 20/1000 of its peace value. The note circulation is roughly 20 trillions, i.e., 500 million gold marks, or $\frac{1}{8}$ of peace circulation. From this alone follows that inflation has to be pushed further; deflation is not possible at all; only devaluation is possible.[81]

---

[77] *Bankarchiv*, No. 24, September 20, 1923, pp. 288–289.

[78] Houghton-Hughes, December 27, 1923, *Houghton Papers*, Correspondence. According to Julius Hirsch, Rathenau had declared in 1919: "Ob im Inland mehr oder weniger Geld umlaufe, das sei für den Stand der Mark auf den Weltmärkten völlig gleichgültig. Dieser sei ausschließlich bedingt durch das Verhältnis von Einfuhr und Ausfuhr." "Im Kampf um die deutsche Währung," *Hirsch Papers*, p. 5. Rathenau's brother-in-law, the banker Fritz Andreae, seems to have been of the same opinion. *Ibid.*

[79] Gert von Klass, *Hugo Stinnes* (Tübingen, 1958), pp. 284 ff. Houghton-Hughes, December 27, 1923, *Houghton Papers*, Correspondence.

[80] *Ibid.*

[81] Dernburg-Hamm, undated, but probably written at the end of June or at the beginning of July 1923. *BA*, R 431/2435.

These different statements clearly show that Allied demands upon Germany were originally of minor importance for monetary decisions. Instead, the adaptation of a war economy to peace time conditions, fear of the effects of a deflationary policy on social and political developments, and perhaps even the intention to wipe out Reich debts were the reasons for the Reich's policy after 1919. However, faced with a wartime budgetary deficit, problems of a new tax system, increased government expenditures for demobilization and then reparation demands, the Reich had no choice but to postpone stabilization. Postponement was especially important as long as German industry could gain through underselling Allied industries, thus keeping production going. This policy, however, proved to be detrimental to passive resistance in 1923, since the German currency was being destroyed as legal tender.

3. STABILIZATION PLANS

If Cuno intended to prevent an economic and financial breakdown of the Reich until Great Britain intervened in the Franco-German struggle, an attempt to curtail inflation and stabilize the mark was urgently needed. Such a policy could of course only be implemented with the support and cooperation of industry, trade, and banking. After a discussion with Havenstein, Cuno demanded on June 22 that each of the above mentioned groups subscribe to 50 million gold marks in dollar treasury bills, which the Reichsbank would then use to stop the fall of the mark.[82] On June 25, the Ministry of Finance notified the central organizations of industry and trade that the banks that had issued the dollar treasury bills in March 1923 would subscribe to their quota immediately if industry and trade would do the same.[83] A meeting between Cuno and the RdI directorate took place, and he requested that industry subscribe to its quota as well.[84]

On June 29 Sorge informed Cuno that after a meeting of the RdI on June 28 the directorate had decided to advise industry to subscribe treasury bills. However, Sorge argued that in contrast to banking, the RdI was unable to determine in advance the amount of bills that would be subscribed by industry, since ownership of foreign exchange was widely spread, while in

---

[82] *Kab. Cuno*, No. 200, June 22, 1923.

[83] *BA*, R 43I/2391.

[84] Martin Blank-Paul Reusch, June 27, 1923, *HA GHH* 193024/3. The dating of this meeting is insecure, since Blank, the representative of the GHH in Berlin, mentions a meeting on June 28, i.e., a day after his letter had been written. It is also possible that he refers to a meeting which took place on June 22. See *BA*, R 43I/2435.

banking a small but strong group existed.[85] The RdI directorate did in fact ask industry on June 28 to subscribe to treasury bills, arguing that everything had to be done to end the Ruhr struggle victoriously. In order to prove that industry had in fact supported Cuno, the members of the RdI were asked to place their orders.[86] The *Wirtschaftsverband der deutschen Reederei* decided at a meeting on June 30 that each member should subscribe dollar treasury bills based on a ratio of $ 1.25 per gross register ton for steamers and motor ships and $ 0.50 for barges and sailing boats. It was confident that 10 million gold marks would be subscribed by shipping industry alone. In order to prove that shipping industry had bought treasury bills, orders should be placed under the code name "Schiffahrtsaktion."[87] Despite these promises, treasury bills were not sold as fast as the Reichsbank had expected, and the mark could not be stabilized either. It remained at about 150.000 marks to the dollar for one week and then dropped sharply again. At a meeting of the *Zentralausschuß* of the Reichsbank von Glasenapp now warned that he would stop all credits if treasury bills were not bought according to the quotas prescribed.[88]

A final summary of the purchase of dollar treasury bills could not be located, but several provisional ones exist. A note dated July 25 reveals that treasury bills worth 50 million dollars were issued (i.e., 210 million gold marks); 35 millions had been subscribed by that date. Of this sum, the banks took 25 millions, the public 2.1, industry 1.46, trade 0.24, shipping industry 1.71 (or 7.182 million gold marks of the 10 million expected). Another 4.4 million dollars were sold against paper marks.[89] A note of July 31 reveals that purchases by industry had slightly increased to 1.56 million dollars. However, at a rate of 4.20 gold marks to the dollar, this amounted to only 6.552 million gold marks while Cuno had demanded 50 millions. Of these 1.56 million dollars, the *AEG* took 300,000, the *Deutsche Kabel-Syndikat* 168,000, *Siemens-Schuckert* 150,000, *Siemens-Halske* 150,000, *A.G. für Anilinfabrikation* 60,000, *Linke-Hoffmann, Luchhammer* (Berliner Werk) 50,000, *Chemische Fabrik Griesheim* 40,000, *Accumulatorenfabrik* 30,000, *Osram* 25,000, *Bemberg* 25,000, *Dynamit-Nobel* 20,000, *Köln-Rottweil* 20,000, *Riedel* 20,000, *Vereinigte Glanzstoffabriken Elberfeld* 20,000, and *Hoechster Farbwerke, Lucius & Brüning* 20,000.[90]

[85] Sorge-Cuno, June 29, 1923, *BA*, R 43I/2435.
[86] RdI, Rundschreiben, *WWA*, Klc, Ab. XVI, No. 1, "Währungsfragen"; also Deutscher Industrie- und Handelstag-Mitglieder, August 26, 1923, *ibid.*
[87] Wirtschaftsausschuß der deutschen Reederei-Cuno, July 2, 1923, *BA*, R 43I/2435, p. 258.
[88] *Ibid.*, R 43I/640, July 7, 1923.
[89] *Ibid.*, R 43I/2439, note June 25, 1923.
[90] *Ibid.*, note August 9, "Industriezeichnungen auf die Dollarschatzanweisungen."

This list only contains chemical and electrical industries while heavy industry is not mentioned at all. To be sure, 470,000 dollar treasury bills that were subscribed are not decoded individually in this list.[91] But even considering that this sum came from heavy industry, the total amount indicates that industry did not fulfill Cuno's demand. Possibly a part of industrial subscriptions is hidden in the amount taken by the banks, and some industrialists may not have followed the RdI's suggestion to buy through the Reichsbank and may have placed orders through private banks. However, this is mere speculation. Whatever the exact subscription of industry, by July 31 about 35 million treasury bills had been placed out of 50 millions. In comparison to March 1923, when only 12.5 millions out of 50 millions had been sold, this was an improvement.

During the summer of 1923, however, a development took place that endangered the supply of food stuffs, and made the collection of foreign currency even more important. The Reichsbank was no longer willing or able to provide the Ministry of Food with foreign exchange for food imports. The Ministry needed 1.5 million gold marks per day and also had an outstanding debt of 25 millions due in August. Fearing food riots and the spreading of social unrest, the Ministry of Food demanded that export industries deliver their "illegally held" foreign exchange quotas.[92] The cabinet had already discussed the situation on July 26 and July 27, and the Minister of Economics had voiced similar fears, arguing that the allotment of foreign exchange for food imports by the Reichsbank was completely unsatisfactory. President Ebert also complained about Havenstein.[93] On August 3, Cuno held a meeting with representatives of the Reichsbank (Havenstein, Friedrich), the banks (Wassermann, Goldschmidt) and industry (Stinnes, von Siemens, von Borsig, Frank, Silverberg, Jordan, Bücher). Fearing a domestic crisis as much as the Ministry of Food, the industrial representatives promised to subscribe to the rest of the dollar treasury bills which could then be used to purchase food stuffs. Twenty industrial groups would each subscribe to 100,000 pounds sterling worth of treasury bills. The banks would take an additional 500,000. Thus the total amount would be roughly 50 million gold marks. But although the domestic situation was obviously critical, the industrial offer was made dependent on several preconditions which, if they were accepted by the government, would "facilitate negotiations" within the RdI directorate. First, the decree about the fixed rate of exchange that had been introduced on June 22 had to be cancelled in the near future, followed

---

[91] *Ibid.* Of the 1.560 million dollars, 1.090 were subscribed by these companies.

[92] *Ibid.*, R 43I/2446, August 3, 1923.

[93] *Kab. Cuno*, No. 222, July 23; No. 225, July 26; No. 227, July 27, 1923.

by a complete cancellation of foreign exchange laws. Second, the Reichsbank must again increase the discounting of commercial bills. Third, export
trade controls were to be cancelled or at least modified. Fourth, loans on
dollar treasury bills were to be allowed. Fifth, the compulsory introduction
of the issue of gold credits by the Reichsbank should not begin before
November.[94]

Despite the careful formulation of these demands, Cuno objected and
declared that he did not regard them as preconditions for industrial cooperation, but as "wishes, which basically were also the wishes of the Reich
government."[95] With few exceptions, these demands had indeed become
something like a program of economic changes that were wide-spread
during the summer of 1923. Although Havenstein had felt that the fixed rate
of exchange had been necessary for political reasons in June, he now demanded its abolition, arguing that the decree endangered necessary imports,
especially food supplies.[96] The Ministry of Economics argued along similar
lines,[97] and the *Verband des Hamburger Einfuhrhandels*, the *Reichsverband
des deutschen Ein- und Ausfuhrhandels*, and the Chamber of Commerce in
Hamburg also protested against the decree.[98]

The credit policy of the Reichsbank after the introduction of fixed rates
of exchange had been attacked by industry, trade, and municipal governments, all arguing that its credit restrictions and the shortage of bank notes
seriously impaired the turnover of goods. The foreign exchange decree and
credit restrictions were also held responsible for the shortage of raw materials and price increases on the domestic market. The Minister of Economics especially protested against the allotment of foreign exchange, while
Havenstein maintained that demands for foreign exchange were far above
the actual need of industry and trade. Despite this opposition, the Ministry
of Economics had for some time demanded that the Reichsbank fulfill all
foreign exchange orders for "vital imports," adapt the rate of exchange
fixed in Berlin to the rate on foreign markets (where the mark was 20–50
percent cheaper), and control credits to industry and trade.[99]

At the same time, the Ministry of Economics had pursued its old idea of
an introduction of gold credits. A proposal concerning the delivery of for-

---

[94] *Ibid.*, No. 237, August 3, 1923. 2.5 million pounds at a rate of 20.43 pounds to a gold
mark are 50.975 million gold marks. The introduction of gold accounts had been rejected
by an expert commission on July 19, 1923. Cf. *BA*, R 431/2445.

[95] *Kab. Cuno*, No. 237, August 3, 1923.

[96] *Ibid.*, No. 230, July 23, 1923. In this letter to Cuno the Reichsbank announced that
it could no longer support the mark.

[97] Becker-Hamm, July 12, 1923, *BA*, R 431/2445.

[98] *Ibid.*, 2446.

[99] *Kab. Cuno*, No. 222, July 23, 1923.

eign exchange earned through exports against gold credits was again forwarded. The scheme was an attempt to regulate the delivery of a certain percentage of foreign exchange to within three days after it had been obtained. It prescribed that these amounts could not be withdrawn before October 1, 1923. The Reichsbank would be allowed to use these funds after a substitute in the form of discounted gold bills had been created. The principal motive of this proposal was to create a stable mark, stimulate the return of foreign exchange held abroad to Germany, and thus overcome the shortage of funds for the purchase of food stuffs and necessary raw materials.[100]

The most difficult problem for a successful implementation of this plan was how to obtain the cooperation of industry and trade. On July 18 Becker asked the RdI, the DIHT, the *Centralverband des deutschen Großhandels* and the *Hauptgemeinschaft des deutschen Einzelhandels* to collaborate in the import of vital goods.[101] Two days later, the Ministry informed the same organizations that the following exception to the *Valutaspekulationsverordnung* had been agreed upon in order to overcome interruptions in the turnover of goods and the transfer of payments. Until August 16, owners of foreign exchange could buy imported goods and goods primarily manufactured with imported raw materials under two conditions: first, that payments had always been made in foreign exchange, and second, that the turnover had not taken place in retail trade and that the seller had a Chamber of Commerce licence, or declared to the purchaser that he would deliver the foreign exchange received within two weeks to the Reichsbank or a person in possession of the above mentioned licence.[102] The purpose of Becker's appeals and of the provision was to accelerate the turnover of goods, which was slowly breaking down since nobody wanted to use a worthless currency in commercial transactions and people only sold goods for stable values. However, although trade with foreign exchange had been forbidden, owners of foreign exchange withheld their quotas or parted from foreign exchange only if this was absolutely inevitable. This attitude had led to a shortage of raw materials for industry. Farmers were also unwilling to sell their products on the domestic market against paper marks, and thus the mark had lost its function as a medium of exchange.

While these developments took place, Cuno demanded on July 10 that the Ministry of Economics prepare a study to investigate not only the establish-

---

[100] "Vorschlag betreffend Exportdevisenablieferung gegen Goldgutschriften," July 17, 1923, *BA*, R 43I/2446.
[101] *Ibid.*, July 18, 1923.
[102] *Ibid.*, July 20, 1923.

ment of a central foreign exchange office, but also the creation of stable wages and salaries, a stable basis for agricultural prices and a limitation of unnecessary imports (luxury goods like tobacco, cocoa, wine, liquor etc.).[103] But in a memorandum prepared in the Ministry of Economics, the hazards of such restrictions were recognized as enormous, since these countries could retaliate and impose similar restrictions on German imports. The attitude of the Brasilian government towards an increase of duty on coffee was an example: when it became known that custom duties would be increased, the Brasilian government informed Berlin that customs on German goods would also be increased. Since Brasil was an important market for German manufacturing industries, coffee imports could not be restricted. Similar hazards existed for imports from Portugal and Spain: from June 1921 to July 1922 Spain had exported goods worth 100 million pesetas to Germany, while Germany had exported goods worth 1 billion pesetas to Spain. Besides economic objections to import restrictions, the Ministry of Economics had another motive: custom revenues for these "luxury imports" had brought 312 million gold marks in 1922. This was not an insignificant contribution to the Reich's budget.[104]

When Becker answered Cuno's letter on July 23, he maintained that for the above reasons imports could not be restricted further. Far more important was a complete revision of the Reichsbank's policy, i.e., an introduction of gold accounts for foreign exchange and the discounting of gold bills. Without such a change, an improvement of Germany's situation was impossible. As to the introduction of a foreign exchange office, technical difficulties did not allow its introduction, but he felt that the Reichsbank could organize controls through its regional branches.[105] His demands concerning the introduction of gold accounts for all foreign exchange earned through exports exactly followed a recommendation of a committee of experts which had been created upon a recommendation from the Reichskanzlei.[106] The meeting of these experts, however, had not led to any con-

---

[103] Cuno-Becker, July 10, 1923, *ibid.*, 2435.

[104] "Einfuhrpolitik und Möglichkeiten sowie Folgen weiterer Einfuhrbeschränkungen," June 9, 1923, *ibid.*

[105] *Kab. Cuno*, No. 22, July 23, 1923.

[106] The necessity of such a study had been recognized during negotiations between the government and interest groups on June 20, 21, and 22. On July 4, Becker had completed a list of experts to be invited and forwarded it to the Reichskanzlei. It was accepted on July 6. The list contains the following names: Wassermann, Urbig, Ritscher, Loeb (crossed out), 2 representatives to be named by the Stempelvereinigung Berliner Banken, one to be named by the organization of Rhenish-Westphalian banks, one by Frankfurt banks; Max Warburg, Alfred Maron (a Dresden banker), Hohenemser (Rheinische Kreditbank), Direktor Kraemer, Abraham Frowein, Rudolf Hilferding (as members of the

crete proposals. Instead, the struggle went on between those who supported
the introduction of gold accounts and those who – like the Ministry of
Finance, the Reichsbank, and members of the banking community – were
opposed to such a policy for the time being. On July 19, the majority of the
experts still rejected gold accounts but were prepared to allow exceptions
for export trade.[107] On the other hand, on July 17 the Minister of Finance
was still opposed to a new currency, for, as long as reparations had not been
adjusted to Germany's capacity to pay, it would only suffer the same fate
as the present mark.[108]

These differences within the cabinet and between the Reichsbank and individual members of the cabinet could not be withheld from the public any
longer, becoming generally known by the beginning of July. The press now
started to discuss changes in the cabinet. The domestic situation had become
especially intolerable, for strikes were spreading, unemployment was increasing, foodstuffs were lacking, and the Communist Party was gaining new
strength and demanding a socialist government. Arguing that "social peace"
was endangered, Georg Bernhard of the *Vossische Zeitung* urged the cabinet
to act at once to prevent complete pauperization of the middle and working
classes, while industry enriched itself. It was "five minutes before twelve."[109]
For Bernhard, the situation was obvious: Hermes had prevented a sound
fiscal policy, Becker and Brauns had contributed to the fiscal ruin of Germany, but Havenstein was mainly responsible for existing conditions.[110]
The party organ of the Center, *Germania*, similarly attacked the financial
policy of Hermes.[111] Gustav Stresemann demanded that Cuno take the
lead and prevent a further radicalization of the public. In a letter to Brockdorff-Rantzau, he argued that the differences between Hermes and Becker
had rendered futile all measures of the cabinet, although he felt that the
Reichstag and Ebert were at least partly responsible. But Stresemann, as
well as Bernhard and most others who wrote about the crisis spared Cuno
from criticism. Stresemann declared that, if necessary, Becker and Hermes
should be dismissed, while the cabinet should be supported in all "national
questions". Despite this criticism of Becker, Stresemann did not say anything

Reichswirtschaftsrat), Professor Warmbold (Stickstoff-Syndikat), Konsul Hugo Mayer
(Getreide-Kommissions-AG.), the President of the Chambers of Commerce in Hamburg
and Bremen, Keinath (DDP) and Franz von Mendelssohn (DIHT), *ibid.*, 2445.
   [107] *Ibid.*
   [108] *Ibid.*, 2435, note Wienstein.
   [109] *Vossische Zeitung*, No. 309, July 3, 1923.
   [110] *Ibid.*, No. 327, July 9, 1923 "Der Primat der Politik." No. 343, July 22; No. 345,
July 24; No. 351; July 27 and No. 355, July 29 "Die Steuertäuschung."
   [111] *Germania*, No. 212, August 3, 1923 and No. 214, August 8.

in public, since, as he was to explain in a letter to the *Generalsekretär* of the
DVP, Truchseß, such criticism would have been directed "above all"
against a member of their own party.[112] Even the leaders of the SPD-
oriented trade unions were reluctant to criticize Cuno, although they were
dissatisfied with his domestic policy and were under pressure from the Metal
Workers Union (DMV) led by Independent Socialists to demand the formation of a new cabinet. However, as long as the SPD Reichstag faction was
unwilling to support a change of government, most union leaders did not increase pressure on the cabinet.[113]

Almost until the end of his Chancellorship, Cuno had done little, if anything, to force the members of his cabinet to cooperate, nor had he determined foreign or domestic policy. Foreign Minister von Rosenberg had,
as I have shown in the preceding chapter, twice changed Cuno's position
towards negotiations. In domestic affairs, Hermes and Becker had more influence on developments than the Chancellor who seems to have been unable
to lead the cabinet. This changed, however, from the middle of July onwards,
and Cuno now took a more active interest in the details of financial and
economic affairs. With a small group of personal advisers in the Chancellory
(several old acquaintances from his work in the Reichsschatzamt and from
industry), he now endeavored to launch some last minute changes. On June
28 Ministerialrat Kempner of the chancellor's office noted that it was useless
to change individual tax laws, as the Ministry of Finance suggested, but that
only a complete revision of the whole system of taxation would do any
good.[114] On July 11, Cuno wrote a letter to Hermes demanding preparation
of appropriate tax bills to support the Ruhr struggle, also reminding the
Minister of Finance that he had repeatedly urged introduction of a special
tax to finance Ruhr expenditures and other tax reforms. A similar request
was made on August 1.[115] As in other fields, Cuno's initiatives came too
late to change developments. However, it is questionable if any other cabinet
would have acted differently once French and Belgian troops had undertaken occupation of the Ruhr.

The Secretary of State in the Chancellory, Eduard Hamm, had also prepared a long memorandum partly based on a resolution passed by the
Taxation and Economic Committee of the Reichswirtschaftsrat.[116] In

---

[112] Stresemann-Brockdorff-Rantzau, July 28, 1923 and Stresemann-Truchseß, August
3, 1923, *Stresemann Nachlaß*, vol. 260.
[113] Bußmann, *op. cit.*, p. 245. "Niederschrift über eine Besprechung zur Ruhrfrage am
7. August 1923 im Büro des ADGB," *Bebel Archiv*, NB 167, 0155 ff.
[114] *BA*, R 43I/2357.
[115] *Kab. Cuno*, No. 216, July 16, 1923 and *BA*, R 43I/2357, August 1, 1923.
[116] *Kab. Cuno*, No. 224, July 25, 1923.

Hamm's view, a complete revision of the tax system, an adaptation of taxation to monetary inflation, anticipated payments of income- and corporation-income taxes, a special Rhein-Ruhr tax, a special tax on real estate, and a gold loan were needed. Besides these modifications of the fiscal system, which were finally being prepared in the Ministry of Finance, Hamm also recommended that gold accounts be created for all foreign exchange earned through exports in order to withdraw foreign currency from industry and make it available to the Reich. Foreign exchange demands should furthermore be restricted by a curbing of imports, a control of foreign exchange purchases, technical improvements of the Reichsbank's foreign exchange policy, and a control of foreign exchange orders. Besides these proposals, which naturally meant conflict with Havenstein, Hamm also recommended a suspension of the printing press, an increase of the discount rate, a valorisation of Ruhr credits, and the issue of Reichsbank bills on a gold basis. In general, the execution of Hamm's proposal would have meant a complete reversal of the policy of the Ministry of Finance and the Reichsbank.

At about the same time another more detailed program was worked out by two of Cuno's confidants: Heinrich Albert, Minister of Reconstruction, and Director Henrich of the Deutsche Werke.[117] This program deserves our special attention, since Cuno accepted it *in toto*. Its purpose was to save Germany from complete "ruin of the currency," from a "catastrophic shortage of food" and from "political chaos." Albert and Henrich severely criticized the Ministry of Finance, since the existing basis for the assessment of taxation was simply "incorrect" and allowed the most solvent taxpayers to evade adequate taxation "by a skilful make-up of balance sheets." An adaptation of taxation to inflation could not stop this development, nor would the "suffering classes of society" have any confidence in similar proposals after they had experienced how the wealthiest groups of society had carried an inadequate tax burden. Temporary measures as proposed by the Ministry of Finance were futile, and the idea of a small gold loan as suggested by the Ministry would not change anything either. Only a huge gold loan of 500 million gold marks (half of the sum to be paid in foreign currency) at 6% interest and redemption after 30 years would stop the depreciation of the mark. Interest on this loan should be paid through a special tax on industry. Agriculture, trade, and banking would also have to subscribe to 50 millions each, while industry would have to take 100 millions. The remaining 250 millions would be sold against paper marks. Since the Reichsbank no longer had the confidence of the public, the loan should be issued through an in-

---

[117] *Ibid.*, No. 229, about July 27, 1923. Other "Wirtschaftsführer" apparently also contributed to the memorandum. See *ibid.*, footnote 1.

dependent board. In addition to these measures, Albert and Henrich recommended severe import restrictions with the exception of food stuffs and coal, the "systematic and ruthless restriction of credits," and the issue of dollar treasury bills against paper marks. They hoped, that, with these provisions, paper marks could be withdrawn from the market, the hoarding of goods could be prevented, and the turnover of goods could be accelerated again.

In connection with this policy, a new tax program and further economic measures had become unavoidable: 1) Income tax should be based upon gold, but the highest rates should not go beyond 20–25 percent; 2) the railway and the postal system would similarly have to be based upon gold; 3) foreign exchange restrictions had to be cancelled; 4) expenditures for public administration were to be cut; 5) all decrees concerning "Zwangswirtschaft" were to be abolished.

Albert and Henrich recognized that their program meant conflict with the parties, but with chaos spreading in Germany they felt that compromises were no longer possible. Instead they suggested that Cuno and Ebert should immediately hold a meeting with economic leaders to solicit their support, while the parties would be informed afterwards. Either they would accept the plan, or they would have to form a new cabinet. If they agreed, a "Vollzugsrat," a council that would implement the program under Cuno's presidency, would be created. The authors of the memorandum were confident that these measures would stabilize the currency.

Cuno followed the course of action described above, and on July 31 and on August 1, he met a group of bankers and industrialists and, with slight modifications, presented the above plan. The Chancellor warned his audience that the Reich had reached the breaking-point. "A capitalist private economy which eliminates the idea of money from the economy, surrenders itself and prepares the ground for Bolshevist chaos." If the "economic leaders" did not support his program, he would resign: "In the most serious hour this government has encountered, I ask industry [Wirtschaft] whether it is ready te make possible an attempt to save the state from ruin."[118] The participants at the meeting were apparently impressed by Cuno's threat and his description of an approaching social and political catastrophe. Nobody

[118] *Ibid.*, No. 234, August 1, 1923. Two separate meetings were held. The bankers Wassermann, Nathan, Salomonsohn, Goldschmidt, Andreae, *Loeb, von Schwabach, Warburg,* and *Hagen* were invited for 3 p.m. on July 31. The underlined could not appear or could not be contracted. Industry was invited for 5 p.m. Silverberg, Stinnes, Vögler, Flechtheim, Henrich, von Siemens, Deutsch, Bücher, Hans Kraemer, Jordan, Reusch, Lammers. These names are marked "yes," while von Borsig, Sorge, Moras, Frowein, and Simson are marked "no!" Minutes for the meeting of August 1 do not exist. See *ibid.*, footnote 1. Instead of a loan at 6% and a redemption after 30 years, Cuno proposed 5% and 12 years.

wanted a repetition of the revolutionary events of 1919. They agreed to support the issue of a 500 million gold mark loan, and also promised to help the Reich out of its immediate difficulties by providing additional foreign exchange for the purchase of food stuffs.

The situation just described was typical of Cuno's Chancellorship. He had to appeal to individual interests to gain support for the Reich and guarantee food stuffs for the next months, while the cabinet and the Reich's bureau-cracy was paralyzed by conflicting policies within the government. Facing social unrest and an uncertain future, these interest groups now decided to support him. At a second meeting already described above, industry, trade and banking decided to subscribe to 2.5 million pounds in treasury bills. In a separate meeting of the RdI on August 7, major industries, with the ex-ception of small iron trade, glass industry, tanner industry, shipping and wharfs – which had not yet agreed on their shares – promised to subscribe their full quotas.[119] Already on August 7, i.e., two days before the written promise from the RdI arrived, the Ministry of Finance had announced that the whole sum had been subscribed. Such an announcement was felt to be necessary to prevent food riots, and Cuno himself asked the Chambers of Commerce in Bremen, Hamburg, and Lübeck to guarantee 20,000, 30,000, and 30,000 pounds sterling respectively for food purchases.[120]

These emergency measures guaranteed the supply of food stuffs for the next few months, and the government had gained some time to prepare the 500 million gold mark loan. However, the depreciation of the mark could not be stopped anymore. When the decree about the fixed rate of exchange was cancelled on August 4, the mark sharply dropped from about 1.3 millions to one dollar to 5 millions on August 8. This new development also en-dangered the subscription of the dollar treasury bills which were traded 40 percent below the rate of the dollar, and on August 9 Kempner alarmed Cuno by demanding that he immediately ask the Reichsbank to intervene. With such a loss, industry could not be expected to subscribe anymore.[121]

A meeting took place the same morning, and now Havenstein promised to throw 50 million gold marks on the market to support the mark again. The money would be taken from the emergency fund just created for food

---

[119] *Ibid.*, No. 235, August 2, and No. 237, August 3, 1923. Bücher-Cuno, August 9, 1923, *BA*, R 43I/2439.

[120] The publication caused protests from director Stimming of the Norddeutscher Lloyd and apparently subscriptions were stopped. In his answer to Stimming, Cuno maintained that publication had been necessary to quieten public opinion, and he demanded that shipping industry take its quota, which Stimming promised. Cf. Stimming-Cuno, August 8, Cuno-Stimming, August 8, and Stimming-Cuno, August 9, 1923, *ibid.*

[121] *RGBl*, I, 1923, p. 760. Kempner-Hamm, August 9, 1923, *BA*, R 43I/2439.

stuffs and be supplemented by the Reichsbank if necessary, while the government had to promise to return these amounts within two weeks from foreign
exchange delivered by industry. But apparently Cuno did not have sufficient
confidence in Havenstein anymore, and Bergmann and Henrich were named
as his confidants who executed the intervention in cooperation with the
Reichsbank.[122]

During this food shortage, cooperation between Cuno and President Ebert
was especially close. Ebert not only met Havenstein in the presence of Cuno,
urging execution of the latter's demands, but also made clear in a cabinet
meeting that he supported the Chancellor's plan.[123] The same could not be
said of Hermes and Becker. Both regarded a 500 million gold mark loan as
impossible. Becker also objected to the control of foreign exchange orders
through the banks as impracticable, while Hermes was still convinced that
an adaptation of taxation to the rate of inflation was sufficient to overcome
preliminary difficulties although he felt that the budget could not be bal-
anced.[124]

This controversy lasted several days, with the Ministers finally accepting the
plan. But when Cuno demanded the introduction of a tax that would charge
every employer one dollar per employee per week as an additional source of
taxation, Becker and Hermes protested. Although Cuno pointed out that
the proposal had come from industry, Becker refused to believe that the
majority of industrialists and bankers would support it. Such a provision,
Becker warned, would never pass the Reichstag, and Hermes, who in the
meantime had submitted several modifications of the tax system including a
so called "Rhein-Ruhr" tax, was unwilling to introduce an "employer tax,"
nor did he intend "to identify himself with it through the formulation of
such a bill" in his ministry.[125] Cuno urged Hermes to reconsider, but the
Minister of Finance did not leave any doubt what the outcome would be.
This tax was considered impracticable since it would lead to price increases
and create additional technical difficulties for the revenue offices.[126]

These differences within the cabinet were finally overcome when a combination of tax measures and a domestic loan were agreed upon to provide the
Reich with additional revenues and, at the same time, lay the foundation for a
long-term program. With this plan, the cabinet appeared before theReichstag.

[122] *Kab. Cuno*, No. 242, August 9, 1923.

[123] *Ibid.*, No. 227, July 27, 1923.

[124] *Ibid.*, and *ibid.*, No. 235, August 2, 1923. Representatives of the Dresdener Bank
also believed that 500 millions was too much. *BA*, R 431/2439, July 30, 1923.

[125] *Kab. Cuno*, No. 235, August 2, and No. 238, August 4, 1923. Minister Albert, who
had originally supported the measure, now argued that it was better if such a proposal
came from the Reichstag.

[126] *Ibid.*, No. 227, July 27, 1927. Undated memo *BA*, R 431/1134.

4. THE RESIGNATION OF THE CABINET

When the Reichstag met, Germany was still in turmoil, although the most serious storm had passed on July 29 when the KPD had organized demonstrations against the cabinet.[127] The Ministries of Interior of several *Länder* had suppressed these activities and the Reich government had also prepared measures to establish a state of emergency, if the need should arise. Reacting to pressure from the rank and file membership, the SPD Reichstag faction demanded a threefold increase of advance payments on corporation income taxes, an increase of turnover taxes, a forced loan, and a special tax upon industry for the duration of the Ruhr struggle.[128] The SPD was in a difficult position, the Left of the party demanding the formation of a socialist government together with the KPD,[129] while the Right was opposed to an overthrow of the Cuno cabinet. A socialist government would lead to "civil war," and the chief journalist of the party organ *Vorwärts*, Friedrich Stampfer, warned in an editorial on August 3: "we do not want the overthrow of Cuno, since we do not want a Great Coalition." He feared that party unity, only reestablished recently would be endangered once again, since the former members of the Independent Socialist Party would not participate in a Great Coalition.[130] A motion by Quessel-Levi to overthrow Cuno was voted down, but future support of the cabinet was made dependent on the government's acceptance of the SPD tax proposals.[131]

When Cuno appeared before the Reichstag on August 8, the KPD demanded his resignation. The Minister of Finance, addressing the Reichstag after Cuno had defended the cabinet's policy, declared that without a change of the foreign policy situation, a final improvement of the monetary situation was impossible. After this obvious attack on Allied reparation policy, he explained the new taxes and the domestic loan.[132] The government's proposals were not discussed the same day, since the parties had agreed to clarify their positions on the tax and stabilization program in separate meetings of the factions first.

---

[127] Ossip K. Flechtheim, *Die KPD in der Weimarer Republik* (Frankfurt, 1969), pp. 172 ff. Wilhelm Ersil, *Aktionseinheit stürzt Cuno* (Berlin, 1963), pp. 163 ff.

[128] *Vorwärts*, No. 353, July 31, 1923 "Ein letzter Ausweg." For comments on the prevailing public mood cf. *Germania*, No. 205, July 27, 1923 "In höchster Not." Also *Westfälische Arbeiterzeitung*, No. 178, August 1, 1923.

[129] For example Arthur Crispien, *Vorwärts*, No. 358, August 2, 1923.

[130] *Ibid.*, No. 360, August 3, 1923; also No. 354, July 31, 1923.

[131] *Rheinisch-Westfälische Zeitung*, No. 406, August 4, 1923.

[132] *RT*, vol. 361, pp. 11749–11758.

When the Reichstag met the next day, Müller-Franken of the SPD opened the debate with an assault on Havenstein and Hermes while sparing Cuno. In the name of his party he declared that the SPD would support the proposed tax measures, but regretted that they had come so late. Marx (Center) and Stresemann (DVP) both stressed that united action by the parties and the government was necessary, but they made it clear that passive resistance was "a national duty" and could not be given up.[133] The BVP and the DNVP also supported the government bills, while Petersen of the DDP sharply criticized Havenstein and Hermes and described them as not being the right men for times of crisis. He also suggested that the Chancellor decide himself whether the Ministry of Economics and the Ministry of Finance should not be united under a single responsible person.[134] Obviously Petersen was thinking of Cuno. Similar ideas had also been discussed in the Henrich-Albert program, and the representative of the HAPAG in Berlin, Arndt von Holtzendorff, had suggested in a letter to Cuno (after the latter had obviously complained of the lack of cooperation in the cabinet), that Bergmann, Henrich, and the last Imperial Secretary of State in the Reichsschatzamt, Graf von Roedern, should form a financial directorate under Cuno.[135] Jakob Goldschmidt of the Darmstädter & Nationalbank also seems to have belonged to this group.[136]

Until Petersen's speech, the debate had hardly produced problems for the cabinet, but when Frölich of the KPD rose and demanded a motion of no confidence and a trial of the cabinet because of a violation of the constitution, a sudden change came about. Ledebour, a former member of the left wing of the USPD, attacked Müller-Franken's speech of the previous day, and appealing to the SPD to form a socialist government together with the KPD, he supported the KPD motion. Dittmann of the SPD followed him, and Ledebour and Koenen (KPD) demanded a meeting of the Reichstag for the next day, a Saturday. The purpose of this meeting was to overthrow the government. In contrast to these deputies, Marx (Center) wanted to gain time. He pointed out that, for the first time since Cuno had become Chancellor, a governmental program had been accepted almost unanimously by all parties, and he proposed that the next meeting take place on Monday which would allow further clarification of party attitudes. This last motion was accepted by the Reichstag majority.[137]

[133] *Ibid.*, pp. 11763–11791, August 9, 1923.
[134] *Ibid.*, pp. 11798 ff, August 10, 1923.
[135] Von Holtzendorff-Cuno, August 6, 1923, *BA*, R 431/2357.
[136] *Kab. Cuno*, No. 250, August 13, 1923.
[137] *RT*, vol. 361, pp. 11820–11824.

The real motive for this proposal became clear when Marx indicated in a meeting with Minister Albert that extra time was needed because it now seemed possible to form a Great Coalition.[138] With this statement, he had clarified the situation and admitted that the Center would no longer support Cuno in case a coalition government could be formed. It is important to note that this statement was made on August 10. As the debate in the Reichstag had shown, the SPD was split. Ledebour and Dittmann did not represent the party, and a clarification of the position of the SPD did not occur until the morning of August 11, when the majority of the SPD decided that the Cuno cabinet no longer possessed the confidence of "the populace." The party also laid down the preconditions for its participation in a new cabinet: an implementation of the tax laws just passed, a monetary reform, increased diplomatic activities to solve the reparation problem, and an application for admission to the League of Nations.[139] With the exception of the last point, the SPD conditions did not differ at all from the cabinet's new policy. In a meeting of the DVP faction on August 10, the party decided after a speech by Stresemann that it would support Cuno, if he intended to remain in office.[140] Cuno was informed of this vote. The same night, a cabinet meeting was held at which emergency measures were prepared to provide the population with food stuffs, and President Ebert, who attended, again supported all proposals.[141]

The next morning a meeting of the Reichstag faction of the Center party was called, and the party formally decided to participate in the formation of a Great Coalition government.[142] Meetings between the parties took place the same afternoon, and Cuno met the leaders of the *Arbeitsgemeinschaft* in the evening to discuss the political situation. While this encounter took place, the decision of the SPD faction became known. Cuno panicked and informed the leaders of the bourgeois parties that he could not govern against this opposition. He seems to have hoped that the party leaders would ask him to remain in office, but they accepted his statement and immediately began negotiations for a Great Coalition. However, not being certain whether such a government could be formed at all, they begged him to postpone his resignation until a decision could be reached.[143] The next

[138] *Kab. Cuno*, No. 248, August 12, 1923.

[139] *Ursachen und Folgen*, V, p. 170.

[140] Stresemann, *op. cit.*, I, pp. 77–78. A different version is given by Marx. *Marx-Nachlaß*, I, p. 186. He reports that Brüninghaus of the DVP told him that the DVP could no longer support Cuno.

[141] *Kab. Cuno*, No. 243, August 10, 1923, 10 p.m.

[142] *Marx-Nachlaß*, I, p. 286.

[143] *Kab. Cuno*, No. 247, August 12, 1923. This meeting gives some details of the events the night before.

morning, Müller-Franken notified Cuno that the SPD would oppose the vote of no-confidence of the KPD but would declare in a separate statement that the cabinet did not have the confidence of the Social Democrats anymore. The SPD was willing to cooperate in the formation of a Great Coalition.[144]

The decision of the SPD alone would not have caused Cuno to resign, but when he recognized that some parties of the *Arbeitsgemeinschaft* wanted a new government, he was determined to leave. In a meeting of the cabinet, Albert, Hermes, Brauns, von Rosenberg, and Luther agreed with the Chancellor, while Gessler, Groener and Becker wanted to go before the Reichstag and bring about a vote of confidence.[145] The latter proposal would have placed some of the parties in a very awkward position, since Becker and Heinze were members of the DVP, Brauns and Hermes belonged to the Center, Oeser was a member of the DDP, and Stingl belonged to the BVP. Cuno had never been attacked by most of these parties and could rely on the support of the DNVP which preferred him to a Great Coalition. The KPD and the SPD alone could not have overthrown the government, yet Cuno, who had never clung to office and had only reluctantly accepted it, did not intend to fight his case before the Reichstag. He was helpless in the face of party tactics, and was only too glad to return to his position with the HAPAG again. Attacks of the press on the cabinet had significantly contributed to this fatalistic attitude. Since July 27, the Center paper *Germania* had repeatedly discussed the formation of a new government.[146] Similar articles appeared in the *DAZ*, and *Vorwärts* wrote on August 12 that the decision of the SPD opened the way for Cuno to leave office, while the *Vossische Zeitung* and the *Frankfurter Zeitung* still blamed Hermes and Becker, the latter paper arguing that a Stresemann cabinet could not pursue a policy different than that of Cuno.[147]

When the Chancellor informed Stresemann (DVP), Marx (Center), Koch (DDP), and Leicht (BVP) after the cabinet meeting of his decision to resign, the party leaders, who had not yet started discussions with the SPD, denied that they no longer supported him. The BVP did not intend to participate in a Great Coalition, and Stresemann reassured Cuno that the DVP would support him, if he remained in office. Stresemann was not willing to let Cuno go yet, and he maintained that if negotiations with the SPD failed, Cuno

---

[144] *Ibid.*, No. 246, August 12, 1923.
[145] *Ibid.*
[146] *Germania*, No. 205, July 27; No. 206, July 28; No. 217, August 8; No. 218, August 9; No. 222, August 13, 1923.
[147] *Vorwärts*, No. 374, August 12; *DAZ*, No. 269, August 12; *Frankfurter Zeitung*, No. 598, August 11; *Vossische Zeitung*, No. 373, August 9.

himself would have to form a new cabinet. Without a definite promise from the SPD, Stresemann, whose name was already mentioned as the only candidate for Cuno's office, was reluctant to accept the burden of Chancellorship. Marx was as unwilling to let Cuno go before a final decision had been reached on the formation of a new government and declared that *Germania* did not represent the Center faction.

Because of these appeals Cuno once more decided to postpone his resignation until the bourgeois parties had talked with the SPD.[148] According to Leicht, negotiations were opened with the understanding that if the SPD was prepared to modify its resolution or renounce it, Cuno should remain in office.[149] The same afternoon the leaders of the bourgeois parties met with a delegation of the SPD and a Great Coalition was decided upon. Although Cuno claimed that neither the KPD nor the attitude of the SPD had finally determined his resignation, he did not say so in his letter of resignation. Marx and Stresemann had both urged him not to mention it, and Stresemann declared that his party could not participate in the formation of a cabinet that was considered to have overthrown Cuno. Upon these appeals and in order to facilitate Stresemann's task Cuno decided not to mention his view of the developments.[150] His resignation came as a complete surprise to President Ebert, after the last days of Cuno's Chancellorship had provided the first real success of the cabinet in domestic affairs.[151]

Fearing the results of food riots and public unrest, the parties had almost unanimously agreed on a common program of taxation. A similar policy had been impossible in March 1923 when party politics had prevented the execution of moderate government bills and the parties had redrafted them to satisfy different interest groups. Now, at a moment of crisis, even industrial representatives supported the tax program, and industry, trade and banking agreed to a 500 million gold mark loan. The fiscal and monetary program which had been developed by the cabinet and had been passed in the Reichstag several days before Cuno's resignation was implemented by Stresemann. A financial directorate was not created, however, and Havenstein and von Glasenapp were not dismissed either.[152]

---

[148] *Kab. Cuno*, No. 247, August 12, 1923. *Marx Nachlaß*, I, p. 301. Because of the attitude of *Germania* Marx later withdrew from its board of directors.

[149] *Kab. Cuno*, No. 248, August 12, 1923.

[150] *Ibid.* See also No. 246 and No. 247. Moldenhauer (DVP) reports in his diary that Cuno felt he was overthrown by the Center. *Moldenhauer Nachlaß*, No. 1, p. 132.

[151] *Ibid.*, No. 246, footnote 12. General v. Seeckt's letter to his sister, August 19, 1923, *Seeckt Nachlaß*, No. 67.

[152] *Kab. Cuno*, No. 250, Havenstein died in November, and Marx wrote later on "Zum Glück starb am 20.11. Havenstein." *Marx Nachlaß*, I, p. 286.

Even in foreign policy, the cabinet's hopes of British intervention were fulfilled. On August 12, Lord Curzon's note to Poincaré became known in Berlin. In this correspondence Curzon announced the illegality of the Ruhr occupation, demanded a fixation of Germany's debts by an impartial committee of experts (since the London Schedule of Payments of 1921 did not take into account German capacity to pay), rejected the French claim that the situation was similar to 1871 (a reference to French reparation payments after the Franco-Prussian war), and declared that "His Majesty's Government, ... regards as doomed to failure the method pursued by the French and the Belgian governments to secure reparations."[153].

On the other hand, von Rosenberg's and Cuno's insistence upon prolongation of passive resistance after it had become a question of prestige, and Cuno's lack of direction in domestic affairs as well as government spending for the Ruhr, led to financial chaos, public unrest, and dissatisfaction with the cabinet. However, as has been shown, party tactics and the ruthless pursuit of individual interests significantly contributed to this development. Considering the constitution of the Reichstag and the influence of interest groups upon politics, it appears unlikely that a different policy might have been possible during 1923. Perhaps the Minister of Finance, who contributed to the complete destruction of the Reich's fiscal system or at least did not take the necessary measures of calculating expenditures and revenues on a gold basis, was right after all when he justified his policy by stating in September 1923 that tax measures that were almost unanimously accepted in August 1923 would never have passed the Reichstag, if the "galloping inflation" that set in in July 1923 had not brought home to the parties the dangers of the situation.[154]

The attitude of the parties during most of Cuno's Chancellorship supports this justification at least partially. Only when it became apparent that a danger of a popular uprising – resulting from the food crisis and the breakdown of the currency system – existed, did the parties of the bourgeois Arbeitsgemeinschaft "flee" into a Great Coalition to bind the SPD and to prevent further strengthening of the KPD, which during the summer of 1923 had been constantly gaining ground. The decision to form a coalition government should have been made earlier, perhaps after Franco-Belgian troops had begun occupying the Ruhr. At that time it would have served to

[153] Rosenberg-London, August 13, 1923, *PA AA*, Büro RM, Reparationen, D 720892. It is possible that Curzon's note which was made public the same day was a last minute attempt to keep Cuno in office, or to aid the formation of a new cabinet. Von Rosenberg had discussed the matter with Lord D'Abernon on August 11 and had announced that Cuno would resign. *Kab. Cuno*, No. 246, August 12, 1923.
[154] *Marx Nachlaß*, I, p. 97.

strengthen Germany's foreign policy position and simultaneously to distribute political responsibility for domestic developments among the major parties. Such a policy might have contributed to a development of foreign policy initiatives and a program to stop inflation. On the other hand, the constant crisis hardly left any time to develop a complete program to stop inflation. Almost until the end of his Chancellorship, Cuno fought the symptoms of inflation but, like previous governments, did not fight its causes. Again, after French and Belgian troops had occupied the Ruhr, hardly any German government could have acted differently. From the Right to the Left, all parties, although for different reasons, were united in their rejections of French coercive policy. British abstention further strengthened German conviction that occupation was an illegal act and contributed to the hope that a final showdown with France would lead to a significant reduction of the reparation liability. Until the end of his Chancellorship, Cuno could count on President Ebert's support, but this certainly was not sufficient in a confrontation that was to be decided both by a realistic estimate of foreign policy initiatives and domestic economic and monetary developments.

CHAPTER VII

THE RETURN OF COALITION DIPLOMACY

I. BRITISH PREPARATIONS

The British note of August 11 had been the result of both careful discussions within the Treasury and diplomatic activities of the Foreign Office in Paris and Brussels during June and July 1923.[1] Treasury officials had examined Cuno's note of June 7 as well as French reparation plans, and they finally reached the conclusion that under certain technical arrangements the German figures came close to Bonar Law's January proposal, while French demands, besides being completely unrealistic, were also unjustified. Despite severe French war-time losses, a priority for the devastated regions could not be admitted. British material losses, especially in shipping, would also have to be accounted for, and the Treasury concluded that Britain was suffering far more from the effects of the war than France. The buildings in the devastated regions could be reconstructed (which was of course true of British shipping as well) but Great Britain had lost her dollar securities and other foreign investments as part of her effort to finance the war. These losses could not be recovered, and from a financial point of view she was thus in a far less favorable position than France.[2]

The Treasury had no intentions of agreeing to any bargaining of the C-bonds against French debts as proposed by Poincaré. In the opinion of the Treasury officials these bonds were worthless, and the real value of the A- and B-bonds did not amount to more than 25 billion gold marks.[3] While these estimates were thus significantly below French demands, the Treasury was also opposed to a combined examination of German reparations and interallied debts, fearing that such a procedure would lead to an agreement

---

[1] Weill-Raynal, *op. cit.*, II, pp. 417–456.

[2] "Note by the Financial Secretary to the Treasury," July 30, 1923, *Cab.*, 24/161, C.P. 358.

[3] "Financial aspects of the French note of 20th August," October 5, 1923, *Cab.*, 24/162, C.P. 410. Poincaré's demand for 132 billion gold marks was also disputed by the *rapporteur* of the French budget Bokanowsky, who calculated the C bonds at 15 billions and the A and B bonds at 50 billions. However, he did not believe that capitalization at 5% was possible, and thus estimated that the real value of the German debt was about 49 billion gold marks.

at the expense of Great Britain.[4] Besides this tactical consideration, the Treasury also stressed that France's economic and fiscal policy did not allow a cancellation of French war debts to Great Britain. According to their estimates, France had a favorable commercial balance and her citizens paid less taxes than British taxpayers. From these facts Treasury experts concluded that France could pay her war debts, while Germany's reparation liability had to be reconsidered. The 132 billions fixed in 1921 and still claimed by Poincaré were only a "judicial valuation" of war damages caused by the Reich, but the sum had "nothing to do with Germany's capacity or obligation to pay.[5]

While the Foreign Office had remained inactive until the summer of 1923 and had not attempted to act contrary to French wishes, Lord Curzon, completely disillusioned with Poincaré's evasive replies to his notes, had demanded separate British action after France had shown its unwillingness to consent to a common Allied answer to Cuno. The legal aspects of such a policy were studied by the Foreign Office and British members of the Reparation Commission, and they reached the conclusion that an independent reparation inquiry was not contrary to the provisions of the Versailles Treaty. They even hoped that such an inquiry would be supported by Italy and Belgium; France – then being isolated – might "fall in line."[6] Sir Eyre Crowe, the permanent undersecretary, believed that the scheme deserved consideration, and he also had a plan in case France refused to yield. He suggested that Britain ought to try to obtain American, Italian, and Japanese approval. Immediately after it had been obtained, the Foreign Office should "inform" Belgium and France that an independent inquiry had begun. If the latter countries should refuse to participate, the German government should be informed; at the same time Sir John Bradbury would raise the question of the legality of the occupation in the Reparation Commission. If it refused to deal with the request, the matter would be submitted to the International Court in The Hague. If France prevented a decision there, an appeal to the League of Nations would follow.[7]

The officials in the Foreign Office were so annoyed over Poincaré's disregard of British suggestions that on Curzon's instructions Crowe urged the Governor of the Bank of England to study the "prospect of putting diffi-

---

[4] *FO.*, 371/8643, C 12173, July 10, 1923.
[5] "Financial aspects ...," *Cab.*, 24/162, C.P. 410.
[6] *FO.*, 371/8639, C 10291, June 9, June 26, and June 28, 1923.
[7] *Ibid.*, 8641, C 11456, June 29, 1923. The participants of the meetings were Hurst, Niemeyer, Fischer-Williams, and Lampson. Crowe's comments were written on June 30, 1923.

culties on French private loans" in Britain.[8] This search for coercive measures was strengthened by the growing conviction that Cuno would make
any number of concessions for a conference on reparations, "including the
cessation of passive resistance."[9]

In the following months the influence of Sir John Bradbury, who during
1923 had become one of Poincaré's most severe critics grew steadily. In a
letter to the Prime Minister, he also favored bringing into action Britain's
financial weapons to force a conference on reparations. He proposed that
the government announce that from January 1, 1924 onwards Britain intended to cover her debts to the United States with German reparation
payments and interallied debts. At the same time, the French Minister of
Finance was to be invited to London "to talk about funding" the French
war loans. If this was refused, the Bank of England should demand immediate cash payments, and in case of default, French gold deposits in
London should be used to cover her debts. In addition to these financial
means, Bradbury as well as Crowe before him proposed that the legality of
occupation ought to be discussed.[10]

While the Foreign Office and the Treasury investigated coercive measures
against France, British observers in Berlin were asked to study the effects of
a German political and economic collapse upon Europe. One of the most
interesting reports was written by Joseph Addison, Counsellor of the British
Embassy in Berlin. Falling back on previous historical examples of French
policy towards Germany he compared Poincaré with the Minister of
War of Louis XIV, Louvois, an advocate of the annexation of the
Palatinate and the Rhineland. Addison reached the conclusion that "no
difference in aims and methods, only a difference of dress" existed
between Louvois and Turenne and Poincaré and Degoutte. Poincaré, he
maintained, wanted to bring about the same state of affairs in Germany
as had been "sanctioned by the Treaty of Westphalia." This policy was,
however, incompatible with the payment of large sums of money and the
delivery of large quantities of material." Thus, in Addison's opinion reparations were only of minor importance to France, while "for the past four
years French policy has been aiming, more or less consciously, at a reconstruction of the past and in the direction of breaking up the unity of Germany – the policeman of Central Europe." But even if Poincaré should succeed, this policy would not work to the advantage of France, since the

[8] *Ibid.*, 8639, C 10294, May 17, 1923.
[9] *Ibid.*, 8640, C 10791, June 18, 1923; C 10381, June 12, Lampson's report about a
meeting with Dufour-Feronce. The quotation is from Joseph Addison's report of June 18.
[10] Bradbury to Baldwin, July 4, 1923, *ibid.*, C 11993.

preservation of the Reich was necessary to the "prosperity and well-being of the trade, industry, and other activities of all countries." Thus a German collapse would affect the whole of Europe and the breaking up of the Reich would hopelessly dislocate the economic structure of Western Europe.[11]

Addison's analysis was highly praised by officials in the Foreign Office. Miles Lampson rated it as an "admirable paper". For Sir Eyre Crowe, the memorandum contained more valuable information than had ever been received from Ambassador D'Abernon, and Lord Curzon being of the same opinion, thanked Addison for his "able" paper.[12] The War Office also believed that Germany was at the brink of collapse and might become a "breeding ground of Communism." However, Communism was not the most immediate danger, since the Reich was strong enough to restore order. Far more dangerous for British interests would be the period after these disturbances would have been quelled. The War Office feared that Germany would turn to a totalitarian form of government. Faced with dictatorship France would, the War Office felt, immediately ask for help.[13]

If Poincaré and the French Ambassador in London had known about these investigations and the proposed countermeasures, they might perhaps have been more willing to reach a compromise with Great Britain. But the Foreign Office had not yet decided on a definite course of action, although Crowe as well als Lord Curzon repeatedly warned Poincaré not to forget that Britain was interested in German reparations; that her concern over the European situation was not less considerable than France's, and she had made as many sacrifices during the war as France. If the cabinet went before Parliament and explained French obstinacy to British overtures, many Liberal, Labour, and Conservative M.P.'s would turn away from France.[14] Besides threatening to inform the public, Lord Curzon used all kinds of diplomatic pressure to show his dissatisfaction. When the Ambassadors of France, Belgium, and Italy asked for an audience, he received them according to their countries' well-behavior towards Britain, meaning that he saw the Italian Ambassador first, followed by the Belgian and finally the French. At another meeting Curzon frankly informed Saint-Aulaire that Britain would go ahead with an inquiry held by international experts.[15]

While Poincaré was still begging for time, hoping for a German breakdown which would allow him to dictate the terms of a settlement, the Bel-

[11] "Probable result of a German collapse," June 26, 1923, *ibid.*, 8641, C 11392.
[12] *Ibid.*
[13] July 2, 1923, War Office, *ibid.*, C 11521. See also "Effects of Economic collapse of Germany," June 29, 1923, *ibid.*, C 11541, and *ibid.*, 8643, C 12112.
[14] *Ibid.*, 8642, C 11639, July 3, 1923.
[15] *Ibid.*, C 11801, July 7, 1923; C 11802 and C 11803.

gian government was impressed by British threats. The Belgian Ambassador informed the Foreign Office that Jaspar was in a very "anxious and agitated frame of mind" on account of Curzon's statements and would do everything in his power to deflect Poincaré from the course he was pursuing, if Curzon would agree to help Belgium. But the British Foreign Secretary did not intend to heed the Belgian plea; instead he sounded out Washington and Rome about an international inquiry.[16]

If Curzon had hoped that the American Secretary of State would agree to a separate inquiry, he was soon to be disappointed, since Hughes was not prepared to act without prior French approval and was apparently waiting for an invitation from all European powers.[17] British Ambassador Chilton could extract no assurances from the Department of State cabling to London: "While unwilling to commit himself, he [Hughes] said that the United States might be able to help in some way when the right moment arrived."[18] Curzon's investigation in Rome was no more successful because the Italian government wanted any conference on reparations to include the discussion of interallied debts as well. Curzon knew only too well that in this case, Britain would be faced with an united Italian, Belgian, and French front, urging British cancellation of debts. When a similar proposal was made by the Belgian Ambassador, he had notified Brussels that he could not "conceive anything more unfortunate than that the whole of that very complicated matter should be reopened and an attempt made to arrive at a new division."[19] In other words, Britain was unwilling to fix reparation claims in connection with interallied debts.

Besides a lack of foreign collaborators, Curzon did not have the full support of the cabinet. Lord Derby, the Secretary for War and former Ambassador to France, and L.S. Amery were opposed to Curzon's policy on the grounds that it was harmful to British interests. Derby believed that, instead of uttering empty threats Britain did not have the power to carry out, Curzon should "save the face" of France and support the Entente by all means.[20] Derby complained to the Prime Minister that Curzon did not inform him of his correspondence with Poincaré but demanded that his comments on Curzon's policy be kept confidential. When the British note of August 11 was sent without the changes suggested by Derby, he threatened to resign, declaring that "though I would take no immediate action I did

---

[16] *Ibid.*, 8643, C 12062, July 16, 1923; C 12343, July 17, 1923. Also *ibid.*, 8647, C 13549.
[17] *Ibid.*, 8643, C 12164, July 12, 1923.
[18] *Chilton-FO.*, July 25, 1923, *ibid.*, 8644, C 12835.
[19] *Ibid.*, 8645, C 12691, July 27, 1923.
[20] Randolph S. Churchill, *Lord Derby. King of Lancashire* (London, 1959), pp. 511 .ff

not see much good in my remaining a member of the government."[21] Derby remained in the cabinet, but the cabinet being divided, it was very difficult for the Foreign Secretary to increase pressure upon France.

On the other hand, after the resignation of Cuno, officials in the Foreign Office were convinced that Poincaré was pursuing an independent policy. Examining French and Belgian replies to the August note, they concluded that they completely ignored the British desire to reach a settlement. They were in "determined opposition to any practical move" towards a settlement. French and Belgian reference to 1871 as an example of prior German bad behavior was "perverse," for it was ludicrous to use the German occupation of France after 1871 to justify occupation of the Ruhr. In reality France had "deliberately set out to upset the political and economic organization of the Reich." Since the Reparation Commission was a French-controlled body, the Foreign Office decided that Britain should go ahead with an independent investigation of Germany's reparation capacity.[22] After studying the demands of the Allies, the Treasury considered it futile to fix reparations at the demand of these powers. If this were done, France would demand as a minimum 26 billions, Belgium 5, Italy and the other Allies 10, and Great Britain 14.2. With a total German debt of 55.2 billion gold marks, the Treasury argued, "we are back in fairy land."[23] In addition to the rejection of these demands, the Treasury also contested the validity of a comparison between the Ruhr occupation and German attitudes after 1871. At that time, French reparation payments to Germany had been easy, since France had received foreign credit. Finally, the British Treasury completely rejected French reparation demands as being unsound and recommended recalling of the banker's committee which had estimated German reparation capacity in June 1922. According to the Treasury "Poincaré knows well what would come" if such a neutral committee gave an impartial view about the 132 billions fixed in 1921.[24]

But despite this new attempt to decide upon a common course of action between the Allies nothing happened, since the Foreign Office was not sure of what Poincaré really wanted: reparations, security or the dissolution of the Reich. The British Ambassador to Washington again reported that President Coolidge, who had become President after Harding's sudden death, had stated in a press conference that it was inopportune for the

[21] Ibid., p. 515, Keith Middlemas, John Barnes, Baldwin. A Biography (London, 1969), pp. 187–191.
[22] FO., 371/8646, C 13539, undated, but written by Lampson at the beginning of August.
[23] Ibid., C 13591, August 8, 1923.
[24] Ibid.

United States to intervene in reparations until Great Britain and France could agree on American help.[25] At the same time, the Belgian Foreign Minister bitterly complained that his country had been pushed into the Ruhr by the British plan submitted at the Paris conference in January 1923. That proposal, Jaspar now maintained, had been so complicated that after 48 hours work only Treasury officials could understand it, yet the Belgian representatives at the conference had been requested to take a position immediately. Since the British plan was the cause of the Belgian dilemma, Jaspar believed it to be especially unfair that Britain would not help Belgium to get out of the Ruhr again.[26] If Belgium wanted British support, she had to break with France first, but this was a course of action Belgium could not pursue, instead, her support for the French position was further strengthened through a 400 million franc loan at very favorable conditions.[27]

With the exception of a Treasury-inspired article in the London Times arguing that France claimed twice as much from Germany as was her due, nothing happened.[28] Incapable of forcing France to agree to a conference and without American support, the British cabinet decided to encourage neutral powers to take the reparation question up in the League and to wait for the Imperial Conference to sound out the views of the Commonwealth countries on British policy.[29] Having reached a deadlock in official negotiations, Lord Curzon retreated for the moment, but now both France and Belgium attempted to influence British policy. However, these feelers were rejected by Curzon, who wanted negotiations according to his own conditions and did not intend to create the impression that Britain agreed to the occupation.[30] Thus a break with France was becoming more and more likely, and Stanley Baldwin, the British Prime Minister, made a last attempt to find out whether he could deal with Poincaré after the Foreign Office had failed. The opportunity for such a meeting arose when Baldwin spent his holidays in a French health resort.[31]

But before Baldwin met Poincaré he received a memorandum prepared by Sir John Bradbury. Bradbury was as opposed as ever to concessions to France, warning the Prime Minister that: "I am myself very firmly con-

---

[25] Ibid., 8649, C 14093, August 15, 1923.

[26] Ibid., 8647, C 13549, August 27, 1923.

[27] Ibid., 8649, C 13905, August 14 and C 14624, August 25, 1923.

[28] Ibid., 8651, C 14669, August 25, 1923.

[29] Cab., 23/46, August 1, 1923.

[30] FO., 371/8554, C 14963, August 9, 1923. The meeting with Poincaré took place on September 19. Ibid., C 15038.

[31] Ibid., C 14950, August 31, 1923.

vinced that no agreement is possible with the present French government which would not be disastrous both to British interests, and the peace of Europe." Bradbury feared especially that the new German chancellor Stresemann might be prepared to find a modus vivendi with Poincaré even at the risk of putting "his signature to impossible future commitments on the model of Wirth and the Schedule of Payments." Such a development would not suit British interests, since even if Stresemann accepted French terms, Germany would be unable to fulfill them. Bradbury thus strongly urged the cabinet not to abandon the British position as laid down in the August note. In addition to these warnings, Bradbury again repeated his demand for a study of the legality of occupation by the International Court in The Hague, and he suggested that the constitution of the Reparation Commission be modified.[32] In another document entitled "British action in event of failure to reach agreement with France," he proposed that, in a meeting with German representatives, British reparation claims should be set at 22% of Bonar Law's January proposal. According to his estimate, Britain would then receive 8.8 billion gold marks from the first series of reparation bonds and 3.6 billions from the second. After an agreement with Germany had been reached along these lines, Britain should then invite the Allies to fund their debts.[33]

The meeting between Poincaré and Baldwin took place in the British Embassy in Paris on September 19. In this two hour tête-à-tête, Baldwin did not bring up Bradbury's provocative scheme but tried hard to establish a common reparation policy, recognizing that without French collaboration a final settlement was impossible. Baldwin wanted to keep the alliance intact, and, requesting that absolute frankness be established between them he warned Poincaré not to be misled by the anti-German Rothermere press. The mood of public opinion in England was changing and an increasing section of the Conservative Party was becoming anti-French, while Labour and the Liberals were already opposed to the Ruhr affair. This changing public attitude, he warned, might have repercussions on British policy towards France. The Prime Minister opened the discussion with a conciliatory

---

[32] Churchill, *op. cit.*, pp. 515 ff. Derby had suggested on September 1 that Baldwin see Poincaré alone. Middlemas/Barnes, *op. cit.*, p. 193.

[33] Bradbury-Baldwin, September 12, 1923, *FO.*, 371/8654, C 15800. Bradbury's view was criticized in a memorandum prepared by Alexander Cadogan of the Foreign Office. He believed that Britain could wait, since her financial assistance was needed for a final settlement. "... we can bide our time, and we should, if asked our opinion, express our views as to the unsoundness of the French plan: we shall then be all the more in a position, when the time comes, to use the leverage we possess in the matter of financial assistance for securing the excision of the more objectionable features." *Ibid.*, 8655, C 16201, September 18, 1923.

attitude towards France and stressed that he also wanted a settlement at the expense of Germany, but he did not leave any doubt that he strongly disapproved of the occupation. Cooperation between France and Britain could not be reestablished as long as occupation continued. On the other hand, Britain wanted a settlement for two reasons:

Firstly because, rightly or wrongly, she attributed the greater part of her unemployment to the present disorganization in the trade of the world, and secondly, rightly or wrongly again, and seeking order and peace she feared that until this great question was disposed of there would be the more probability of disorder and fighting in a Europe which had already suffered too much.[34]

At this first meeting between a British Prime Minister and Poincaré after the disastrous clash in January 1923 which had led to the Ruhr occupation, Baldwin tried to find out what Poincaré intended to do after passive resistance had been abandoned. The French Minister President, however, although he politely appreciated the "frankness" with which Baldwin had spoken, refuted his approach. Returning Baldwin's frankness, he told him that the French government was not master of the French press and that ninety-nine percent of the population supported his Ruhr policy. He further argued that without occupation France would have "found herself in a worse plight than before 1914." But the real motive behind his policy was the fact that French claims had been "jeopardized" ever since 1919. He made it clear that he still resented that Britain had not participated in the seizure of productive pledges and maintained that if she had supported coercive measures, Germany would never have dared to resist. Thus, it was really the British who had brought about military occupation. He did not want British intervention and had thus opposed Lord Curzon's mediation at a moment when Germany could not keep up resistance any longer. Prestige played a great role in Poincaré's thinking, and he further justified his opposition by stating that in the case of British mediation "Germany would have capitulated under British demands, but not French pressure." Poincaré was as intransigent as towards Lord Curzon, and at the end of their meeting informed Baldwin that 1) France would not tolerate a discussion of reparations in the League of Nations; 2) French conditions for a settlement had been laid down in the French Yellow Book; and 3) Germany would have to give up passive resistance before a practical solution could be worked out. On the other hand, Poincaré knew only too well that he was dependent on British good will, and assured Baldwin that a final solution would be reached by all the Allies. This last remark may have been the

---

[34] *Ibid.*, 8655, C 16201, September 19, 1923. Although the meeting was held in September, the report is dated October 16. Middlemas/Barnes, *op. cit.*, pp. 197–201.

result of the Prime Minister's warning against unilateral action and his hints to the pending security question and interallied debts.[35]

Although a communiqué was published stating that a common attitude existed and future agreements between the Allies were possible, the meeting did not bring any immediate change of policy. Instead, the communiqué which was apparently drafted by Sir William Tyrell to placate the French and was bitterly resented by the hardliner Curzon, surprised the British press and caused uneasiness in some parts of the government as well as in Berlin.[36] On September 21, only two days after Baldwin's departure from Paris, the British news agency Reuter warned that, although suspicion as to French goals in the Ruhr had apparently been dispelled, only Baldwin himself could interpret the results of the discussion; a cabinet meeting would be held in order to prepare the Imperial Conference in October, and the convocation of an international conference on reparations would probably be the first issue on the agenda.[37] The Reuter communiqué was the first attempt to smooth over the waves created by the Paris statement. On September 27 Baldwin himself intervened and tried to set the matter right by stating in a public speech that his meeting with Poincaré had been good "to clear the atmosphere." The Entente was important for Great Britain, since otherwise there would be no settlement. However, the Imperial Conference would deal with reparations.[38]

At first sight, Baldwin's statement appears to be far more conciliatory than Curzon's correspondence with Poincaré. But developments at the Imperial Conference, and Baldwin's answer to Poincaré's complaints about Curzon's speech before the conference, reveal that the Prime Minister essentially differed very little from Curzon. The British Foreign Secretary had given up all hope of French collaboration and was "tired of making proposals" in Paris which were constantly being rejected.[39] Angered by this obstinacy, he declared before the Imperial Conference on October 5 that the sum fixed by the London Schedule of Payments in 1921 bore no relation to Germany's capacity to pay. British experts considered the figures to be economically unsound, but Poincaré had nevertheless been unwilling to reduce the sum without the seizure of productive pledges. Although Curzon admitted that Germany had prolonged passive resistance for too long a period, he stated that any government which would not have followed

[35] Ibid.
[36] White, op. cit., p. 155. Middlemas/Barnes, op. cit., p. 201. Zimmermann, op. cit., pp. 216–218. Weill-Raynal, op. cit., II, p. 496 f.
[37] Weill-Raynal, op. cit., II, p. 496 f.
[38] FO., 371/8656, C 16964, September 27, 1923. Baldwin's speech at Northhampton.
[39] Curzon, October 1, 1923, ibid., C 17007.

such a policy would have been driven out of office. Britain had tried to hold
the scales between the rival parties, but now that passive resistance had
finally been given up, he was expecting a proposal from France. A settlement
without British cooperation, he warned Poincaré, was not feasible. At the
end of his speech, he repeated the position already made public by the
August note: the Ruhr occupation was not justified, but he had not expressed
his opinion publicly until Poincaré had raised the legal issue.[40]

When Poincaré was informed of Curzon's speech, he immediately protested to Baldwin. The British Prime Minister answered in a letter to his
"dear colleague" in Paris in polite but determined words completely rejecting this criticism, and reminded Poincaré that despite their meeting on
September 19, their countries still regarded reparations from completely
different angles. Curzon's speech was not, as the French Minister President
had explained in his letter, an unfriendly act towards France, but a reasonable evaluation of the situation. "His Majesty's Government feel bound to
maintain the accuracy of Lord Curzon's statement that the sum bore no relation to what Germany could pay, but was arrived at by lumping together
the demands of the various claimant powers." Germany's capacity to pay
had thus "never to this day been approached by the Reparation Commission." The occupation of the Ruhr was disastrous for the "collection of
reparations, and Curzon's statement, that Italy had denounced military occupation and had not participated was correct as well." Since all powers had
presented their plans by now, the Prime Minister demanded that France
submit a plan of her own. If Poincaré had thought that Baldwin was easier
to deal with than Curzon, this answer certainly dampened his hopes. It also
indicated that the pro-French groups in the cabinet around Lord Derby
were also losing their influence.[41]

Despite Baldwin's request, Poincaré did not intend to discuss reparations
at this stage. France could not endorse the creation of an international
committee of experts according to Hughes' December proposal, and Peretti
de la Rocca warned Belgium and Italy that the British initiative was dangerous at a moment when passive resistance was finally being discontinued and
Germany was ready to submit proposals to the Reparations Commission.
The British demand for an international conference would serve only to
strengthen German hopes of evading reparation payments.[42]

Again Poincaré succeeded in preventing the convocation of an internatio-

---

[40] *The Times*, October 6, 1923.
[41] Baldwin-Poincaré, October 17, 1923, *MAE*, Allemagne 482, fol. 34–40. Derby-
Baldwin, October 9, 1923, Churchill, *op. cit.*, p. 516.
[42] *MAE*, Allemagne 482, October 21, 1923, fol. 49–53.

nal conference, but the longer he waited for a German breakdown, the stronger British opposition to French policy became. This was due more than anything to the fear that France might create a French-dominated industrial giant on the Continent. Several branches of British industry had profited from the elimination of German competition at the beginning of 1923, but now France and Belgium had confiscated stocks in the Ruhr and started selling them on the world market. Fearing that the sales of this material would lead to low prices for British dye-stuffs, the Board of Trade had already urged the British Dyestuff Corporation on July 7 to buy as large an amount as possible of German dyestuffs "now dumped by France." Similar advice to other industries followed, and soon British industry demanded protection from French exports from the Ruhr as well.[43]

As a result, a discussion took place at a cabinet meeting on September 25, about how to

safeguard British industry against the dangers of dumping which would threaten it (and more particularly the steel industry, in which there is already overproduction) if in the course of separate negotiations between the French and German governments and between French and German industrialists, German industry should fall under the control of that of France.[44]

Immediately after this meeting France and Belgium were asked to stop the dumping of German goods, and both these countries promised that excessive dumping of seized stocks on Allied countries would be prevented.[45]

Not only did the British cabinet try to influence Belgium and France, but Lord Curzon also advised the German Ambassador in plain language not to deal separately with France: "Did I [Curzon], for instance, hear that such negotiations were on foot or still more had been conducted, I should not feel disposed to lift a little finger to help Germany in any of her future troubles." Sthamer assuaged Curzon by declaring that Stresemann would not agree to a separate understanding with France, and Curzon in return told him that at the Baldwin-Poincaré meeting in Paris a common Anglo-French reparation strategy had not even been discussed.[46]

But despite German promises,[47] rumors about a Franco-German in-

[43] FO., 371/8735, C 11681, July 7, 1923; C 12014, July 10, 1923.
[44] Cab., 23/46, September 25, 1923.
[45] Ibid., October 15, 1923. FO., 371/8658, C 13389 and 8748, C 19423. MAE, Ruhr 31, fol. 86–89.
[46] FO., 371/8656, C 16799, September 27, 1923. Sthamer's report is in PA AA, Büro RM, Reparationen, D 721240–242.
[47] These massive warnings and Sthamer's assurances were not regarded to be sufficient by Curzon and, on October 16, Lord D'Abernon asked for an audience in the German Foreign Office, again repeating the previous warning. Stresemann reconfirmed Sthamer's statement, but Lord D'Abernon visited the Wilhelmstrasse several times during the fol-

dustrial understanding circulated in London, and finally the National
Federation of Iron and Steel Manufacturers sent representatives into the
Ruhr to elicit the truth.[48] British fears of a separate Franco-German industrial agreement at the expense of Great Britain were increased when the
Counsellor at the German Embassy suggested to representatives of British
industry that, if Britain did not cooperate with the Reich, German industry
would be forced to deal with France alone. These hints served their purpose.
Negotiations about Anglo-German industrial cooperation, which had
broken down in June, were resumed. As a result of these talks in London
an agreement between the British Dyestuff Corporation and the Deutsche
Teerinteressengemeinschaft was signed.[49]

However, British suspicion about Franco-German cooperation received
new impetus when the contracts between Ruhr industrialists and the
MICUM were signed which regulated the resumption of reparation deliveries after the end of passive resistance on September 26. Immediately
Lord D'Abernon went to the *Wilhelmstraße* and insisted that the contracts
must not contain any clauses detrimental to British industry. The Germans,
still interested in British help against France, handed over copies of the contracts to Lord D'Abernon in order to allay his fears.[50]

British apprehension towards a potential French-dominated pact between
French and German industry caused the Foreign Office to act. The moment
to "stand up against France had come."[51] Benevolent neutrality towards
French Ruhr and Rhineland policy had necessarily to come to an end. In
essence, this decision meant that Britain would not yield to French pressure
any more, and, in the hope of German collaboration, would resist the creation of an Independent Rhineland Republic, prevent French control of the
railway system in the occupied zones, and refuse to allow the creation of a
separate currency in this area. In short, Britain intended to prevent French
political and economic supremacy on the Continent. Except for a break of
diplomatic relations, the Foreign Office would use British political, economic,

---

lowing weeks to obtain further information on developments, while strongly arguing
against any agreement. *FO.*, 371/8748, C 18976, October 31, 1923. *PA AA*, Büro RM,
Reparationen, D 721697, November 7. and D 721707, November 8, 1923.

[48] *FO.*, 371/8748, C 19420, November 8, 1923; C 19025, November 2, 1923.

[49] *Ibid.*, Büro RM, Reparationen, October 11, 1923, D 721364. The report about this
contract is in *Nachlaß Maltzan*, Allgemeine Verhandlungen, November 17, 1923.

[50] Weill-Raynal, *op. cit.*, II, pp. 464 ff. Stresemann, *op. cit.*, I, pp. 160 ff. Reports about
the first MICUM contracts are in *PA AA* Sonderreferat W., Verhandlungen Krupp, Wolff,
Becker mit der MICUM. For D'Abernon's visit see *ibid.*, Büro RM, Reparationen, D
7216697, November 7, and D 721708, November 8, 1923, D 721730, November 10, 1923.
The contracts are in *BA*, 38/204–223.

[51] *FO.*, 371/8749, C 20414 and C 18249 October 19 and 22.

and financial power to stop France and obtain an international conference on reparations.

2. THE NEW OPPONENTS: STRESEMANN AND POINCARE

In contrast to British influence upon events at the end of 1923, the German government could do nothing but wait and block French demands for a separate agreement. From the moment Gustav Stresemann became Chancellor, both his domestic and his foreign policy were largely directed towards obtaining the withdrawal of Franco-Belgian troops from the Ruhr. During the first phase of his Chancellorship, his policy did not differ from that pursued by the previous cabinet. Like von Rosenberg and Cuno, he hoped that France could be isolated by Britain drawing Belgium and Italy on her side.[52]

Accepting Cuno's note of June 7 as the basis of his reparation policy, he at the same time opposed French Rhineland policy.[53] On September 2, he repeated Cuno's January proposal about a peace pact for all countries bordering on the Rhine and extended the period of the treaty.[54] With this speech, German policy was slightly modified and Stresemann's policy of appeasing France began. In a memorandum written as late as July 27, Stresemann, at that time nothing more than an influential party leader, had still been uncertain of which alternative to take; whether to pursue a policy leaning towards Britain or one of cooperation with France. In the first case, Britain would have to help Germany finance the Ruhr and contribute to the creation of a new currency. With British help, a future confrontation with France would also become possible. If on the other hand, Britain did not support him, cooperation between French and German industry would become a necessity. In July 1923, Stresemann apparently was still open to both alternatives, but was also considering the possibility of military conflict with France.[55] He abandoned this kind of speculation after he had become Chancellor in August 1923. Instead he attempted to find out about Poincaré's real intentions in the Ruhr. In a meeting with French Ambassador de Margerie, he inquired what he could do to reach a compromise con-

---

[52] Stresemann, *op. cit.*, I, p. 98. Werner Weidenfeld, *Die Englandpolitik Gustav Stresemanns: Theoretische und praktische Aspekte der Außenpolitik* (Mainz, 1972), p. 174.

[53] *Die Zeit*, No. 196, August 26, 1923. The speech was made at a breakfast of the Deutscher Industrie- und Handelstag and is partly printed in Stresemann, *op. cit.*, I, p. 92, but the editors wrongly refer to the note of May 2.

[54] Stresemann, *op. cit.*, I, pp. 100 ff.

[55] "Denkschrift Stresemann, 27.7.1923," *PA AA*, Nachlaß Stresemann, Politische Akten, 1923 V, Bd. 250, H 145801 ff.

cerning the internationalization of the railway system. He suggested that French coal demands should be satisfied by voluntary agreements which would fix deliveries to France at a certain percentage of Ruhr production, and demanded to know how French and German industry could cooperate and what Poincaré wanted as reparations in kind.[56]

This meeting with de Margerie, although it ended the diplomatic isolation of the French Ambassador and improved relations between the Wilhelm-straße and the French Embassy did not mean that Stresemann had decided in favor of yielding to military pressure. The same day, he received a visit from the British Ambassador and warned D'Abernon that the situation had become intolerable. If Britain did not act soon, Germany might be forced to reach an agreement with France. He also demanded financial help from Great Britain, which was denied.[57] Like Cuno, Stresemann had simply over-estimated British power and willingness to help against France. His attempt to exploit British fears about a German collapse failed as did his initiative to open direct consultation with France. Hoping for a dissolution of the Reich, Poincaré refused to enter into formal negotiations. He also rejected Belgian demands for a conference with Stresemann.[58] Instead he requested that the French Ambassador to Poland investigate the possibility of sending Polish miners into the Ruhr. France intended to exploit the pledges her-self.[59] The French Minister President also warned Pierre de Margerie not to fall into Stresemann's traps, that German proposals were only designed to put France "at the mercy of international financiers."[60]

Since Poincaré was unwilling to deal with him, Stresemann had to admit, on October 1, that negotiations with France had failed, although he had given up passive resistance on September 26.[61] The new Chancellor's official and private attempts to contact Poincaré had been as unsuccessful as Cuno's unyielding attitude towards France earlier in the year.[62] However, when he gave up passive resistance, the Reich was in a far more difficult position than under Cuno. The fall of the mark had continued, public unrest had grown,

[56] Stresemann, op. cit., I, p. 101.
[57] Ibid., p. 105. De Margerie's report is in MAE, Ruhr 28, September 5, 1923, fol. 42 ff. Weidenfeld, op. cit., p. 181.
[58] MAE, Ruhr 28, September 12, 1923, fol. 157 and September 13, 1923, fol. 170.
[59] Ibid., Ruhr 27, August 25, fol. 182. Poland agreed to send workers. Ibid., August 30, 1923, fol. 223–225.
[60] Ibid., Ruhr 28, September 14, 1923, fol. 174. Zimmermann, op. cit., p. 214.
[61] Stresemann, op. cit., I, p. 149. Weidenfeld, op. cit., p. 182.
[62] Hoesch-Stresemann, September 9, 1923, PA AA, Büro RM, Reparationen, D 736482. For Stresemann's policy towards France see Michael-Olaf Maxelon, Stresemann und Frankreich. Politik der Ost-West-Balance (Düsseldorf, 1972), p. 88, p. 96, p. 105, and passim.

and finally the government did not have sufficient means to prolong passive resistance any more. Faced with the bankruptcy of the Reich, Stresemann was forced to give in. Under these circumstances passive resistance had lost all meaning.

The German Foreign Office had already recognized the desperate situation at the beginning of September and, hoping to prevent a French-controlled Ruhr and Rhineland, on September 10 had asked the Ministry of Economics to prepare a study of what the temporary neutralization of the occupied areas would mean for the Reich's economic life. The Foreign Office suggested that Switzerland might be a possible trustee and also requested an investigation into the creation of an international trust that should receive pledges upon part of German industrial working capital. Unexploited coal fields, state forests, the capital of the coal syndicate, and fiscal income were considered to be adequate pledges.[63] The demand for such an investigation shows that the Foreign Office was prepared for the worst – the temporary loss of the Reich's sovereignty over Germany's most productive industrial region.

When de Margerie's announcement that Germany had given up passive resistance reached the Quai D'Orsay, Poincaré was not in Paris. Jules Laroche, Assistant Director for political and commercial affairs of the Foreign Office, who was in charge in Peretti's absence, immediately phoned Poincaré. Laroche, who apparently had been sceptical about the eventual success of the Ruhr enterprise, now congratulated the Minister President to his personal victory. But Poincaré, who had not answered the cables of the French Ambassador in Berlin demanding negotiations refused to deal with Stresemann even now.[64] Laroche and René de Saint-Quentin, the Councellor of the French Embassy in Berlin, both believed that Poincaré was waiting for the economic and political disintegration of the Reich to solve French security problems and put the Reich at the mercy of France.[65] Even the French Prime Minister, Millerand, felt that Poincaré stubborn attitude prevented negotiations with Germany before Great Britain and the United States intervened.[66]

Developments in Paris during the last months of 1923 reveal that Poincaré, obsessed with the idea of obtaining reparations and security, overestimated his control of developments in Germany and had greatly underesti-

---

[63] *PA AA*, W. Rep., Besetzung des Ruhrgebiets, H 226848–849, September 10, 1923.

[64] Jules Laroche, "Quelques aspects de l'affaire de la Ruhr," *Revue D'Histoire Diplomatique* 63 (1949), pp. 180–182.

[65] René de Saint Quentin, "L'occasion manquée de la Ruhr," *ibid.*, pp. 177–179.

[66] *Ibid.*, p. 178. Auguste F. Saint Aulaire, *Confession d'un vieux diplomate* (Paris, 1953), p. 672.

mated France's dependence upon Britain and the United States. Hoping to gain time for the implementation of foreign policy goals that had existed partly since 1919 but had taken more concrete shape during 1923, Poincaré lost the chance to deal with Germany. The French Minister President who wrote most of the notes himself, carefully rejected his opponent's arguments and refuted Ambassadors abroad and advisers at home if they did not share his opinion. Moreover, he had informed the French Embassy in Berlin and his Belgian ally that he would not deal with Stresemann.[67] To him, the German proclamation ending resistance was not acceptable, and President Ebert's speech – maintaining that the occupation had been illegal – was "real provocation". In face of this, he insisted that France would not negotiate but would arrange the end of resistance in negotiations with local authorities.[68] This meant in fact, a weakening of the ties between the occupied areas and unoccupied Germany and could only help, if carried out successfully, in establishing total French control of Ruhr industries. This was indeed obtained through the MICUM agreements which were signed at the end of October and in November, granting France the exploitation of the Ruhr for reparation purposes. In this respect, Poincaré had won a victory over German tycoons. Nevertheless, exploitation of Ruhr coal mines neither solved reparations nor the security problem. However, it could be used, Poincaré hoped, to influence British and American policy towards interallied debts and as a pledge for further Allied negotiations.[69] Thus in the following months both German reaction to exploitation of the pledges as well as Anglo-American attitudes were of the utmost importance for a successful implementation of French policy. But as the following developments show, neither the United States nor Great Britain were willing to combine new reparations talks with a discussion of interallied debts. Even with victory in the Ruhr, Poincaré had simply overestimated the impact of his pledges on Allied negotiations.

3. THE CREATION OF THE DAWES COMMITTEE

After Stresemann had given up passive resistance, the British Foreign Office again contacted the United States and the other European powers about

[67] Zimmermann, op. cit., pp. 50–53. MAE, Ruhr 29, September 28, 1923, fol. 219, and September 29, 1923, fol. 258–260.
[68] MAE, Ruhr 28, September 29, 1923, fol. 258–260. Ursachen und Folgen, V, No. 179, pp. 203–204.
[69] Denise Artaud, "A propos de l'Occupation de la Ruhr," Revue D'Histoire Moderne et Contemporaine 17 (1970), pp. 11 ff.

a conference on reparations. Without American participation and financial power, a solution to the reparation question was not feasible and Curzon tried to obtain American consent to an international conference first. If France would not participate, he was also prepared to act without her collaboration and, as earlier in the year, he asked Hughes whether the Unites States would take part in such an inquiry.[70]

The American position, made clear by Secretary Hughes on October 12, was that the United States government would participate if the conference were kept an advisory one, all final decisions being left to the government at home. Hughes did not want to discuss German responsibility for the war, nor should the Reich's liabilities be cancelled. Like Curzon, he was also opposed to a combined discussion of reparations and interallied debts, but in contrast to the British Foreign Secretary, he did not think that a conference without French participation would do any good.[71] The presence of former Prime Minister Lloyd George in Washington and his public advocacy of the adaptation of the Hughes Plan of December 1922 greatly facilitated the American decision but also led to immediate reactions in Paris. Peretti de la Rocca rejected the Hughes Plan on October 15, arguing that it would have been useless to undertake an inquiry in December 1922. At that time, Germany had neither acquired the will to pay, nor had the government been willing to undertake stabilization, while the failure of passive resistance had finally led to changes in Germany. Apparently the right moment for American intervention had come, and Peretti also invited the Americans to discuss the obvious connection between reparation credits to Germany and interallied debts.[72] Paris also warned Italy and Belgium against any discussion of German debts with independent experts, because this would only increase German hopes for a reduction of her liability. This was a development Poincaré would not tolerate, and, furthermore, the Reparation Commission was the only legal agency to consider reparations. This commission of course had the right to invite experts to participate in an inquiry.[73] Although Hughes further clarified the American attitude in a meeting with the Counsellor of the French Embassy, Laboulaye, and even hinted that he would favor a re-

---

[70] FO., 371/8658, C 18042, October 10, 1923. Ibid., 8657, C 17662. See Gescher, op. cit., p. 195.

[71] FO., 371/8657, C 17706, October 12, 1923. Ibid., C 17912 October 16, and 8658, C 17930.

[72] Ibid., 8658, C 18042, October 10, 1923. For the reaction in Paris cf. MAE, Allemagne 482, fol. 2 ff, October 11 and Peretti-Jusserand, October 15, ibid., fol. 15 f.

[73] Peretti-Brussels, Rome, London, Washington, October 21, 1923, ibid., fol. 49 ff. Cf. also Peretti's discussions with British Ambassador Crewe on October 20. FO., 371/8658, C 18059.

duction of French debts to the United States once reparations had been settled, Poincaré rejected the British initiative, although he was certainly pleased about Hughes' remarks. He feared, however, that any expert meeting would only serve to show Allied disunity. Thus only the Reparation Commission remained as the legal agency for discussion of reparations.[74]

Poincaré's intransigent attitude led to increased activities by Hughes, Baldwin, and the British delegate to the Reparation Commission, Bradbury. When the French Counsellor met Hughes again on October 29 to explain Poincaré's attitude and informed Washington that German experts would not be allowed to participate in an inquiry held by the Reparation Commission, Laboulaye met an unmerciful Hughes who seemed to take pleasure in reminding the French that their reparation policy had been unsuccessful. Hughes even claimed that neither Poincaré's diplomatic communications nor his public speeches "indicated his desire to secure reparations." Two days later, in another unpleasant meeting, Hughes declared that if the experts could not consider comprehensively Germany's capacity, "the inquiry would be abortive."[75]

Faced with French opposition, the British Prime Minister made a speech at the National Unionist Association Conference at Plymouth, pleading with Poincaré to reconsider his decision and warning that the creation of separate states within Germany "would at once break the Treaty of Versailles."[76] As this last remark shows, reparation was not the only issue between France and Britain. British distrust of French policy towards Germany increased when an attempt to create a Rhenish Republic was made in the Belgian zone and was followed by a similar step in the French zone. Although French support for the Separatist Movement had been clearly recognized by British observers, the French High Commissioner maintained that France had been neutral. But now that the Separatists were actually in power, France would support them and Tirard declared that "the French

[74] Laboulaye-MAE, October 23, 1923, *MAE*, Allemagne 482, fol. 63 ff. *FO.*, 8658, C 18460, October 26, 1923, Cf. *Hughes Papers*, Box 174, Folder 74 b, France, Memo about a meeting between Hughes and Laboulaye on October 26. Bariety, *op. cit.*, p. 263 f.

[75] Memo Hughes, October 29, 1923, *Hughes Papers*, Box 174, Folder 74 b, France. Hughes stated: "It did not appear that thus far France had been sucessful in producing reparation payments and if matters went on in that way they would not be secured at all. Of course, if M. Poincaré did not wish to obtain reparation payments, he could take the course leading to that. But if he did wish reparation payments, the Secretary hoped that M. Poincaré would not put any unnecessary obstacles in the way of securing them." The meeting on October 31 took place because Poincaré had some "misgivings as a result of what the Secretary had said in his last interview." *Ibid.* Also *MAE* Allemagne 482, fol. 151 f, October 30.

[76] *PA AA*, W. Rep., Öffentliche Reden zur Reparationsfrage, October 25, 1923.

public would never tolerate their being overthrown by Prussian reactionaries."[77]

Shortly before this incident, the Belgian Foreign Minister had intervened in London demanding to know what Britain would do if an independent Rhenish state were in fact created. In his opinion, an Allied conference should be held to discuss the matter.[78] But the Foreign Office was not prepared to participate in any conference at all. Instead, it strongly warned that the foundation of such a state would impair the workability of the Treaty of Versailles "so much so that in certain important aspects the latter would automatically cease to operate and would require complete revision.[79] When Poincaré argued that article 18 of the Weimar constitution allowed the creation of a separate state within the Reich, Curzon repeated the warning, adding that Britain would step down from all interallied commissions.[80]

Parallel to these developments, the British delegate on the Reparation Commission attempted to increase pressure on France, suggesting that the commission should be enlarged to include a neutral, a German, and an American representative. Stresemann also demanded an examination of Germany's capacity to pay according to Article 234 of the Versailles Treaty, but France prevented a decision although the German note was discussed in the Reparation Commission.[81] The discussion of the note, however, indicates that important changes had occurred. The temporary differences between Great Britain and Italy as a result of the Corfu incident no longer influenced Anglo-Italian cooperation in reparations and the Italian delegate accepted Bradbury's proposal for an impartial inquiry.[82] The Belgian government informed Paris that it was useless to investigate Germany's capacity for a limited period as Poincaré had suggested to Hughes on October 25; everybody knew that Germany's capacity was "zero" at the moment.[83]

Faced with isolation in the Reparation Commission and recognizing the seriousness of British threats and American annoyance, Louis Barthou, the French President of the Reparation Commission, also moved away from

[77] FO., 371/8685, C 18303, October 24, 1923. Ibid., 8686, C 18744, October 29, 1923. Ibid., 8685, C 183 78, October 25, 1923.
[78] Ibid., C 18382, October 26, 1923. Ibid., C 18050, October 20, 1923. See also Erdmann, op. cit., pp. 71 ff.
[79] FO., 371/8686, C 18941, October 30, 1923.
[80] Ibid., C 18935 and C 18941, November 2 and November 20, 1923.
[81] Hoesch-AA, PA AA, Büro RM, Reparationen, D 724452–456, October 17, 1923. Bergmann, op. cit., p. 273.
[82] FO., 371/8659, C 18703, October 31, 1923. White, op. cit., p. 149. For the Corfu incident see Middlemas/Barnes, op. cit., p. 194 f.
[83] MAE, Allemagne 482, November 1, 1923, fol. 172.

Poincaré's intransigent position. On October 30, the Reparation Commission unanimously accepted a motion submitted by Bradbury stating that paragraph 18, of Annex II of the Versailles Treaty had not yet been interpreted by the Reparation Commission.[84] With this decision, the Commission indirectly contested Poincaré's interpretation of the paragraph which was the basis of his legal arguments, although the decision was not made public at that time. Nevertheless, the vote shows that the French delegate, no longer supported by Belgium and Italy, had finally yielded. The legality of the Ruhr occupation could thus be decided upon, if such a need should arise. The British delegate had obtained a powerful weapon in case France should reject an expert inquiry, and it is doubtful whether Poincaré could have vetoed a decision of the Commission which he had declared to be impartial.

During these weeks, Bradbury's influence upon the course of reparation policy further increased.[85] His British colleague on the Reparation Commission, Frederick Leith-Ross, also warned against deliberations that did not take into account the political and social consequences of a huge reparation liability. In economic theory, he felt, it was possible "to reduce the German nation to a position of hewers of wood and drawers of water for the rest of the world," but this would definitely mean "political trouble" in Germany.[86] This pessimistic outlook was shared by Sir Otto Niemeyer of the Treasury who argued that it was useless to have Germany accept figures "in desperation" which she could not fulfill.[87] British reparation experts had decided that Germany's capacity to pay would have to be reconsidered. This did not mean that they would give up their claims, but it foreshadowed a reduction of the London Schedule of Payments. They wanted a reasonable settlement, and Bradbury was determined to obtain an international inquiry despite Poincaré's objections. Initially he had been unwilling to accept a committee under the control of the Reparation Commission fearing that it would be under French control. Instead he had favored the recalling of the old bankers' committee.[88] If Bradbury and the Treasury really intended to obtain French participation, the proposal could not have been worse, since Poincaré would never have agreed to such a committee. The scheme

[84] *FO.*, 371/8659, C 18916, October 30, 1923. For Bradbury's intentions see *ibid.*, C 18627, October 26, 1923.

[85] Bradbury-Treasury, October 16, 1923, *FO.*, 371/8658, C 17977.

[86] *Ibid.*, 8657, C 17823, October 17, 1923.

[87] *Ibid.*, 8658, C 17924, October 11, 1923. Niemeyer's comments were made in connection with a plan submitted by the Minister President of South Africa, Smuts.

[88] *Cab.*, 24/162, C.P. 438, November 2, 1923. *Ibid.*, 23/46, October 29, 1923.

was obviously a tactical measure to show alternative proposals which would greatly embarrass France.

The French Ambassador to London also sent disturbing reports to Paris. Sir Eyre Crowe, who had always been a loyal supporter of the Entente, had announced that the British cabinet would go ahead with the investigation "with or without" France. Crowe again warned that Britain would not tolerate the destruction of the Versailles Treaty, nor could she allow the "disguised annexation" of Germany's "richest regions."[89] After this audience Saint-Aulaire was convinced that British opinion could not be changed any more. Two days later the British Ambassador delivered a note to the French Foreign Office repeating that his country would not allow the creation of a separate Rhenish state, which would complicate reparation payments and would lead to a revision of the Versailles Treaty. Britain would never give up her rights under the Treaty.[90]

Faced by British threats and American dissatisfaction, Poincaré was in a difficult position. In his public speeches as well as in his parliamentary statements he still claimed at the end of October that he would not allow a reduction of the sums fixed in 1921. However, an international inquiry meant – as Poincaré knew only too well – that French reparation claims would most certainly be reduced while neither Britain nor the United States were prepared to cancel French debts. Thus he refused demands for an impartial inquiry, and asked the French Ambassador to Washington to inform Hughes discreetly that he did not understand how the Americans could study German reparation debts while explaining to the French that they did not have the power to study French debts to the United States.[91] When the Belgians finally accepted an expert inquiry, Poincaré was highly incensed. Belgium was "deserting" France, and he bitterly complained that the Belgians had agreed to a study of Germany's capacity of payments, such an investigation having been the goal of British policy since 1921, "pushed by German, British, and American bankers."[92] Several stormy meetings between French and Belgian representatives took place during the following days in Paris and Brussels.[93] But the damage had been done, Poincaré had lost control of his Ruhr partner.

However, Poincaré did not give up that easily. He immediately informed all powers that 1) the experts could not reduce the sum fixed in the London

[89] MAE. Allemagne, 483, November 8, 1923, fol. 26–32.
[90] Ibid., Rive gauche 35, November 10, 1923, fol. 289 ff.
[91] Ibid., Allemagne 482, November 2, 1923, fol. 183–187.
[92] Ibid., November 3, 1923, fol. 190 f. Ibid., Allemagne, 483, November 6, 1923, fol. 9.
[93] FO., 371/8659, C 18937, November 2, 1923. "Visite de l'Ambassadeur de Belgique à M. Peretti," MAE, Allemagne 482, November 3, 1923, fol. 200.

Schedule of Payments, 2) any reduction would have to be decided upon unanimously by the Reparation Commission, 3) only Germany's present ["actuelle"] capacity could be investigated, 4) the inquiry could not deal with the legality of the occupation. But even when Poincaré announced that the investigation should be limited to Germany's capacity until 1930, Hughes rejected any participation and reminded the French of his previous proposals. Nevertheless, the Americans tried to obtain mediation between France and the United States through a diplomatic demarche in Brussels.[94] The initiative led to nothing. But discussions between Ambassador Fletcher and Jaspar further clarified the Franco-Belgian position. For Jaspar, Hughes held the key for the solution of all difficulties: the Americans only had to reduce interallied debts and the European powers would immediately scale down their claims on Germany.[95] The Belgian hint, however, did not find approval in Paris. Poincaré knew that Washington did not favor such a discussion. The occupation of the Ruhr and the Rhineland as well as the MICUM treaties guaranteed French control of important pledges and could also serve French purposes in future negotiations. Only after Germany had paid her debts could interallied debts be dealt with. Thus two developments were possible: either a long occupation, since Germany could not pay at the moment or Anglo-American participation in French coercive policy, including credits to Berlin once the Germans had given in to all demands. However, Poincaré himself would not publicly plead for a reduction of interallied debts. "Nos créanciers sont avertis: nous n'avons plus rien de dire; c'est à eux de prendre les décisions qu'il leur conviendra; sans que nous les provoquions."[96] Apparently, he hoped to create a situation sufficiently unpleasant for his country's former Allies that they would themselves open discussions.

Hughes did not react, instead, the Americans made public their disapproval of French strategy.[97] In France, the opposition in the Chamber demanded an examination of Germany's capacity. It was obvious, that Poincaré was becoming increasingly isolated, and, on November 10 he ordered Louis

[94] Poincaré-Embassies, November 2, 1923, MAE, Allemagne 482, fol. 183 ff; November 3, 1923, ibid., fol. 198 f. Jusserand-Poincaré, November 6, 1923, ibid., Allemagne 483, fol. 1 ff. Also ibid., fol. 33 f. Cf. memos about the meetings between Hughes and French representatives in Hughes Papers, Box 174, Folder 74 b, France, especially November 5, 7, 9. Also FO., 371/8660, C 19072, November 3, 1923.
[95] Herbette-Paris, November 7, 1923, MAE, Allemagne 483, fol. 20 f. Cf. Fletcher-Hughes, November 5, 1923, Henry P. Fletcher Papers, Box 10, November 1923.
[96] Poincaré-Washington, November 8, 1923, MAE, Allemagne 483, fol. 40 f.
[97] Gescher, op. cit., pp. 197–202. Link, op. cit., pp. 203–207; FR, 1923, II, pp. 77 ff. Laboulaye-Paris, November 13, 1923, MAE, Allemagne 483, fol. 70.

Barthou to create an expert committee under the Reparation Commission.[98] This advisory body should serve two purposes: first, the final outcome of reparations would still be controlled by France, since according to Poincaré's interpretation of its function, a reduction of the German debt could only be decided upon unanimously. An international committee, however, would be far more difficult to control. Second, Poincaré had saved face. The Reparation Commission was the lawful agency for studying reparations according to the provisions of the Versailles Treaty – a view which he had endlessly repeated in his public speeches.

On November 13, Louis Barthou demanded that Germany's capacity to pay until December 1926 be investigated, and he also allowed discussion of the German note of October 24. Bradbury had waited a long time for this moment. He wanted an impartial inquiry, and, full of irony, he declared that the French delegate was like a philosopher who had invented a "pill to treat the trembling of the earth." An inquiry of Germany's capacity to pay could not be limited.[99] But nothing final was decided on at this meeting, since Bradbury recognized the powerful position he was now in. The presentation of the German note would enable him to demand a total investigation. The Germans pleaded their case on November 27, but before this meeting was held, a British "ultimatum" had been delivered to the meeting of the Council of Ambassadors on November 19.

The meeting had been called at France's request in order to discuss countermeasures against the return of the Crown Prince to Germany and to discuss the resumption of the work of the Interallied Military Control Commission. When the French delegate, Jules Cambon, declared that France intended to take separate military and territorial measures against Germany if the Allies did not force Germany to yield to French demands, the British were brought to the limit of their endurance. Lord Crewe, British Ambassador to Paris, declared that if France undertook such a step, Britain would recall her representatives from the Interallied Military Control Commission, from the Council of Ambassadors, and from the Reparation Commission. The Italian Ambassador immediately supported Crewe, while the Belgian delegate announced that he could only agree to a unanimous decision. Faced by this opposition, France yielded. French isolation was not kept secret, and British representatives in Paris did everything to make

[98] *MAE*, Allemagne 483, December 3, 1923, fol. 100–111. In this letter to Barthou, Poincaré's reminded the French delegate of his instructions of November 10. Growing opposition to Poincaré is described by Zsigmond, *op. cit.*, pp. 325–326.

[99] *FO.*, 371/8661, C 20098, November 13, 1923. Niemeyer-Bradbury, November 16, 1923, *ibid.*, C 20094. Weill-Raynal, *op. cit.*, II, pp. 510–511.

Crewe's statement generally known. According to the American Ambassador to Paris, Herrick, the British Embassy informed Reuter correspondents about what had happened at the conference. The Chief of British Naval Intelligence spread the news in Paris, and Herrick also speculated that the British had informed the American press, since an article appeared in the New York World.[100]

After this serious encounter, which, if France had not yielded, would probably have meant the end of the Entente, the Belgian delegate to the Reparation Commission, being only too anxious to prevent a complete break between France and Britain, notified Barthou that a reparation inquiry limited to 1926 would be futile. At the same time, Sir John Bradbury stubbornly clung to his intention to obtain a total inquiry and made Barthou aware of his adverse feelings.[101] Completely isolated and recognizing the seriousness of British threats, Barthou pleaded with Delacroix not to demand publicly that the inquiry should be unlimited. It would put Poincaré and himself in a very "awkward position" because of their previous statements. But if the question were not raised publicly "he would be quite prepared to propose himself any reduction of the total debt."[102]

Since Barthou was willing to agree to an unlimited inquiry, Sir John Bradbury proposed that two committees of experts be created. The first was to study German means for payment, the second, German assets abroad. But the latter committee was to be only "whitewash" and had no real value but to satisfy France.[103] In order to facilitate French acceptance, Bradbury dropped his demand for neutral and German participation. After Delacroix and Bradbury had dealt with Barthou, it was Logan's turn to influence the French delegate. In their meeting, Barthou finally agreed to write a letter to the United States government, being careful not to create the impression that the expert inquiry would be limited in its scope of investigation.[104] The committee of experts, which later became known as the Dawes Committee, was thus created without official American participation, and the "unofficial" American observer to the Reparation Commission, James

---

[100] White, *op. cit.*, p. 186 f. Gescher, *op. cit.*, p. 202. The term "ultimatum" was used by Herrick in a report to Hughes. See Herrick-Hughes, November 25, *Hughes Papers*, General Correspondence, 1922–1923, Box 48.

[101] *FO.*, 371/8662, C 20977, November 27, 1923. *MAE*, Allemagne, 487, July 3, 1924, fol. 30. Weill-Raynal, *op. cit.*, II, p. 511 f.

[102] Kemball-Cook-Bradbury, November 27, 1923, *FO.*, 371/8662, C 20977. This letter reports about a meeting between Delacroix and Barthou. It contains important information of discussions among reparation experts.

[103] *Ibid.*, C 20619. November 27, 1923.

[104] *FR*, 1923, II, pp. 98–104.

Logan, urged his British colleagues on November 28 not to mention his name in connection with the decision.

He [Logan] fears very much ... the political difficulty which the United States government may have in taking the matter up again, and he does not wish to get Hughes back up by any statement that he [Logan] was favorable to the scheme or anything of that sort.[105]

Bradbury had taken the initiative, and when he visited London to inform Lord Curzon about his success, the latter was pleasantly surprised by the break-through. He had not known that negotiations in the Reparation Commission were still going on. However, Curzon immediately agreed with Bradbury's suggestion that the governments should remain in the background, and he also approved the proposal that Washington should not yet be informed officially. On November 30, after the two committees had been finally decided upon, Bradbury asked the Foreign Office to notify Hughes.[106] On December 1, the British Foreign Office invited the United States to participate, but Hughes, who had already been briefed on Barthou's position by the American Ambassador to Paris, was still hesitant: he would have to wait for a copy of Barthou's assurances before he could make a final decision.[107] These letters arrived in Washington on December 6, and on December 11 the United States decided to allow their experts to participate in the inquiry.[108]

Hughes' active role in the constitution of the Dawes Committee has been repeatedly overestimated so that it is necessary to discuss his policy for a moment.[109] In later days, Hughes would claim that his foreign policy was basically influenced by a concern for the reactions in foreign countries to his reparation proposals and by an equal concern about whether "any action would run counter to an established US policy."[110] Obviously, the Secretary of State referred to the principle of non-entanglement. However, of far

[105] *FO.*, 371/8662, C 20747, November 28, 1923.

[106] *Ibid.*, C 20619, November 27, 1923. Apparently negotiations began with a discussion of German assets abroad. Then Bradbury proposed to discuss Germany's capacity to pay. Recognizing the importance of American participation, Miles Lampson suggested that it would be more tactful to send the drafts of the agreement to Washington. He hoped that Hughes might be "susceptible to flattery" and would accept a scheme which, although not directly based upon the American Secretary's New Haven speech, resembled his original proposal. *Ibid.*, C 20912, November 30, 1923. Lampson's comments were written on December 1.

[107] *FR*, 1923, II, pp. 102 ff.

[108] *Ibid.*, C 20198, December 1, 1923.

[109] For example Link, *op. cit.*, pp. 203 ff.

[110] Mitchell interview with Hughes, November 11, 1941, *Houghton Papers*, Mitchell Reference Files.

greater importance were limitations imposed on his policy by the insecurity created by the non-ratification of the Versailles Treaty in Congress. Only when pressure from American business groups in favor of intervention and fears in the Department of State about Poincaré's Ruhr policy increased after the termination of passive resistance, did Hughes take a more active part in developments in Europe. From then on, Ambassador Houghton's warnings about French goals were also taken seriously.[111]

Contemporary observers in the United States recognized Hughes reluctance to act, which was partly caused by his fear that the European nations would demand a reduction of interallied debts in return for their cooperation in reparations. From this attitude John F. Dulles concluded that the solution of the reparations stalemate "was worked out not by, but despite, the Republican administration."[112] Basil Miles, the American representative on the International Chamber of Commerce, similarly believed that British diplomacy had won a temporary success by further isolating France and "by placing the United States" on record as again refusing to help.[113] Both statements have to be taken with some caution, the first being made as part of an anti-Republican election campaign, while Miles had always urged intervention and was annoyed at Hughes' policy. But there is ample evidence to doubt at least the validity of earlier interpretations of Hughes' foreign policy. From November 8 until November 28, the Department of State had not (as William Phillips, the Acting Secretary of State, admitted on November 30) communicated with Poincaré at all.[114] In other words, Hughes, after having shown his dissatisfaction with Poincaré on November 9, had not felt justified in cooperating with Britain in a separate inquiry. He was still not convinced that the American public would favor such a step, nor that France would allow it on US terms.

However, American public opinion was slowly changing, although not as a result of Hughes' policy. Instead Fred I. Kent, who had already tried to mediate between Germany and France during the summer of 1923, had

---

[111] *Ibid.*, November 4, 1941. Also Dwight-Houghton, September 29, 1923, *ibid.*, Correspondence. Werner Link, "Die Ruhrbesetzung und die wirtschaftlichen Interessen der USA," *Vierteljahrshefte für Zeitgeschichte* 17 (1969), pp. 372–283.

[112] *Dulles Papers*, II, Correspondence 1922–1925, Box 135, Folder 1924, July 18, 1924.

[113] Miles-Bedford, December 4, 1923 and Bedford-Miles, December 6, 1923, *Kent Papers*, Correspondence. In contrast to Miles, Bedford objected to the intervention of American business without prior approval by the Department of State.

[114] *FR*, 1923, II, p. 101 f. However, on November 12 Hughes had explained his position in a cable to Ambassador Herrick in Paris. *Ibid.*, p. 97. For Herrick's reports from Paris cf. Herrick-Hughes, November 16, 20, 25, 29, 30, *Hughes Papers*, General Correspondence 1922–1924, Box 4 b.

started a campaign to influence public opinion and gain the support of influential business groups. The purpose of the campaign was to put pressure upon the hesitant Republican Administration. Carefully eliminating any hints about the legality of the Ruhr occupation, he made a speech before the annual meeting of the American Bankers Association in September 1923. In this speech he repeated his formula, developed before the International Chamber of Commerce meeting in Rome, and suggested a partial cancellation of interallied debts in return for European collaboration in a final settlement of reparations and connected problems.[115] Kent's suggestions were unanimously accepted by the American Bankers Association. The reception of the speech in Europe was overwhelming. Representatives from European banks including the Banque de Paris et des Pays Bas, the Banque Nationale Française Du Commerce Extérieur, the Banca d'Italia, the Banco di Roma, the London Joint City and Midland Bank, and the Bank of England, as well as representatives from the Chambers of Commerce in Paris and Lyon, the Comité National des Conseillers du Commerce Extérieur de la France, and the Société Générale pour favoriser le développement du Commerce et de l'Industrie en France applauded his speech and wished him success in his undertaking.[116]

During the following weeks, Kent made several other speeches all over the United States, and he managed to obtain the support of the Merchants' Association of New York, the American Farm Bureau, the Investment Bankers' Association, the National Association of Manufacturers, the National Association of Credit Men, and the Federal Council of Churches.[117] An Emergency Foreign Policy Conference of American Producers also demanded US intervention,[118] and the American Farm Bureau Convention in Chicago passed the following resolution:

---

[115] Kent-Houghton, September 20, 1923, *Houghton Papers*, Berlin Correspondence. The meeting took place in Atlanta City on September 26. He informed the Secretary of Commerce about his plan and although Hoover did not like the combination of interallied debts and reparations, he felt that a public discussion might be a good idea. Hoover-Kent, September 25, 1923, *Kent Papers*, Correspondence.

Kent, who did not like Hughes' policy did not inform the Secretary of State, whereas he did announce his intentions in a letter to Ambassador Houghton, who also favored American intervention. Kent-Houghton, September 20, 1923, *Houghton Papers*, Berlin Correspondence.

[116] Kent-Houghton, October 15, 1923, *Houghton Papers*, Berlin Correspondence. *Kent Papers*, Speeches 1923.

[117] Kent-Houghton, January 17, 1924, *Houghton Papers*, Berlin Correspondence. Cf. US Chambers of Commerce Bulletin, October 19, 1923, *Hoover Papers*. Secretary of Commerce Official File, Foreign Trade 1923, Box 131.

[118] *Baruch Papers*, VIII, Special Memoranda 1924–1928.

We urge the immediate adaptation by the American government of a vigorous foreign policy designed to carry out America's obligation resulting from the war aims and the terms of the armistice which ended the war, and thus to restore peace and prosperity in Europe.[119]

Influenced by an ever increasing majority of American interest groups, Hughes finally acted at the end of 1923. This is not to deny that Hughes himself thought that American intervention was necessary, since the European situation affected the domestic economic development of the United States; but Hughes was not willing or able to force France to agree to an international conference. Moreover, he knew only too well that he could wait until the European nations unconditionally demanded American help because of her financial strength.[120]

4. THE END OF COERCION

The view that Poincaré was not influenced by American attitudes in 1923 is also supported by the fact that Louis Barthou had agreed to an unlimited investigation without prior approval from Poincaré.[121] Annoyed by this independent action, the French Minister President again instructed Barthou on December 3 that the investigation was to be limited to 1926. A reduction of Germany's liability was not possible, and French experts would not participate in such an inquiry. In addition, Poincaré warned that neither the legality or result of the occupation, nor French contracts with German industrialists could be discussed. France would not give up the railway system, which was also a "pledge for French security." Instead, Poincaré proposed that the Allies join France in the creation of an international railway company in order to prevent German industry from controlling the system again.[122] In this letter, which can be regarded as Poincaré's instructions for negotiations with the Reparation Commission, he also informed Barthou that France intended to maintain control over certain Ruhr coal mines in such a way as to "assure once and for all our coke requirements. ..." French industry would also have to be protected against a future German

---

[119] *Ibid.*, Special Memoranda 1918–1923, Folder 1923.

[120] The attitude of the United States government towards Europe, Lord Curzon bitterly complained, "has in it no element of altruism at all. They are governed exclusively by what they regard as their own interest, and by an overpowering fear of being involved in the entanglements, perils, and dangers of Europe." Middlemas/Barnes, *op. cit.*, p. 203. The quotation is from the Jones Papers. Jones was Deputy Secretary to the Cabinet.

[121] *MAE*, Allemagne 483, November 28, 1923, fol. 96–97.

[122] *Ibid.*, December 3, 1923, fol. 100–111.

export offensive, and a special tax of twenty-six percent should be applied to all exports as a "brake against dumping." The flight of German capital abroad, although a "delicate" question, since foreign banks were involved, was to be investigated as well. If France did not receive satisfaction on this point, she would neither agree to a moratorium nor to a change in the modus of payment. At the end of his instructions, which would – had they become known in Britain and the United States – have destroyed the chances for an inquiry even before it had started, he again urged Barthou to be careful and not let himself be carried away by the political chaos existing in Germany. In such difficult times it was nearly impossible to conduct a thorough inquiry "in cold blood."

Poincaré's goals were directly opposed to British plans, but when Barthou, under the effect of Poincaré's instructions, informed Bradbury that the German liability could not be reduced, the British expert rejected this new attempt to impose limitations upon an inquiry. Great Britain and the United States were in the possession of Barthou's letter in which he had agreed to an unlimited inquiry.[123] In general, Poincaré was forced to accept an inquiry which did not fulfill his wishes. Neither the United States nor Great Britain had agreed to a combination of reparations and interallied debts. In fact, although France was still in possession of the Ruhr, had forced German industry to sign the MICUM agreements, and was again attempting to change the status of the Rhineland, the Ruhr adventure had brought Poincaré not an inch closer to his goal: to force the Allies into a reduction of interallied debts before any change of the German reparation liability could be obtained. In this respect the European stalemate resembled the situation before the Ruhr occupation when Hughes had made his proposal for an international inquiry and when Cuno had likewise forwarded such a plan. However, at the end of 1923 there were some advantages for France: the investigation took place in co-operation with the Reparation Commission and she was still holding her pledges. Nevertheless, these pledges were to prove of dubious value in the following months.

Although Poincaré had finally accepted an investigation of the German situation, he did not give up attempts to create difficulties in the Ruhr and in the Rhineland. But apparently Sir John Bradbury was no longer worried about French obstruction, since he knew that Britain had a "weapon of overwhelming power" with which to force France into line. On November 14, the Foreign Office had requested that the Treasury prepare a study about British means of influencing French policy. On December 3, Sir Otto Nie-

[123] *FO.*, 371/8663, C 22245, December 24, 1923; C 22712, December 27, 1923 and C 22294.

meyer informed Crowe in a note – which he considered to be private until
the Chancellor of the Exchequer had approved it – that the British government had the means of causing a

fall in the French franc sufficiently serious to shake the confidence of the French
peasant in his national securities. A lively fear of this result would make the French
government very susceptible to pressure.[124]

Niemeyer, chief financial adviser to the Treasury, argued that French reparation policy was depriving Britain of reparation receipts, and suggested
that Britain recover these losses from her Allied debtors. Britain could, for
example, indicate to France and to her other Allies that she was willing to
grant liberal terms, if these countries would fund their debts. If this suggestion were not followed, sanctions should be applied. First, Britain should
use French "gold deposits [in London] to payment of interest on maturing
bills until these are exhausted." Although Great Britain had already declared
that these deposits could not be returned until French debts were paid,
Niemeyer was convinced that the threat would have its effect. "Public application of this sum to interest would mean that the Bank of France would
have to take the ... 35 millions out of the reserves (where they still figure).
This would seriously compromise their proportion of reserves and therefore
their credit. There is no doubt that the French government would be ex-
ceedingly unwilling to face this measure." Niemeyer then proposed several
other measures, including the sale of French Treasury bills held by the Bank
of England. The French government having

... ex hypothesis refused to meet these bills, the sales price would naturally be
very low and this very fact would destroy French credit in most of the world
markets. This in return would react on the franc and on French international
credit.

As embarrassing to the French government would be the exchange of
French for German bonds. If further threats were necessary (which he did
not believe) an import levy could be raised on goods from defaulting countries. He estimated that retaliation was unlikely, since France was more
vulnerable than Great Britain. However, Niemeyer was convinced that these
measures would not have to be executed and expected that the "threat alone
would be sufficient." In summary, he declared that the

exaction of short-term French debts could be made a very potent lever to bring
about conditions likely to induce France in order to avoid most serious financial

[124] Niemeyer-Crowe, December 3, 1923, *ibid.*, 8662, C 22023.

difficulties to a general settlement of reparations, provided H.M.G. were prepared to use this lever resolutely it would be essential that the French government should believe that Britain really meant business.[125]

The Foreign Office, convinced that British threats at the meetings of the Council of Ambassadors had been sufficient, did not apply financial pressure for the moment. Members of the French Senate also informed London that they would attempt to modify Poincaré's position, and thus Lampson asked Bradbury on December 6 not to do anything to "corner either Poincaré or Barthou."[126] But when French policy did not change, Lampson urged the Treasury to write an official letter. The Senior Clerk of the Central European Division believed that the Treasury had an "overwhelming case" and he felt that Niemeyer's suggestion should be taken up, if France did not yield now.[127] At this point, the results of a British General Election influenced developments. The Conservative Party lost and it became clear that the Labour Party would for the first time in British history form a cabinet. French government officials were unpleasantly surprised by this development, since Labour's opposition to the Ruhr policy was known, and British observers in Paris felt that Poincaré would now modify his position.[128]

Nevertheless, when the official Treasury scheme was received in the Foreign Office, Lampson again reasoned in favor of putting financial pressure upon France. Sir Eyre Crowe suggested that a cabinet meeting should be called, while Lord Curzon was annoyed that the Treasury had taken that much time to write an official note. Still under the influence of the election shock, he felt that the delay had "prevented this government" from executing the proposal. Now he hoped that the question would be taken up by the new cabinet.[129] But when the Treasury memorandum was discussed in the Foreign Office upon the request of the new Prime Minister, Ramsay

---

[125] All quotations are from *ibid.*

[126] *Ibid.*, C 21256, December 6, 1923.

[127] *Ibid.*, C 22023, December 26, 1923. Attached to this note is a bill of the *Trésor public de Paris* issued on January 1, 1923 and due on January 1, 1924.

Adding to British wrath was the fact that France was making loans for political purposes in Eastern Europe, while she did not pay interest on her debts to Great Britain. *Cab.*, 24/163, C.P. 441. *FO.*, 371/9388, C 20196, November 20, 1923. For future development cf. *FO.*, 371/9682, C 1000, January 7, 1924; C 886, January 10, 1924 and note January 16, 1924; C 2006 February 2, 1924; C 1293, January 24, 1924.

[128] *FO.*, 371/8662, C 21595, December 5, 1923; C 21523, C 21236, and C 21550. Middlemas/Barnes, *op. cit.*, pp. 211–249.

[129] *FO.*, 371/9682, C 203, January 1, 1924. See now Stephen A. Schucker, *The End of French Predominance in Europe: The Financial Crisis of 1924 and the Adaption of the Dawes Plan* (Chapel Hill, 1976) pp. 51 ff.

MacDonald, it was decided not to act since the Dawes committee had finally started with the investigation of reparations.[120]

Although the above mentioned measures were not implemented, they show how far Anglo-French relations had deteriorated by the end of 1923. From now on British policy towards Poincaré was characterized by a careful investigation into French activities both in the Rhineland and in the Ruhr. This was shown especially in the discussions of a separate Rhenish currency again opened by French High Commissioner Tirard[131] and French attempts to remain in control of the railway system on the left bank of the Rhine for security purposes.[132] Both demands were systematically blocked by the British. The Bank of England and London Clearing Banks opposed the creation of a separate currency once they had been informed of Reichsbank opposition. The railway experts of the Dawes Committee also decided that the railways had to remain in German hands, although an international board of trustees would control the enterprise in order to reduce the deficit. However, they rejected repeated French attempts to place these lines under Allied or League control.[133] The fall of the French currency at the end of 1923 and again in 1924 furthermore strengthened British hopes that France had overextended her financial resources and would become more and more dependent upon financial help both from Great Britain and the United States.[134] Although the French Minister of Finance claimed that the depreciation of the currency was "brought about in order to influence our foreign

[130] Ibid., C 1974, January 24, 1924. Crowe's and Lampson's comments are in ibid., C 1540, January 28, 1924.

[131] For the negotiations see Tirard's report. MAE, Ruhr 31, October 19, 1923, fol. 74–82. Ibid., September 5, 1923, fol. 86 ff. Zimmermann, op. cit., p. 85, p. 128. Karl-Dietrich Erdmann, Adenauer in der Rheinlandpolitik nach dem Ersten Weltkrieg (Stuttgart, 1966), p. 119 f.

[132] The railway question cannot be discussed here. Rich material is in PA AA, Handakten Direktoren, Eisenbahnfrage. MAE, Ruhr 30. Ibid., Allemagne 484 and also in the Houghton Papers, Berlin Correspondence. Of special interest are demands for the creation of a private railway company, a long standing demand of German industry, private American initiative to obtain working capital for such an enterprise and French demands upon Germany.

[133] For the bank issue see especially: FO., 371/869, C 20652, November 26, 1923; C 21148, October 5, 1923. According to this report German participants in the meetings with Tirard were Hagen, Pferdmenges, von Schröder, von Oppen, Wippermann, Hirschland. Also ibid., 8691, C 21364, December 10, 1923; C 21364, December 12 and C 21607, December 15. Boyle, op. cit., p. 172 f. Zimmermann, op. cit., p. 256. The railway issue is described in Moulton, op. cit., pp. 167 ff, 261 ff.

[134] Miles Lampson of the Foreign Office noted happily that the fall of the franc may have "an important reaction on M. Poincaré's success in the election." FO., 371/10533, W 532, January 9, 1924. The quotation is from ibid., W 483, January 19, 1924. Bradbury felt that the French financial situation made an agreement to the committee's recommendations "almost essential." Ibid., 9739, C 14525, March 12, 1924.

policy," American and British financial conditions for loans in support of the franc were remarkably modest and only demanded the reduction of public expenditures and a new tax package to balance the budget. These technical demands, however, made French dependence upon the Allies only too obvious.[135]

Even now, Poincaré only reluctantly gave up his scheme for a revision of the Versailles Treaty. This was especially shown by his treatment of the Rhenish question at the end of 1923, while negotiations for an allied reparation inquiry were under way. Partly, the French Minister President was dependent on suggestions brought forward by the French High Commissioner Tirard, but in a meeting between Tirard, Peretti de la Rocca and Poincaré on October 30 in Paris, he ordered Tirard to go ahead with the creation of a Rhenish state under the jurisdiction of the League. Such a state was France's final goal, but if the population wanted a separate state within the Reich, this possibility should also be complied with. In order to influence the population, a separate Parliament, diplomatic representatives, independent railways, independent civil servants and an independent budget could be promised, while reparation demands upon this state would be cancelled. However, it was necessary to act immediately because of international and domestic developments.[136]

---

[135] For French suspicion concerning speculation see the statement by French Minister of Finance, de Lasteyrie. His speech was printed in the Information Bulletin of the French Bureau of Information in the United States on September 17. He stated that the depreciation of the currency was "caused almost exclusively by speculative influences. There exist, in France, large foreign balances which can be transferred with the utmost ease upon instruction from abroad and which can be used to launch attacks against our Franc and bring about its fall. Without the slightest doubt ... some of these attacks were brought about in order to influence our foreign policy." *Otto Kahn Papers*, Correspondence 1923, Box 199. At the beginning of January 1924 when the franc dropped again, he attributed it to the unfavorable French budgetary situation and to German holdings of francs which were being used as a weapon, while the director of the Economic Branch of the *Banque de France*, Jules Decamps, argued that budgetary expenditure and the decline of exports were the cause of the currency depreciation. See *FO.*, 371/10533, W 352, January 9, 1924. Rudolf, Kuczynski, "Zur Finanzlage Frankreichs," *Wirtschaftsdienst*, 15 (1924), p. 413. Cf. Weill-Raynal, *op. cit.*, pp. 599 ff. Petit, *op. cit.*, p. 70 reports that London banks had already promised in August 1923 to support the franc, if France accepted the Curzon note. Petit was *Inspecteur Général des Finances* and had access to French Treasury papers when he wrote his study. The discussions of a loan with the Morgan Bank have now been described in detail by Schucker, *op. cit.*, pp. 91 ff, 108 ff.

[136] *MAE*, Rive gauche 34, October 30, 1923, fol. 188 ff. See Zimmermann, *op. cit.*, p. 236 f. Already in May 1923 Poincaré had declared that not the form of government, but "des conditions que nous saurons ... imposer" would be decisive. *MAE*, Rive gauche 30, May 24, 1923, fol. 426. In November Poincaré developed further detailed instructions for the creation of a Rhenish State within the Reich. Cf. Poincaré-Tirard, November 6, 1923, *ibid.*, Rive gauche 35, fol. 188 f.

This document more than anything else explains Poincaré's policy and Tirard's negotiations in Germany. Tirard supported the Separatist Movement in order to create an autonomous state under League protection. If this failed, negotiations with Louis Hagen, Konrad Adenauer and other well-known Rhinelanders might still bring about a Rhenish state within the Reich. Understandably neither Poincaré nor Tirard wanted to be directly identified with such a policy. It had to be executed by prominent German citizens.[137] The majority of politicians and industrialists from the Rhineland, however, were opposed to the creation of an autonomous state, but some were prepared to accept a separate state within the Reich, if it were created after a referendum of the population according to the German constitution.[138]

Thus, while negotiations for the creation of an inquiry into reparations were going on and even after the Dawes committee had started with the investigation, French attempts to create a separate Rhenish state and respectively an Allied-controlled railway system to control Ruhr industry and establish ties for future economic co-operation continued.[139] During this difficult period the British Foreign Office was closely watching every French move, and Poincaré was too brilliant a lawyer not to recognize France's difficult situation if Britain should decide to bring the Rhenish question and Separatist activities before the International Court in The Hague, a threat repeatedly mentioned in correspondence between London and Paris.[140] In

---

[137] French documents clearly show Tirard's support of the Separatist Movement. Cf. for example *MAE*, Rive gauche 34, October 25, 1923, fol. 50. *Ibid.*, Rive gauche 37, "Notes sur les conversations de M. Tirard en vue de la création d'un Etat Rhénanie," fol. 160 ff. The report covers the period from October 26 to December 4, 1923. *Ibid.*, Rive gauche 34, December 2, 1923, fol. 216–217.

Despite his negotiations with Adenauer, Tirard did not trust him at all. He believed that Louis Hagen was a far better person for French purposes. Poincaré similarly distrusted Adenauer. *Ibid.*, October 30, 1923, fol. 168 f. *Ibid.*, Rive gauche 37, December 3, 1923, fol. 140.

[138] Erdmann, *op. cit.*, pp. 79 ff. *MAE*, Rive gauche 37, November 25, 1923, fol. 1 f. This is a report from François-Poncet about a meeting with Otto Wolff and Ottmar Strauss of the *Phoenix AG für Bergbau- und Hüttenbetriebe* who both favored the creation of an independent Rhenish state within the Reich.

[139] For relations between French and German industry and British attitude see: Erdmann, *op. cit.*, pp. 181–183, pp. 372 ff; Schmidt, *op. cit.*, pp. 159–163. *FO.*, 371/9760, January 24, 1924, C 11549; C 1651, February 2, 1924. Also Jean-Noel Jeanneney, *François de Wendel en République. L'Argent et le Pouvoir 1914–1940* (Paris, 1976), pp. 168–174.

[140] *MAE*, Rive gauche 38, December 9, 1923, fol. 313. Zimmermann *op. cit.*, p. 267. *Cab.*, 23/46, January 17, 1924 has Curzon's statement before Parliament. *MAE*, Rive gauche 40, fol. 33–38. Wiedenfeld, *op. cit.*, pp. 205–206. *MAE*, Rive gauche 38, January 5, 1924, fol. 269–270. *Ibid.*, January 10, 1924, fol. 322. *Ibid.*, Rive gauche 39, January 26, 1924, fol. 233; *ibid.*, Curzon-Crewe, January 19, 1924, fol. 249–155. Curzon again warned that the treaty would require complete revision. Poincaré refuted the British thesis on January 28. See *ibid.*, Rive gauche 40, fol. 175–176. Another British warning was sent on

the end Poincaré yielded to British pressure, while the Separatist Movement died away and its leaders left hurriedly for France. The myth of an independent Separatist Movement in the Rhineland could no longer be supported once Tirard had given up support for Dorten and other separatists.

During this period the German government simply tried to hold out as long as possible and yield as little to France as existing circumstances allowed. This did not mean that Germany wholeheartedly supported the Dawes investigation or felt that she would be treated justly. But the Dawes Committee and British and American attitudes towards French Ruhr and Rhineland policy had at least created the hope that these powers would become a counterweight towards French attempts to disorganize the Reich and subject Germany to French economic control until reparations had been paid. Although German politicians and industrialists would complain later about the harshness of the terms, they had been notified that the United States did not have an interest in the investigation of capital flight from Germany. Visiting London in January 1924, the American Secretary of Treasury, Andrew Mellon, assured the German Ambassador that the Republican Administration would not assist in locating German capital in the United States. Mellon foresaw "insuperable difficulties" and doubted whether such an investigation could be successful. He believed that expatriated capital was negligible in comparison with Germany's national wealth.[141] The expert committee did in fact rely upon estimates, and nothing was done to determine where German capital was deposited abroad. The experts were of the opinion "that it would be neither proper nor useful to request the disclosure of specific transactions which in general would have been entered into under an implied condition of secrecy."[142]

When France and Germany accepted the Dawes plan under American and British pressure in 1924, the reparation struggle which had started at the Versailles Peace Conference and had constantly influenced international economic and political developments as well as the domestic scene in all the countries concerned, had come to an end. However, a final decision on German payments had not been reached, interallied debts had not been solved either and the Ruhr was still occupied. These problems would still occupy an important position in international relations during the next years, but the war-like atmosphere which had determined the first years of the post-war period had given way to a period of greater economic and political co-oper-

February 4. *Ibid.*, Rive gauche 41, fol. 57–60. *Ibid.*, January 8, 1924, fol. 235–236. The same day he warned Tirard *ibid.*, fol. 249 ff. *Ibid.*, Rive gauche 42, February 11, 1924, fol. 15–23.
[141] *PA AA*, Büro RM, Reparationen, D 722303, January 5, 1924.
[142] Moulton, *op. cit.*, 293 ff. The quotation is on p. 294.

ation in Europe. From 1924 onwards, the European political climate constantly improved, and despite the pessimistic outlook of many allied economists upon Germany's capacity,[143] the Reich was able to pay reparations until the world economic crisis led to a modification and then to a final cancellation of reparations at the Lausanne conference in 1932. However, during the whole period, payments were largely made possible by American loans to Germany.

[143] Bradbury, for example, did not consider the plan as "a solid foundation for the restoration of international credit." *FO*, 371/9739, C 14525, March 12, 1924. Professor Edwin W. Kemmerer of Princeton University, who participated in the drafting of the report noted in his diary on March 24, 1924 that "all technical men believe that demands in the report will be too high for Germany to pay." *Kemmerer Papers*, Diary 1924. He would have liked to see a final amount established, but French experts objected, insisting that the fixation of a final sum was not the duty of the commission. If American representatives on the committee had insisted upon an inquiry, French objections, Kemmerer argued, "might very well have destroyed the usefulness of the other part of their [the experts] work. It seemed to me politically impossible to get anything definite on this particular phase of the subject." Kemmerer–W.W. Cumberland, June 25, 1924, *ibid.*, Correspondence. See also Schmidt, *op. cit.*, pp. 221–225 and Link, *op. cit.*, pp. 248–250. Professor Jenks, another American adviser, was equally pessimistic, but felt that it was "worth while to make an attempt and go ahead," since possibility of later revisions remained. Jenks-Kemmerer, May 24, 1924, *Kemmerer Papers*, Correspondence. Jenks had also informed Hughes about his opinion.

CONCLUSIONS

This study has sought to analyze decision-making processes during a crucial period of the Weimar Republic, which basically covers the period of the Cuno cabinet but finds a preliminary end with the creation of the Dawes Committee after Cuno had already resigned. During this period a cabinet which had no sound parliamentary basis struggled both against powerful domestic interest groups and the overwhelming power of France determined to control Germany as long as reparations, interallied debts and French security had not been solved. This confrontation was the logical outcome of differing economic and political strategies in Germany and in the Allied countries, which had already become apparent during the Versailles peace conference and determined international relations during the 1920's. At Versailles, all the problems that were to prevent economic and political stabilization of Europe were clearly recognized by Allied statesmen and their economic and financial advisers. However, politicians were convinced that the presentation of Allied unity – even though decisions on the most important problems had to be subordinated to this goal – was more important than a final decision on the sums to be requested from the defeated nations or on the modes of payment. On the other hand, it should be noted that precise figures reached in the political turmoil at Versailles would have been unrealistically high, and thus, with few exceptions, the financial advisers preferred that an amount be fixed after a detailed examination of Germany's financial resources. Such an investigation did not, however, take place until the Dawes Committee named both the amount of a preliminary liability and the means of transfer.

The situation was further complicated by differing Allied goals in postwar Europe. The French saw the problem of peacemaking in terms of their national security. Consequently, French politicians wanted to reduce and control German economic and military potential as long as possible. This could be obtained through territorial demands, military control, and reparations. Reparations – besides contributing to French reconstruction – were thus also a means to keep the Reich in a state of continued weakness and dependency. Representatives of the United States and Great Britain, on the other hand, were less concerned with political objections and from the beginning stressed the significance of economic factors. While initially Germany's "bad faith," her unwillingness to execute the provisions of the treaty, largely influenced the attitude of Allied reparation experts, soon more and more economists, bankers, industrialists and politicians in the Allied countries recognized the need for a revision of the reparation clauses. With hardly any exceptions, Allied governments pursued a revisionist policy. This development was first started in Great Britain, which was most severely hit by the continuing economic crisis and by a German export offensive made possible by low wages and a depreciating currency.

Faced with increasing unemployment at home and strong German competition on the world market, British politicians were soon ready to reduce Germany's reparation liability. As a maximum goal, British policy envisaged the complete reduction of interallied debts followed by a partial cancellation of reparations, but, because of objections in the United States to a solution that would have meant the loss of American war loans to Europe, nothing came of it. While Britain was prepared to cancel part of the debts of her European allies under the condition that a settlement of reparations could be reached, the United States did not intend to abolish war debts and carefully avoided being drawn into a discussion of interallied debts and reparations. This study suggests that the United States government, fearing increased pressure for a cancellation of interallied debts while faced with an unwilling public and Congress at home, was far less active in the solution of the reparation issue than has been described in literature. The American Ambassador to Germany, Alanson B. Houghton, who had suggested a partial cancellation of interallied debts in return for a reduction of reparations and the establishment of peace in Europe, had no influence on Hughes' policy at all. His warning about French intentions in 1923 were not considered to be sound. Only when France still resisted a discussion of reparations after passive resistance had come to an end did the State Department recognize that Houghton's warnings had been only too justified: France was pursuing political goals through the occupation of the Ruhr.

If British reparation policy was clearly revisionist, and the United States policy negative and lacking in initiative, French policy was intransigently opposed to any change, although, as her Rhineland policy in 1923 shows, France under Poincaré was in fact a revisionist power in a somewhat different sense. Under Briand, France had, although reluctantly, accepted the British lead and had moved closer to David Lloyd George who was working for a modification of reparation terms. Briand had also studied French coercive measures, including the occupation of the Ruhr in order to force German payments, but had not carried them through in face of British opposition. He knew, in any case, that from an economic point of view occupation could not hope for success.

With Poincaré coming to power, French policy slowly changed and finally led to the seizure of productive pledges. From the beginning of his period in office, Poincaré had been a ruthless fighter for the protection of French rights. Having promised the execution of the treaty terms when he came to power, he was in a difficult position when British demands for a modification of reparations increased during 1922. Faced by an increasing financial deficit as a result of the war and the reconstruction of the devastated regions, he recognized that France would not receive sufficient reparations to cover these costs. However, his position was further complicated by the unwillingness of French industry to allow significant deliveries of reparations in kind. Taking Germany's bad will for granted and having promised the execution of the treaty, Poincaré, supported by a nationalistic chamber, had no intention of following British requests for modification. His objections to British reparation policy further hardened when Britain, pushing for a solution of the stalemate, demanded the refunding of French war debts to Britain. In consequence, he decided to take productive pledges in the Ruhr, which served to force German payments and could also be used in a final reparation settlement. But even more important, the seizure of Germany's most productive region could also serve, Poincaré hoped, to influence Allied decisions on war debts. It was obvious by 1922 that a new agreement with Germany was necessary; considering his previous experience with international financial experts, Poincaré knew that reparations would be reduced or that the Reich would at least be granted a moratorium for payments. Having spent billions on reconstructions in the hope of huge payments from Germany, the French financial situation would have been desperate. This would have been especially bitter since France's Allies did not show any readiness to reduce French war debts to Great Britain and the United States. With France and Belgium holding the Ruhr and Great Britain and the United States interested in a recovery of European trade, the Ruhr might also be a pledge for negotiations over reparations and interallied debts. On the other hand, if Great Britain did not follow France into the Ruhr and thus increase pressure on Germany (a hope Poincaré never gave up) France could also try to settle a number of unsolved issues. Since the return of Lorraine in 1919, France urgently needed Ruhr coke for the smelting of Lorraine iron ore. An industrial deal between Ruhr and Lorraine industries, having failed repeatedly because of German industrial opposition, could now perhaps be forced upon Ruhr tycoons. Occupation also provided France with a chance to reopen the question of security and to try once more to win the military frontier denied in 1919. With this in mind Poincaré attempted to create a Rhenish State within the Reich by supporting the Separatist Movement. The foundation of such a state, possible under article 18 of the Weimar Constitution would have solved French security problems on condition that it could have been placed under League of Nations control, would be demilitarized and would have loosened ties with the Reich in other fields as well, as provided for in French planning. It should be noted, however, that although Poincaré hoped for the disintegration of the Reich, these changes could not be carried through against the will of the majority of the population. Thus in the end French policy in 1923 proved to be based on misconceptions of political realities in the Rhineland.

The British Cabinet, uncertain about French intentions until the autumn of 1923 and split as to an appropriate policy towards France while partly paralyzed by developments in the Near East, did not and could not act immediately. However, once British politicians recognized that the Franco-German struggle in the Ruhr might lead to an abolishment of the Versailles Treaty, they intervened. Concern for the prosperity of British trade and industry, the effects of political chaos in Germany, and fear of a French-dominated economic giant on the continent motivated British policy. Without allies and incapable of forcing a French retreat alone, British politicians – greatly aided and sometimes led by the British members of the Reparation Commission – finally succeeded in arranging a study of the whole reparations problem. When this happened, the United States joined the investigation and from then on determined the outcome of reparations.

During the first years of the Weimar Republic, Germany was a revisionist power par excellence. Politicians, bankers, and industrialists had never accepted the Treaty of Versailles. From 1919 onwards, they tried especially to modify the reparation clauses, which were considered to be unbearable. Rathenau's policy of "fulfillment" was no exception to this policy. More than anything it was designed to show that fulfillment was impossible. Like his predecessors Cuno tried to free reparations from politics, an attempt that could only fail since he did not recognize that reparations for France was a political question of foremost importance. In view of French determination, Cuno can hardly be blamed for the occupation of the Ruhr. As a basis of his reparation policy, he had accepted Wirth's note of November 14, 1922 and when French and Belgian troops moved into the Ruhr he had only been Chancellor for six weeks. Although he was certainly further to the Right than Wirth and his cabinet, his effort to reach an agreement on reparations was not even disputed by the French Ambassador to Berlin. This was again shown by his attempt to reach an agreement for a conference of international experts at the end of 1922. Given the nature of the Reichstag majority, it is unlikely that he could have gone beyond Wirth's note, which had also been endorsed by the SPD. Cuno's proposal for a peace pact with France in December 1922, a last desperate attempt to prevent occupation, came too early to be a success. It would take more time before Stresemann and Briand could finally reach an agreement ending the atmosphere of extreme nationalism and distrust between these two countries, thus opening the way to normalization. However, German reparation offers, prepared after close consultation with spokesmen from industry, banking and trade, were hardly sufficient to be acceptable to any allied country. Again, with the parties divided and paralyzing each other, it is questionable if any other policy could have been pursued.

On the other hand, Cuno's decision to prolong passive resistance in order to have a final showdown with Poincaré in the expectation of a French retreat is more debatable. Germany was ill-prepared for such a policy and her hope of British intervention prevented a search for a more realistic policy. In this sense, Cuno's policy was shortsighted. However, any different policy, like an agreement with France after occupation had taken place, would have led to a serious domestic crisis. Cuno himself would never have undertaken such a step and it is doubtful whether President Ebert, incensed by what he considered a violation of the treaty by France, would have gone along with it. The majority of the parties and the Länder certainly would not have accepted submission to French coercion at a moment when that country was not supported by Great Britain. Since the majority of the population regarded occupation as part of an "imperialistic" scheme to control Germany, it was easy for the cabinet to take a strong stand and organize passive resistance.

Yet when it came to financing resistance and preparing Germany for a long struggle with France, Cuno clearly failed. This was due to a large extent to the attitude of the bourgeois parties in the Reichstag and industrial interest groups who were not prepared to base the government's policy upon a sound budget. These groups prevented the balancing of the budget and the modification of the tax system until the moment when the Reich's fiscal system had broken down completely. In the end, these omissions and the financing of the Ruhr struggle through the printing press accelerated the collapse of the Reich. Cuno's attempt to regain Germany's economic freedom and to reduce reparations to what he considered an economically feasible sum had failed. To be sure, German offers during 1923 always re-

mained below allied expectations and thus perhaps prevented British inter
vention. These unsatisfactory proposals were the result of conflicting evaluations of the Reich's financial and economic situation in the cabinet, Cuno's
inability to determine an adequate final offer, and the demands of most
influential industrialists, bankers and politicians on the Right for a reduction
of the liability lower than the figures fixed by the cabinet, which were already
far below Allied demands. In short, more than any other cabinet, Cuno had
to compromise endlessly on reparation initiatives. Yet, it may also be argued
that French policy during 1923 showed that future developments did not depend so much on higher offers from Germany as on total submission of the
Reich to French demands and the introduction of means to guarantee deliveries in kind and in cash.

In a broader context, Allied indecision at Versailles, Germany's determi-
nation to reduce reparations and French attempts to force an "integral"
execution of the peace treaty thus poisoned the postwar atmosphere in
Europe and led to a new war fever during the occupation of the Ruhr.
Bearing the reparation policy in mind, it may be said that the First World
War did not come to an end until 1924, when Great Britain and the United
States had modified reparations and had brought home to both Germany
and France the fact that they could not change the Treaty of Versailles
unilaterally and without prior consultation with the other major powers.

BIBLIOGRAPHY

I. PRIMARY SOURCES

A. Germany

1) *Bundesarchiv Koblenz*

Reichskanzlei, R 43 I
Reichsfinanzministerium, R 2
Reichsministerium für den Wiederaufbau, R 38

2) *Politisches Archiv des Auswärtigen Amts, Bonn*

a) *Büro des Reichsministers*
Reden des Reichskanzlers über auswärtige Politik
Reparationsfragen
Reparationen 5 secr.
Maßnahmen der Entente bei Nichterfüllung der Reparationen
Internationale Geschäftsleutekonferenz
Deutsch-Englische Industrie Cooperation
Ruhrgebiet
Frage des Abbruchs der Beziehungen
Frage der Aufgabe des passiven Widerstandes

b) *Sonderreferat Wirtschaft*
Verhandlungen der Sechserkommission des bergbaulichen Vereins mit der MICUM
Verhandlungen Krupp, Wolff, Becker, u.a. mit der MICUM
Die Aktion der amerikanischen Handelskammer
Wirtschaftliche Vereinigungen

c) *Wirtschaftsreparationen*
Organisation der Sachleistungen, Vorschläge, Seydoux: Abschluß von Abkommen mit Frankreich über Sachleistungen und Lauf der Sachleistungen (Verhandlungen mit Tannery, Loucheur, Rathenau)
Lieferungsabkommen zwischen de Lubersac und Stinnes
Besetzung des Ruhrgebiets
Sonderakte Kohle, Koks, usw.

Pläne bzw. Vorschläge zur Regelung der Reparationsfrage
Allgemeine Reparationsfrage
Vorarbeiten zum Memorandum v. 7.6.23
Kommissionsarbeiten zur Bereitstellung des Reparationsmaterials
Die amerikanische Vermittlung in der Reparationsfrage

d) *Handakten, Direktoren*
Schubert
Ha. Pol. Ritter

3) *Historisches Archiv der Gutehoffnungshütte* (HA GHH)

4) *Werksarchiv der MAN Augsburg*

5) *Westfälisches Wirtschaftsarchiv, Dortmund* (WWA)

6) *August Bebel Archiv, Berlin*

7) *Private Papers*

Moritz J. Bonn (Bundesarchiv Koblenz)
Wilhelm Cuno (Archiv der Hamburg-Amerika-Linie, Hamburg)
Otto Geßler (Bundesarchiv Koblenz)
Wilhelm Groener (Microfilm)
Julius Hirsch (New York)
Ago von Maltzan (Politisches Archiv des Auswärtigen Amts, Bonn)
Paul Moldenhauer (Bundesarchiv Koblenz)
Arnold Rechberg (Bundesarchiv Koblenz)
Paul Silverberg (Bundesarchiv Koblenz)
Gustav Stresemann (Politisches Archiv des Auswärtigen Amts, Bonn)
Hans von Seeckt (Microfilm)

B. France

Ministère des Affaires Etrangères, Europe 1918–1929 (MAE)

Allemagne
Rive gauche du Rhin
Ruhr

C. Great Britain

Public Record Office

Minutes of the British Cabinet
Records of the British Foreign Office, Record Group 371

D. United States

1) *Library of Congress, Manuscript Division*
   Henry T. Allen Papers
   Leonard P. Ayres Papers
   Henry P. Fletcher Papers
   Charles E. Hughes Papers

2) *Herbert Hoover Presidential Library*
   William R. Castle Papers
   Benjamin Strong – Montagu Norman Correspondence

3) *Hoover Institution*
   James A. Logan Papers
   Louis Loucheur Papers

4) *Princeton University*

   Bernard Baruch Papers
   John F. Dulles Papers
   Otto Kahn Papers
   Edwin W. Kemmerer Papers
   Fred I. Kent Papers

5) *Warren D. Harding Papers (Microfilm)*

6) *Alanson B. Houghton Papers (Corning)*

7) *Ellis L. Dresel Papers*

II. GOVERNMENT PUBLICATIONS

Akten der Reichskanzlei, Weimarer Republik, *Das Kabinett Cuno*, bearbeitet von Karl-Heinz Harbeck (Boppard, 1968).

–, *Das Kabinett Fehrenbach*, bearbeitet von Peter Wulf (Boppard, 1972).

–, *Das Kabinett Marx I/II*, bearbeitet von Günter Abramowski (Boppard, 1973).

–, *Das Kabinett Müller I*, bearbeitet von Martin Vogt, (Boppard, 1971).

–, *Das Kabinett Scheidemann*, bearbeitet von Hagen Schulze (Boppard, 1971).

–, *Das Kabinett Wirth I/II*, bearbeitet von Ingrid Schulze-Bidlingmaier (Boppard, 1973).

Auswärtiges Amt, *Aktenstücke über den französisch-belgischen Einmarsch in das Ruhrgebiet*, 4 Bde, (Berlin, 1923).

–, *Die den Alliierten seit dem Waffenstillstand übermittelten Angebote und Vorschläge zur Lösung der Reparations- und Wiederaufbaufrage* (Berlin, 1923).

–, *Die Pariser Konferenz, 2. bis 4. Januar* (Berlin, 1923).
Documents on British Foreign Policy, First Series, vol. XV and XIX (London, 1967/1974).
France, Assemblée nationale, *Débats Parlementaires, Chambre des Députés*, 1922 f.

Inter-Allied Conferences on Reparations and Inter-Allied Debts, held in London and Paris, December 1922 and January 1923, Cmd. 1812 Miscellaneous No. 3 (London, 1923).

Ministère des Affaires Etrangères, Documents Diplomatiques, *Documents relatifs aux négotiations concernant les garanties de sécurité contre une agression de l'Allemagne* (Paris, 1924).

Reparation Commission, *Report on the Work of the Reparation Commission from 1920–1922* (London, 1923).

United States, Department of State, *Papers Relating to the Foreign Relations of the United States*, 1921 f.

Verhandlungen des Reichstags, I. Wahlperiode (1920–1924).

Verhandlungen der Sozialisierungskommission über die Reparationsfrage, 3 Bde. (Berlin, 1921/22).

III. ALMANACS, HANDBOOKS AND ENCYCLOPEDIAS

Neue Deutsche Biographie (Berlin, 1953 ff).

HORKENBACH, CUNO, *Das Deutsche Reich von 1918 bis heute* (Berlin, 1930).

KENT, G.O., *A Catalogue of Files and Microfilms of the German Foreign Ministry Archives 1920–1945*, 3 vols. (Stanford, 1961 f).

MICHAELIS, HERBERT und ERNST SCHRAEPLER (Hrsg). *Ursachen und Folgen – Vom deutschen Zusammenbruch 1918 und 1945 bis zur staatlichen Neuordnung Deutschlands in der Gegenwart. Die Weimarer Republik*, Bd. 5 (Berlin, 1961).

PINNER, FELIX, *Deutsche Wirtschaftsführer* (Berlin, 1925).

Reichsgesetzblatt, 1921 ff.

Reichshandbuch der Deutschen Gesellschaft, 2 Bde. (Berlin, 1930).

SCHULTHESS, *Europäischer Geschichtskalender*, 1921 ff.

SCHWARZ, MAX, *MdR. Bibliographisches Handbuch des Reichstags* (Hannover, 1965).

IV. NEWSPAPERS AND MAGAZINES

Bankarchiv
Berliner Börsen Courier

Berliner Tageblatt
Deutsche Allgemeine Zeitung
Deutsche Bergwerkszeitung
Frankfurter Zeitung
Germania
Münchener Neueste Nachrichten
Neue Preussische Zeitung
Rheinisch-Westfälische Zeitung
Vorwärts
Vossische Zeitung
Westfälische Arbeiter-Zeitung
Die Zeit

The Economist
The Manchester Guardian Weekly
The Times

L'Eclair
L'Europe Nouvelle
Le Figaro
L'Humanité
La Journée Industrielle
Le Matin
L'Oeuvre
Le Petit Parisien
Le Populaire
Le Temps
L'Usine

V. PUBLISHED PAPERS, DIARIES, AND MEMOIRS

ALLEN, HENRY T., *My Rhineland Journal* (Boston and New York, 1923).

AMERY, L.S., *My Political Life*, 2 vols. (London, 1953).

BARDOUX, JACQUES, *De Paris à Spa, la bataille diplomatique pour la paix française* (Paris, 1921).

–, *Lloyd George et la France* (Paris, 1921).

BONN, MORITZ J., *So macht man Geschichte* (München, 1953).

BONNET, GEORGE, *Vingt Ans de Vie Politique 1918–1939* (Paris, 1969).

BRAUN, OTTO, *Von Weimar zu Hitler* (Hamburg, 1919).

BRECHT, ARNOLD, *Aus nächster Nähe. Lebenserinnerungen 1884–1927* (Stuttgart, 1966).

BROCKDORFF-RANTZAU, GRAF, *Dokumente und Gedanken um Versailles*, 3. ed. (Berlin, 1925).

CAMBON, PAUL, *Correspondance*, t. 1–3 (Paris, 1946).

CUNO, WILHELM, *Der Krieg nach dem Kriege. Wirtschaftspolitische Reminiszenzen und Ausblicke* (Düsseldorf, 1931).

D'ABERNON, VISCOUNT, *An Ambassador of Peace; Pages from the Diary of Viscount D'Abernon*, 3 vols. (London, 1929–1930).

DAWES, RUFUS C., *The Dawes Plan in the Making* (Indianapolis, 1925).

DUISBERG, CARL, *Abhandlungen, Vorträge und Reden aus den Jahren 1882–1921* (Berlin und Leipzig, 1923).

–, *Abhandlungen, Vorträge und Reden aus den Jahren 1922–1933* (Berlin, 1933).

EBERT, FRIEDRICH, *Schriften, Aufzeichnungen, Reden*, 2 Bde. (Berlin, 1926).

FRANÇOIS-PONCET, ANDRÉ, *De Versailles à Potsdam, la France et le problème allemand contemporain* (Paris, 1948).

FRIEDENBURG, FERDINAND, *Die Weimarer Republik* (Hannover und Frankfurt am Main, 1959).

HERRIOT, EDOUARD, *Jadis*, 2 vols. (Paris, 1952).

HOUSE, EDUARD M., *The Intimate Diary of Colonel House*, ed. by Charles Seymour, 4 vols. (London, 1929).

HOUSE, EDUARD M. and CHARLES SEYMOUR, *What really happened at Paris* (London, 1921).

JOUVENEL, BERTRAND DE, *D'une guerre à l'autre* (Paris, 1940).

KAHLENBERG, FRIEDRICH P. (Hrsg.), *Die Berichte des Eduard David als Reichsvertreter in Hessen, 1921–1927* (Wiesbaden, 1970).

KESSLER, HARRY GRAF, *Aus den Tagebüchern, 1918–1937*, hrsg. von Wolfgang Pfeiffer-Belli (München, 1965).

LAROCHE, JULES, *Au Quai d'Orsay avec Briand et Poincaré, 1913–1926* (Paris, 1957).

LLOYD GEORGE, DAVID, *The Truth about the Peace Treaties*, 2 vols. (London, 1938).

LOUCHEUR, LOUIS, *Carnets Secrets 1908–1932*, présentés et annotés par Jacques de Launay (Bruxelles, 1962).

LUTHER, HANS, *Politiker ohne Partei* (Stuttgart, 1960).

"LUTHER ERINNERUNGEN," in: *Beiträge zur Geschichte von Stadt und Stift Essen*, 73 (1958).

MANGIN, L.E., *La France et le Rhin. Hier et Aujourd'hui* (Genève, 1945).

MARIAUX, FRANZ (Hrsg.), *Paul Silverberg, Reden und Schriften* (Köln, 1951).

MEISSNER, OTTO, *Staatssekretär unter Ebert, Hindenburg, Hitler* (Hamburg, 1950).

MERTON, RICHARD, *Erinnernswertes aus meinem Leben* (Frankfurt am Main, 1955).

MORDACQ, GÉNÉRAL, *Le Ministère Clemenceau. Journal d'un Témoin*, t. 1–3 (Paris, 1930–1931).

MORDAL, JACQUES, *Versailles ou la Paix Impossible* (Paris, 1970).

NOLLET, CHARLES M., *Une Expérience de Désarmement. Cinq Ans de contrôle militaire en Allemagne* (Paris, 1932).

PINON, RENÉ, *Le Redressement de la Politique Française 1922* (Paris, 1923).

–, *La Bataille de la Ruhr 1923* (Paris, 1923).

RABENAU, FRIEDRICH VON, *Seeckt. Aus seinem Leben 1918–1936* (Leipzig, 1940).

RECOULY, RAYMOND, FOCH, *My Conversations with the Marshal* (New York, 1929).

REYNAUD, PAUL, *Mémoires. Venu de ma Montagne* (Paris, 1960).

RIDDELL, LORD, *Intimate Diary of the Peace Conference and After, 1918–1923* (New York, 1934).

SAINT-AULAIRE, AUGUSTE F.CH. DE BEAUPOIL, *Confession d'un vieux diplomate* (Paris, 1953).

SCHACHT, HJALMAR, *My First Seventy-Six Years; the Autobiography of Hjalmar Schacht* (London, 1955).

SCHWABACH, PAUL, *Aus meinen Akten* (Berlin, 1927).

SEVERING, CARL, *Mein Lebensweg*, 2 Bde. (Köln, 1950).

SEYDOUX, JACQUES, *De Versailles au Plan Young* (Paris, 1932).

STAMPFER, FRIEDRICH, *Die ersten 14 Jahre der deutschen Republik* (Offenbach, 1947).

STEHKÄMPER, ERNST, (Hrsg.), *Otto Wiedfeldt als Politiker und Botschafter der Weimarer Republik. Eine Dokumentation zu Wiedfeldts 100.Geburtstag am 16. August 1971* (Essen, 1971).

STEHKÄMPER, HUGO (Hrsg.), *Der Nachlass des Reichskanzlers Wilhelm Marx*, 4 Bde. (Köln, 1968).

STOCKHAUSEN, MAX VON, *Sechs Jahre Reichskanzlei. Von Rapallo bis Locarno. Erinnerungen und Tagebuchnotizen 1922–1927*. Bearb. von Walter Görlitz (Bonn, 1954).

STRESEMANN, GUSTAV, *Vermächtnis*, 3 Bde., hrsg. von H. Bernard (Berlin, 1932).

TARDIEU, ANDRÉ, *The Truth about the Treaty* (Indianapolis, 1921).

TIRARD, PAUL, *La France sur le Rhin. Douze Années d'Occupation rhénane* (Paris, 1930).

WARBURG, MAX, *Aus meinen Aufzeichnungen* (New York, 1952).

ZECHLIN, WALTER, *Pressechef bei Ebert, Hindenburg und Kopf* (Hannover, 1956).

VI. MONOGRAPHS AND SPECIAL STUDIES

ABRAHAMS, PAUL P., "American Bankers and the Economic Tactics of Peace 1919," *Journal of American History*, LXV (1969).

ALBERTIN, LOTHAR, *Liberalismus und Demokratie am Anfang der Weimarer Republik. Eine Vergleichende Analyse der Deutschen Demokratischen Partei und der Deutschen Volkspartei* (Düsseldorf, 1972).

ALBRECHT-CARRÉ, RENÉ, *Britain and France. Adaptations to a Changing Content of Power* (New York, 1970).

ALDCROFT, DEREK H., *The Inter-War Economy: Britain 1919–1939* (London, 1970).

ANDERLE, ALFRED, *Rapallo und die friedliche Koexistenz* (Berlin, 1963).

ANGELL, JAMES W., *The Recovery of Germany* (New Haven, 1929).

ARNS, GÜNTER, "Friedrich Ebert als Reichspräsident," *Historische Zeitschrift*, Beiheft 1971.

ARTAUD, DENISE, "A propos de l'Occupation de la Ruhr," *Revue d'histoire moderne et contemporaine*, 17 (Mars 1970).

–, *La Reconstruction de l'Europe* (Paris, 1973).

BANE, L.S. and RALPH H. LUTZ, eds., *The Blockade of Germany after the Armistice 1919* (Stanford, 1919).

BARDOUX, JACQUES, *Lloyd George et la France* (Paris, 1923).

BARIÉTY, JACQUES, *Les Relations Franco-Allemandes après la Première Guerre Mondiale* (Paris, 1977).

–, "Les Réparations Allemandes après la Première Guerre Mondiale: Objet ou Prétexte à une Politique Rhénane de la France (1919–1924)," *Bulletin de la Société d'Histoire Moderne*, Série 5, No. 6, 1973.

–, "Le Rôle de la Minette dans la Sidérurgie Allemande et la Restructuration de la Sidérurgie Allemande après le Traité de Versailles," *Centre de Recherches Relations Internationales de l'Université de Metz*, 3 (1973).

BARTHELÉMY, JOSEPH, "Chronique de Politique Extérieure," *Revue Politique et Parlementaire*, 340 (1923).

BARTHOU, LOUIS, "French Rights and German Obligations," *Current History*, XVII (1923).

BARUCH, BERNARD M., *The Making of the Reparation and the Economic Sections of the Treaty* (New York, 1920).

BAUMONT, MAURICE, *La Faillite de la Paix* (Paris, 1950).

–, *La Grosse Industrie Allemande et le Charbon* (Paris, 1928).

BEAVERBROOK, LORD, *The Decline and Fall of Lloyd George* (London, 1963).

BEHNSEN, HENRY and WERNER CENZMER, *Die Folgen der Markentwertung für uns und die andern* (Leipzig, 1921).

BERBUSSE, EDWARD JOSEPH, "Diplomatic Relations between the United States and Weimar Germany, 1919–1929." Unpublished doctoral dissertation, Georgetown University, 1951.

BERG, PETER, *Deutschland und Amerika. Über das deutsche Amerika-Bild der zwanziger Jahre* (Lübeck und Hamburg, 1963).

BERGMANN, CARL, *Der Weg der Reparationen* (Frankfurt, 1926).

BERTELSMANN, HEINZ-OTTO B., "The Role of the German Parliament in Foreign Affairs, 1919–1926. Four Tests of the Weimar Republic." Unpublished doctoral dissertation, Columbia University, 1956.

BETTELHEIM, CHARLES, *Bilan de l'Economie Française, 1919–1946* (Paris, 1947).

BIARD D'AUNET, "Le Règlement de la Paix," *Revue Economique Internationale*, 2 (1923).

BISCHOF, ERWIN, *Rheinischer Separatismus 1918–1924, Hans Adam Dortens Rhein-staatsbestrebungen* (Bern, 1969).

BLAKE, ROBERT, *The Unknown Prime Minister. The Life and Times of Andrew Bonar Law, 1858–1923* (London, 1955).

BOIS, JEAN-PIERRE, "L'Opinion Catholique Rhénane devant le Séparatisme en 1923," *Revue d'histoire moderne et contemporaine*, 21 (1974).

BONN, MORITZ J. and MELCHIOR PALYI (Hrsg.), *Festgabe für Lujo Brentano zum 80. Geburtstag* (München und Leipzig, 1925).

BONNEFOUS, EDOUARD, *Histoire Politique de la Troisième République*, 5 vols. (Paris, 1959).

BONNET, GEORGES, *Le Quai d'Orsay sous Trois Républiques* (Paris, 1961).

BORSKY, G., *The Greatest Swindle in the World. The Story of German Reparations* (London, 1942).

BOYLE, ANDREW, *Montagu Norman. A Biography* (London, 1967).

BRELET, M., *La Crise de la Métallurgie. La Politique Economique et Sociale du Comité des Forges* (Paris, 1923).

BRENIER, HENRI, *Why France is in the Ruhr* (Marseille, 1923).

BRESCIANI-TURRONI, CONSTANTINO, *The Economics of Inflation. A Study of Currency Depreciation in Post-War Germany* (London, 1937).

BRY, GERHARD, *Wages in Germany, 1871–1945* (Princeton, 1960).

BÜCHER, HERMANN, *Finanz- und Wirtschaftsentwicklung Deutschlands in den Jahren 1921–1925* (Berlin, 1925).

CADOUX, GASTON, "Etappes et Résultats de la Bataille de la Ruhr," *Revue Politique et Parlementaire*, 350 (1924).

CALMETTE, GERMAIN, *Les Dettes Interalliées* (Paris, 1926).

–, *Recueil de Documents sur l'Histoire de la Question des Réparations* (Paris, 1924).

CASTILLON, RICHARD, *Les Réparations Allemandes. Deux Expériences 1919–1932, 1945–1952* (Paris, 1953).

CHASTENET, JACQUES, *Les Années d'illusions 1918–1931* (Paris, 1960).

–, "Une Occasion manquée. L'Affaire de la Ruhr," *La Revue de Paris*, 66 (1959).

–, *Poincaré* (Paris, 1948).

CHAUMEIX, ANDRÉ, "Les Alliés, la Ruhr et l'Orient," *Revue de Paris*, 32 (1923).

–, "L'Europe et la Question de la Ruhr," *Revue de Paris*, 33 (1923).

CHURCHILL, RANDOLPH S., *Lord Derby. King of Lancashire* (London, 1959).

CONZE, WERNER, "Deutschlands weltpolitische Sonderstellung in den zwanziger Jahren," *Vierteljahrshefte für Zeitgeschichte*, 9 (1961).

COUPAYE, LÉON, *La Ruhr et l'Allemagne* (Paris, 1922).

COWLING, MAURICE, *The Impact of Labour 1920–1924* (Cambridge, 1971).

CRAIG, GORDON A. and FELIX GILBERT (eds.), *The Diplomats 1919–1939* (Princeton, 1953).

CZADA, PETER, "Ursachen und Folgen der großen Inflation," *Schriften des Vereins für Sozialpolitik, Gesellschaft für Wirtschafts- und Sozialwissenschaften*, Neue Folge, Band 73 (1973).

–, "Große Inflation und Wirtschaftswachstum," *Industrielles System und politische Entwicklung in der Weimarer Republik*, hrsg. v. Hans Mommsen, Dietmar Petzina, Bernd Weißbrod (Düsseldorf, 1974).

DEUERLEIN, ERNST, *Deutsche Kanzler von Bismarck bis Hitler* (München, 1968).

DIECKMANN, HILDEMARIE, *Johannes Popitz. Entwicklung und Wirksamkeit in der Weimarer Republik* (Berlin, 1960).

DITTRICH, ERICH, *Die deutsch-französischen Wirtschaftsverhandlungen der Nachkriegszeit* (Berlin und Leipzig, 1931).

DOEHN, LOTHAR, *Politik und Interesse. Die Interessenstruktur der Deutschen Volkspartei* (Meisenheim am Glan, 1970).

DOMBROWSKI, ERICH, "Die Wirkungen der Reparationsverpflichtungen auf die Wirtschaftsführung der Deutschen Reichsbahn-Gesellschaft," Phil. Diss. (Berlin, 1931).

DUROSELLE, JEAN-BAPTISTE and PIERRE RENOUVIN, *Introduction to the History of International Relations* (New York, 1967).

–, *Les Relations Franco-Allemandes de 1914 à 1950* (Paris, 1967).

EINZIG, PAUL, *In the Centre of Things* (London, 1960).

ELLIS, HOWARD S., *German Monetary Theory 1905–1933* (Cambridge, 1937).

ELSTER, KARL, *Von der Mark zur Reichsmark* (Jena, 1928).

EPSTEIN, KLAUS, *Matthias Erzberger and the Dilemma of German Democracy* (Princeton, 1959).

ERDMANN, KARL-DIETRICH, *Adenauer in der Rheinlandpolitik nach dem Ersten Weltkrieg* (Stuttgart, 1966).

ERDMANN, LOTHAR, *Die Gewerkschaften im Ruhrkampf* (Berlin, 1924).

ERSIL, WILHELM, *Aktionseinheit stürzt Cuno* (Berlin, 1962).

–, "Über die finanzielle Unterstützung der rechts-sozialistischen und bürgerlichen Gewerkschaftsführer durch die Reichsregierung im Jahre 1923," in: *Zeitschrift für Geschichtswissenschaft*, 6 (1958).

EULENBURG, FRANZ, "Die handelspolitischen Ideen der Nachkriegszeit," *Weltwirtschaftliches Archiv*, 25 (1927).

EULER, HEINRICH, *Die Außenpolitik der Weimarer Republik 1918–1923. Vom Waffenstillstand bis zum Ruhrkonflikt* (Aschaffenburg, 1957).

EYCK, ERICH, *A History of the Weimar Republic*, 2 vols. (Cambridge, Mass., 1962–1963).

EYNERN, GERT VON, *Die Reichsbank. Probleme des deutschen Zentralnoteninstituts in geschichtlicher Darstellung* (Jena, 1928).

FAULKNER, HAROLD U., *From Versailles to the New Deal. A Chronicle of the Harding-Coolidge-Hoover Era* (New York, 1950).

FAVEZ, JEAN-CLAUDE, *Le Reich devant l'Occupation Franco-Belge de la Ruhr en 1923* (Genève, 1969).

FELDMANN, GERALD D./HEIDRUN HOMBURG, *Industrie und Inflation. Studien und Dokumente zur Politik der deutschen Unternehmer* 1916–1923 (Hamburg, 1977).

FELDMANN, GERALD D., "The Social and Economic Policy of German Big Business," *American Historical Review*, 75 (1969).

FELIX, DAVID, *Walter Rathenau and the Weimar Republic. The Politics of Reparations* (Baltimore, 1971).

–, "Reparations Reconsidered with a Vengeance." *Central European History*, 2 (1969).

FISCHER, WOLFRAM, *Herz des Reviers, 125 Jahre Wirtschaftsgeschichte des Industrie- und Handelskammerbezirks Essen-Mühlheim-Oberhausen* (Essen, 1965).

–, *Deutsche Wirtschaftspolitik 1918–1945* (Opladen, 1968).

FLECHTHEIM, OSSIP K., *Die KPD in der Weimarer Republik* (Frankfurt, 1969).

FÖRST, WALTER (Hrsg.), *Zwischen Ruhrkampf und Wiederaufbau* (Köln und Berlin, 1972). (= Beiträge zur Neueren Landesgeschichte des Rheinlandes und Westfalens, Bd. 5).

FRAENKEL, ERNST, *Military Occupation and the Rule of Law. Occupation Government in the Rhineland 1918–1923* (London, 1944).

FRASURE, CARL, *British Policy on War Debts and Reparations* (Philadelphia, 1946).

FURST, GASTON A., *De Versailles aux Experts* (Paris, 1927).

GEIGENMÜLLER, ERNST, "Botschafter von Hoesch und die Räumungsfrage," *Historische Zeitschrift*, 200 (1965).

GESCHER, DIETER-BRUNO, *Die Vereinigten Staaten von Nordamerika und die Reparationen 1920–1924* (Bonn, 1956).

GEYER CURT, *Drei Verderber Deutschlands. Ein Beitrag zur Geschichte Deutschlands und der Reparationsfrage von 1920–1924* (Berlin, 1924).

GILBERT, MARTIN, *The Roots of Appeasement* (London, 1966).

GLÜCK, GEBHARD, "Die britische Mitteleuropapolitik nach dem I.Weltkrieg," Phil. Diss. (Erlangen, 1962).

GLUM, FRIEDRICH, *Das parlamentarische Regierungssystem in Deutschland, Großbritannien und Frankreich* (München, 1965).

GOSSWEILER, KURT, *Großbanken und Industriemonopole. Staat, Ökonomie und Politik des staatsmonopolistischen Kapitalismus in Deutschland 1914–1932* (Berlin, 1971).

GRADL, BAPTIST, *Die Geschichte der Reparations- und Sachleistungen* (Berlin, 1933).

GRAEFRATH, BERNARD, *Zur Geschichte der Reparationen* (Berlin, 1954).

GRAHAM, FRANK, D., *Exchange, Prices and Production in Hyper-Inflation: Germany 1920–1923* (Princeton, 1930).

GRASTY, CHARLES H., "France's Invasion of the Ruhr," *Current History*, XVII (1923).

GREER, GUY, *The Ruhr-Lorraine Industrial Problem. A Study of the Economic Interdependence of the two Regions and their Relations to the Reparation Question* (London, 1925).

GRIESER, HELMUT, *Die Sowjetpresse über Deutschland in Europa 1922–1932. Revision von Versailles und Rapallopolitik in sowjetischer Sicht* (Stuttgart, 1970).

GULICK, EDWARD V., *Europe's Classical Balance of Power. A Case History of the Theory and Practice of one of the Great Concepts of European Statecraft* (New York, 1955).

HALLGARTEN, GEORGE W.F., *Hitler, Reichswehr und Industrie. Zur Geschichte der Jahre 1918–1933* (Frankfurt am Main, 1955).

HALPERIN, WILLIAM S., *Germany tried Democracy. A Political Study of the Reich from 1918–1931* (New York, 1965).

HARDACH, GERD, *Weltmarktorientierung und relative Stagnation. Währungspolitik in Deutschland 1924–1931* (Berlin, 1976).

HAUGS, PETER, *Reichspräsident und parlamentarische Kabinettsregierung. Eine Studie zum Regierungssystem der Weimarer Republik in den Jahren 1924–1929* (Opladen, 1968).

HAUPTS, LEO, *Deutsche Friedenspolitik 1918–1919. Eine Alternative zur Machtpolitik des Ersten Weltkriegs?* (Düsseldorf, 1976).

HELFFERICH, KARL, *Geld und Banken*, 6th ed. (Leipzig, 1923).

HERTZMANN, LEWIS, *DNVP. Right-Wing Opposition in the Weimar Republic* (Lincoln, 1963).

HESSE, FRIEDRICH, *Die deutsche Wirtschaftslage von 1914–1923. Krieg, Geldblähen und Wechsellage* (Jena, 1938).

HESTER, JAMES MCNAUGHTON, "America and the Weimar Republic. A Study of the causes and effects of American policy and action in respect to Germany, 1918–1925." Unpublished doctoral dissertation, Oxford, 1955.

HIRSCH, JULIUS, *Die deutsche Währungsfrage* (Jena, 1924).

HIRST, FRANCIS W., *The Consequences of the War to Great Britain* (London and New Haven, 1934).

HOFMANN, HANNS HUBERT, *Der Hitlerputsch. Krisenjahre deutscher Geschichte 1920–1924* (München, 1961).

HOHLFELD, KLAUS, "Die Reichsexekution gegen Sachsen im Jahre 1923, ihre Vorgeschichte und politische Bedeutung," Phil. Diss. (Erlangen-Nürnberg, 1964).

HOLTFRERICH, CARL-LUDWIG, "Internationale Verteilungsfolgen der deutschen Inflation 1918–1923," *Kyklos*, 30 (1977).

HORTZSCHANSKY, GÜNTER, *Der nationale Verrat der deutschen Monopolherren während des Ruhrkampfes 1923* (Berlin, 1961).

HORWITZ, LEO, *Endkampf um die Reparationen. Zur Krise des politischen Schuldensystems* (Leipzig, 1931).

HOWARD, JOHN E., *Parliament and Foreign Policy in France* (London, 1948).

HOWARD, MICHAEL, *The Continental Commitment. The Dilemma of British Defense Policy in the Era of the Two World Wars* (London, 1972).

HUPERZ, JOSEPH, "Die Sachlieferungen nach Frankreich," Phil. Diss. (Berlin, 1930).

IGNOTUS, "Etudes et Portraits. Le Chancelier Cuno," *Revue de Paris*, 32 (1923).

Institut für Zeitgeschichte (Hrsg.), *Deutsche Geschichte seit dem Ersten Weltkrieg* (Stuttgart, 1971).

JACOBSON, JAN, *Locarno Diplomacy. Germany and the West, 1925–1929* (Princeton, 1972).

JAEGER, HANS, *Unternehmer in der deutschen Politik (1890–1918)* (Bonn, 1967).

JAMES, ROBERT R., *Memoirs of A Conservative. J.C.C.Davidson's Memoirs and Papers 1910–1937* (London, 1969).

JEANNENEY, JEAN NOËL, *François de Wendel en République. L'Argent et le Pouvoir 1914–1940* (Paris, 1976).

JORDAN, W.N., *Great Britain, France and the German Problem, 1918–1939* (London, 1943).

KASTNING, ALFRED, *Die deutsche Sozialdemokratie zwischen Koalition und Opposition, 1919–1923* (Paderborn, 1970).

KATZ, EMIL, *Les Prestations en Nature* (Paris, 1928).

KAYSER, JACQUES, *Ruhr ou Plan Dawes? Histoire des Réparations* (Paris, 1926).

KESSEL, EBERHARD, "Seeckts politisches Programm von 1923," *Spiegel der Geschichte. Festgabe für Max Braubach zum 10. April 1964*, hrsg. von Konrad Repgen und Stephan Skalweit (Münster, 1964).

KEYNES, MAYNARD, *The Economic Consequences of Peace* (London, 1920).

–, *A Revision of the Peace Treaty* (London, 1922).

KING, JOSEPH, *The Ruhr. The History of the French Occupation of the Ruhr; its Meaning and Consequences* (London, 1924).

KLASS, GERT VON, *Hugo Stinnes* (Tübingen, 1958).

–, *Albert Vögler* (Tübingen, 1968).

KOHLHAUS, HEINZ-HELLMUT, "Die Hapag, Cuno und das Deutsche Reich 1920–1933." Phil. Diss. (Hamburg, 1952).

KÖLLER, HEINZ, *Kampfbündnis an der Seine, Ruhr und Spree. Der gemeinsame Kampf der KPF und KPD gegen die Ruhrbesetzung 1923* (Berlin, 1963).

KOSZYK, KURT, *Zwischen Kaiserreich und Diktatur. Die sozialdemokratische Presse von 1914 bis 1933* (Heidelberg, 1958).

KROHN, CLAUS-DIETER, *Stabilisierung und ökonomische Interessen. Die Finanzpolitik des Deutschen Reiches 1923–1927* (Düsseldorf, 1974).

KRÜGER, PETER, *Deutschland und die Reparationen 1918–1919. Die Genesis des Reparationsproblems in Deutschland zwischen Waffenstillstand und Versailler Friedensschluß* (Stuttgart, 1973).

-, "Die Rolle der Banken und der Industrie in den deutschen reparationspolitischen Entscheidungen nach dem Ersten Weltkrieg," *Industrielles System und politische Entwicklung in der Weimarer Republik*, hrsg. v. H. Mommsen, D. Petzina, B. Weißbrod (Düsseldorf, 1974).

-, "Die Reparationen und das Scheitern einer deutschen Verständigungspolitik auf der Pariser Friedenskonferenz im Jahre 1919," *Historische Zeitschrift*, 221 (1975).

KUCZYNSKI, R., "Zur Finanzlage Frankreichs," *Wirtschaftsdienst*, 15 (1924).

-, (Hrsg.), *Deutschland und Frankreich, ihre Wirtschaft und ihre Politik 1923–1924* (Berlin, 1924).

KUNHEIM, HUGO E., *Die Wirkungen der Ruhrbesetzung auf die Wirtschaft und Politik Großbritanniens* (Berlin, 1929).

LANGE, HERMANN, "Ideen und Praxis der sozialdemokratischen Außenpolitik in der deutschen Republik 1918–1926," Phil. Diss. (Erlangen, 1949).

LANSBURGH, ALFRED, "Die Politik der Reichsbank und die Reichsschatzanweisungen nach dem Krieg," *Schriften des Vereins für Sozialpolitik*, 166 (Leipzig, 1924).

LAROCHE, JULES, "Quelques Aspects de L'Affaire de la Ruhr," *Revue d'Histoire Diplomatique*, 63 (1919).

LAUBACH, ERNST, *Die Politik der Kabinette Wirth 1921–1922* (Lübeck und Hamburg, 1968).

LAUFENBURGER, HENRY, "La Collaboration économique franco-allemande," *Revue Politique et Parlementaire* (October 1924).

LAURSEN, KARSTEN and JØRGEN PEDERSEN, *The German Inflation 1918–1923* (Amsterdam, 1964).

LECKEBUSCH, GÜNTHER, *Die Beziehungen der deutschen Seeschiffswerften zur Eisenindustrie an der Ruhr in der Zeit von 1850–1930* (Köln, 1963).

LEFFLER, MELWYN, "The Origins of Republican War Debt Policy 1921–1923: A Case Study in the Applicability of the Open Door Interpretation," *Journal of American History*, LIX, 4 (1972).

LEWINSOHN, RICHARD (MORUS), *Die Umschichtung der Europäischen Vermögen* (Berlin, 1925).

LIBAL, GISELA, *Aspekte der britischen Deutschlandpolitik 1919–1922* (Göttingen, 1972).

LICHTENBERGER, HENRI, *The Ruhr Conflict* (Washington, 1923).

LIEFMANN, ROBERT, *Vom Reichtum der Nationen. Untersuchungen über die sogenannten Reparationsfragen und die internationalen Verschuldungs- und Währungsprobleme* (Karlsruhe, 1925).

LIESEBACH, INGOLF, "Der Wandel der politischen Führungsschicht der deutschen Industrie von 1918–1945," Phil. Diss. (Basel, 1951).

LINK, WERNER, *Die amerikanische Stabilisierungspolitik in Deutschland 1921–1932* (Düsseldorf, 1970).

–, "Die Ruhrbesetzung und die wirtschaftlichen Interessen der USA," *Vierteljahrshefte für Zeitgeschichte*, 17 (1969).

LINKE, HORST GÜNTHER, *Deutsch-sowjetische Beziehungen bis Rapallo* (Köln, 1970).

LOCHNER, LOUIS P., *Herbert Hoover and Germany* (New York, 1960).

LOYRETTE, JEAN E.L., "The Foreign Policy of Poincaré. France and Great Britain in relation with the German problem (1919–1942)." Unpublished doctoral dissertation, Oxford, 1955.

LUCKAU, ALMA, *The German Peace Delegation at the Peace Conference* (New York, 1941).

LUEKE, ROLF, *Von der Stabilisierung zur Krise* (Zürich, 1958).

MAIER, CHARLES, *Recasting Bourgeois Europe: Stabilization in France, Germany and Italy in the Decade after World War I* (Princeton, 1975).

MAIZELS, ALFRED, *Industrial Growth and World Trade. An Empirical Study of Trends in Production, Consumption and Trade in Manufacturers from 1899–1959 with a Discussion of Probable Future Trends* (Cambridge, 1963).

MANTOUX, ETIENNE, *The Carthagenian Peace, or the Economic Consequences of Mr. Keynes* (London, 1946).

MARKS, SALLY, "Reparations Reconsidered: A Reminder," *Central European History*, 2 (1969).

MASCHKE, ERICH, *Es entsteht ein Konzern. Paul Reusch und die GHH* (Tübingen, 1969).

MAXELON, MICHAEL-OLAF, *Stresemann und Frankreich. Deutsche Politik der Ost-West-Balance* (Düsseldorf, 1972).

MAYER, ARNO J., *Politics and Diplomacy. Containment and Counterrevolution at Versailles, 1918–1919* (New York, 1967).

MAYER-JESSE, ILSE, "Die deutschen Reparationen nach dem Weltkrieg 1918–1933." Phil. Diss. (Wien, 1951).

MCDOUGALL, WALTER A., "French Rhineland policy and the Struggle for European Stabilization: Reparations, Security, and Rhenish Separatism 1918–1924." Unpublished doctoral dissertation. University of Chicago, 1974.

MCFADEYAN, Andrew, *Reparations Reviewed* (London, 1938).

MENDERSHAUSEN, HORST, *Two Postwar Recoveries of the German Economy* (Amsterdam, 1955).

MENZEL, KARL-HEINS, "Die Gebundenheit der britischen Außenpolitik am Ende der Regierungszeit Lloyd Georges und ihre Auswirkungen auf Deutschland," Phil. Diss. (Hamburg, 1951).

MIDDLEMAS, KEITH (ed.), *Thomas Jones. Whitehall Diary*, 3 vols. (London, New York, Toronto, 1969).

MIDDLEMAS, KEITH and JOHN BARNES, *Baldwin. A Biography* (London, 1969).

MILLER, KENNETH E., *Socialism and Foreign Policy in Britain to 1931* (The Hague, 1967).

MIQUEL PIERRE, *La Paix de Versailles et l'Opinion Publique Française* (Paris, 1972).

–, *Poincaré* (Paris, 1961).

MOMMSEN, HANS, DIETER PETZINA, BERND WEIßBROD (Hrsg.), *Industrielles System und politische Entwicklung in der Weimarer Republik* (Düsseldorf, 1974).

MORSEY, RUDOLF, *Die deutsche Zentrumspartei, 1917–1923* (Düsseldorf, 1966).

MOULTON, HAROLD G., *The Reparation Plan*, repr. (Westport, 1970).

MOULTON, HAROLD G. and CONSTANTINE E. MCGUIRE, *Germany's Capacity to Pay* (New York, 1923).

MOULTON, HAROLD G. and LEO PASOLVSKY, *Russian Debts and Russian Reconstruction*, repr. (New York, 1972).

MOWAT, CHARLES, *Britain between the Wars, 1918–1940* (Chicago, 1955).

MÜLLER-JABUSCH, MAXIMILIAN, *Franz Urbig zum 23. Januar 1939* (Berlin, 1939).

NAUMANN, HANS-GÜNTHER, "Über die wirtschaftlichen Auswirkungen des Versailler Vertrages," *Geschichte in Wissenschaft und Unterricht*, 21 (1970).

NETZBAND, KARL-BERNHARD and HANS PETER WIDMAIER, *Währungs- und Finanzpolitik der Ära Luther, 1923–1925* (Tübingen, 1964).

NICOLSON, HAROLD, *Curzon: The Last Phase. A Study in Post-War Diplomacy* (London, 1934).

NORRIS, JACK K., "France and the Ruhr," M.A. Thesis, Georgetown University, 1951.

NORTHEDGE, F.S., *The Troubled Giant: Britain among the Great Powers, 1916–1939* (New York, 1967).

NOYES, PIERREPONT B. and PAUL FULLER, *The French Occupation of the Ruhr. Its Impact and Consequences from the American Viewpoint* (New York, 1923).

OBERMANN, KARL, *Die Beziehungen des amerikanischen Imperialismus zum deutschen Imperialismus in der Zeit der Weimarer Republik, 1918–1925* (Berlin, 1952).

OLTMANN, UWE, "Reichsarbeitsminister Heinrich Brauns in der Staats- und Währungskrise 1923–1924. Die Bedeutung der Sozialpolitik für die Inflation, den Ruhrkampf und die Stabilisierung," Phil. Diss. (Kiel, 1968).

OSTERROTH, NIKOLAUS, *Der deutsche Arbeiter und der Ruhreinfall* (Berlin, 1923).

OSTHOLD, P., *Die Geschichte des Zechenverbandes* (Berlin, 1934).

PAINLEVÉ, PAUL, "The French Opposition to Poincaré's German Policy," *Current History*, XVIII (1923).

PARRINI, CHARLES P., *Heir to Empire. United States Economic Diplomacy 1919–1923* (Pittsburgh, 1969).

PAWLIKEK, EGON, *Die deutschen Sachlieferungen unter dem Dawes und Young Plan* (Nürnberg, 1934).

PEDERSEN, JØRGEN, "Einige Bemerkungen zur deutschen Inflation," *Zeitschrift für die gesamte Staatswissenschaft*, 122 (1966).

PETIT, LUCIEN, *Histoire des Finances Extérieures de la France. Le Règlement des Dettes Interalliées* (Paris, 1932).

Politik in Bayern 1919–1933. Berichte d. württembergischen Gesandten Carl Moser von Filseck. Hrsg. und kommentiert v. Wolfgang Benz (Stuttgart, 1971).

POLLARD, SIDNEY, *The Development of the British Economy 1914–1967*, 2nd ed. (London, 1969).

RATHENAU, WALTHER, *Gesammelte Reden* (Berlin, 1924).

RATZ, URSULA, *Georg Ledebour. Weg und Wirken eines sozialen Politikers* (Berlin, 1969).

RECOULY, RAYMOND, "La Barrière du Rhin: Droits et Devoirs de la France pour assurer sa Sécurité," *La Revue de France* (July 1923).

–, "Après l'Occupation de la Ruhr," *La Revue de France* (February 1923).

REICHERT, JAKOB W., *Rathenaus Reparationspolitik. Eine kritische Studie* (Berlin, 1922).

RENOUVIN, PIERRE, "Les Buts de Guerre du Gouvernement français, 1914–1918," *Revue Historique*, 235 (1966).

RESPONDEK, E., *Die wirtschaftliche Zusammenarbeit zwischen Deutschland und Frankreich* (Berlin, 1929).

RHODES, BENJAMIN D., "Reassessing Uncle Shylock; the United States and the French War Debt, 1917–1929," *Journal of American History*, 55 (1969).

RINGER, FRITZ, *The German Inflation of 1923* (New York, 1969).

ROESELER, KLAUS, "Unternehmer in der Weimarer Republik," *Tradition*, 13 (1968).

ROLLITZ, HORST, *Verfall und Wiederaufbau der französischen Währung seit dem Kriege, 1914–1932* (Berlin, 1933).

RONDE, HANS, *Von Versailles bis Lausanne. Der Verlauf der Reparationsverhandlungen nach dem ersten Weltkrieg* (Stuttgart und Köln, 1950).

RÖSSLER, HELMUTH, *Ideologie und Machtpolitik 1919. Plan und Werk der Pariser Friedenskonferenz* (Göttingen, 1966).

–, (ed.), *Die Folgen von Versailles 1919–1924* (Göttingen, 1969).

RUGE, WOLFGANG, *Die Stellungnahme der Sowjetunion gegen die Besetzung des Ruhrgebietes. Zur Geschichte der deutsch-sowjetischen Beziehungen von Januar bis September 1923* (Berlin, 1967).

RUPIEPER, HERMANN-JOSEF, "Industrie und Reparationen: Einige Aspekte des Reparationsproblems 1922–1924," *Industrielles System und politische Entwicklung in der Weimarer Republik*, hrsg. v. Hans Mommsen, Dieter Petzina, Bernd Weißbrod (Düsseldorf, 1974).

–, "Die britische Rheinlandpolitik im Spannungsfeld der anglo-französischen Beziehungen, 1919–1924," *Problèmes de la Rhénanie 1919–1930*, Centre de Recherches Relations Internationales de l'Université de Metz (Metz, 1975).

SAINT-QUENTIN, RENÉ DE, "L'Occasion Manquée de la Ruhr?," *Revue d'Histoire Diplomatique*, 63 (1949).

SALEWSKY, MICHAEL, *Entwaffnung und Militärkontrolle in Deutschland, 1919–1927* (München, 1966).

SAUVY, ALFRED, *Histoire Economique de la France entre les deux Guerres*, 2 vols. (Paris, 1965–1967).

SCHAEFER, DIETER, *Der deutsche Industrie- und Handelstag als politisches Forum in der Weimarer Republik. Eine historische Studie zum Verhältnis von Politik und Wirtschaft* (Hamburg, 1966).

SCHIECK, HANS, "Der Kampf um die deutsche Wirtschaftspolitik nach dem Novemberumsturz 1918," Phil. Diss. (Heidelberg, 1959).

SCHMACKE, ERNST, "Die Außenpolitik der Weimarer Republik unter Berücksichtigung der Innenpolitik. (Von Rapallo nach Locarno)," Phil. Diss. (Hamburg, 1951).

SCHMIDT, ROYAL S., *Versailles and the Ruhr: Seedbed of World War II* (The Hague, 1968).

SCHNEE, HEINRICH und HANS DRAEGER, *Zehn Jahre Versailles*, 3 Bde. (Berlin, 1929–1930).

SCHOENTHAL, KLAUS-FERDINAND, "American Attitudes towards Germany 1918–1932." Unpublished doctoral dissertation, Ohio State University, 1959.

SCHROEDER, ERNST, *Otto Wiedfeldt. Eine Biographie* (Essen, 1964).

SCHUKER, STEPHEN A., *The End of French Predominance in Europe: The Financial Crisis of 1924 and the Adoption of the Dawes Plan* (Chapel Hill, 1976).

SCHULTZE, ERNST, *Ruhrbesetzung und Weltwirtschaft* (Leipzig, 1927).

SCHULZ, GERHARD, *Zwischen Demokratie und Diktatur. Verfassungspolitik und Reichsreform in der Weimarer Republik* (Berlin, 1963).

SCHWABE, KLAUS, *Die Vereinigten Staaten, die deutsche Friedenspolitik und das Scheitern des Wilsonfriedens. Deutsch-amerikanische Beziehungen vom Kaiser zur Republik 1918–1919* (Freiburg, 1969).

SCHWARZ, ALBERT, *Die Weimarer Republik* (Konstanz, 1958).

SCHWARZ, GOTTHART, *Theodor Wolff und das Berliner Tageblatt. Eine liberale Stimme in der deutschen Politik, 1906–1933* (Tübingen, 1972).

SCHWOB, MAURICE, *The Ruhr Problem. An Independent Rhineland-Westphalia* (Nantes, 1923).

SEITZY, WOLFGANG, "Die Entente Cordiale am Vorabend der Besetzung des Ruhrgebietes," Phil. Diss. (Tübingen, 1952).

SIMON, HUGO F., *Reparationen und Wiederaufbau* (Berlin, 1925).

SINGER, KURT, *Staat und Wirtschaft seit dem Waffenstillstand* (Berlin, 1924).

SOUTOU, GEORGES, "Les Problèmes du Rétablissement des Relations Économiques entre la France et l'Allemagne, 1918–1929," *Francia*, 2 (1973).

–, "Die deutschen Reparationen und das Seydoux Projekt 1920–1921," *Vierteljahrshefte für Zeitgeschichte*, 25 (1975).

SPETHMANN, HANS, *12 Jahre Ruhrbergbau. Aus seiner Geschichte, vom Kriegsanfang bis zum Franzoseneinmarsch*, 5 vols. (Berlin, 1928–1932).

–, *Der Ruhrkampf, 1923–1925* (Berlin, 1933).

STREET, C.J.C., *Rhineland and Ruhr* (London, 1923).

STUCKEN, RUDOLF, "Die wertbeständigen Anleihen in finanzwirtschaftlicher Betrachtung," *Schriften des Vereins für Sozialpolitik*, 166 (1924).

–, *Deutsche Geld- und Kreditpolitik 1914–1963*, 3rd ed. (Tübingen, 1964).

TARDIEU, ANDRÉ, "The Policy of France," *Foreign Affairs*, I (1922).

–, "A Defense of French Policy," *Current History*, XVIII (1923).

TÖTTER, HEINRICH, "Das Versagen der deutschen Presse im Ruhrkampf. Die Methoden der französischen Pressepropaganda und ihr Zusammenspiel mit der deutschen Linkspresse," Habilitationsschrift Publizistik (Köln, 1940).

TRACHTENBERG, MARC, "French Reparation Policy 1918–1921." Unpublished doctoral dissertation, University of California, Berkeley, 1974.

TRENDELENBURG, E., *Amerika und Europa in der Weltwirtschaftspolitik des Zeitabschnitts der Wirtschaftskonferenzen* (Berlin, 1943).

TREUE, WILHELM, *Die Feuer verlöschen nie. August-Thyssen-Hütte, 1890–1926* (Düsseldorf, 1960).

TURNER, HENRY A., *Stresemann and the Politics of the Weimar Republic* (Princeton, 1963).

UFERMANN, PAUL, *Könige der Inflation* (Berlin, 1924).

UHLEMANN, MANFRED, *Arbeiterjugend gegen Cuno und Poincaré. Das Jahr 1923* (Berlin, 1930).

VAGTS, ALFRED, *Deutschland und die Vereinigten Staaten in der Weltpolitik*, 2 Bde. (London, 1935).

-, "M.M. Warburg & Co. Ein Bankhaus in der deutschen Weltpolitik 1905-1933," *Vierteljahrsschrift für Sozial- und Wirtschaftsgeschichte*, 45 (1958).

Verein für Hamburger Geschichte, *Carl Melchior. Ein Buch des Gedenkens und der Freundschaft* (Tübingen, 1967).

VERGÉ, ARMAND, *La Bataille des Réparations 1919-1924* (Paris, 1924).

VIETSCH, EBERHARD VON, *Arnold Rechberg und das Problem der politischen West-Orientierung Deutschlands nach dem 1. Weltkrieg* (Koblenz, 1958).

WANDEL, ECKHARD, *Die Bedeutung der Vereinigten Staaten von Nordamerika für das deutsche Reparationsproblem 1924-1929* (Tübingen, 1971).

WATT, DONALD S., *Studies in the Formulation of British Foreign Policy in the Twentieth Century* (London, 1965).

WEIDENFELD, WERNER, *Die Englandpolitik Gustav Stresemanns. Theoretische und praktische Aspekte der Außenpolitik* (Mainz, 1972).

WEIKARDT, CHARLES, "Das Rheinland in den deutsch-britischen Beziehungen 1918-1923: Eine Untersuchung zum Wesen der britischen Gleichgewichtspolitik," Phil. Diss. (Bonn, 1967).

WEILL-RAYNAL, ETIENNE, *Les Réparations allemandes et la France*, 3 vols. (Paris, 1947).

WENGST, UDO, *Graf Brockdorff-Rantzau und die außenpolitischen Anfänge der Weimarer Republik* (Bern/Frankfurt, 1973).

WENTZCKE, PAUL, *Einbruch und Abwehr im Rheinisch-Westfälischen Industriegebiet*, 2 vols. (Berlin, 1930-1932).

WERTH, ULRICH, "Die Reparationspolitik der Kölnischen Zeitung, 1920-1924," Phil. Diss. (Köln, 1935).

WERTHEIMER, RUDOLF, "Der Einfluß der Reichspräsidenten auf die Gestaltung der Reichsregierung," Jur. Diss. (Heidelberg, 1929).

WHITE, DAVID GLEN, "Einige Kapitel aus der großen Politik zur Zeit der Ruhrbesetzung," Phil. Diss. (Berlin, 1939).

WILLIAMSON, JOHN G., *Karl Helfferich 1872-1924. Economist, Financier, Politician* (Princeton, 1971).

WINGEN, OTTO, *Weltverschuldung und Deutschlands Reparationslast* (Berlin, 1927).

WINKLER, HEINRICH-AUGUST (Hrsg.), *Organisierter Kapitalismus. Voraussetzungen und Anfänge* (Göttingen, 1974).

WOLFERS, ARNOLD, *Britain and France between two Wars* (New York, 1966).

WOLFF, S., "Das Comité des Forges und seine Politik," *Wirtschaftsdienst*, 33 (1924).

WRIGHT, GORDON, *Raymond Poincaré and the French Presidency* (Stanford, 1942).

YOUNG, KENNETH, *Arthur James Balfour* (London 1963).

ZIMMERMANN, LUDWIG, *Deutsche Außenpolitik in der Ära der Weimarer Republik* (Göttingen, 1958).

–, *Frankreichs Ruhrpolitik von Versailles bis zum Dawes Plan*, hrsg. von Walther Peter Fuchs (Göttingen, 1971).

ZSIGMOND, LASZLO, *Zur deutschen Frage 1918–1923. Die wirtschaftlichen und internationalen Faktoren der Wiederbelebung des deutschen Imperialismus und Militarismus* (Budapest, 1964).

ZUYLEN, PIERRE BARON VON, *Les Mains Libres, la Politique Extérieure de la Belgique, 1914–1940* (Brussels, 1950).

ZWOCH, GERHARD, "Die Erfüllungs- und Verständigungspolitik der Weimarer Republik und die deutsche öffentliche Meinung," Phil. Diss. (Kiel, 1950).

INDEX

Accumulatorenfabrik, 200
Addison, Joseph, 220f
Adenauer, Konrad, 14, 96n, 120, 252
ADGB (Allgemeiner Deutscher Gewerkschaftsbund), 98f, 107, 139, 145, 148, 158, 206n
Adler, Carl, 184n
Albert, Heinrich, 22, 148, 207, 210n, 212, 214
AEG (Allgemeine Elektrizitätsgesellschaft), 34n
A.G. für Anilinfabrikation, 200
American Bankers Association, 245
Amery, L.S., 222
Andreae, Fritz, 208n
Asquith, Herbert H., 132
August-Thyssen-Hütte, 109
Ayres, Leonhard P., 3n, 4n
Balfour, Lord Arthur, 84
Baldwin, Stanley, 136, 152, 161n, 168, 224–230
Ballin, Albert, 16
Banque Nationale Française Du Commerce Extérieur, 245
Banque de Paris et des Pays Bas, 245
Barrère, Camille (French Ambassador in Rome), 141n
Barthou, Louis (President of the Reparation Commission), 55, 76, 79n, 80, 88, 94, 150, 166, 237f, 241f, 246f
Baruch, Bernard, 2, 5
Batocki, Adolf von, 14
Bauer, Gustav, 98
Beckerath, Herbert, 196
Becker, Jacob, 155
Becker, Dr., Johann, 23, 26, 63, 65, 148f, 159n, 160, 185, 187, 190, 201, 204, 210, 214
Bemberg, 200
Bemelmans, A., (Belgian delegate on the Reparation Commission), 46, 53
Bendixen, Friedrich, 196f
Berckemeyer, Hans, 184n
Bergen, Diego, v, 141n

Bergeon, Charles, 94n
Bergmann, Carl (German reparations expert), 6n, 19, 44f, 55n, 61f, 71, 73, 108, 143, 148f, 161n
Berliner-Handels-Gesellschaft, 185n
Bernard, Georg, 22, 24n, 147, 204
Bernstein, Eduard, 101
Bierwes, Heinrich, 186n
Blackett, Basil P. (British Treasury), 46
Blank, Martin, 199n
Bleichröder, S., 186n
Blumenstein, 184n
Blunzig, 143n
Böhm, 182n
Bokanowski, Maurice, 230
Bonn, Moritz J., 18, 103, 148, 161n
Borsig, Ernst von, 35n, 201, 208n
Boyden, Roland, 10, 74, 91, 119
Bradbury, Sir John (British delegate on the Reparation Commission), 10, 43f, 50f, 58, 64, 73f, 81, 150, 218f, 224f, 236f, 241f, 247
Brand, Robert H., 11
Brandt, Alexander von, 58, 60n
Braun, Otto, 98, 148
Brauns, Heinrich, 23, 98n, 148, 204, 214
Brecht, G., 153
Breitscheid, Rudolf, 26, 63, 131, 138, 155
Briand, Aristide, 9, 10, 81, 256, 259
Brockdorff-Rantzau, Ulrich Graf v., 205, 206
Bromberg, 184n
Brugère, Charles, 125
Brüninghaus, Willi, 213n
Bücher, Hermann, 32, 36f, 61, 68, 99, 107n, 152f, 157–160, 201
Burges, Franz, 139
BVP (Bayerische Volkspartei), 23, 27, 63, 155, 178, 214f
Cachin, Marcel, 96
Cadogan, Alexander, 225n
Cambon, Jules, 241
Cambon, Paul, 95
Carp, Werner, 144, 186n